Adult Education
in the
American Experience

Harold W. Stubblefield
Patrick Keane

Adult Education in the American Experience

*From the Colonial Period
to the Present*

Jossey-Bass Publishers • San Francisco

Substantial discounts on bulk quantities of Jossey-Bass books
are available to corporations, professional associations, and other
organizations. For details and discount information, contact the
special sales department at Jossey-Bass Inc., Publishers.
(415) 433-1740; Fax (415) 433-0499.

For sales outside the United States, please contact your local
Paramount Publishing International office.

Manufactured in the United States of America. Nearly all Jossey-Bass
books and jackets are printed on recycled paper that contains at least
50 percent recycled waste, including 10 percent postconsumer waste.
Many of our materials are also printed with vegetable-based inks;
during the printing process these inks emit fewer volatile organic
compounds (VOCs) than petroleum-based inks. VOCs contribute to
the formation of smog.

Library of Congress Cataloging-in-Publication Data

Stubblefield, Harold W.
   Adult education in the American experience : from the colonial
period to the present / Harold W. Stubblefield, Patrick Keane. —
1st ed.
      p.   cm.—(Jossey-Bass higher and adult education series)
   Includes bibliographical references and index.
   ISBN 0-7879-0025-7
   1. Adult education—United States—History.   I. Keane, Patrick.
II. Title.   III. Series.
LC5251.S735   1994
374′.973—dc20   94-26314
                                                                      CIP

FIRST EDITION
HB Printing   10 9 8 7 6 5 4 3 2 1   *Code 94106*

The Jossey-Bass
Higher and Adult Education Series

Consulting Editor
Adult and Continuing Education

Alan B. Knox
University of Wisconsin, Madison

Contents

Preface

Today more than ever, American society depends on adult education systems to spread information and knowledge, develop skills, and shape attitudes. The knowledge explosion after World War II, the advent of the knowledge economy and the information society, and the diffusion of electronic communication call for new ways of thinking about education for adults. Various forms of adult education now pervade American life, and the belief that education must extend through adulthood has become commonplace. But previous periods of transition also used learning processes to help adults cope with changing social conditions, be more productive, enjoy life, and understand themselves and the world.

How to write this history is a matter of dispute among adult education scholars. In recent decades, historical study has focused on critical revision. The traditional eulogy of eminent leaders and of the programs of mainstream institutions now sits uneasily in an increasingly egalitarian and multicultural society. Correspondingly, some are now challenging the way in which history is taught in public schools. Groups long excluded from much historical consideration now seek their roots, and television finds a growing audience for its dramatizations of past events and issues. Inevitably, such realities as illiteracy, unemployment, and discrimination in-

fluence the current generation's more critical interpretation of the
past and bring vitality to historical studies in adult education.

But no single book has described and interpreted the evolution and role of adult education in the sweep of American history—
a richer and longer role than previous accounts suggest. In *Adult
Education in the American Experience* we critically address the
broad context of adult learning and its relationship to social, economic, and political movements. We emphasize adult education's
potential, evident from efforts during colonial times to control its
scope as well as from the lifelong learning concept of our own
postindustrial society. Using recent studies, we integrate the development of the major forms of adult education.

Audience

This book is intended for several audiences, but primarily for adult
education practitioners and scholars, who need a comprehensive
history of adult education in the United States that interprets their
work in relation to the larger field of adult education and to national history. A description of the evolution of institutional settings, programs, and clienteles reveals adult education's holistic
nature, and an analysis of factors that have affected public access to
adult education provides a critical perspective of the field. We hope
that this book will facilitate broader understanding of ideology and
practice and will be a point of departure for other studies.

Not just for specialists, this book is also for legislators who
allocate resources for education, educators who train primary and
secondary school teachers, and citizen activists. Though the concept
of lifelong education has recently been popularized, life-span education is an old practice. A thorough historical account may help
policy makers, educators, and citizens gain a more comprehensive
view of education and its relation to policy planning, teaching, and
action.

Overview of the Contents

The term *adult education* has many meanings and therefore often
confuses consumers. Programs ranging from literacy for the under-

educated to continuing education for professionals are called adult education. Even the boundaries of adult education are not certain: at one extreme, adult education is considered to include all life experiences through which adults learn; at the other, it includes only organized learning experiences. Whatever the definition, systematic study of adult education began in the 1920s, and this book belongs to that scholarly tradition.

An introductory chapter (Chapter One) discusses various definitions of adult education and offers an assessment of the achievements and shortcomings of earlier adult education histories, a discussion of the contributions of the revisionist educational historians, and a summary of the themes that will follow. This chapter also explores formative influences, showing how adult education occurred as part of the cultural transmission process among Native Americans and the early European settlers in the thirteen colonies. We identify adult education activities during (1) the colonial period, (2) the formation of a new nation and expansion prior to the Civil War, (3) the accommodation to new social and economic forces from the end of the Civil War through World War I, (4) the decades of prosperity, depression, and the second World War, and (5) the postwar era of movement into the postindustrial society.

Part One examines how adult education developed in the colonial and post-Revolutionary periods. Chapter Two traces an Atlantic information network that helped independent study and research in the colonies, the rise and limitations of a literate culture, and the Puritan impact. Chapter Three deals with the more structured apprenticeship education and evening schools and notes the conflict between the rhetoric of opportunity and the reality of stratification.

Part Two treats the development of adult education in the early national and antebellum periods through the Civil War. The educational aspirations of independence—with the attendant paradoxes and lack of progress—are covered in Chapter Four. Next, the forms of adult education for social reform are juxtaposed with the prevailing ideology of individual improvement. The rising tide of antebellum "improvement" is discussed in Chapter Five, which shows how literacy, publishing, libraries, evening schools, and uto-

pian communities proliferated. Chapter Six analyzes three important and interrelated innovations of the period—mechanics' institutes, lyceums, and an incipient professionalizing process—and
describes how the common factors of middle-class involvement and
direction reflected the dominant educational ethos. The focus of
Chapter Seven is on organized labor's response to adult education.
Labor's enthusiasm for education's role in workers' achieving their
aspirations is shown to have dissipated amid changing social and
economic conditions. Chapter Eight examines (white) women's
adult education and shows how increased formal provision of education largely complemented ascribed roles, whereas independent
study and workplace or community learning proved more empowering. Chapter Nine addresses the "civilizing mission" of Native
American education, the contributions of Sequoyah and the Choctaws. It also outlines the African-American commitment to education, from the "hush harbors" to the churches, and the nature of the
slaveholders' provision of literacy education.

Part Three explores the development of adult education in
the formation of modern America during the period from the end
of the Civil War through the end of World War I. In Chapter Ten,
the focus is on institutional innovations to expand the dissemination of knowledge and culture, the creation of an educational system for agriculture, and the emergence of training and education for
industrial work. Chapter Eleven addresses initiatives for social
change by women, farmers, industrial workers, African Americans,
and Native Americans, and initiatives by the dominant culture to
frame an education appropriate for the station assigned these
groups. Chapter Twelve analyzes methods to cope with the new
urban, industrial, and immigrant society—for example, social settlements and "Americanization"—and explores the consequences of
World War I for adult education.

The topic of Part Four is the development of adult education
from the end of World War I through World War II. How adult
education became recognized as an educational domain, the expansion of institutions to foster learning and education, and the growing importance of the workplace in education are covered in
Chapter Thirteen. Chapter Fourteen analyzes several educational

initiatives that were guided by visions of a better society—education for conflict resolution, women as citizens, African-American education, and workers' education. Adult education during the New Deal and World War II—two national emergencies that made extensive use of adult education—is discussed in Chapter Fifteen.

Part Five treats the influences and changing forms of adult education from the end of World War II through the 1980s. The continuing institutionalization of adult education in higher education and the workplace, and the growing importance of adult education, are shown in Chapter Sixteen. Chapter Seventeen describes how Americans addressed social issues and civic concerns through informal learning and action. Chapter Eighteen explores efforts by various agencies to foster a conceptual and organizational coherence within adult education in the transition to the postindustrial society. A concluding chapter identifies several patterns, recurring themes, and changing and conflicting ideologies that manifested themselves as adult education became a mass undertaking.

Acknowledgments

Our acknowledgment of others is always a subjective and incomplete process, for innumerable contacts over the years have necessarily shaped our contributions. Three series of events provided particular stimulus. We met when Keane was teaching at Northern Illinois University during the 1981 Adult Education Research Conference held there. Informal discussions among the participants spawned a series of history mini-conferences that attracted a network of interested contributors. A proposal that we write the history chapter for the 1989 *Handbook of Adult and Continuing Education* instigated our collaboration and provided a broad outline for this book. In 1988, the Syracuse University–Kellogg Project on Resources for Educators of Adults brought both authors to the Cazenovia Lake conference to promote adult education resource materials. Several historical research conferences for visiting scholars enabled Stubblefield to conduct research at the George Arents Research Library; that proved particularly helpful for the section on the Adult Education Association of the U.S.A. Stubblefield is grateful for the assistance of Jan Carlton and Arlene Tavoularis, librarians at Virginia Tech's Northern Virginia Graduate Center, in securing materials from the campus library and through interlibrary loan.

Falls Church, Virginia   Harold W. Stubblefield
August 1994   Patrick Keane

The Authors

Harold W. Stubblefield is professor of adult education at the Virginia Polytechnic Institute and State University. He received his B.A. degree (1955) in social science from Murray State College, both his B.D. degree (1958) in theology and his Th.M. degree (1960) in pastoral counseling from the Southern Baptist Theological Seminary, and his Ed.D. degree (1973) in adult education from Indiana University. After completing his doctorate and before coming to Virginia Tech, he served for one year on the faculty at Indiana University.

Stubblefield's research and writing activities have focused on the history of adult education in the United States and the development and organization of adult education as an academic discipline. He is editor of *Continuing Education for Community Leadership* (1981) and author of *Towards a History of Adult Education in America* (1988), as well as recipient of the 1988 Imogene Okes Award for Outstanding Research in Adult Education. He has contributed several chapters to edited collections. He was chair of the Commission of Professors of Adult Education and a consulting editor for *Adult Education Quarterly*. He has also served on the board of directors of the American Association for Adult and Continuing Education, the Association for Voluntary Action Scholars, and the Virginia Association for Adult and Continuing Education.

Patrick Keane was professor of continuing education at Dalhousie University (Halifax, Nova Scotia) from 1970 until his retirement in 1992. He received his B.A. degree (1958) from the University of Manchester, both his postgraduate certificate in education (1959) and his M.A. degree (1964) from the University of Bristol, and his Ph.D. degree (1970) from the University of Bath. Prior to his appointment at Dalhousie University, Keane held positions in England as resident tutor at the Dillington House Residential College of Adult Education, principal of Devizes College of Further Education, and extramural tutor and adult education adviser of the Cornwall Adult Education Joint Committee. In 1981, he was visiting professor of adult education at Northern Illinois University.

Keane has specialized in nineteenth-century adult education in England, Canada, and the United States. His articles have treated internationalism in early adult education, methodology issues, mechanics' institutes, workers' education, libraries, museums, and the role of the state in adult education. His articles have been published in such journals as *Studies in Adult Education, International Journal of Lifelong Education, Convergence,* and *Adult Education Quarterly.*

1

Formative Influences
on Adult Education
in America

A publicly funded, hierarchical system for educating America's children and youth has gradually taken shape through the development of common schools, high schools, colleges and universities, and community colleges over a period of approximately 150 years. Provisions for educating adults, however, did not take shape around a single institutional form. In some instances, activities grew out of the efforts of individuals to improve themselves in various ways. In others, they were initiated by an institution to achieve some larger institutional purpose. In still other instances, people with a common interest formed associations for specific educational purposes or used education to achieve a broader social purpose. Only since the 1920s have scholars studied these educational activities conducted by individuals or offered by a sponsoring agency as part of a larger phenomenon called adult education.

Applying the term *adult education* to a variety of educational activities gives coherence to otherwise discrete activities, at the same time raising questions about what constitutes a history of adult education. To address these questions, this chapter explores definitions of adult education, describes early efforts to write a history of adult education as well as new revisionist approaches, and advances the themes of this study. The final section of the chapter examines

1

learning and education as part of the cultural transmission process among Native Americans and the early European settlers.

Definitions

In Western Europe and the United States, adult education, as a distinct form, accompanied the rise of democracy and the industrial revolution. The first popular use of the term *adult education* occurred in England in the early nineteenth century; in the United States, the term grew out of the late-nineteenth-century educational outreach (by public schools, universities, public libraries, and museums) to adults. Educators, advocates of popular education, and encyclopedists recognized that many activities could be organized under this generic category. Historian Herbert Baxter Adams preferred the term *popular education* or *educational extension*, while librarian Melvil Dewey used the term *home education*. By the 1910s, however, the term *adult education* was preferred for designating and classifying educational programs for adults (Stubblefield and Rachal, 1992).

In the early 1920s, the Carnegie Corporation's initiatives became the catalyst for a social movement. Carnegie mapped the field, commissioning several studies of adult education in libraries, university extension, correspondence study, and chautauquas and lyceums. Lyman Bryson, a professor of and leader in adult education, saw this development as a signal shift in the social significance of adult education: "Lifelong learning is an ancient ideal in the history of civilization, but adult education as an organized social movement is comparatively new in American life" (1936, p. 3). Carnegie's exploratory work culminated in 1926 in the organization of the American Association for Adult Education (AAAE). Though independent, the AAAE functioned largely as an agent of the Carnegie Corporation, which provided most of its funding. As the conduit for the Carnegie Corporation's grant activities in adult education, the AAAE supported research studies on adult learning abilities, experimental projects, conferences, and publications. A fuller account of the AAAE will be presented later, but of interest here is how the AAAE defined and classified adult education.

The AAAE's first efforts to identify agencies engaged in adult education resulted in two handbooks that listed alphabetically and then described participating institutions (Rowden, 1934, 1936). A picture of adult education as a differentiated field of activity emerges in a book of articles from the *Journal of Adult Education* (Ely, 1936) and in a book on the literature of adult education (Beals and Brody, 1941). Ely depicts a field comprising social purposes, a history, agencies and specialized programs, teachers, content, and method. Though the attempts to frame the field varied widely and encompassed diverse educational activities, the AAAE had interest only in liberal education, focused on the study of human thought through books and on the study of public issues through discussion. On divisive social issues, the AAAE believed that adult educators should remain neutral: they were teachers, not social activists.

A widely quoted and influential definition of adult education in the AAAE tradition appeared in the first textbook of adult education by Lyman Bryson (1936). Bryson defined adult education as "all the activities with an educational purpose that are carried on by people engaged in the ordinary business of life" (Bryson, 1936, pp. 3-4). Following this definition, Bryson argued that a thirty-year-old man in a doctoral program is engaged in schooling, while a sixteen-year-old high school graduate seeking to improve himself is engaged in adult education. Bryson regarded adult education as a voluntary activity characterized by the self-direction of adult learners who were attempting to improve their personalities: personal improvement was the fundamental motive of individuals for learning, and *liberal education* was the term that best described this kind of education. From the perspective of the agencies providing adult education, their purposes ranged from the remedial to the occupational to the relational to the liberal (education for the new leisure) to the political. This definition emphasized adult education as the provision of institutions, and the participation of individuals as motivated by the desire for self-improvement.

For an organizationally diverse field such as adult education, that definition provided a conceptual framework for collaboration among those who saw the social importance of extending educational opportunities to adults. Such a definition also provided the conceptual framework for the few persons who sought to understand the historical background of this new social movement. From this perspective, activists and historians began to map the contours of its institutional development.

Early Efforts

Framing a history of adult education began with descriptive studies of institutional settings. When the AAAE commissioned James Truslow Adams to write a history of adult education (*Frontiers of American Culture*, 1944), it chose a historian who "possessed no professional or technical knowledge of adult education" (p. x). Adams recognized that "education for adults, in innumerable forms, had been in process from the beginning of our history" (p. 136). He found an "adult education jumble," which gave him a feeling of helplessness when he tried to rationalize his task (p. 128). C. Hartley Grattan was likewise commissioned by the Fund for Adult Education, a project of the Ford Foundation, to write a history of adult education. Also a recognized historian without expertise in adult education, Grattan produced his *In Quest of Knowledge* in 1955. He described it as "neither a formal nor a complete history; it is rather a long essay, using historical materials" (p. v).

The third major contributor to the field was Malcolm S. Knowles, whose book *The Adult Education Movement in the United States* was published in 1962 and updated in 1977. Differing from his predecessors, Knowles was a professional adult educator, not a historian, and the work was an outgrowth of his doctoral dissertation rather than commissioned by a foundation. As the first executive director of the Adult Education Association of the U.S.A. (1951–1959), a former state official, and a YMCA educator, Knowles focused on the evolution of institutions for adult education. Perhaps because of his administrative background, he envisaged something that eluded his predecessors—a systematic classification of the field. Nevertheless, like them, he continued in the descriptive tradition, identifying important features and functions but seldom analyzing the forces that shaped them.

Revisionist Influences

Even though these early works remain serviceable in some respects, more recent appraisals suggest their limitations (Stubblefield, 1991).

Since the 1960s, a number of revisionists have been attacking traditional views of the history of education. Although they have focused their attention on the schooling of children and presented varying interpretations, they nevertheless provided conceptual frameworks applicable to adult education. Such cultural revisionists as Bernard Bailyn and Lawrence Cremin emphasized the educational impact of nonacademic agencies, the sociopolitical context of such agencies, and the need for primary source documentation in educational history (Bailyn, 1960; Cremin, 1965). It should be noted, however, that while Bailyn and Cremin considered adult education a part of culture, they did not classify it as a separate entity. Adult educators had already accepted such "revisions" and thus found the cultural revisionists' school compatible with their efforts.

More challenging were the views of such radical revisionists as Michael Katz (1968, 1975), Colin Greer (1969), Marvin Lazerson (1971), Clarence J. Karier (1973), Samuel Bowles and Herbert Gintis (1976), and Michael Apple (1979). While sharing in an educational perspective broader than that of the public schools, they also judged the schools to have been instruments of middle-class exploitation of poor children. This judgment led to questions about the conflict and struggles glossed over in descriptive essays on adult education (Davenport, 1982).

Other writers have advanced critical interpretations of adult education's development: Robert Carlson (1975), Frank Adams (1975), Kathleen Rockhill (1976), and Maxine Seller (1978). Studies of scientific and learned societies, the women's movement, university extension, and the education of African Americans have likewise contributed to a reappraisal of the history of adult education (Oleson and Brown, 1976; Rothman, 1978; Oleson and Voss, 1979; Taylor, Rockhill, and Fieldhouse, 1985; Neufeldt and McGee, 1990). The revisionists argue for a more inclusive historiography—for example, to include the history of women's efforts—suggesting both compensatory and critical approaches (Hugo, 1990).

Such new viewpoints are prompted by a written history that derives largely from our Eurocentric culture, dominant since Europeans arrived on the American continent and came into contact with the indigenous peoples, and that reflects an increasingly multicultural and egalitarian American society. Rather than contributing to a traditional melting-pot ideology of cultural coherence, the tendency now among historians and educators is to contribute to an ideology of difference. In response, others have argued that a stress on gender, race, and class leads to an overly deterministic Marxist analysis: such an approach denies any transcendent values in American education, instead presenting an ideology of political correctness that excludes "adverse reflection" on any group and includes an "equal portrayal" of their contributions (Hirsch, 1987; Bloom, 1987; Cheney, 1988; D'Souza, 1991).

At the heart of the controversy is the question of whether there is any such thing as objective, disinterested scholarship committed to rational inquiry, or whether there are simply permutations of conscious or unconscious ideology. Historian Carl Becker concluded that it is impossible to present all the facts and that those presented reflect the writer's own agenda; hence innumerable interpretations of the same event are possible (Becker, 1959). The fact that revisionists hold differing views emphasizes the need to conduct ongoing research and to confront old biases. Otherwise, claims to "objectivity" and "rational inquiry" will be viewed suspiciously, as though the writer has a political agenda. Nevertheless, the pressure to meet all the demands for "inclusion" might well inhibit some potential contributions to a field relatively undeveloped. As Tyack (1976) suggests, some interpretations "fit certain times and places better than others" and "call attention to different actors, motives and evidence" (p. 388).

Purposes and Themes

This field clearly has some room for eclecticism, for we are, as Stubblefield has shown, still working *Towards a History of Adult Education in America* (Stubblefield, 1988). This book is one such contribution, and like earlier ones will undoubtedly incur criticism, for the process of historical inquiry is ongoing and vibrant, and new perspectives are an inevitable part of growth.

In our exploration of the development of adult education, five major themes have emerged. First, Americans value education in adulthood and have created many educative systems for adults, to serve a variety of purposes. Early histories by Adams, Grattan, and Knowles traced the institutional development of adult education. A fragmented system emerged as each institution—as diverse in organization and purpose as religion, business and industry, communication, health, education, and government—addressed specific educational needs of the adults who fell within its purview. Efforts to bring these institutions into a loosely coupled system began in the late nineteenth century and were formally organized in 1926 with the formation of the AAAE, followed by the Adult Education Association of the U.S.A. (1951 to 1982) and the American Association for Adult and Continuing Education (1982 to the present). Adams, Grattan, and Knowles believed that adult education opportunities in the United States developed and expanded within the context of the democratization of culture and knowledge. A formal education system accessible to the general population, as well as an inclusive economic and political system, enabled many to achieve whatever their abilities and ambition warranted. But these early historians glossed over, if not ignored, the harsher realities of American life. A fuller account of the historical development of adult education will include other themes.

Second, for many, the United States was indeed a land of opportunity that rewarded ability, initiative, and hard work. But other factors circumscribed the opportunities for several groups: women, Native Americans, African Americans, immigrants, and industrial workers and farmers found their life chances and educational opportunities limited by virtue of their gender, race, class, or national origin. In assigning these groups a marginal or subservient status, the dominant culture also prescribed an education appropriate for that status, using education to instill its own values and ensure its continued domination. Unwilling to accept their prescribed status, members of these groups, on their own initative or with the assistance of members of the dominant culture, created alternative educational systems.

Third, a dynamic society called for new forms of adult education. Many early Americans required only a limited education that would give them the basic literacy skills necessary for life in a literate culture. Educational requirements increased as the United States changed from an agricultural society to an industrial society and then to an information society. Children and youth gradually spent longer periods of time in educational institutions. A common school education at a minimal level gave way to high school, to community college, college, and graduate or professional school. For those at the minimal level, adult education provided remedial instruction. Increasingly, for the professionally and technically trained, it provided a means of maintaining competence. For this latter group, at least, education had become lifelong.

Fourth, creating forms of adult education became a way to shape individuals and society. Such ventures as lyceums, lecturing, chautauquas, Great Books, and the National Training Laboratory clearly bore the characteristics of adult education. Other ventures, such as reform movements and social campaigns, used adult education to achieve a broader social purpose. Through voluntary action, Americans worked for abolition, woman's suffrage, temperance, prison reform, improved working conditions in factories, antilynching legislation, health reform, literacy education, civil rights, women's liberation, and farmers' and workers' rights. Educative delivery systems were created around these issues, and adult education became an agency for change and for many, an arena of activity. Women, in particular, found in voluntary associations a way to have a public voice and a space of their own—as did African Americans, Native Americans, workers, farmers, and other ethnic groups.

Fifth, adults began to use existing information systems: newspapers, magazines, and books brought adults into contact with the larger world of culture and knowledge, informing them of events that touched their lives and making knowledge accessible for their part-time study. In a print culture, the ability to read became the avenue for participation. The twentieth century has seen the invention and broad dissemination of radio, television, telecommunications, and computers, which gave people not only words but images and instant access to information. Electronic communication generated new delivery systems for education, which overcame the barriers of time and distance.

But access to the more advanced information systems requires expensive equipment. Just as books were once affordable only for the wealthy, advanced information systems are now only for the economically advantaged and employees of large organizations. While the development of public libraries made print media accessible to the entire population, we have yet to see what present or future public institution will make electronic information systems accessible to everyone.

As these themes suggest, adult education is not a single institutional entity; therefore, to define adult education is a critical problem. Many of the activities identified in this book as adult education fall outside the boundaries of the education-as-schooling that society normally regards as education. To identify what is— and what is not—adult education, we drew upon Cremin's (1970) definition of education as an intentional and organized activity to transmit or to acquire knowledge, skills, or attitudes. With far more modest intentions and achievements than Cremin's, we have sought to understand the nature of adult education as a distinct entity among the varieties of education, as an agency in American society, and as part of adult experience. Educators of adults, in their infinite variety, have created specialized areas of practice organized around institutional settings, subject matter, clientele, and delivery systems. These areas were brought under the umbrella of adult education, even though some practitioners in these fields may not regard themselves as "adult educators."

Formative Influences

An elaborate educative system has evolved to disseminate the knowledge that a modern society requires. All human societies, however, require forms of learning and education for their survival and perpetuation. In the earliest days of this country, adult learning and education occurred as part of the process of cultural transmission. From these beginnings, more intentional forms of learning developed.

Native Americans

Adams, Grattan, and Knowles based their narratives on the fundamental assumption that adult education came over with the colonists and was subsequently adapted and assimilated into a new society. This assumption rested largely on the recorded activities of

English colonists along the Atlantic seaboard and neglected any contributions made by French, Spanish, Russian, or other colonists elsewhere. Such a view of cultural transmission also relegated Native Americans to an essentially passive role in a savage wilderness, rather than recognizing them as partners in an acculturation process.

This section focuses on the thirteen colonies. It is, however, important to realize that the perspective we present is that of the new colonists, who furnished the only written record. European and Native American contact indeed preceded the settlement of Jamestown, and in any event, it would be ethnocentric to date Native American culture only from the time of European contact. Historian J. H. Parry asserts that "Columbus did not discover a new world; he established contact between two worlds, both already old" (1966, p. 55). Not only did Columbus believe that he had reached Asia, but evidence now suggests the Vikings reached Newfoundland circa A.D. 1,000. There is also speculation about even earlier Roman and Phoenician visits to the New World. The search for "original discoverers" will doubtless be matched by a search for the "original inhabitants."

Certainly, the Iroquois, Mohawk, and Onondaga Indians encountered by Jacques Cartier in 1535–1536 were not the primitive savages of legend. Donald Creighton (1944) concludes that "these tribes, with their skill in agriculture and their talent for political organization, had advanced far beyond the other native societies in northeastern North America in the development of their culture" (p. 5). Thus, Cartier saved himself from scurvy by learning and adopting a pharmacological remedy from Native American folklore.

Similarly, it was from the Native Americans that the Europeans learned of maize or Indian corn, white and sweet potatoes, tomatoes and some beans, and maple sugar. The new arrivals displayed a substantial dependence on certain Indian knowledge and skills; Francis Jennings (1976) emphasizes that Atlantic Coast Indians "fed the earliest colonizers and taught them how to grow crops under new conditions of soil and climate. Indians guided explorers and traders over established trails and routes through the wilderness that was otherwise so mysterious and frightening to the newcomers, and Indians gave instruction in transportation and survival techniques" (p. 40). This instruction, derived from a knowledge base assembled long before Jamestown's foundation, led Robert Berkhofer (1987) and others to advocate a "New Indian History," encompassing cultural pluralism. Here, one seeks "the dynamics of a tribe's history before white contact and then proceeds with how its leaders and others coped creatively with the altered circumstances of the tribe over time" (p. 36).

In writing a history such as this, one faces certain perceptual constraints. In the oral–aural Native American culture, "education and socialization were transmitted verbally without the technological advances of writing and printing" (French, 1987, p. xii). Such knowledge was transmitted by storytellers and orators, or absorbed through experience of family life, economy, religion, or government. The Native Americans organized the knowledge into a personal, dynamic account of ever-changing events, unlike the more abstract and dispassionate European style of learning. For historians, the concepts and interpretations of the majority culture relegated Native American beliefs to mythology. On balance, the attention devoted by anthropologists to education in preliterate societies, as well as the current interest in oral history, reveals the limitations of printed sources: formal history, however well documented, necessarily represents an incomplete picture of events.

Unless this question of factuality is resolved, perceptions of the education of the preliterate Native American will remain constrained. Roanoke colonists, returning to England after their first year in the New World, described an Indian culture whose members had acquired the skills for physical, psychological, and social survival and who were anxious to learn from the settlers (Quinn, 1955). One colonist recalled that the Indians "have no such tooles, nor any such craftes, sciences and artes as wee; Yet in those things they doe, they shewed excellencie of wit" (p. 104, p. 371). The recognition of different but refined knowledge and skills complemented the premise of missionary activity—that Native Americans were educable in aspects of European culture. In 1624, Richard Eburne, a settlement promoter, emphasized more than the religious potential: he contended that the Native Americans were capable of learning European arts and sciences. Lacking "acceptable" Indian accounts, one is left with a limited understanding of education among preliterate inhabitants, although a social organization and culture clearly existed when the Europeans arrived.

New Settlers

The European settlers had little interest in the social organization and culture of Native Americans. Beyond having to learn some survival techniques, the new arrivals saw themselves more as teachers than as learners. As the heirs of Western civilization, their journey to Jamestown in December 1606 was prompted by twin desires: they hoped both to emulate Spanish and Portuguese financial success in Mexico, Peru, and Brazil and to share in the civilizing and Christianizing of the Native Americans. While the thirteen colonies attracted diverse groups of settlers, we will focus on the English cultural patterns because they prevailed.

The Reformation witnessed the closing of monastic and convent charity schools and the dispersal of most early church libraries (Kelly, 1962). The state took a more active role in educational reform, and educational philanthropy became an interest of the prosperous merchant classes as well. The government promoted regular instruction in archery, uniform textbooks in Latin, and a mandatory system of apprenticeship for skilled employment. The emphasis was understandably on the education of children and youth, but opportunities soon proliferated for adults.

In practice, independent study was being facilitated, especially by the increased publication of works in the vernacular. In the Elizabethan age, numeracy and vernacular literacy were probably common to skilled workers and yeomen farmers (Kelly, 1962; Bennett, 1965), and the new secular and scientific studies found a more congenial home among adult learners than they did in either the schools or universities. Stimulated by geographical discoveries and improved military techniques, the late sixteenth century witnessed the publication of almanacs and of scientific and technical textbooks (Taylor, 1954). Such works were often intended for those lacking in formal education and might be supplemented by formal courses in mathematics, cartography, horology, navigation, surveying, and gunnery. Both authors and instructors tended to come not from educational institutions but from among the ranks of practitioners (Taylor, 1954).

The sporadic nature of such instruction was remedied after 1597 through the endowment of Gresham College, London, which offered public lectures in astronomy, geometry, civil law, medicine, divinity, music, and rhetoric. Intended for "the common benefit of the people of this city," the lectures proved popular with merchants and skilled workers who lacked proficiency in Latin (Kelly, 1962, p. 26). Participation in other forms of instruction generally required the payment of fees, but the market for courses was evidently growing, particularly in the capital. In 1615, John Keane, a London physician, was offering Latin, Greek, and "arithmetic . . . the mathematical sciences . . . as of geodaesie, geographie . . . the use of the globes, the hemisphere in plano, the astrolabe, cross staffe, circumferentor and plane table" (Taylor, 1954, p. 204).

Already, the English merchant, as a personification of the self-made individual, had inspired a popular literature of attainable success. Among the many success stories of the period were Richard Johnson's *Nine Worthies of London* (1592) and William Perkins's *A Treatise on Vocations* (1603). "Success-minded immigrants sometimes carried Perkins' book with them to the New World" (Wyllie, 1954, p. 11). Such scientific studies influenced the ambitious merchants, sailors, and craftworkers who scented opportunities in the New World.

Socially, the early settlers included a few upper-class magnates like Lord Baltimore, first proprietor of Maryland, but mainly ranged from landed gentry, merchants, and professional people to yeoman farmers, storekeepers, skilled tradespeople, and substantial numbers of indentured servants (Bailyn, 1986). Virginia, and later other colonies, offered fifty acres of land to colonists for each passage paid, enabling planters to expand their holdings when they brought over indentured servants. The latter repaid the passage money by working for a specified number of years (Handlin, 1986). The indentured servants ranged from university-educated Puritan ministers to illiterate servants. Their motivations varied, too: some were actively seeking better outlets for their talents; others were fleeing persecution, imprisonment, or poverty; yet others had been dispatched by public authorities as "undesirables." These last were sought for a Scottish expedition to New York in 1669, specifically, "strong and idle beggars, vagabonds, egyptians, common and notorious whoores, theeves and others dissolute and louse persons banished or stigmatized for gross crymes" (Gouldesborough, 1961, p. 56).

The new settlers represented not a cross section of English society but those elements subject to economic, social, or theological constraints. Fischer (1989) has interpreted their cultural inheritance as that of the British subcultures represented in four waves of emigration. The first wave, the Puritans from the east of England, settled in New England from 1629 to 1641. The second wave, from 1642 to 1675, comprised fleeing royalists and indentured servants en route from southern England to Virginia. In the third wave, from 1675 to 1725, Quakers from the English midlands headed for Pennsylvania. The final wave, in the eighteenth century, comprised Irish emigrants moving to the backcountry.

Among free settlers as well as indentured servants, the overriding perception of the New World was of a place open to talent, ingenuity, and investment. However, Fischer sees three contrasting sets of values: the Quakers recognized freedom for all; the backcountry settlers prized uniform community values with no right of dissent; and members of the Virginia elite sought to preserve or enhance their own privileges. Handlin concludes that while "the colonists did not challenge hierarchical social arrangements," the conception of rank was "significantly modified by accelerated movement from one level to another" (1986, pp. 196–197). Social privilege was an important factor in the colonies, as in England.

Colonial Concerns

The colonists inherited the tradition of education, particularly formal education, as a privilege related to rank. Beyond the differences of opportunity, as between the isolated backcountry settlers and the prosperous tidewater planters, there were attitudinal differences. In the formative years, for example, Virginia lacked the educated elite found in Massachusetts. "In the first fifteen years of Virginia's history, we have record of only two or three men with university training who settled within her borders. But in the first fifteen years of the history of Massachusetts, at least fifty religious leaders with university training became pastors of her churches" (Jernegan, 1931, p. 133). The Virginia ruling elite, mainly wealthier planters, was followed by small farmers and planters, indentured servants, and slaves. This elite was deeply interested in the education of gentlemen, and yet it feared any general expansion of education.

In the thirteen colonies, there were also fundamental differences between the Native American inhabitants, the soon-dominant white inhabitants, and the subjugated African Americans. Despite differences of educational emphasis, the white settlers displayed a conscious desire to entrench their cultural standards. Such commitment, while adapted to the frontier environment, brooked little interference from cultures deemed inferior: the concept of a "civilizing mission" assumed the formation of a Western (Christian) polity. This polity and the role of education were to be interpreted differently by the various religious denominations. Religious differences compounded national differences, as among the Scottish, Swedish, German, Dutch, and French settlers. However, in both political and cultural terms, an English (Protestant) ethos became dominant and was the primary influence on education in the thirteen colonies.

Above all, the gospel of utility, of preparation for an independent productive role in society, influenced education. Such a role was enjoined upon the colonists by two factors: the need for practical survival skills in the New World and the Puritan ethic stressing work and study for salvation. William Penn's Quakers might replace the authority of the Bible with individual responsibility to uphold the word of God, but they nevertheless remained committed to the Puritan work ethic. Penn's *1682 Frame of Government* envisioned his colony as "the Holy Experiment." In it, everyone would be "taught some useful trade or skill, to the end none may be idle" (Morris, 1946, p. 4). As colonial industry and commerce expanded and Britain attempted to limit the emigration of its skilled workers, colonial skill training took on enhanced value.

Summary

Early histories of adult education grew out of the efforts of philanthropic foundations and adult education associations, from the

1920s through the 1950s, to promote adult education as a new and distinct educational domain. Focusing on institutional development, these histories illuminate the pervasiveness of educational activities for adults throughout American history and across American society. A full account would include education for subordinate groups, the uses of adult education through voluntary action, and the function of information systems in continuing adult learning. We need to define adult education so that it can be identified as a distinct activity within preliterate American experience. Learning as a process of cultural transmission is reflected in the experience of Native Americans and the early settlers.

      Native American culture existed before European settlement, and it promoted the settlers' survival. Nevertheless, the lack of written documentation has encouraged denigration of Native American culture. Some contemporary European testimony to Indians' skills and knowledge base (aside from the evangelists' conviction that Indians could be educated in the Christian faith) has, however, come down to us. Today, there is a growing interest in preliterate societies and in oral history, but non–Native American historians are still constrained by questions of documentation. When English settlers arrived and proceeded to establish what were to become the thirteen colonies, the formative influences, essentially those of the (Protestant) English, reflected a growing shift from church to state in the nature and control of education. Colonial education was also associated with rank, particularly in Virginia, and later chapters will examine the manner in which such received values were retained or transformed.

PART ONE

Adult Education in Early America

2

Informal and
Literary Endeavors

The thirteen colonies remained very much a part of the transatlantic community, within which informal learning opportunities flourished especially in the areas of business and daily life for the literate: correspondence networks, an ever growing selection of both domestic and imported literature, and community activities influenced by world travelers. From all of these sources, libraries and temporary societies would eventually develop.

Informal Education

Much of adult education in the early colonial period owed less to formal institutions, educational or otherwise, than to everyday living. Dupree (1976) notes the existence of an informal correspondence network: mail formed an integral part of ships' cargoes "from the time Thomas Hariot rode Raleigh's ships to Roanoke, to the continuous trade of the Quaker merchants of Philadelphia" (p. 22). The correspondence related not only to commerce but to affairs among relatives and friends.

Henry Oldenburg, secretary of the Royal Society from 1663 to 1677, established a vast correspondence network "that reached America peripherally at least" (Frick, 1976, p. 78), which gave individuals broader opportunities than the local associations could provide. The Royal Society also supported isolated efforts at scientific research and self-education. For example, Frick (1976) shows that the "botanizing parsons . . . the first effective naturalists in Virginia" were aided by their correspondence with Henry Compton, bishop of London, in the 1690s (pp. 79–80).

Similarly, Peter Collinson was the "philosophical broker" of the Anglo-American scientific link in the early eighteenth century. Collinson, a Quaker merchant in London, had a correspondence network that reached from Philadelphia to Peking. He sent the Library Company of Pennsylvania "the earliest accounts of every new European improvement in agriculture and arts, and every philosophical discovery" (Frick, 1976, p. 70) as well as assisted in the European publication of many early American scientific works.

Literature relevant to the lives of ordinary people developed slowly because Harvard College housed the colonies' only printing press for over three decades beginning in 1638. The Harvard press published more scholarly works. However, later works published in the thirteen colonies were more didactic, including catechisms, almanacs, broadsheets, pamphlets, chapbooks, manuals or primers for school use and self-education, magazines, and weekly newspapers.

Harvard monopolized the production of almanacs by regularly assigning the task to a young mathematician, who prepared scientific and theological publications that sold for threepence. By the late eighteenth century, almanacs, whose authors varied from physicians to self-educated craftworkers, had evolved into "veritable textbooks of political theory and economic innovation," becoming, next to the Bible, the colonies' "most widely read literary production" (Sidwell, 1968, pp. 278, 286). Although essentially calendars, they often took the form of cookbooks, home medical guides, farming journals, political treatises, or collections of poetry and prose. Benjamin Franklin's famous *Poor Richard's Almanac* (1732–1757) proclaimed the virtues of hard work as an avenue to success and prosperity. The almanac was described as the "most despised, most prolific, most indispensable of books, which every man uses and no man praises . . . [and was] the only literary necessity even in households where the Bible and the newspaper are still undesired or unattainable luxuries" (Tyler, Vol. 2, [1878] 1949, p. 120).

The first newspaper was published in Boston in 1690, but by 1725 the colonies had five newspapers and by 1765, twenty-five, two of which were in German. None was published in either Delaware or New Jersey (Mott, 1950; Kobre, 1944). Newspapers provided local information as well as reprints from English papers; letters from readers; sermons; essays; advertisements; and reports on inventions, discoveries, and experiments. Medical innovations were also reported: a 1759 Boston newspaper describes Dr. Sylvester Gardiner's two successful gallstone operations (Bridenbaugh, [1955] 1964a, p. 201). Three short-lived American magazines appeared in 1741, including one by Benjamin Franklin, and by 1783 some twenty-two journals had been published in the colonies, although only one was still in circulation (Cremin, 1970, p. 392).

Despite high production costs and uneven quality, newspapers and magazines contributed substantially to the self-education of colonists, even to those unable to afford a personal copy or dependent on others to do the reading. These newspapers were published by men who frequently aspired to influential roles in an expanding, highly competitive market (Wroth, 1938). The distribution of these publications was aided by the growth of bookstores in Boston, New York, Philadelphia, Charleston, and Savannah: by 1750, there were 121. Although colonial publishing suffered from a chronic lack of capital, bookstores stocked numerous imports from England as well.

The cost of books—and therefore of access to them—is a subject of speculation, given the complexities of the book trade, the extent of competition, and the changing state of the economy. Colonial Virginia, for example, lacked subscription and circulating libraries, so it seems that "except for an inexpensive almanac, prayer book or Bible, neither books nor the local bookstore figured prominently in Virginians' search for information, instruction, or entertainment" (Stiverson and Stiverson, 1983, pp. 165, 173).

Access to books was limited to a relatively small elite—those with access to libraries and other educational institutions; the newly literate public had yet to acquire the habit or means of purchasing books. Samuel Goodrich, a successful publisher and author, recalled eighteenth-century Connecticut farmers' limited access to books: beyond some religious books and pamphlets, families tended to have only "the Bible and Dr. Watts's Psalms and Hymns . . . a volume or two of sermons, (and) Doddridge's *Rise and Progress of Religion*" (Hall, 1983, p. 1). As independence approached, it was the newspaper, the almanac, and assorted pamphlets that informed or incited the populace (Bailyn, 1967)—for example, Thomas Paine's 1776 *Common Sense,* which popularized the "natural rights" philosophy that was to be embodied in the Declaration of Independence.

Individual travelers—government employees, merchants, clergy, and new settlers who traveled within the colonies or voyaged across the Atlantic and back—also had an impact. Ministers seeking to cultivate Puritan values played a dominant educational role in the nucleated communities of New England, as did clergy in the small Finnish, Swedish, and French Dissenting communities of the middle colonies and the Dutch villages of New Netherland. However, in the farmlands of Virginia, neither church nor community exercised that degree of influence. In the seaports of Boston, New York, and Philadelphia, such influences as town meetings, militia musters, and churches contributed to the informal education of the inhabitants.

Colonial seaport taverns and coffee houses also played an educational as well as a social role. Taverns stocked newspapers, made public announcements, hosted club meetings and dances, held public readings and theatrical entertainment, and provided a venue for literate customers to share their knowledge with illiterate companions. Many taverns provided furnished rooms for social, professional, or business purposes. In 1729, at the Spring Garden tavern, New York City, a group of lawyers initiated such a venture: they "formed a private corporation of members of the legal profession, arranging to meet there on the first Wednesday in each month to discuss matters affecting their group and professional interests" (Bridenbaugh, [1938] 1964b, p. 428). Although taverns remained associated with debauchery and drunkenness despite municipal licensing and supervision, some gave birth to formal educational agencies. Coffee houses, popular with public officials, army and navy officers, and the gentry, often provided newspapers, public announcements, and even writing materials. Associated with relaxation and entertainment, taverns and coffee houses in the seaport towns attracted a diverse clientele. Political groups found these gathering places to be useful for influencing public opinion.

As prosperity and newfound leisure encouraged recreation and entertainment, New York's traditional joviality was balanced by Boston's reserve. Between 1709 and the 1730s, according to Bridenbaugh, New York progressed from banning live theater to supporting sold-out houses, while in Boston theater was outlawed. At the same time, in Philadelphia the Quakers, too, outlawed theater and frowned on dancing classes and fencing academies. Clearly, many factors affected access to learning opportunities.

Literacy

Colonial Massachusetts and Connecticut each had an established church, Puritan or Congregational, that was integrated into the life of the community it served. The Puritan obligation to seek salvation required that literacy be promoted to enable everyone to read the Bible. In New England, therefore, each congregation needed both a pastor to supervise church activities and a teacher to deliver sermons and catechize youth. Education soon became a public responsibility. In 1644, Massachusetts required every town with fifty householders to have a teacher of reading and writing and those with one hundred householders to have a grammar school. Harvard, the first institution of higher education established in the colonies, exemplified the Puritan commitment to a liberal classical education, and about half of its graduates entered the ministry. Parents felt obligated to be literate, not just for their own salvation, but in order to teach their own children. The practices of reading aloud and of repeating religious texts when books were scarce inevitably influenced "the pace and quality of reading as a style. Reading in early New England was an act that took place slowly and with unusual intensity," and while the mother taught reading, the father taught writing (Hall, 1983, p. 23).

For example, Cotton Mather, the son of New England Puritan leader Increase Mather, was first educated at home and then at the Boston Latin School. He entered Harvard College at the age of twelve, and by 1679, the sixteen-year-old Mather had hatched plans for a Young Men's Association. Four years later, he inaugurated it and, with his father, founded a Boston Philosophical Society (Levin, 1978, p. 92). Ordained in 1685 and active in philanthropy, Cotton Mather later devoted attention to education and scholarship. For him, the goal of education was piety—knowing the scriptures and acting on their precepts. He wrote about the educational responsibilities of parents and clergy, the training of ministers, and the role of voluntary associations. In 1693, Cotton Mather recorded that "a company of poor Negroes, of their own accord" asked him to help establish a society "for the welfare of their miserable nation that were servants among us" (Levin, 1978, p. 235). This society combined learning the catechism with the encouragement of mutual assistance among its members.

By 1710, Mather had formulated plans for discussion groups to promote community improvement (Mather, 1966). In his *Bonifacius: An Essay Upon the Good*, he envisaged regular meetings to help one's neighbors, distribute approved books, and discuss questions of public and private morality. Membership was restricted to men, but the benefits were intended for the community in general. Fundamental to the scheme was the eradication of ignorance and of perceived social injustice (Levy, 1979). Benjamin Franklin, who visited Mather in 1724, expanded and secularized the idea of a voluntary society with his *Junto*.

Mather, in his effort to promote piety and benevolence and combat declining religious influences, contributed to teaching and learning with some 468 printed works: religious sermons and tracts, biographies and histories, poetry and prose, a diary, and private correspondence. His *Bonifacius: An Essay Upon the Good* may have been the first American publication on adult education, reprinted at least eighteen times in the United States and Britain between 1807 and 1845 (Levy, 1979).

Education, equated with a preordained standard of behavior and obligation, also implied an acceptance of the status quo, with its subservient roles for women, Indians, and slaves. Thus, "as in eighteenth century Virginia, the book in colonial New England was closely tied to certain structures of authority" (Hall, 1983, p. 20). "The purpose of biblical literacy was fundamentally conservative in both aims and method. Interpretation of biblical passages was doctrinaire, and the method of recitation used to teach reading emphasized memorization" (Stevens, 1987, p. 106). However, by the eighteenth century, church and community were no longer coterminous, and the colonial family was losing its cohesive power as it responded to the new environment. Its younger members were scenting possibilities for individual fulfillment outside their family, community, and church. To the Puritan establishment, the purpose of education was to achieve "the good life," but to others this had a more secular connotation. For some, productivity had replaced salvation as a goal, as illustrated in Benjamin Franklin's 1748 caution that "time is money" (Bridenbaugh, 1968, p. 45). Differing interests often overlapped, as seen in general opposition to the Stamp Act and to the possible appointment of an Anglican bishop in the colonies. Puritan ministers now indulged in political education through preaching, publishing, and correspondence.

Between 1630 and 1776, most skilled white male immigrants were apparently literate. The less skilled, male and female, improved their literacy in adulthood, the motivation not entirely religious (Galenson, 1981, p. 17). It seems probable that by the end of the eighteenth century, there was nearly universal male literacy in New England and two-thirds male literacy in Virginia and Pennsylvania (Lockridge, 1974). The semiliterate and illiterate had to acknowledge the preeminence of the fully literate and rely on an oral medium for their own access to knowledge. Whether the motivation was religious or secular, advances made by white males served to highlight the handicaps faced by white females, and even more, those faced by Native Americans and African Americans. Puritan ideals, having promoted selective improvement of opportunities, gave literate New Englanders attitudes not very different from those of their illiterate neighbors. Brown (1976) ascribes these inequalities of opportunity to a conflict between Puritan modernity and Puritan traditionalism: concepts of individual autonomy and literacy conflicted with biblical models of family government and church polity. For example, around 1700, "the admission policy of Congregational churches in Boston resulted in exclusion of many artisans and tradesmen from membership, although not from attendance at services" (Bridenbaugh, [1938] 1964b, p. 258). The cultural elite thus continued to tolerate fundamental social inequalities.

Public Lectures

Public lectures functioned more as a supplement for the literate public than as an alternative for the semiliterate or illiterate public. As early as 1726, Isaac Greenwood was lecturing in Boston on mechanical philosophy, and in 1734 on astronomy. Professor John Winthrop of Harvard College responded to the public's fears resulting from a 1755 earthquake by lecturing on the subject. Four years later, he delivered two public lectures on the ever-popular subject of astronomy (Bridenbaugh, [1955] 1964a, [1938] 1964b). Electricity was also a popular topic, proving both entertaining and educational: the 1743–1744 lecture tour by Dr. Adam Spencer stimulated Benjamin Franklin to undertake his own experiments, and William Claggett of Newport began his own lectures. In 1765, William Johnson hoped that his Charles Town lecture on electricity would entertain the more cultured members of the town; later, he found that audiences in Boston and New York were equally appreciative (Bridenbaugh, [1955] 1964a). When engineer Christopher Colles left Philadelphia to install the Manhattan waterworks in 1774, he also delivered a series of public lectures on pneumatics and hydraulics. Such lectures doubtless contributed to a public appreciation of municipal improvements as well as to Colles's own career, for the project was to dwarf the earlier waterworks' schemes at Bethlehem and Providence (Bridenbaugh, [1955] 1964a). Boston, New York, Philadelphia, Newport, and Charles Town developed into established cultural centers, comprising a regular circuit for itinerant lecturers whose popular scientific speeches and demonstrations were open to anyone able to pay modest to high fees—which in practice meant largely the leisured, business, and professional classes.

With smallpox epidemics and the absence of a colonial medical school, public medical lectures achieved some popularity as well. Although the College of Philadelphia did not appoint its first medical faculty member until 1765, Dr. Adam Thomson delivered a public lecture there on the treatment of smallpox in 1750. Attracting much public interest as well as stimulating professional controversy, the lecture was subsequently published. In 1754–1756, Dr. William Hunter delivered annual lectures and demonstrations on anatomy in the Colony House in Newport, and in 1765, Dr. William Lee Perkins did the same in Boston (Bridenbaugh, [1955] 1964a). Such ad hoc public lectures supplemented the apprenticeship training of medical practitioners and served a public need.

Colleges promoted many public lecture courses to raise money and encourage enrollments. Long (1976, 1984) identifies scientific and medical lectures offered by the College of Philadelphia and King's College, New York, in 1766 and 1767 respectively. While medical lectures and demonstrations were solely for males, females could accompany them to other lectures. Courses were available both day and evening and were intended to be entertaining and understandable to an audience that also included people with little medical knowledge. Fees for these short courses varied from gratis to ten pounds. The lectures might be supplemented by a printed syllabus, illustrations, demonstrations, "preparations," and a solar microscope; they provided continuing professional education, general cultural development, or sometimes just simple entertainment. An evident weakness was their ad hoc nature, as well as a dependence on the resources of agencies with other commitments. Similar lectures were also popular in England (Long, 1984).

Libraries, Societies, and Institutions

Colonial governments usually lacked the power, the inclination, or the funds to meet the educational needs of the various segments of the public. Accordingly, people resorted increasingly to voluntary associations committed to specific functions, thereby avoiding the ever-unpopular taxation. Groups of like-minded individuals gathered to meet their own cultural and social interests. Some of the resulting associations were primarily social; others were specifically educational from the outset. In part, this trend represented a move from a popular culture toward an elitist culture, one that reflected social and/or economic status.

The Boston Public Library was founded in 1673, thanks to Robert Keayne's donation of books twenty years earlier. Keayne, a successful Puritan merchant, contributed to Harvard College (Bridenbaugh, [1938] 1964b) and showed his affection for books in his famous will, in which he bequeathed to his son a book "bound in leather, all written with my own hand, which I esteem more precious than gold" (Bailyn, 1965, p. 29). Another such library, established at Charleston, South Carolina, after 1698, became a provincial library in 1700, under the supervision of public trustees. In New York, also in 1700, the governor's chaplain, Rev. John Sharp, donated a library for free public use, but it subsequently merged with the collection of a proprietary library (Department of the Interior, 1876). Private libraries were brought over by the colonists or amassed over the years. An individual library might embrace the classics, religious works, practical treatises on medicine, law, and agriculture, as well as literary or historical works. Such libraries were valued both for their intrinsic qualities in self-education and as adjuncts to a more formal education.

Anglican Virginia was judged by one of its seekers of knowledge to be a literary desert (Hall, 1983). In a defense of "Cracker Culture," McWhiney (1988) allows that "a few Southerners read and collected books, but usually they were considered curiosities by their neighbors" (p. 198). He also notes the saying, "only partly in jest, that more Southerners wrote books than read them" (p. 206). While New England developed its own literary culture, Virginians "long remained content to import their culture, like their furniture and clothing, from England" (Stiverson and Stiverson, 1983, p. 139). However, despite the increased study of colonial literary culture and identification of many books, Richard Beale Davis's works (1978) illustrate the continuing difficulty of measuring their impact.

Parochial lending libraries, to which the laity had some access, were introduced first in Annapolis, Maryland, in 1696. Rev. Thomas Bray, a commissary of this colony's newly formed Anglican parishes, concluded in 1700 that such libraries would aid the work of the clergy and the education of the laity. In the previous year, he had cooperated in founding the Society for Promoting Christian Knowledge, which he envisioned as a religious educational program for Indians, poorer planters, and the nonconforming Quakers. By 1701, Bray had obtained a royal charter for the Society for the Propagation of the Gospel in Foreign Parts, which organized a major effort at religious conversion, soliciting the participation of clergy and schoolteachers. Bray's society instituted parish libraries, largely religious in content but embracing the classics, literature, medicine, commerce, economics, law, and politics (Searcy, 1963;

Calam, 1971). Established in Anglican parishes from Boston to Charleston, these libraries were an important educational resource for the privileged.

Proponents of learned societies believed that they could offer something more than the informal education of a small library. Many early scientists looked toward a society with regular membership meetings, demonstrations and/or research, and published proceedings or transactions. Increase Mather launched a Boston Philosophical Society as early as 1683; Cotton Mather described it as composed of "agreeable gentlemen, who met once a fortnight for a conference upon improvements in philosophy and additions to the stores of natural history" (Bates, 1965, p. 3).

In 1727, Benjamin Franklin, then a working printer, launched his Society of the Leather Apron, or Junto, in a Philadelphia tavern. This society functioned as a mutual improvement club for about thirty years and became a model for others; the first members included a copier of deeds, a self-taught mathematician, a surveyor, a shoemaker, a joiner, a merchant's clerk, and a gentleman of independent means. Franklin claimed that the Junto was the best club of its kind in the province, thus revealing a self-serving side of his character, which prompted John Quincy Adams to note that Franklin's love of ease and dissipation would "prevent any thorough reformation of anything—and his cunning and silence and reserve render it very difficult to do anything with him" (Levin, 1987, p. 107).

In 1730, noting that the absence of a good bookstore south of Boston obligated Junto members to import books from England, Franklin and the Junto members combined their personal collections in a common library. In the next year they initiated a fifty-member subscription library with a two-pound entrance fee in the Junto's building. Nonsubscribers borrowed books for a small weekly charge. A year later, an order for books was sent to Peter Collinson, noted earlier as a Quaker merchant in London, who served as "an unpaid buyer and unsolicited adviser to the Company" (Frick, 1976, p. 80). Such public interest in an information system needs to be seen within the context of the limited colonial resources noted by Franklin. Yet subscription libraries proved attractive, suddenly doubling in number in the last decade of the

eighteenth century (Hall, 1983, p. 44). They were unevenly distributed, however: colonial Virginia, for example, lacked both
circulation and subscription libraries.

Some early ventures began with more social goals, such as
the Winyaw Indigo Society, founded about 1740 in South Carolina,
where Georgetown planters met monthly in the Old Oak Tavern.
In 1756, one year after receiving a royal charter, the society initiated
an educational project by adding an apprenticeship endowment
and a free school for poor children to an established library.

Franklin and others founded the American Philosophical Society in Philadelphia in 1743, but many American scientists continued to aspire to membership in the Royal Society in England,
which had shown early interest in fostering scientific study and
research in the colonies (Stearns, 1970). The American Philosophical Society began as something of a club for aristocrats who liked
to dabble fashionably in scientific experiments. Cotton Mather's
election to membership in 1713 was followed by that of some fifty-
three other colonists before the close of the War of Independence.
In the period 1720–1742, the total published contributions of six
Bostonians in the society's *Philosophical Transactions* exceeded
those of the other four Americans and nine Englishmen (excluding
those from Oxford and Cambridge) who contributed (Bridenbaugh,
[1938] 1964b, p. 454).

In 1753, the governing body, on which Benjamin Franklin
served, awarded him a medal for his experiments in electricity. His
growing reputation as a scientist, educator, publisher, and municipal improver (Cohen, 1990) eventually helped his role as a diplo-
mat in London and Paris. In addition to the society's occasional
financing of research in America and its members' patronage of
American scientific collections, the society's secretaries maintained
a substantial correspondence network. The *Philosophical Transactions* proved to be both an information source and a model for
subsequent American societies.

The other major influence on American development in the
area of learned societies was the Society of Arts, established in
England in 1754 to improve agriculture and manufacturing. Its
colonial involvement included "exchanging seeds, by sending a
sawmill to America, and by despatching agents to study technolog-

ical problems . . . dispensing large sums of money for potash in Massachusetts, silk in Georgia, and viniculture in New Jersey" (Hindle, 1976, pp. 86–87). The secretaries conducted extensive correspondence with such important figures as Benjamin Franklin or the Charleston naturalist Alexander Garden. Elected to membership in 1755, Garden shared the results of his own experiments and attempted to establish a local society but was unsuccessful.

Models like the American Philosophical Society and the Society of Arts prompted several colonial developments. These included the Society for Encouraging Trade and Commerce (Boston, 1763), the Society for the Promotion of Arts, Agriculture and Oeconomy (New York, 1764), American Society for Promoting and Propagating Useful Knowledge (Philadelphia, 1766), the Society for Encouraging Manufactures (Charleston, 1771), and the Society for the Promotion of Useful Knowledge (Virginia, 1774).

In January 1769, remaining members of the dormant American Philosophical Society joined forces with the recently founded American Society for Promoting and Propagating Useful Knowledge in Philadelphia. Benjamin Franklin now presided over the "Proprietary–Anglican–Presbyterian" inheritance of the former and the "den of liberal Quakers" from the latter (Hindle, 1956, pp. 128–129). The Quakers had espoused the more utilitarian model of the Society of Arts, while the American Philosophical Society had increasingly followed the "pure science" model of the Royal Society. College faculty now provided leadership and the provincial assembly began making regular grants. With the 1771 publication of its *Transactions,* the society achieved recognition as a reputable learned body. It was also a fairly exclusive (white male) publicly funded body. Nonlocal in nature, elected members lived elsewhere in America and in Europe, but even its "most outstanding scientific figures" were largely amateurs (Hindle, 1956, p. 140).

In 1780, Boston followed Philadelphia's lead by establishing its own learned society, the American Academy of Arts and Sciences. Thanks to John Adams, the Massachusetts constitution included the obligation to promote such societies. The society's charter identified its aims: "to cultivate every art and science which may tend to advance the interest, honor, dignity, and happiness of a free, independent, and virtuous people" (Whitehill, 1976, p. 153). Many of its founders were Harvard graduates, mostly lawyers and judges, followed by clergymen, medical men, and "a leavening of prosperous merchants and gentlemen of inherited property" (Whitehill, 1976, pp. 158–159). In 1780, the society mounted a scientific expedition to observe a solar eclipse from nearby Penobscot Bay. The event was facilitated by an otherwise hostile British garrison—clearly learning took precedence over politics!

As Reingold (1976) traces the professionalization of American science, he terms most early supporters of such societies "cultivators" rather than "amateurs." He differentiates them from "practitioners," employed in scientific occupations, or "researchers." Cultivators might progress to the other categories but "were quite often concerned with their own self-education, rather than the increase or dissemination of new knowledge. Not being interested in publishing, the cultivators tended to regard what they did as a source of pleasure—a form of relaxation, a hobby. It was even a sport" (Reingold, 1976, p. 41). We may thus regard the society membership of the "agreeable gentlemen" of Boston or the "outstanding scientists" of Philadelphia as largely the self-education of a privileged elite.

The establishment of early medical societies presaged continuing professional education for practitioners: the Boston Medical Society, in operation as early as 1735, published articles and held demonstrations. Other often transitory local societies soon followed in the Northeast. In 1766, the New Jersey Medical Society became the first colony-wide body, with its members "striving to promote their professional interests . . . (and) medical science" (Bates, 1965, p. 18). Boston physician John Warren was similarly inclined, aiding the establishment of the Boston Medical Society in 1780, the Boston Humane Society in 1780, and the Massachusetts Medical Society in 1781 before becoming a professor of anatomy and surgery at Harvard University in 1782 (Bates, 1965). The Massachusetts society initiated its own library in 1782, later began publication of *Medical Communications,* and sponsored the establishment of local societies.

Other practitioners who attempted some continuing education in colonial times included navigators and sea captains. The Boston Marine Society of 1742 progressed from social and philanthropic aims to the collection and dissemination of information on "the variations of the needle, the soundings, courses, distances, and all other things remarkable on this coast" (Bates, 1965, p. 20). The Salem Marine Society of 1766 similarly recorded its members' observations, and these remain with us today.

Beyond their use by specific social, occupational, or religious groups, these "information systems" benefited relatively few. However, as independence approached, there was a growing interest in more diverse needs and in such basics as the promotion of agricultural education.

Summary

The colonial population was part of an Atlantic information network serving literary, religious, and business purposes. This network helped independent study and early scientific research. The network was enhanced by early colonial publications and by a growing number of bookstores.

The Puritan commitment to salvation encouraged literacy, but with strictly conservative aims and methodology. New England's literate white males had attitudes that proved very similar to the beliefs and attitudes of the illiterate, thus supporting the status quo. For some though, literacy helped them to be successful in a more secular and utilitarian world.

Informal education influenced the literate and the illiterate, the prosperous and the poor, the free and the enslaved. The Puritan ministers had to contend with the influences of the taverns, coffee houses, theaters, town meetings, militia musters, and workplace: it was in these "schools for the people" that information was exchanged, opinions heard and debated, and contacts often established with a wider world.

Lectures in particular served the male and female members of "polite society," and a lecture circuit developed on the Eastern seaboard. Parish libraries reached a wider public, sometimes even Native Americans and African Americans. The "mutual improvement" principle was evident in the voluntary societies that were initially an elite phenomenon, but which laid a foundation for more popular agencies.

3

The Evolution of
Regulated Access

Apprenticeship, "the most fundamental educational institution of the period" (Seybolt, [1917] 1969, p. 22), and the evening schools that followed it, merit exploration. Their scope and their potential for expanding access to learning, including access for women and minorities, was significant.

Apprenticeship

Surgeons as well as shoemakers were trained through the traditional system of apprenticeship, which usually included the rudiments of reading, writing, and arithmetic, and close moral, religious, and social supervision. Customarily, it lasted for seven years or until the age of twenty-one for males or marriage (or the age of eighteen) for females. The apprentice traditionally lived with the teacher, and their mutual obligations were specified in a legal contract known as an indenture (Towner, 1955, 1966; Quimby, 1963). For example, a Portsmouth, New Hampshire, agreement of 1676 identified the master's responsibilities: to "teach and instruct [the apprentice] or cause to be taught and instructed in the art and mystery as a mason . . . teaching him to read and allowing him three months towards the latter end of his time to go to school to write . . . " (Seybolt,

34

[1917] 1969, p. 29). Local schoolteachers increasingly provided the general education, often because of the inabilities of masters or mistresses. Apprentices were obligated to apply themselves diligently in their work and learning, to respect trade secrets, and to observe a moral code.

Benjamin Franklin, born in 1706, is often hailed as an exemplary apprentice, owing largely to his uninhibited self-promotion. The tenth son of a Boston tallow and candle maker, he completed his formal schooling at the age of ten. He read extensively before his 1718 apprenticeship to an older brother as a printer. In his *Autobiography,* Franklin described his early interest in seafaring, understandable since many Boston youths entered that trade to learn "the art and mistry of navigation and of a mariner" (Bridenbaugh, [1938] 1964b, p. 46). But young Ben's father arranged the printing apprenticeship, and Ben gained access to books and to writing, availing himself of the printing trade's resources for independent study. Ben's dissatisfaction and eventual flight at the age of seventeen indicate the tensions between the aspirations of parents and those of their children inherent in the system. That he continued in the printing trade in Philadelphia and London, however, becoming prosperous and retiring at the age of forty-two, indicates the value of the skills he acquired. The apprenticeship system may also have contributed to his often utilitarian approach to educational issues.

Colonial apprenticeship copied many of the English patterns: close moral and technical supervision, learning by emulation of demonstrated skills, and some public supervision of its operation. In its integration with general education and its accessibility, it was probably superior to the original English form. While the colonies ignored the English property requirements for entry to highly skilled apprenticeships, substantial premiums were often still required for training as physicians, lawyers, silversmiths, or goldsmiths, and launching such businesses remained expensive. The colonies also differed in generally not developing craft guilds. In England, guilds accepted a limited number of apprentices, supervised their training, and evaluated their competence to establish a business and enroll other apprentices. Philadelphia did incorporate limited forms of guilds for tailors and cordwainers in 1718, and for a "carpenters' company" in 1724; the latter sought instruction in the science of architecture, presumably for its already qualified members (Bridenbaugh, [1938] 1964b).

Rorabaugh (1986) attributes the general absence of colonial guilds with powers of enforcement to "vast distances, shortages of skilled labor, a largely agricultural population, and a poorly developed legal system," noting that "one consequence was shoddy workmanship" (pp. 4–5). Cremin (1970) concludes that physicians, lawyers, and other professionals trained under the colonial apprenticeship system also displayed "a sharp decline in professional standards" in comparison with those educated at university (p. 223). However, a concern with the low standards that resulted from easy access and inadequate supervision seemed less likely to promote regulation than did a public hostility toward some of the practitioners because of their inadequate services.

Few colonial towns and parishes outside New England had the communal power and resources to enforce a high quality of apprenticeship instruction. While court-arranged apprenticeships were routinely recorded to secure compliance, few places outside Boston, Philadelphia, and New York recorded private agreements. Apprenticeship in the middle and Southern colonies was also inhibited by the influx of indentured servants and by Southerners teaching crafts to their slaves. In order to exclude occupations requiring only nominal instruction, the colonies followed a Massachusetts precedent that confined apprenticeship to skills benefiting the commonwealth (Seybolt, [1925] 1971). However, systematic instruction might have proved unenforceable in towns that required apprenticeships, at minimum cost, as a way to take care of the indigent.

Early colonial legislation provided for the apprenticeship of the idle, the dissolute, the illegitimate, the orphaned, and the poor. In 1671, authorities in Barnstable, New Hampshire, arranged such apprenticeships ("with the consent of their parents if it may be haid [sic] and if the parents shall oppose them") with the help of the magistrate (Handlin, 1986, p. 165). Varying levels of access to education and training are evident: on the one hand, there were independent, voluntary agreements, exemplified by Benjamin Franklin; on the other hand were mandated, tax-supported agreements, some of which did not even identify a trade.

The greater insistence on reading, writing, and arithmetic often attributed to colonial apprenticeships must be qualified. While seventeenth-century New England legislation promoted literacy, in the South legislation provided not for literacy but for trade education. Thus the region south of Philadelphia placed less emphasis on general education than did the North (Morris, 1946).

The close supervision of apprentices led inevitably to charges and countercharges of exploitation and idleness, which led to court intervention. Apprentices quickly established a tradition of riotous conduct and desertion and were sometimes discharged for drinking or inattention. Conversely, they were quick to assert that the fundamental teaching function was being ignored. Thus, one York Court, Virginia, agreement provided for instruction in tailoring, reading, and writing, but in 1690 the master was charged for not honoring the agreement. Such types of allegations and defensive statements merit consideration.

Certainly, it was common to delay the bulk of the instruction until the latter part of the apprenticeship. This stratagem guaranteed cheap labor from an unskilled apprentice who was unlikely to have other opportunities. Inevitably, this situation prompted many apprentices to abscond (including the relatively privileged Ben Franklin), leading some employers to offer rewards and threaten penalties. Tensions continued beyond the colonial period, and in Boston in 1791, a "6 pence reward" was offered for "Mathias Fanning, an apprentice young man about nineteen years of age" (Seybolt, [1917] 1969, p. 31). Other apprentices were cast adrift before the completion of their training if their employers were unable to continue in business.

The European preindustrial ideas of "rank" or "estate" were still evident in colonial apprenticeships, particularly in cases of gender or race. Women were usually apprenticed in such traditional occupations as spinning or weaving, while the parish apprenticeship of female orphans often involved only "housewifery" or domestic work (Jernegan, 1931). A Massachusetts act of 1642 required a combination of basic education, religious education, and trade training, as exemplified in a 1656 Watertown, Massachusetts, agreement: a widow's daughter was apprenticed to an Ipswich ropemaker "until she comes to the age of eighteen years, in which time [she] is to serve [the family] in all lawful commands, and the [master] is to teach her to reade the English tongue, and to instruct her in the knowledge of God and his ways" (Jernegan, 1931, p. 119). Women were more likely to be exploited or abused, as with Margerie Goold who, in 1663, "accused John Lumbrozo, her master, of trying to rape her, while offering her scriptural proof that it was the right thing to do" (Handlin, 1986, p. 168).

In New England and New York, African Americans and Native Americans were often apprenticed to agriculture and trades, as were slaves and free African Americans in the South. Since indentured workers tended to become farmers on completion of their service, skilled workers were in demand in the South. Thus, "young Negro slaves could be apprenticed by masters to free white artisans," and in seventeenth-century Virginia, there were "many Negro mechanics, especially carpenters and coopers, and Negro women who had been taught to take part in domestic manufacture" (Jernegan, 1931, pp. 10–11). By 1777, Jernegan writes in 1931, a small textile factory in Williamsburg, Virginia, was advertising that "Negro girls are received as apprentices" (p. 18). Such slaves might work for their owners, for those to whom they were apprenticed, or for those to whom they were hired out, or they might even enjoy industrial freedom in return for part of their wages.

The institution of apprenticeship is credited with having "often served as a step toward freedom" for African Americans, although discrimination persisted toward them and toward Native American apprentices (Morris, 1946). Indeed, as early as 1715, there were complaints that Native American apprentices "bound out for a limited time to be taught by Christians were being sold into slavery" (Adams, 1946, p. 21). In 1744, opposition to slave apprenticeships surfaced in South Carolina. White shipwrights resented the competition, and the general assembly felt that they deterred white tradespeople from immigrating. In 1750, similar concerns led Georgia to permit only coopers, among craftsmen, to take African Americans as apprentices (Jernegan, 1931).

There was a fundamental difference between white males in the professionalizing apprenticeships and in the skilled trades and all other apprenticeships: the former would be recognized as competent to manage their own businesses, not merely as technically competent to perform a skilled role. Regardless of gender or race, the apprenticeships in nominal trades often provided little more than basic general education. Conversely, even systematic instruction in skilled trades for females and minorities could not redress existing social inequities.

Colonial apprenticeship, an integral part of the educational process, also served social, economic, religious, and humanitarian roles. To some, it offered the potential for social and economic advancement; to others, it reinforced certain social imperatives by constraining freedom and mobility. For newcomers to trades and professions, it was the chief source of occupational expertise; for the poor, orphaned, and illegitimate, it was also an important source of elementary and religious education. For all social classes, apprenticeships offered greater access to prized knowledge and skills.

Evening Schools

Evening schools were recorded in New Amsterdam in 1661, New York City in 1690, Boston and other New England seaports at the end of the seventeenth century, Philadelphia and Charleston at the beginning of the eighteenth century (Seybolt, [1925] 1971, pp. 9–12). Typically private ventures, their curriculum began with elementary courses in reading, writing, and arithmetic. Some offered more advanced courses in classical and modern languages, or in business and technical subjects, or made provision for social or leisure activities. Depending on local interests and needs and the availability of instructors, evening schools offered a rich assortment of courses even before the middle of the eighteenth century: algebra, astronomy, bookkeeping, chronology, English, ethics, French, geography, geometry, German, Greek, gauging, Hebrew, history, Latin, logarithms, logic, metaphysics, natural philosophy, navigation, rhetoric, surveying, and trigonometry (Seybolt, [1925] 1971, p. 32). By 1723, New York City had an academy in which a Yale graduate offered a liberal college education by evening study. Between 1765 and 1789, Savannah, Georgia, was offering such courses as music, dancing, fencing, drawing, and self-defense.

The students, who usually worked during the daytime, included apprentices, young women (often in separate classes), and young men preparing for college. The apprentices were frequently entitled to some instruction as part of their agreement, but access for others was constrained by the cost of fees. The schools furnished theoretical instruction as a supplement to practical training. Fee schedules differed widely, from forty shillings per month for "young gentlemen" attending a 1744 Charleston French course, to six shillings per quarter for a 1768 Newport course on writing and arithmetic, to three dollars entrance fee plus three dollars monthly for a 1789 Savannah dancing class (Seybolt, [1925] 1971, p. 43). Accommodation varied from existing school buildings to private houses, from "a sail loft in Philadelphia [to] public rooms of taverns" (Long, 1975a, p. 33). Long shows how cooperative efforts were attempted: a 1768 *Pennsylvania Gazette* published a joint advertisement for ten evening schools (1984, p. 20). Seybolt attributed much of the success of these schools to the growing needs of apprentices.

Occasionally, sponsored ventures are recorded, such as a trade school that was established in Nazareth, Pennsylvania, in 1757, by the Moravian church. The reading, writing, and arithmetic were supplemented by courses in blacksmithing, gunsmithing, locksmithing, weaving, carpentry, and masonry; church members were assigned "automatically and dogmatically" to take the courses (Bridenbaugh, 1964c, p. 131).

As competitors in an uncertain market, the private evening schools tended to be very responsive to immediate needs limiting class sizes or emphasizing effective teaching as interests changed (Seybolt, [1925] 1971). Nathaniel and Mary Gittens promised the latter in a 1744 *South Carolina Gazette* advertisement: he taught male students writing and arithmetic, and she taught female students drawing. Such instructors might be day school teachers, or have vocational experience, or claim a college education. Few were as blunt as Thomas Carroll in advertising his intended school in the *New York Mercury* in 1765: he stated that some unfortunate events compelled him to teach and that he would accept only those who had scholarly skills (Seybolt, [1925] 1971, pp. 62–63).

Such instructors were condemned as "unscrupulous, self-serving, and of doubtful origins and attainments" (Kendall, 1973, p. 16). Certainly, they were a diverse group, mostly lacking in professional preparation and particularly subject to market forces for their survival. However, many teachers in the publicly supported day schools, at least some college professors, and numerous apprentice mistresses and masters faced similar handicaps and attracted similar criticism. To what extent evening school instructors were unethical, incompetent, or unpopular remains a subject for additional research. Certainly, the private venture evening school was under fewer restraints than established institutions such as apprenticeships, town day schools, or colleges. Nevertheless, evening schools' survival did depend on meeting the needs of the communities; the evening school instructor might offer social and economic opportunities, either for a modest fee or as part of an apprenticeship agreement. But these schools were unable to redress fundamental inequalities of gender, race, or class—unlike the Quaker or Moravian evening schools, the private venture ones were businesses intended to provide a service for those best able to afford it.

Education of Women

Clearly, gender, race, social class, and religion were among the factors influencing participation in colonial adult education. The Puritans followed the teaching of St. Paul to Timothy: "Let the woman learn in silence with all subjection. But I suffer not a woman to teach, nor to usurp authority over the man but to be in silence" (1 Timothy 2:11-12). The Puritans believed that women should be literate in order to ensure salvation, not to encourage independent intellectual growth. White women clearly had less access to formal education than did white men. Long (1975b) argues, though, that the traditional focus on "dame" schools—schools that provided basic reading and writing skills to young girls—ignores the rich and diverse opportunities for informal learning available to women.

But even the daughters of a Puritan minister in cultured Boston might find their parents skeptical of their educational aspirations. Stirred by reading poetry, Jane Coleman wrote some of her own; her father then warned her that "writing poetry was indulgent; she should spend her time in reading and devotion" (Kerber, 1988, p. 22). Well before her death in 1729 at age twenty-seven, she displayed remorse for having read fiction and was worried about her salvation. Her father attributed the elopement of her younger sister,

Abigail, to ideas that she derived from a lifetime of reading, particularly novels. This judgment typified a widespread tendency to denigrate colonial women who managed to gain access to books.

Benjamin Franklin, a champion of self-improvement, accepted that women might be rational beings capable of the pursuit of happiness. However, his *Reflections on Courtship and Marriage* (1746) assumed that female education should focus on preparation for marriage and motherhood and on household management, not on challenging the status of women. His own wife, however, managed not only the household but also the printing business during Franklin's periodic absences. His views were an improvement over the Puritan concept of female irrationality, but they still excluded women from fully developing their intellect. Thus Kendall (1973) characterizes women's education as an instrument of social control, which kept women in existing roles, subservient to men.

There were no colonial institutions offering formal higher education to women; the only options were independent study, attendance at public lectures, or sampling the usually segregated classes in evening schools. Long (1976) concludes that women "were generally offered the same subjects available to men" (p. 58). However, this does not mean that women were able, socially or economically, to take full advantage of such opportunities: rather, as Long acknowledges (p. 51), education was viewed as a function of social roles for both men and women and those for women "centered around the home." Great stamina and initiative would have been needed to challenge such views.

The status of women reflected that of their fathers or, if married, their husbands, and female literacy rates reveal this. One 1740s study found that nine out of ten of the wealthiest 90 percent of women in Windsor, Connecticut, signed their names on deeds (Auwers, 1980, pp. 204–214). Eliza Lucas Pinckney commented that leisured colonial women regarded an inability to compose a good letter as "almost inexcusable in one of our sex" (Norton, 1980, p. 262).

For women who worked as teachers or apprentice mistresses, "appropriate roles" meant "the domestic arts" or the instruction of other females. Some became tutors for young children, teaching reading, writing, arithmetic, perhaps sewing, and occasionally music and French.

Despite the handicaps they faced, some women gained the skills and confidence needed to manage estates and business ventures. Through keen observation and informal learning rather than formal classes or apprenticeship training, many widows were able to take over inherited businesses (Holliday, 1922).

In 1775, John Adams confessed to his own educational limitations, but he did not doubt that his wife, Abigail, with her "totally homemade education," was well qualified to educate their young children (Levin, 1987, p. 41). Abigail, in fact, concluded that few women could aspire to be "learned" because of their obligation to perform "most domestic cares and duties" (Levin, 1987, p. 29). She *persevered* nevertheless and found expression in a rich heritage of letter writing. The uncommon few who did aspire to be "learned" included Hannah Williams of South Carolina, credited in 1704 with a remarkable knowledge of zoology, and Eliza Lucas Pinckney, who devoted considerable time to an independent study of the classics (Holliday, 1922). Conversely, a traveler concluded in 1775 that the ladies of aristocratic Virginia spent their time largely on household duties and entertainment: "They seldom read, or endeavor to improve their minds" (Burnaby, 1775, p. 58). However, even in cultured Boston in 1773, it was recognized that few women "have been sufficiently instructed in their own language to write it with propriety and elegance" (Bridenbaugh, 1964a, p. 377).

Nonprivileged women also faced extraordinary difficulty. An assortment of informal learning opportunities did not compensate for the relative lack of alternate social roles and formal education. Instead, influential opinion remained critical of women who aspired to continue their education, particularly if they were not white and upper middle class. Change did not seem to be on the horizon. "Apart from Mrs. Adams's letters, there is little evidence that American women before the 1780s perceived their lack of educational opportunity as a circumstance that called for a societal remedy" (Norton, 1980, p. 263).

Education of Minorities

Adult minorities (Native Americans and African Americans) differed in levels of formal and informal education, as well as in levels of limitation prescribed by their assigned social roles. Some slaves brought craft skills with them from Africa, and all were quickly engaged in learning their new roles in America (Stavisky, 1949). Specifically, some slaves brought "skills in metallurgy, woodworking, and leather," which slaveowners learned, used, and supplemented (Foner, 1974, p. 4).

Some have held laudatory views of the education of African Americans before 1835, characterizing it as a period of enlightenment, with their education similar to that of white people. The anticipation of manumission, instead of indefinite slavery, is believed to be responsible for providing for skill development, religious needs, citizenship, and general improvement. Phillips regarded the education on Southern plantations as the best "yet invented for the mass training of that sort of inert and backward people which the bulk of American Negroes represented" (Cremin, 1970, p. 412). This attitude is reminiscent of Cotton Mather's condescending contribution to the education of African Americans in 1693. Comparable paternalism can be seen in the efforts of the Society for the Propagation of the Gospel to teach African Americans to read in South Carolina beginning in 1702 and in New York City beginning in 1704 (Klingberg, 1940; Reid, 1945).

In addition to these real difficulties for African American education, early legislation outlawed the education of slaves: in 1740, South Carolina declared it illegal to teach slaves to write. Such legislation conflicted with practical necessity for some plantation slaves, but it shows the conflicting values of the period. Indeed, the justification for instructing the slaves was not derived solely from the needs of the plantation. In colonial Charleston, "slave craftsmen were even hired out," while "in the North, where trade and manufacturing grew, slaves continued to move into the skilled trades" (Foner, 1974, p. 4).

Education for Native Americans attracted substantial attention, with institutional provision in schools and colleges, apprenticeship, training in colonists' homes, and education in England. The original 1606 charter of Virginia proclaimed the need to spread Christianity. A 1660 Essex, Massachusetts, petition on Indian apprenticeships said that "an Indian may have the same distribution of justice with ourselves" (Morris, 1946, p. 388). In practice, as Bailyn (1960) notes, "In Virginia, Maryland, and especially Massachusetts, the first and most carefully planned efforts in education were directed not at the settlers, but at the Indians" in order to convert them to Christianity (pp. 37–38).

In 1649, nine self-sustaining "praying Indian" towns were established in Massachusetts. They were intended to exemplify "visible civility," provide schools for Indian children and adults, and "alter previous ways of life in a number of rigorously mandated particulars" (Jennings, 1976, p. 251). John Sassamon, a praying Indian, was sent to Harvard College in 1653 to prepare for teaching the Wampanoag Indians to read. Other efforts included a projected East India Company school and college at Henrico, Virginia, abandoned after the 1662 massacre and a short-lived Indian College at Harvard, which published an Indian Bible (Adams, 1946, p. 18). This phase of development ended in 1675 when King Philip led the Wampanoag and their allies into a revolt.

At the end of the seventeenth century, an English charity fund enabled the College of William and Mary to enroll Native American students, although in segregated classes. Declining enrollments and the withdrawal of funds due to the War of Independence ended this venture. Between 1745 and 1753, the Scottish-based Society for the Propagation of Christian Knowledge funded a self-supporting Indian community at Bethel, New Jersey, which provided apprenticeships and an adult evening school for Delaware Indians (Adams, 1946). This venture lasted until 1753, when white settlers forced the Delawares to move to Pennsylvania; further pressures forced the Indians on to New York during the Revolution.

The same society funded the Rev. Eleazer Wheelock's charity school at Lebanon, Connecticut, in 1755, and his subsequent Dartmouth College in Dresden, New Hampshire, in 1769 (Adams, 1946). In the former, Native American males were taught reading, writing, arithmetic, English, Greek, and Latin. Females learned reading and writing in school and housekeeping and sewing in local homes. Both were also prepared for careers as missionaries, mainly among the Iroquois. Although Wheelock devoted considerable energy to Christianizing Indians at his Lebanon school, Dartmouth College had a broader focus on liberal education and "Indian education was a secondary concern" (Adams, 1946, p. 20).

English efforts at educating Native Americans and African Americans were fragmentary. Such literacy and religious education as was provided was, for African Americans, overshadowed by the more immediate concerns of slavery, especially among slaves with skills, who had to compete with white journeymen. "Throughout the colonial period free white craftsmen fought a losing battle to exclude Blacks from most of the skilled trades" (Foner, 1974, p. 4).

Whether or not formal education was provided is not the major issue here—rather, the issue concerns the perceptions and attitudes of the majority culture that provided that education. The dominant culture used education, formal or informal, to instill its own values and safeguard its predominance. Among Native Americans, exceptional individuals did overcome the manifest obstacles and succeeded in the majority culture, but "access to occupations was sufficiently restricted by social covenant and convention to make any substantial education a luxury" (Cremin, 1970, p. 360).

Literacy and Christianity spread, if unevenly, among Native Americans and African Americans. However, neither the colonial missionary endeavor nor the informal learning by association had transformed these minorities into prospective partners by the end of the colonial period; the results of education and emancipation evidently did not provide much challenge to the dominant culture. Frustration with its modest achievements undoubtedly influenced that major Anglican proselytizing body, the Society for the Propagation of the Gospel in Foreign Parts, to shift its emphasis to work among Dissenters. Fundamentally, it had offered only a circumscribed education intended to enhance social control rather than effect reform. With the War of Independence, the society ceased its activities in the colonies. Some time would elapse before the colonists' early interest in minority education was revived.

Summary

Apprenticeship was the most pervasive form of colonial education. It provided for technical competence; moral and religious instruction; and some reading, writing, and arithmetic. Its opportunities tended to be segregated in terms of gender, class, and race. Legal enforcement of the provisions was often uneven, and disputes were common. The system had the potential to offer substantial social and material advancement but was constrained by the desire to maintain the status quo.

Evening schools proliferated in the seventeenth century, serving apprentices entitled to free instruction as well as men and women able to pay modest fees. The curriculum met liberal, vocational, and leisure interests, and instructors were often day school teachers or practitioners. Most schools were private venture institutions, necessarily responsive to changing needs and interests, but a few were sponsored institutions. The fee-paying institutions served a growing and competitive market and respected the dominant values and orthodoxies of that market.

Some women benefited from such schools, as they did from public lectures, or the opportunities for independent study. Nevertheless, even women fortunate enough to continue their education were constrained by a Puritan heritage of traditional female roles. Some managed to gain the skills and confidence to become schoolteachers, tutors, apprentice mistresses, or midwives and to manage the business or estate of an absent or deceased husband. Most women faced denigration of any intellectual aspirations that were independent of their husband or father (if they were unmarried).

Minorities also found that their educational provision was circumscribed by their assigned social roles. The early colonists accepted an "obligation" to "civilize" the Indians, but lost enthusiasm after several unsuccessful attempts. In the eighteenth century, the Society for the Propagation of Christian Knowledge funded both formal schooling and apprenticeship, but these foundered in the face of prejudice and indifference. Some black slaves arrived from Africa with valued skills, but their owners usually limited any subsequent education and training to those skills supportive of the plantation economy. While evangelizing was generally acceptable, reading, and especially writing, were matters of contention. Minority education, both of Indians and of African Americans, was constrained by such limitations as slavery, likely competition with white workers, and the fragmentation of denominational efforts. The real issue was not a question of *how much* or *what type* of education was provided, but *why* such education was provided: to keep minorities subservient in a society that was dominated by values which did not relate to them. Even then, few of the minorities who received that education managed to use it for their own social improvement.

PART TWO

The Early National and Antebellum Eras

4

Education's Role
in Building
the New Republic

Independence revealed colonial education's weaknesses in developing an enlightened populace. Although no unified movement had developed, adult education flourished, comprising early reform movements as well as a series of often compartmentalized "causes" that served the needs of different groups of adult learners. This chapter discusses some of the people's aspirations and the activists who promoted the various causes.

Ideologies and Expectations

Despite optimism, confidence, and idealism, more than a generation would elapse before social and economic change followed political change. The earlier class, gender, and race relationships persisted, influencing educational provision. However, there was a belief that the new nation was destined to become "the cultural as well as the political capital of the world" and that the electorate "would eagerly support American artists, poets, and playwrights who would soon rival Rembrandt, Milton, and Shakespeare" (Ellis, 1979, p. ix). Innovation, improvement, and social and economic ambition were becoming apparent. The Declaration of Independence proclaimed that "all men are created equal," although Thomas Jefferson, its major archi-

51

tect, hardly intended this to apply to women and minorities. The 1787 Ordinance on the Northwest Territory initiated a colonial policy that recognized equality rather than subordination in a territory. The ordinance provided for education by setting aside revenue from the sale of some land to support public education. It also gave the Northwest Territory the eventual right of entering the Union on an equal basis with the original states. A compact with the territorial inhabitants outlawed slavery and guaranteed civil rights and liberties. However, no educational provisions were included in the federal constitution, ratified in 1789, and the new state constitutions were noticeably vague.

While the Jeffersonian Revolution of 1800 was to shift power from the Federalist and commercial Northeast to the agrarian states, the latter were still under the influence of a planter aristocracy. Thus, Virginia and the Carolinas successfully combated many egalitarian influences for another half-century. In the South generally, tradition was indeed strengthened after 1800 by a growing reliance on the tobacco crop: "The old quasi-aristocratic system of economic and political organization gained renewed vitality. . . . The drive for education came primarily at the university level. Other social improvements found comparatively little support" (Brown, 1976, p. 114). Slaveholders, who dominated the political process, tended to be hostile to educating both their slaves and the nonslaveholding white population.

Elsewhere, deliberate attempts were soon made to promote cultural independence alongside nationalism, republicanism, and economic independence. This promotion was reflected in the patriotic flavor of textbooks, which aimed to encourage an educated electorate. Noah Webster in particular sought to promote American education and culture as a democratic and cohesive force. His work was to reflect the language of the ordinary citizen, excluding foreign phrases and providing a standard spelling and pronunciation. He first produced a speller as part of *A Grammatical Institute of the English Language* (1783), and went on to the *American Dictionary of the English Language* (1828). Webster saw many advantages in a reformed American spelling: it would simplify learning, remove prejudice, contribute to national unity, encourage the domestic publishing industry, reduce the price of books, and curb "an astonishing respect for the arts and literature of their parent country" (Webster, 1789, pp. 393–398). His democratic ideals were limited by the conviction that "education is always wrong which raises a woman above her station" (Perkins, 1988, p. 72).

Republican ideas of education embraced children and adults, individual and national purposes, and private and public responsibility (Rudolph, 1965). In 1779, Thomas Jefferson's *Bill for the More General Diffusion of Knowledge* proposed education for everyone, appropriate to each person's age and abilities, although in practice, it sought to produce a white male intellectual elite to serve the new nation's civic and political needs. It was radical in assuming state responsibility for the free basic education of all white children but conservative in limiting scholarship access to secondary and higher education and in assuming that leadership by the intellectual elite would be acceptable to citizens of the new republic. Elsewhere, Jefferson briefly envisaged the education of white females, Native Americans, and African Americans; the establishment of public libraries; and, along with George Washington, John Adams, and Dr. Benjamin Rush, the establishment of a national university. His schemes failed to win legislative support, although Washington left a small endowment for the national university.

In 1796, Washington urged the promotion of educational institutions; his goal was supported by the founding fathers, and their successors were expected to support it as well. To overlapping themes of nationalism, democracy, and an enlightened citizenry, Rush and others added practicality. Thus, the founding fathers questioned the value of the classics in promoting the well-being of the new nation. Rush, a controversial Philadelphia physician and signer of the Declaration of Independence, campaigned for a broad program of social reform (Butterfield, 1951), which embraced the education of women, temperance, emancipation, prison reform, and other issues. In criticizing slavery, he contended that blacks had the potential to benefit from education. In criticizing the penal system, he again stressed the role that education could play in rehabilitation. Rush's views typified the Enlightenment ideology, with education serving national purposes, promoting progress, and transmitting the shared basic values of a self-governing people.

The educational aspirations that followed independence predictably focused on white children and youth, on schools and colleges, and on formal instruction to achieve perfection. In actual practice, the education of adult Indians was to be based on colonial precedents, whereas the education of whites was to be based on republican ideals. Such beliefs have since been seen as "idealizing traditional rather than liberal values, precapitalist rather than capitalist codes of behavior" and being not "premodern" but actually "antimodern" (Ellis, 1979, p. 34). This belief system involved many paradoxes, some of which appeared in early adult education ventures. Thus, an explicit commitment to progress and creativity was often matched by an implicit commitment to social control and the avoidance of controversial issues. As Grattan (1955) concludes, "Between the end of the American revolution and the eighteen thirties, the intellectual and social climate in the United States was not too favorable to elaborate experiments in adult education" (p. 147).

While the new republic recognized that "all men are created equal," it nevertheless saw white male property holders as the electorate—although initially the wage earners among that group were considered to lack the economic freedom needed for republican citizenship. The New Jersey state constitution of 1776 had given the vote to "free" property holders, but women and blacks were disfranchised in 1807 "on the grounds that their votes could be easily manipulated" (Norton and others, 1982, p. 141). The new citizen body had nevertheless increased due to a general lowering of colonial property qualifications and to the fact that many states made land grants to returning veterans. However, it was not until about 1817, when Monroe became president, that Northern states abolished the property ownership requirement.

At the same time that participation in the political process broadened, efforts for social change were initiated. Often the education of adults was merely a service component in broader social campaigns, such as the religious revivals of the Second Great Awakening, the temperance movement, the development of utopias, abolition, and women's rights. Such campaigns were influenced by economic development that both created and intensified social problems. Economic progress also increased the number of people with the income, education, and leisure to find solutions.

New England's long cultural tradition and commitment to morality and education found expression in individual efforts at self-improvement. Thus, in 1786, Royall Tyler, hoping to marry the daughter of John Adams, sought to erase a blemished reputation by "assisting in a course of lectures on natural philosophy" (Levin, 1987, p. 220). The abilities of New Englanders—for example, the sailors who studied navigation—impressed Europeans: in Genoa, in 1817, the crew's navigation skills on a passing Salem, Massachusetts, vessel amazed astronomer Van Zach. He noted that "even the Negro cook could compute lunars, and knew the advantages of one method of computation over another" (Brown, 1976, p. 139). In Boston, conservative reformer Edward Everett (1832) noted the proliferation of adult education institutions and the number of inventions, discoveries, and improvements from those of "humble origin, narrow fortunes, small advantages, and self-taught"—a familiar eulogy of individual potential (p. 14).

Frontier pioneers from New England also sought to develop a cultured society, one that supported their concepts of individualism and progress. Inclined to disregard such issues as free choice and predestination, which were great concerns in Puritan culture, the pioneers were ripe for the pursuit of social and cultural progress. Timothy Flint, Calvinist president of Yale, traveled extensively in the Mississippi Valley. He concluded that despite the backwoodsmen's worship of progress, they "are not yet a reading people . . . [they] are too busy, too much occupied in making farms and speculations, to think of literature" (Flint, [1826] 1932, p. 171). These "speculations," and the labor shortage in fast-growing Cincinnati, nevertheless helped the development of some education and training. As early as 1811, a papermaker felt obligated to entice a prospective apprentice by offering cash, clothes, and night school. By the 1820s, women were moving beyond their traditional apprenticeships in spinning, weaving, and knitting to the more prosperous ones in chair making and cabinet making (Ross, 1985). Soon, the relatively successful Westerners would join the laboring classes of the Eastern seaboard and use their new suffrage (males were no longer required to be property owners in order to vote) to bring about the Jacksonian Revolution of 1828.

Adult Educators as Reformers

Andrew Jackson, who had proclaimed his belief that "man can be elevated," urged "perfecting our institutions" in pursuit of that goal (Wecter, 1937, p. 100). The embracing scope of "useful knowledge" attracted wide support among the old elite classes (for example, ministers) as well as among the new ones (industrialists). Support also came from the multiple reform movements, from writers and publishers catering to the newly literate publics, and from civic leaders serving community interests from the Northeast to the frontier. Promoters of educational ventures were varied, motivated by their own cultural, political, and economic aspirations, as well as by the specific and local contexts that influenced their target participants. "Before the 1820s, reform more commonly was a sideline for men, and some women, who had social position, or at least gainful employment. . . . For women, it was virtually the only way to have public influence" (Walters, 1978, p. 13). Later, educational ventures were to provide career prospects for some men and women, when despite the influence of voluntarism and self-help, a substantial market developed for "professional" lecturers in adult education.

Josiah Holbrook, a Connecticut traveling science lecturer, was the original lyceum founder, to be discussed later. Supporters of the national American Lyceum included the presidents of Yale College; Columbia College; Illinois College; Washington College, Connecticut; and Washington College, Pennsylvania. Other contributors were Daniel Webster, the famed orator and senator from Massachusetts; novelist Washington Irving; Alexander Dallas Bache, already an eminent scientist at the Franklin Institute; John Griscom, a Columbia College scientist; Stephen Van Rensselaer, founder of the Rensselaer Polytechnic Institute; and John Lowell, a prosperous Bostonian soon to launch the Lowell Institute (Hayes, 1932).

Adult education attracted a rhetoric of social progress and human perfectibility. With mechanics' institutes in particular, it also attracted the early support of those interested in economic development and a disciplined and intelligent labor force. Thus, Edward Everett (1840) advocated adult education on the premise that "an intelligent class can scarce be, as a class, vicious" (p. 83). Horace

Mann, while secretary of the Massachusetts Board of Education (1837–1848), urged upon industrialists the economic value of education and accordingly supported the development of mechanics' institutes and lyceums. De Witt Clinton, governor of New York, achieved his fame by association with the technological advances and economic opportunities of the Erie Canal, completed in 1825. He also supported the New York Scientific and Mechanic Institution, several learned societies, a state board of agriculture, and county agricultural societies. The chief promoter of Boston Mechanics' Institute was Timothy Claxton, a minor employer who made scientific apparatus; the first president of the Franklin Institute was James Ronaldson, a major cotton manufacturer and type founder; David Bell, a president of Buffalo Mechanics' Institute, was a substantial builder of locomotives and steamboats; and an early president of the San Francisco Mechanics' Institute was Andrew Hallidie, a prosperous engineering employer who introduced the famous cable cars. The evolution from small craft shop to factory and from mutual respect to regular moral preachment was instigated by these types of leaders. Hallidie reincorporated the institute and created a new governing board of trustees with close ties to the mechanic arts and industry (Keane, 1984b). A similar evolution of control succeeded in Cincinnati despite resistance by journeymen critical of new industrial "aristocrats" (Ross, 1985).

Later on, we will discuss the contributions of others who saw that adult education would play an important part in their struggle. Women's education in the (male) egalitarian republic received support from across the social and economic spectrum, although, as we shall see, to different degrees and for different reasons and with promoters as varied as Abigail Adams and Frances Wright. There were many contributions from those who saw women's education as a service component in the wider issue of women's rights. George Guess, a Sequoyah, recognized the importance of education in the struggle of Native Americans, as Frederick Douglass saw its significance in the struggles of African Americans.

Perhaps the most colorful collection of educational promoters was the group that accompanied William Maclure, the "father of American geology." In 1826, Maclure took these promoters on his "boatload of knowledge" to the utopian community of New Harmony, Indiana—among them, Marie Duclos Fretageot, a cultivated and cosmopolitan French teacher. She supervised the community's boarding school, directed the printing press, and advocated educational opportunities for women equal to those for men. Others advocating a role for adult education in radical social change included newspaper editor Horace Greeley, Unitarian minister Rev. William Ellery Channing, and transcendentalist writer Orestes Brownson. Such advocates covered the spectrum from male conservative to female utopian, from Native American to immigrant, from citizen to escaped slave, and from New Englander to Californian. Their objectives, too, were diverse.

In a period of substantial economic and social change, the motives of antebellum reformers have been interpreted variously— for example, the evangelical reformers have been seen both as radical activists whose religious beliefs inevitably led them to an involvement in broader social reforms and as essentially conservative people, concerned with social control (Thistlethwaite, 1967). The latter interpretation views their work as "an implicitly conservative reaction against the anxieties engendered by the disorders of libertarian society" (Berthoff, 1971, p. 256).

Self-Fulfillment as Reform

In the early 1830s, the diminishing influences of such established social institutions as the church and the community and the emergence of economic and geographical mobility resulted in rampant individualism. This individualism was moderated by the formation of voluntary associations, which became the preeminent instrument of reform.

In 1831–1832, Alexis de Tocqueville noted the importance of voluntarism in American society, a trend that mirrored the English experience, as Lord Macaulay pointed out in 1823: "This is an age of societies. There is scarcely an Englishman in ten who has not belonged to some association for distributing books, or for prosecuting them" (Jarman, 1970, p. 246). In the eighteenth century, such societies were largely a white male middle-class manifestation, but they took on a more democratic flavor in the nineteenth century. The societies filled two needs for both countries: "consistency with the revolutionary new individualism of private economic enterprise, and yet the capacity to cope with the social anxieties that were byproducts of that same economic revolution" (Berthoff, 1971, p. 254).

We can attribute the popular acceptance of education for adults to its promotion of individual improvement, not to any change that it cultivated in the prevailing social structure. The philosophy of transcendentalism extended the promise of Christian perfectionism to all who sought it. However, this was expected to come through self-culture, not institutional reform. However, to the poorer white males who obtained citizenship, and to the women and minorities who did not, the limitations of "individual improvement" were apparent at the outset. It seemed an ideology appropriate only for the fortunate and prosperous.

As capitalism developed, the elite among the skilled laborers also began to contemplate policies of their own. Nevertheless, as late as 1849, the Sunday School Union denounced proposals that placed the reform of society ahead of individual perfectibility. "Instead of making the invisible, intangible, and irresponsible composition which we call society the scapegoat for the sins and sufferings of the visible, tangible, and responsible individuals who compose it . . . we should . . . hold the individuals to answer for the burdens and griefs of society" (Griffin, 1967, p. 93). Many educators of adults encouraged a perfect society by promoting a succession of individual reformations, by relying on self-improvement, not on the political process. The importance of inherited genius, or of inherited wealth, was minimized in the eulogy of self-improvement. Therefore, all could aspire to the promised success by developing those separate aptitudes that were embodied in the prevailing faculty psychology. Such development was encouraged by a "historic congeniality" between Protestantism and business, which meant that Congregational ministers, in particular, were active in promoting self-improvement and material success (Wyllie, 1954, p. 55).

In the 1840s the rise of a new "science" of phrenology also encouraged the ideals of self-improvement, promising to identify by cranial readings those traits of character and ability that merited cultivation or restraint. Not only associated with self-improvement, this science was also marketed to the business community as an effective tool in selecting suitable employees, "a contributor to existing social stability, not . . . a way of undermining it" (Horlick, 1971, p. 34).

For all these reasons, it was not only possible but obligatory for adults to continue their education. Promoters promptly condemned any apathy or resistance within their target audiences. In 1845, one promoter told Cincinnati workers not to complain of exploitation, but instead to attend to education and self-improvement (Ross, 1985, p. 88).

The sciences quickly became an integral part of self-improvement, and even the conservative Boston merchant class showed an interest in Newtonian science as it related to navigation. However, like Federalists generally, they had little interest in the natural sciences, engineering, or technology, especially if such knowledge was associated with democracy, or with the philosophical radicalism and atheism of the French Revolution (Struik, 1968). Such diffidence had been apparent when the Boston Mechanick Association (1795) had "engaged in discussions of mechanical problems and scientific instruments, and occasionally even published transactions" (Bates, 1965, p. 26). Thus by 1802, there were only some twenty-one full-time college posts in science nationwide, and often-short-lived scientific societies, such as the Chemical Society of Philadelphia (1792), the Connecticut Academy of Arts and Sciences (1799), the East India Marine Society (1799), and the American Botanical Society (1806) (Kerber, 1972). By 1825, times had changed, even in Boston, where a committee chaired by the influential Unitarian minister William Ellery Channing saw a "useful knowledge" of the sciences as an answer to community immorality. The committee proposed a survey of books in Boston Apprentices Library and called for a study of "the nature and operation of institutions lately formed in Great Britain, and particularly Scotland, for giving lectures to young mechanics on the scientific principles of their various arts" (Brown, 1956, p. 165).

Even more striking was Boston educator Emerson's 1822 advocacy of chemistry and natural philosophy in women's education. Later, Ohio lawyer Timothy Walker (1831) could argue that advances in science and technology would create the leisure necessary for a generally accessible culture. Even astronomy, which utilitarians condemned as "stargazing," was defended by Joel Poinsett of the Smithsonian in 1841; he argued that it was supportive of mathematics, the physical sciences, and "the advancement of the mechanic arts" (Miller, 1965, p. 278).

Not everyone wished to advance the mechanic arts: the *Philadelphia National Gazette* editorialized in 1830 that it would be more profitable to rely on a workforce that was "comparatively uneducated" (Commons, Vol. 5, 1910, pp. 113–114). However, reform was clearly in the ascendant, with the sciences accepted as "useful" and popular in early adult education.

Summary

With independence came the expectations of an enlightened citizenry and of a cultural development that stressed practicality. Prevailing aspirations revealed certain paradoxes. Race, gender, social class, and religion determined suitability for citizenship and for educational development. New England was the home of many reform campaigns, while in Virginia, the legislature rejected Jefferson's educational proposals. Frontier settlers, impressed with material progress, were to prove supportive of the innovations in adult education associated with the Jacksonian Revolution.

Adult education promoters almost defy classification. They included old elites, new elites, upholders of the status quo, and challengers of the status quo. The voluntary associations channeled much of the enthusiasm, the more mainstream among them predictably committed to mainstream values. The associations as a whole promoted individual improvement, not wider social reform, and their ideals were accepted even by the utopian communities. They offered few prospects to poor citizens, women, and minorities. The physical sciences in particular were associated with these educational endeavors.

5

The Spread
of Literacy

Fundamental to a society that allowed greater political participation and economic opportunity was the improvement of educational access and expansion of facilities for independent study. Primary among such facilities were libraries, which complemented the growth of literacy and of publishing. Reading instruction was being developed, from the basics in evening schools to the high culture of perfectionism in utopian communities. The expansion of "book learning" and conflicts over its "appropriateness" are explored in this chapter.

Libraries and Publishing

Literacy, like illiteracy, was "stratified by occupation, wealth, race, ethnicity, nativity, gender, age, and population density" (Stevens, 1987, p. 102). In the early nineteenth century, its general level was clearly increasing. Learning from the successful religious press, reformers made efforts to promote literacy by producing and distributing cheap popular reading materials. Secular entrepreneurs included newspaper editors, publishers, agricultural reformers, and abolitionists. Libraries and reading rooms, an important form of voluntary association, aided their work, paralleling the rise of such major publishing companies as Harper Brothers, who began business in New York City in 1817. Following the initial publication of the New York *Sun* in 1833, the new "penny press" also aided the growth of literacy. Before the penny press developed a social conscience, critics charged that it "soon determined what their grubby readers wanted and gave it to them with relish. Robbery, riot, and rape was the recipe" (Bode, 1960, p. 252).

Horace Greeley's two-cent *New York Tribune,* launched in 1841, was an effective didactic instrument, containing perceptive editorials, informed civic and political comment, and cultural information, all written according to high ethical standards. Daily press, largely partisan and Whig, entered the reading rooms of the voluntary societies, thus challenging the societies' initial policies of excluding controversial material. Between 1840 and 1860, there was an estimated rise in the number of dailies nationwide from 138 to 373, and in weeklies from 1,266 to 2,971 (Bode, 1960, p. 251).

Another improvement was the grouping of books in "libraries" of related works, thus forming a possible curriculum. Intent on serving a growing market for literature and useful knowledge, other publishers imitated Harper's Family Library and Harper's Library of Select Novels. With no international copyright, it was possible to produce dime versions of foreign classics and newly popular novels. Beginning in 1818, Benjamin Silliman's *American Journal of Science and Arts* combined selections from foreign journals with contributions from American science.

A fundamental difficulty for the new reading public, particularly skilled workers wishing to study scientific and technical works, was to find material on a level suited to their literary accomplishments. The Society for the Diffusion of Useful Knowledge, founded by Henry Brougham, an internationally regarded adult educator, in London in 1826, partly overcame this problem by gathering some very able writers to produce authoritative, yet simple, popular "libraries" for cheap distribution. Two years later, in Boston, such eminent people as Daniel Webster, Josiah Holbrook, and Edward Everett sought to emulate Brougham with a lyceum named for his society. The venture became a commercial success on both sides of the Atlantic. However, in 1841, some New York workers were still encountering difficulties in finding suitable reading material. In the *N. Y. S. Mechanic,* they complained of "interminable volumes" full of "blind technicalities, quotations of foreign languages, and a dry, uninteresting style" (Calvert, 1967, p. 37). Meanwhile, writers produced numerous how-to manuals on character and morality and on basic skills and operations for those without apprenticeship training, and many entered the lecture circuit. All forms of print were prospering simultaneously in an increasingly literate population. As the total population increased from 17 to 31 million between 1840 and 1860, the number of literate Americans rose from 6.44 million to 15.3 million (Bode, 1960, p. 116).

Religious societies were a major influence on the increasingly literate culture. The American Bible Society (1816) and the American Tract Society (1824) both strove to sustain the nation's fundamentally Protestant character by providing ample materials for the growing reading public. The former sold or donated King James Bibles to local affiliates, with its output rising from 6,410 Bibles in 1816 to 240,776 Bibles in 1856 (Bode, 1960, p. 142).

Between 1840 and 1855, the annual distribution of tracts by the American Tract Society increased from three million to over twelve million, while bound volumes increased from 325,000 to over one million (Bode, 1960, p. 133). The society employed hundreds of colporteurs (combined missionaries and salespeople) to encourage Protestants and to convert Catholics. The society also published a colporteur's manual, identifying its publications and their message and stressing an avoidance of any denominational controversy. In addition to the colporteurs' visits to individuals, families, and public meetings, tracts were placed in the libraries of the growing array of voluntary societies. Combined, these two societies strengthened the religious influence on American culture by providing easily understood examples and references for instructors and students in secular adult education. Both secular and religious adult education were criticized for attempting to exclude controversial issues. In particular, the abolitionists criticized the American Bible Society for refusing to teach illiterate slaves to read the Bible.

Agricultural Societies

Agricultural societies also played a part in reform. Initially, an elite of such agricultural reformers as George Washington, Thomas Jefferson, John Adams, and James Madison had attempted to show the benefits of modern science. However, working farmers proved skeptical of "book farming" and were disinclined to emulate the experiments of the great estates. In 1811, Elkanah Watson began to pioneer societies of working farmers in New England, starting with the Berkshire Agricultural Society. Later, he actively lectured and published on the merits of agricultural innovation. By obtaining some state assistance and combining fairs, demonstrations, prize giving, and social activities, promoters launched many societies before the harsh economic climate of the late 1820s. Many continued to regard working farmers as " 'anti-intellectual,' practical men . . . intolerant of theories," but, in the 1830s, a popular agricultural press gathered support in the Northeast (Rossiter, 1976, p. 282).

"Commercial agriculture" now promised an alternative to farmers' growing migration to the more fertile soils of the West. A group of literate, middle-class farmers developed, intent on learning and applying the new scientific knowledge. By 1841, New York was the leading innovator in agricultural improvements, with an eight-thousand-dollar annual state grant to support such ventures as a state agricultural society, *Transactions* (a state publication), the county agricultural societies, and county fairs. After 1840, agricultural societies and journals increased nationally. By 1858, there were some 912 societies, and two years later there were some fifty to sixty journals with a combined circulation of 250,000 (Rossiter, 1976, p. 290).

Mechanics' and Apprentices' Libraries

The early 1820s witnessed the growth of a series of mechanics' and apprentices' libraries. Some of these were additions to trade societies of skilled workers, dating from the late eighteenth century, while others were freestanding separate foundations. The library departments of mechanics' institutes and lyceums were similar in intent and will be discussed later. The trade societies, combining welfare and fraternal roles, had been open to employers and journeymen alike. However, New York printers heralded changing times with their 1817 decision to exclude any printer who became an employer.

They concluded that "the interests of journeymen are separate, and in some cases opposite to those of employers" (Laurie, 1989, p. 51).

Even as journeymen came to identify their separate interests, many continued to lack the human and material resources to develop such libraries. Much depended on the purely local relationships of the political and economic power structure, and the litany of successful foundations doubtless ignores innumerable controversies and failures. Thus, when religious and civic leaders promoted the Brooklyn Apprentices Library, working mechanics displayed "considerable indifference" and refused any contribution (Jackson, 1941, p. 507).

In 1785, twenty-two mechanics founded the General Society of Mechanics and Tradesmen of the City of New York to aid members in sickness and distress (Bennett, 1926). In 1820, the society established a library of four hundred volumes (Lamb, 1889), and by 1829, some sixteen hundred apprentices were using its ten thousand volumes (Ditzion, 1940, pp. 199–200). In 1821, the Providence Association of Mechanics and Manufacturers of Rhode Island also established a library. But Portland, Maine, which was the site of a small lumber industry, needed ten years to muster support for the establishment of the Maine Charitable Mechanic Association in 1815. The association's sixty members then elected "a worthy shoemaker" to direct the venture. They sought to relieve "the distress of unfortunate mechanics and their families, to promote inventions and improvements in the mechanic arts, by granting premiums for said improvements, and to assist young mechanics with loans of money" (Maine, 1965, p. 3). In 1820, the association inaugurated a library for "cultivation of the mind." In 1817, Salem Charitable Mechanic Association, Massachusetts, began "to extend the means of usefulness by encouraging the ingenious, by assisting the necessitous, and by promoting mutual good offices with each other" (Hurd, 1888, p. 180). In 1820, a donation of books made possible the inauguration of a library, which accumulated some three hundred volumes within two months.

Similar libraries also started in Boston, Detroit, and Philadelphia in 1820; Lowell, Massachusetts, in 1825; Portsmouth, New Hampshire, in 1826; and Lancaster, Pennsylvania, in 1828 (Department of the Interior, 1876). In Lancaster, the Linnaean Society, the

Agricultural Society, the Law Association, and the Medical Society also established libraries in the nineteenth century (Kieffer, 1944). While the latter libraries served a defined membership, the mechanics' and apprentices' libraries frequently evolved into public libraries, and often provided lectures, debates, and discussions.

While mechanics' and apprentices' libraries seemed largely a local phenomenon, they were not entirely separate from other reform agendas. William Wood, who promoted the Boston library in 1820, was a liberal merchant involved in such activities as promoting Greek and Polish independence. He went on to act as a consultant when libraries were established in New York City, Albany, Philadelphia, New Orleans, and other centers (Ditzion, 1940). In New York City, Wood spent months visiting employers and employees while compiling a list of 740 prospective members (Bennett, 1926). In 1820, the promoters of the Apprentices Free Library of Philadelphia included Robert Vaux, an abolitionist and educator; Daniel B. Smith, a pharmacist and member of several learned societies; Robert Eyans, a public-spirited flour merchant engaged in literary and scientific studies; and Thomas Kimber, Quaker bookseller and stationer (Ditzion, 1940). Library promoters thus varied— from self-employed tradespeople who launched mutual benefit societies for their enlarged families, to prosperous merchants and professionals involved in a wider reform agenda. These libraries initially sought donations of books for three purposes: as a fundamental service for members' occupations, for moral and spiritual development, and for intellectual growth.

Thus, there was potential for an educated citizenry as well as for employers to exercise social control. Apprentices had traditionally submitted to such control, but skilled workers were increasingly sensitive to their own interests and often dubious of book-based knowledge. However, these libraries had a novelty value, which prompted participation and emulation. By midcentury, there were changes, as at the Charleston Apprentices' Library, South Carolina, where a membership of "mechanics whom the civic-minded were trying to lead along the path to literature" had changed to one of "the sedate middle class and . . . the fashionable rich" (Bode, 1956, p. 159). Possibly, the class consciousness noted among New York mechanics in 1817 had drifted south and such educational leadership was no longer acceptable in Charleston.

Sheriff Noah of New York City sent information on American libraries to Egerton Smith, editor of the *Liverpool Mercury*, which helped the founding of a mechanics' and apprentices' library in Liverpool, England, in July 1823. This link was strengthened in January 1824 with a gift from the New York Apprentices' Library of a banner and thirty books. The pride of the donors doubtless matched the recorded appreciation of the recipients: it was an opportunity for the donors to display their American skill and initiative in a city through which so many immigrants passed on their way to the United States.

Mercantile Libraries

Boston and New York established mercantile libraries in 1820. These were followed by Philadelphia in 1821, Cincinnati in 1835, Baltimore in 1839, St. Louis in 1846, Pittsburgh in 1847, Portland, Maine, in 1851, Portsmouth, New Hampshire, in 1852, San Francisco in 1853, Peoria, Illinois, in 1855, Brooklyn in 1857, and yet others later in the century (Department of the Interior, 1876). The mercantile libraries sought to promote business education, with an impetus that came not so much from employers as from the young clerks and merchants (Ditzion, 1940).

In 1820, the founders of the New York Mercantile Library noted their own youth with pride, but they soon needed the moral and financial support of employers. That these highly motivated and relatively favored clerks needed employers' support implies social conservatism as well as limited resources. Such later ventures as the San Francisco Mercantile Library Association, unable to secure the support of any employers, were obligated to charge onerous membership fees of three dollars a quarter. These libraries often prospered by expanding their programs or by amalgamating with other institutions. To a lending and reference library, some added a reading room, a museum, a gymnasium, a debating society, lectures, classes, or "a sort of business college" (Department of Interior, 1876).

Public Libraries

Despite these developments in agriculture, industry, and commerce, independent study and research in the sciences remained constrained by limited holdings even in such major libraries as the Library of Congress, the Astor Library of New York, the library of the Peabody Institute of Baltimore, and the Boston Public Library. Confirmation of this came as late as 1876, with the Smithsonian Institution's survey of learned society libraries. The survey found that "there are considerably less than a dozen which demand special notice," and even the combined federally supported scientific libraries in Washington had "many lamentable deficiencies" (Gill, 1876, p. 184). There were many volumes in the surgeon general's office (40,000), the Essex Institute, Salem (30,655), the Philadelphia Academy of Natural Sciences (30,000), and West Point Military Academy (25,000). However, "in no instance could any bibliographical study on an extensive scientific subject be prosecuted to a satisfactory conclusion in any one city, although the means for so doing are best provided in Philadelphia" (Gill, 1876, p. 188).

The goal—to serve the general public—still remained, although membership fees continued to constrain access to most libraries. In 1839, Horace Mann, secretary of education for Massachusetts, surveyed that state's library facilities. He identified 299 subscription or social libraries with 180,028 volumes, valued at $191,538 and accessible to 25,705 persons. There were also 10 to 15 town libraries with some 3,000 to 4,000 volumes accessible to all citizens, and about 50 district school libraries with about 10,000 volumes. Mann argued that reading should be promoted as the great instrument of self-culture, and that every schoolhouse should contain a library suited to both old and young. He advocated a system of public libraries integrated into a broad community education program.

Promotion of the public library took account of the growing number of citizens who had passed through the public school system but who lacked the opportunities to continue their reading. Some libraries had progressed to virtual public status with their membership and holdings, but any public funding was at best an ad hoc arrangement. Thus, in 1827, the town of Castine, Maine, took over responsibility for its social library. In 1833, Peterborough, New Hampshire, voted to maintain a free town library, as did Orange, Massachusetts, thirteen years later (Curti, 1964). The same three states pioneered legislation permitting tax-supported public libraries. Eighteen thousand district school libraries and thirty thousand Sunday school libraries supplemented the provisions by public libraries, according to an 1859 survey (Rhees, 1859).

Despite the earlier New England municipal libraries, it was the 1852 Boston example set by Edward Everett, an early supporter of adult education, that launched and publicized the public library movement. A Unitarian clergyman and former president of Harvard, Everett wrote to Mayor Quincy in June 1851, donating a collection of books. He also urged public funding for a library open "to the citizens at large" to help "independent study and research" (Grattan, 1962, p. 44). George Ticknor (1876), a Harvard professor of Spanish and French, was equally committed to independent study and supported the proposal. He advocated the public funding of "popular books, tending to moral and intellectual improvement," "pleasant literature" but not "such poor trash as . . . novels" (Grattan, 1962, p. 45). This support of "improvement" reflected the utilitarian policies of the "useful knowledge" movement. Approval of the library was granted in 1852, and it began operation two years later with support and a substantial donation from the mayor.

The public library experiment was blossoming, and by 1854, ten other Massachusetts towns were so provided. Bode (1956) notes that each of these "were either actual or potential caretakers of the libraries of decaying lyceums" (p. 245). Elite middle-class libraries usually still had the resources to retain their independence. However, many lyceums, mechanics' institutes, and mercantile libraries seem to have coalesced amicably with each other and with later public foundations. Among early public libraries there was thus an adult education heritage, which in later years some sought to reestablish. In effect, responsibility for the pervasively Victorian didactic role had passed from voluntary agencies to elected public bodies.

Self-Culture

Writers and publishers had urged public libraries to support the self-culture eulogized by the Unitarian Rev. William Ellery Channing, who saw formal education as preparation for lifelong independent study by all people. This conflicted with the notion that most people only needed training to prepare them for their work. Channing's controversial, socially responsive Christianity rated self-culture as a more effective tool in problem solving than was political action. Along with others of like mind, such as Ralph Waldo Emerson, he made quite an impact on adult education. However, so did Orestes Brownson, a supporter of the New York Working Man's party, who argued that Channing's self-culture was an inadequate substitute for more radical reforms (Welter, 1975).

Balancing Channing's spirituality was the social activism of Elihu Burritt, "the learned blacksmith" (Curti, 1937). His independent study included learning to speak French, German, Greek, Hebrew, Italian, and Spanish. His contributions progressed from lyceum lectures to work in the peace movement of the 1840s and the abolition movement of the 1850s and to efforts to avert the Civil War. Henry Ward Beecher (1846), a famous public lecturer, was another prominent dispenser of advice on independent study and traditional values, as indicated in his *Lectures to Young Men*. Young women received similar attention from other writers, as we shall see.

Evening Classes

The colonial provision of freestanding adult evening classes continued into the early national period. In the second quarter of the nineteenth century, some evening schools also started under public auspices.

Prominent among the voluntary agencies was the Society of Friends, or Quakers, who promoted Bible reading among the illiterate poor. Dr. Thomas Pole, a Quaker physician in Philadelphia and a member of the American Philosophical Society, had become involved in the work of the Bristol Adult School Society (1812) in England. Coolie Verner (1967) concludes that this "was undoubtedly the first organization established solely to promote the education of adults" (p. 8).

Other groups in Britain and the United States soon emulated the Bristol venture. In 1814, Pole published *A History of the Origin and Progress of Adult Schools,* which put him into contact with others interested in adult education, particularly other Quakers. The book dealt with such learning principles as self-motivation, memory, reinforcement, practice, evaluation, awareness of results, variation in the learning task, and progression from the simple to the complex. It referred to such factors as instructors' personal qualities, the continuing education of instructors, small-group teaching, and ability grouping. It recommended the formation of reading and discussion circles, noted the importance of peer-group support, and discussed the multiple roles of adulthood. There were notes on administration and supervision, with proposals for record keeping, applicant interviews, progress reports, attendance reports, and the reduction of "drop outs." Even the learning environment received attention: there was a recommendation to hold classes "in the dwellings of the poor, where small companies of neighbors acquainted with each other, may be collected for the purpose of receiving instruction in a more private way" (Verner, 1967, p. 39). Pole's manual drew recognition from the duke of Kent, in England, who said that "he considered the subject of adult education an object of national importance" (Verner, 1967, p. 94).

In the United States, correspondence networks, which we noted earlier, served as a conduit for Pole's ideas, and in 1815, Samuel Wood of New York reprinted Pole's manual. In the same year, Sarah Whitehead of Philadelphia and Divie Bethune of New York each reported enthusiastically on adult schools in their cities, established according to Pole's principles. Pole's manual on the adult school experiment provided a pioneer analysis of some problems and possibilities in educating adults. That many of these schools taught only reading limited their effectiveness. The objective was the moral reformation of low-income adults in order to make them law-abiding and efficient producers who accepted the status quo. The venture sought not to redress inequality, but to socialize behavior in accordance with dominant middle-class values.

Public evening schools developed first in New York City, Boston, and Louisville, their goal to provide an elementary education for young adults employed in the daytime. In New York City, a few classes were provided between 1825 and 1842 by the Public School Society, a publicly supported private agency whose functions, after 1842, were undertaken by the new Board of Education (Berrol, 1976). Due to increased immigration, by 1845 over one-third of the city's population was foreign-born, (Rosenwaike, 1972), a development that paralleled increasing industrialization. Such factors created a need for English language courses and vocational courses, and spawned the Americanization programs that later established the importance of evening schools.

Evening high schools developed in Cincinnati (1840), Boston (1847), and New York City (1850). Allowing for disagreements on foundation dates (Knowles, 1962), it seems that only about a dozen public school systems operated evening schools by the time of the Civil War. Their objectives were largely to teach established daytime curricula to young adults who had entered the workforce, many of whom were foreign-born. Before the Civil War, coping with the daytime schooling of children took all the attention of these public agencies, and few of them had the resources for elective evening programs. A general public responsibility for the latter would await the impact of larger social forces, although in Baltimore, and perhaps elsewhere, some public support for these programs did occur by midcentury. We shall explore separately the way in which voluntary agencies strove to provide evening classes as part of broader programs of adult education.

Utopian Experiments

Education played a role of varying importance in the voluntary associations formed to establish the proliferating utopias and religious cults of the early nineteenth century (Bestor, 1950; Manuel, 1966). Such associations exemplified the ideology of perfectionism and (Protestant) religious pluralism believed by many to be particularly suitable for the new republic. To realize the promise of America required an educated and disciplined commitment to new values, represented by a variety of social and ideological viewpoints. These associations extended the notion of individual perfectibility to one of communal perfectibility, using education as the driving force of social change. The reformers planned to effect change in small communities, which would then become educational models for wider use. In some cases, they envisaged communal ownership of property. Their utopia demanded intellectual as well as physical effort, and it involved a rejection both of the gradualism inherent in traditional self-improvement and of the violence associated with class struggle. It promised speedy, radical, yet peaceful change without involvement in the political process.

In a particularly influential experiment, Robert Owen, believing that character and behavior are entirely the products of environmental influences, sought to create a perfect society at New Harmony, Indiana, in 1825. Owen's experiment was preceded by a model society at New Lanark, Scotland, and meetings with interested Americans (Harrison, 1969). Professor John Griscom of Columbia College introduced Owen to many intellectual and political leaders in New York; in Philadelphia, Owen's host was Dr. James Rush, son of the renowned social reformer Benjamin Rush. There, Owen's itinerary included lecturing at the Franklin Institute and a discussion of his social ideas at the Athenaeum. In Washington, he met with President Monroe, John Quincy Adams, and a group of Choctaw and Chickasaw chiefs, before lecturing in the Hall of Representatives (Bestor, 1950). Owen then gathered supporters for his project, and in January 1825, he purchased a twenty-thousand-acre property from the Rappites, a German communitarian sect at Harmony, Indiana. There he offered prospects of infinite perfectibility to the "ignorant, poor, oppressed, and consequently vicious and miserable" (Owen, 1825, p. 1).

Among Owen's supporters was William Maclure, a prosperous geologist much influenced by the educational ideas of Swedish educator Johann Heinrich Pestalozzi (Maclure, 1831–1838). Maclure believed that political and economic equality was impossible without recognizing that "knowledge is power"—but only the provisions of useful knowledge, not classical education, would empower the producing class. He sought to influence character reformation by replacing competition and discord with the cooperation and harmony of a communitarian socialist environment. A Society for Mutual Instruction, with its own publishing unit, would provide the education. While Maclure, not Owen, had spearheaded the educational efforts among adults, in 1826 it was Owen who introduced an evening lecture series on trades and occupations, "delivered in place of systematic discussions of mineralogy, chemistry, or mechanics, on the theory that one useful thing is as much a part of science as another" (Bestor, 1950, p. 193). Maclure rejected this curriculum theory as well as lecturers chosen solely for experience and the relegation of students to passive attendance.

This initiative by Owen did not put an end to the influence of experts. The community included Pestalozzian teachers and some of Maclure's scientist friends. Publications and the content of the lecture program itself soon reflected their expertise. Thus, Maclure and his colleagues had their students debate with recognized experts in established fields of inquiry. By 1826, Owen, less committed to such educational horizons, was moving from cooperative to communist ideals. He rejected private property, the institution of marriage, and organized religion.

At New Harmony, Owen and Maclure faced over eight hundred people of great educational and social diversity, and a gulf between intellectuals and others persisted despite proclaimed egalitarian principles. Owen's son, Robert Dale Owen, described the settlers as "a heterogeneous collection of radicals, enthusiastic devotees to principle, honest latitudinarians, and lazy theorists, with a sprinkling of unprincipled sharpers thrown in" (Owen, [1874] 1967, p. 286). Occupationally, they varied from farmers to professionals, but included few skilled craftworkers. The new lifestyle sought to overcome traditional frontier isolation with a demanding intellectual and recreational program: "the weekly dance on Tuesday night, the concert on Thursday or Friday, the public discussion on Wednesday, the frequent lectures on everything from the circulation of the blood to the circulation of wealth, the unhampered discussions of religious ideas, the meetings of the Female Social Society and the Philanthropic Lodge of Masons, the parades and the drills . . . " (Bestor, 1950, p. 168).

Social discontent appeared, for which some blamed the emphasis on education. While the broader vision faded, belief in education's potential to effect change still attracted reformers. Indeed, Maclure's Society for Mutual Instruction was followed by his Workingmen's Institute at New Harmony in 1837 and his endowment of libraries in Indiana and Illinois (Lockwood, 1905). In New Harmony, he had invested capital, provided a library and scientific apparatus, and encouraged other scientists to conduct research.

Some accorded him recognition as New Harmony's cofounder (Harrison, 1969), and some saw his contributions as more enduring than Owen's (Wilson, 1964). Although the experiment failed by 1827, other Owenite communities struggled on for several years. Robert Dale Owen, who remained in Indiana, created traveling libraries that circulated among the villages of Indiana.

Horace Greeley, founder of the *New York Tribune,* and Albert Brisbane, an adherent of French socialists Charles Fourier and Saint-Simon, launched another utopian venture, the Fourierist Phalanx. This was the last major attempt to establish communitarian alternatives to prevailing economics. Some fifty cooperative agricultural settlements, or phalanxes, arose in the East and Midwest, and most proved very short-lived. The most enduring (1843–1854) at Red Bank, New Jersey, attracted many visitors and the attentions of such reformers as William Ellery Channing and Parke Godwin. Greeley had risen from poverty to champion several reform movements, including improved labor conditions, women's rights, abolition, and popular education. His Fourierism aimed to win the support of a broad spectrum of reformers interested in effecting social change. He emphasized that "before education can become what it should and must be, we must reform the social life whence it proceeds" (Greeley, 1853, p. 219). Thus, while education was provided in the phalanxes, the Fourierists viewed its potential in cautious terms (Greeley, 1868; Van Deusen, 1964). In a time of economic depression, the venture proved attractive, but individualism and outside opportunities soon intruded into the demanding and spartan life-style.

Ann Lee, who launched the Shaker religious communities in the Northeast in the late eighteenth century, did not live to see the expansion after 1830 of her perfectionist sect. Attracting many of the poor and uneducated, this highly disciplined movement, encompassing celibacy and agricultural communism, stressed the development of vocational skills. However, it offered few cultural activities and discouraged higher education as potentially disruptive.

Many other largely short-lived utopias developed in the same period, with education playing some part in their millennial agenda. Among them were the Hopedale Community (1840), founded in Milford, Massachusetts, by Adin Ballou, a minister of the Universalist church; Brook Farm (1841), near Boston, by the Unitarian minister George Ripley; Fruitlands (1843) at Harvard, Massachusetts, by the transcendentalist Bronson Alcott and the ascetic Charles Lane; and the long-lasting Oneida Community, New York, led from 1848 by John Humphrey Noyes. Brook Farm benefited from an outstanding intellectual commitment and included many societies, lectures, and cultural activities; it attracted distinguished reformers before its demise in 1847. Oneida's founder, Noyes, had attended Dartmouth College, Andover Theological Seminary, and Yale and came from a different world from that of the eighty-seven members, who were largely farmers and artisans (Lockwood, 1966). Noyes established a library, with education as the community's "central object and inspiration," and " groups of members set about reading zoology, algebra, French, or phrenology with ingenious enthusiasm. Eventually, some twenty men and women went away at community expense for medical and scientific training at Yale university and musical studies in New York City" (Lockwood, 1966, p. 189). Economic success helped such innovations, and Thoreau's *Walden* (1854) and Louisa May Alcott's *Little Women* (1868) communicated the ideals.

In these experiments, education's role varied from relatively minor in the Shaker communities to veritable saturation at New Harmony. The embodiments of utopian educational ambitions were the perfect beings imagined by Bronson Alcott. The education of such beings necessarily took place outside the larger society, and they were expected to be models for society to emulate. As the larger society failed to follow their lead, their potential was never fully realized.

Apparently no utopian community realized its goals (Harrison, 1969). With a few charismatic leaders and a motley assortment of members, disputes seemed inevitable, including disagreement over the role of education. The industrial capitalist society from which the utopians had fled was increasingly shaping the educational and other social provision of the age in its own image. Accordingly, "the majority of labor reformers turned away from utopianism in the 1840s, lost or muted their millennial zeal, and directed their attention to achievable, short range objectives" (Walters, 1978, p. 190).

Summary

Literacy was increasing, helped by cheap, popular reading materials in libraries and reading rooms. The American Bible Society and the American Tract Society published extensively, while colporteurs lectured to reinforce Protestantism. The benefits of literacy did not extend to illiterate slaves, who were not permitted to learn to read the Bible.

Despite working farmers' skepticism of both "book learning" and the success of elite farmers, agricultural societies promoted modern science. In the 1830s, a popular agricultural press developed, and state grants helped agricultural innovation. For the next two decades, both agricultural societies and agricultural journals continued to increase, as did the pace of innovation.

Small employers founded mechanics' and apprentices' libraries, which collected "useful works" and "polite literature" and often admitted other family members. A social tension was sometimes evident between artisan members and promoters from the business and professional classes.

Mercantile libraries also developed, providing materials on business education as well as "polite literature" for young clerks and budding merchants. A public avowal of the "rags to riches" philosophy did not deter some established merchants from indifference or hostility toward these ventures.

Despite substantial library growth in this period, no one city in the United States possessed adequate library facilities for independent, advanced scientific study.

As William Ellery Channing and others praised lifelong independent study, Horace Mann urged public library provision to make it possible. After several local ventures, Boston's 1852 public library succeeded in publicizing this movement. Later, various self-supporting libraries progressed to municipal status.

Voluntary agencies and religious groups such as the Quakers established evening schools for African-American and white students, patterned after Thomas Pole's pioneer study of adult education principles. These schools aimed to instill dominant middle-class values. By the 1840s, industrialization and increased immigration created a need for evening vocational and English language programs. By the Civil War, about a dozen public school systems were engaged in this work.

Rejecting such projects, radicals sought to establish models for change in self-contained utopian communities. Here, adult education might be used as an instrument to attain communal perfectibility. After such noteworthy ventures as Robert Owen's 1825 experiment at New Harmony, Indiana, a host of others often proved short-lived, their heterogeneous membership unable to sustain the ambitious intellectual and physical goals of charismatic leaders.

6

The "Elaborate Experiments"

Aside from the many ad hoc ventures in adult education, a few complementary projects blossomed nationwide and merit particular attention because of their impact. Dominant middle-class values lay beneath their innovative, often impressive contributions; as Grattan (1955) notes, the conservative "intellectual and social climate in the United States was not too favorable to elaborate experiments in adult education" in the early national period (p. 147). In the 1820s, the temper of the times facilitated innovation in diffusion of knowledge to the general population. Three such ventures—mechanics' institutes, lyceums, and the incipient professionalizing process that accompanied their development—are described here.

Mechanics' Institutes

Reflecting the utilitarianism of Jeremy Bentham (1789), the mechanics' institutes were championed by liberal reformers on both sides of the Atlantic in the 1820s, praised for their promotion of "useful knowledge." The reformers, who were middle-class utilitarians, sought to advance qualities that matched their own ideas of progress and the modern personality (Inkeles and Smith, 1974). Already having formed (exclusive) learned societies, they now decided to form societies appropriate to skilled workers and apprentices. Between 1815 and 1825, American scientific societies had increased in number from seven to twenty-three, the greatest increase in any decade between 1785 and 1865 (Bates, 1965), so the assumption was made that a modernizing society needed to continue the education of its "mechanics." Such education, it was thought, might enable the mechanics to effect fundamental scientific and technological discoveries and so help social and economic progress.

The possibilities for advancement dazzled the workers after an era of social and political conservatism. The experiment started with much fanfare, not only in the United States but in Britain, Canada, Australia, and New Zealand. In fact, the institutes formed the first large-scale international venture in adult education and often maintained links with institutes in other countries (Keane, 1985a, 1985b). Their programs displayed remarkable similarity, offering lectures, scientific demonstrations, classes, a library, and a museum. Later, some would hold examinations and award certificates; sponsor public exhibitions of art, science, and technology; arrange musical concerts; establish schools for members' children; and even meet such entertainment and recreational interests as picnics, river cruises, chess, and other "approved" games. Temperance was implicit in their operations; they identified role models who displayed morality, industry, and ingenuity, and programs specifically avoided controversial politics, economics, or theology.

There has been no in-depth exploration of the full scope and interaction of American mechanics' institutes. One study identified over sixty institutes in twenty-three states and the District of Columbia, largely between 1820 and 1850 (Treffman, 1981). One hundred and sixty societies in Indiana and Illinois benefited from geologist William Maclure's library grants at midcentury; some of these societies probably merit recognition as mechanics' institutes. Certainly, Maclure's own New Harmony Workingmen's Institute was said to be "modeled after the noted mechanics' institutes" (Lockwood, 1905, p. 323). However, the utopian socialism of the New Harmony community separated it from the industrial morality of mainstream institutes. Nevertheless, New Harmony still sought grants under Maclure's contested 1840 will (Keane, 1984b).

Actual dates of foundation may vary from inaugural meetings

to formal incorporation, but some merit recognition: the New York Mechanic and Scientific Institution, 1822; the Franklin Institute, Philadelphia, 1824; the Maryland Institute, Baltimore, 1825; the Middlesex Mechanics' Institute, Lowell, Massachusetts, 1825; Boston Mechanics' Institute, 1826; Rochester Mechanics' Institute, 1826; Pittsburgh Mechanics' Institute, 1827; Newark Mechanics' Association, New Jersey, 1828; Paterson Mechanics' Society, New Jersey, 1828; Ohio Mechanics' Institute, Cincinnati, 1828; Buffalo Mechanics' Institute, 1828; Lexington Mechanics' Institute, Kentucky, 1829; New York City Mechanics' Institute, 1830; Chicago Mechanics' Institute, 1837; Kentucky Mechanics' Institute, Louisville, (1840s); St. Louis Mechanics' Institute, Missouri, 1841; Augusta Mechanics' Association, Maine, 1841; Metropolitan Mechanics' Institute, Washington, D.C., 1853; New Orleans Mechanics' Institutes, 1853; Richmond Mechanics' Institute, Virginia, 1854; San Francisco Mechanics' Institute, 1854; and Tennessee Mechanics' Institute, Nashville, 1855.

There was an assumption that "an unmistakable Yankee form and emphasis" characterized the products of educational borrowing (Ross, 1942, p. 2) and that American institutes, unlike earlier British institutes, "featured diversity" (Sinclair, 1974, p. 14). These institutes did, indeed, reflect their local communities in each country. They varied from fully democratic to oligarchic and from miserably poor to relatively prosperous, revealing the inability of skilled workers in either country to sustain this adult education venture without middle-class support—a crucial factor in the subsequent development of adult education.

The aims reflected reformers' views that education should be accessible, "functional and general," with some "training in natural sciences, and in language and mathematics" (Brown, 1976, p. 103). George B. Emerson (1827), a Harvard-educated Unitarian reformer, identified the institutes' objectives: to give to "persons whose time is chiefly occupied with the business of labor, knowledge of a kind to be directly useful in their daily pursuits" (p. 273).

The assumed community of interests proved to be another controversial issue. The middle-class promoters sought to co-opt skilled workers into the dominant middle-class culture by concentrating on their material aspirations. The term "mechanic" at that time included "apprentice," "journeyman," and "master" or "mistress," implying a differentiation by evolving status. The institute might also contribute to an existing associational life, embracing family, workshop, church, and benevolent society, or it might help the expression and emulation of craft skills in which "ingenious mechanics" traditionally prided themselves by providing systematic education to improve those skills.

As industrialization proceeded, there were clearer distinctions between "mechanic" and "manufacturer," with fewer opportunities for upward mobility. As late as 1854, voting and office holding in the new San Francisco Mechanics' Institute were limited to a class of shareholding members (Keane, 1984b). Even among institutes that proclaimed each member's right to vote and hold office, onerous and sometimes expert committee functions deterred journeymen, many of whom worked a sixty-hour week. This situation led to some resentment, particularly when workers sensed more general threats to their skills and status. Institute administrations routinely faced criticism of their policies (Claxton, 1839) and many proved unable or unwilling to respond to a more demanding student body.

A source of dissonance lay in the curriculum. While its initial scientific emphasis proved generally attractive, its practical application had to be taken on trust. In 1826, skilled workers in places like Cincinnati still tended to work in unmechanized shops that employed less than twenty people. Here, they "preserved traditional patterns of learning and practicing the mysteries of the craft" (Ross, 1985, p. 7). It was some time later that "some entrepreneurially minded mechanics began emerging from the cocoon of artisan culture and entering the web of capitalist relations" (Leary, 1986, p. 39). That "useful knowledge" frequently aided such role models among the ranks of the mechanics has long been an article of faith. However, it must be pointed out that initially, no coherent scientific and technical curriculum existed. When a curriculum emerged, the institutes did not have adequate human and material resources to teach systematically. Additionally, the existing structure of industry offered few opportunities for mechanics to apply their newly learned skills. All these potential problems were ignored when the institutes formulated their objectives.

Gradually, promoters came to realize that it was too ambitious to expect skilled craftworkers to be transformed into engineers and inventors within a generation. Therefore they needed to adapt the curriculum to the target audience or the target audience to the curriculum. The Franklin Institute, Philadelphia, abandoned its target group of mechanics. Instead, it instituted a more profitable program serving a mixed public, with a research and publication program intended to win national recognition among the new professional classes (Sinclair, 1974). Conversely, like most other institutes, the New York City Mechanics' Institute reconciled itself to "the diffusion of knowledge and skill, but [was] little concerned with their advancement" (Hindle, 1976, p. 104). More challenging to the founders were students' demands for a more liberal (and even recreational) program.

The institutes did not intend to promote an artisan culture, nor to recognize the multiple social aspirations of their members. Thus, in the 1830s, Newark Mechanics' Association persevered with a science program. Simultaneously, a separate Journeymen Mechanics' Debating Society addressed issues of conscience, and several trade unions formed. A result was that the association "failed to grow, and remained composed of an elite of craftsmen" (Hirsch, 1978, p. 87). In 1835, the New York City Mechanics' Institute placed its reading room at the disposal of delegates attending a convention of the National Trades Union, a gesture appreciated by organized labor (Curoe, 1926). A more long-term policy shift took place at the Ohio Mechanics' Institute, which decided to assuage a public thirst for entertainment, recreation, and novelty. This change probably saved the institute from the demise that many other institutes experienced. By mid-century, fundraising, through public exhibitions, had enabled it to offer its 850 members expanded facilities and educational programs in a substantial new building. Institutes in Louisville, Kentucky, and San Francisco followed suit. To some supporters, such public and entertaining innovations detracted from the high ideals that launched the institutes. The definition of "success" remained a bone of contention.

Achieving viability by enlarging the scope of the fee-paying target audience had the potential to be divisive. The original clientele, skilled workers and apprentices, was by implication white, male, and native or "old immigrant" from northern Europe. Gradually, the institutes accepted female members, and even children were allowed into the institute schools. There was also a growing middle-class membership that initially held leadership positions but that also reflected the use of the embracing term *mechanic* to include employers. However, in 1854, the institute in Cincinnati went further with a "money-making scheme" (Mead, 1951, p. 144): it overcame inhibitions regarding controversial issues and offered a course of lectures on slavery. This attracted a substantial enrollment, including many African Americans. Subsequently, members criticized the lecture committee for offering popular programs with "brilliant oratory or attractive humbug," instead of practical discourses suited to mechanics (Mead, 1951, p. 198).

Such resentment at changes in curriculum and membership reflected employees' fears of threats to their status and skills and led some mechanics to resign. These employees often shared a common national and/or religious heritage, were largely indifferent to the interests of unskilled workers, and were predictably hostile to different immigrant groups. Other mechanics, still aspiring to upward mobility, continued to support the surviving institutes after mid-century. Thus, in 1854, Chicago Mechanics' Institute was offering programs that were "practical or technical, and were offered as a rule by local men, the best informed and most scientific men in the city" (Bode, 1956, p. 172). However, the Morrill Land Grant College Act (1862) reflected changes that were overtaking these "most scientific men." Under the Morrill Act, states received gifts of land from the federal government on which to establish colleges that would teach the practical disciplines of agriculture and the mechanical arts. These land-grant colleges would incorporate into a higher education curriculum the subjects taught in the mechanics institutes. The elitism of university-educated engineers was about to replace the democratic connotation of useful knowledge. Realizing this, Chicago's mechanics unsuccessfully demanded a university college under the Morrill Act (Ross, 1942). San Francisco Mechanics' Institute proved more successful, since the University of California arranged for extension courses to be held at the institute (Keane, 1984b).

The institute experiment had unintentionally pioneered a modest international movement. It embraced the identification of adult learning interests, needs, and handicaps and recognized the limitations of voluntarism and the merits of educational marketing. Uncritical emulation had given way to the development of information networks and some alternative programming. However, challenges to the prescriptive nature of this unresearched experiment continued. The viability of specialized programs for this special public often proved illusory, leading many to judge the institutes a "failure." Conversely, the popularity and profitability of general programs for larger publics were to many an embarrassment rather than a "success," a situation that still exists today in some educational institutions. Few institutes proved sufficiently market-oriented to survive; only those in San Francisco and New York remain.

Lyceums

The lyceums were a second "elaborate experiment." After use by various natural history societies, the term *lyceum* was appropriated by Josiah Holbrook for an adult education venture that he publicized in the October 1826 *American Journal of Education*. Following the precedent set by his Yale mentor, Benjamin Silliman, Holbrook delivered a series of public science lectures in New England; then, wanting an institutional framework for such ventures, he proposed the formation of mutual education associations for adults. His plans followed current mechanics' institute practice: exclusion of politics and religion, a stress on sciences and useful knowledge, development of libraries and museums, and encouragement of temperance and morality. However, Holbrook did not want to serve only one specific public; he sought participation by the community, and he also wished to improve the common schools. Rather than the informal linkages developed by the institutes, he planned an impressive structure of county, state, and national lyceums and later proposed an international organization. By November 1826, he had published the *American Lyceum of Science and the Arts*, which offered guidance on the rationale and structure of lyceums.

It is an oversimplification to assume, as have some historians, that the lyceum concept originated in Britain (Bode, 1956). Indeed, when British educators introduced lyceums in the 1830s, they acknowledged an American model with more popular and less rigorous objectives than the institutes'. Lecturer William Ellery Channing saw the objective of the American lyceums "not [as] the improvement of science . . . so much as its extension" (Struik, 1968, p. 276). This was a more modest aim than that of the institutes. In 1829, founders of Salem Lyceum in Massachusetts identified their objectives: "our own improvement in knowledge, the advancement of popular education, and the diffusion of useful information throughout the community generally" (Stephens and Roderick, 1984, p. 141). This suggests a distinctly American experiment.

In 1826, Holbrook initiated the first lyceum in Millbury, Massachusetts, enrolling some forty farmers and mechanics and agreeing on a fee of one dollar to cover books and scientific apparatus. By the following January, delegates from eight neighboring lyceums had established the Worcester County Lyceum in Leicester. These delegates comprised "a high proportion of ministers and doctors" (Bode, 1956, p. 14), thus paralleling the middle-class leadership of the institutes. Farmers, like mechanics, lacked the time and expertise to participate fully in formation of policy.

The lyceums spread more rapidly than did the institutes. After flourishing in New England, they spread to the Atlantic states, the South, the Midwest, and even Britain. Horace Mann, the influential Massachusetts superintendent of education, endorsed lyceum membership. The Boston Society for the Diffusion of Useful Knowledge, the lyceum that Daniel Webster initiated in Boston in November 1828, attracted distinguished support, including Holbrook, Edward Everett (later governor of Massachusetts), William Russell (editor of the *American Journal of Education*), and local educators George B. Emerson and Timothy Claxton (Hayes, 1932). It inaugurated a lecture series at the Boston Athenaeum in 1829–1830 and proved to be "the forerunner of the Lowell Institute" (Rossiter, 1971, p. 603).

Holbrook also initiated a lyceum model village in Berea, Ohio, in 1837. Seeking to attract "influential friends of science and the moral enterprises of the age," he proposed to combine "a liberal, a practical, and an economical education" with farmwork (Noffsinger, 1926, p. 101). Like many contemporary utopian schemes, this venture soon foundered: by 1842, its fifty inhabitants had departed after an educationally stimulating but economically disappointing experiment (Sheldon, 1842).

Meanwhile, town lyceums proliferated until the late 1830s, retaining a degree of stability until the Civil War. Specific sections of the public promoted some lyceums, such as ladies' lyceums, Negro lyceums, army lyceums, seamen's lyceums, teachers' lyceums, college lyceums, the United States Naval Lyceum, or the Beriah Sacred Lyceum, New York (the latter originated in a Sunday School class). The Baltimore Union Lyceum separated first into ward lyceums, and then into ladies', mothers', teachers', apprentices', and seamen's departments. Later "each town lyceum became an adult school" (Hayes, 1932, p. 32). Supporters of the Salem Charitable Mechanic Association of 1817 added a library by 1820 and a lecture program by 1828 (Dennis, 1906). They joined with others to inaugurate Salem Lyceum (later the Essex Institute) in January 1830, thereby adding a new foundation, open to the community at large.

Transcendentalism, a philosophy of self-culture derived from Unitarianism, provided the lyceum movement with the support of such literary figures as Nathaniel Hawthorne and Henry David Thoreau (Salt, 1896; Scudder, 1947). The lyceum also attracted the services of George Combe, Henry Ward Beecher, William Ellery Channing, Ralph Waldo Emerson, Horace Mann, and Walt Whitman. Other distinguished lecturers included William Makepeace Thackeray, author of *Vanity Fair* (1847), and Louis Agassiz, professor of natural history at the Lawrence Scientific School. Later, such controversial figures as abolitionist Wendell Phillips gained a hearing, although it took longer for such feminists as Frances Wright to be accepted. Nevertheless, there was some resentment of the lyceums' "no controversy" policy, and by 1856, radicals decided to establish a rival lyceum at Manchester, New Hampshire. In the Midwest, antislavery lectures were profitable and thus overcame opposition and were included in the curriculum (Bode, 1956; Mead, 1951).

Timothy Claxton, curator of the Boston Society, personified the new cohort of adult educators. A largely self-educated scientific instrument maker who had supervised a Baptist Sunday school, he had "never made any particular profession of religion" (Claxton, 1839, p. 63). He served as vice president of the Methuen Social

Society for Reading and Social Inquiry and was a founder and administrator of the Boston Mechanics' Institute. In 1831, he went on to become president of the Boston Mechanics' Lyceum and an influential proponent of adult education. He made models and apparatuses for lyceums, lectured regularly, and witnessed the publication of some of his students' papers in the *Essayist*. From 1832 to 1835, Claxton and other lyceum members edited the *Young Mechanic*. Claxton displayed his commitment to adult education during an 1836 visit to England, where he promoted lyceums based on the American model (Claxton, 1839).

He became critical of the increasingly formal education of mechanics' institutes and, like his friend George W. Light, secretary of the Boston Society, promoted "friends educating friends" rather than relying on outside lecturers; he urged members to "acquire a habit of doing their own studying and speaking" (p. 137). Light found the goal of mutual improvement incompatible with a reliance on lecturers; instead, the *Young Mechanic* eulogized the careers of those who shared with friends the benefits of their independent study (Calvert, 1967, p. 35). This theme was repeated by three South Carolinians planning a lyceum: criticizing a reliance on outside lecturers and "formal exercises," they urged a priority on educational materials to aid in individual study (Stephens and Roderick, 1984).

Claxton (1839) also advocated a specialization of function among lyceums; Holbrook went farther by proposing an embracing scheme to culminate in a national organization—the American Lyceum, which held conventions, first in New York in 1831, and then annually until 1839. The American Lyceum attracted delegates from as far away as Illinois and Ohio; prominent among them were educators, ministers, and such distinguished leaders as Stephen Van Rensselaer, founder of the Rensselaer Institute, and Professor John Griscom of Columbia College. Distinguished lecturers addressed issues not just in terms of the citizenry, but also of women and minorities. They made recommendations for the development of people's colleges, traveling libraries, and an American museum of natural history.

By 1837, a gathering momentum led Holbrook to propose an international adult education agency, the Universal Lyceum, and to nominate British educator Henry Brougham as its first president (Bode, 1956). Meanwhile, both British and Swedish educators were recommending adoption of Holbrook's system for their own countries (Curti, 1964). In practice, it was the local town lyceum, not the higher administrative structures, that enjoyed some stability.

Before 1839, the lyceums spent much time promoting public schools. Nevertheless, Hayes (1932) credited lyceums with constituting "the first adult education school system in the United States" (p. 35). Lyceums mobilized community support for adult education at the same time that public lecturing was moving beyond its association with the business and professional classes. Lyceum attendance had both social and educational benefits, enabling the local establishment to bathe in the reflected glory of guest lecturers (Jackson, 1941). Thus, an 1847 geology lecture at Portsmouth Lyceum, New Hampshire, attracted 1,000 of the town's 7,900 citizens (Brown, 1976). Despite the initial broad community involvement, lyceum promoters, administrators, and lecturers promoted prevailing middle-class views of individual responsibility and social improvement, views that originated in Puritan New England but, through cultural receptivity and improved transportation, were easily adapted for a more critical frontier environment.

Competition from proliferating voluntary agencies and the threat of civil war ensured that divisive issues would be included in the programs of the surviving lyceums. However, the established white, middle-class, Protestant culture prevailed. It was challenged less by critical social ideology than by rising preoccupation with entertainment. The lyceums had been a leading, socially approved, agency that encouraged local talent and ingenuity and that brought eminent literary and scientific figures to previously isolated communities. With the Civil War, lyceums often took on a more patriotic and charitable role, bequeathing such assets as libraries and museums to later public bodies.

Lecturing

A third "elaborate experiment" was an incipient professionalizing process that occurred in the public lecture movement. Many contributors to adult education, seeking to professionalize their basic disciplines, founded national associations: geology and dentistry (1840), medicine (1847), civil engineering (1852), pharmacy (1854), schoolteaching and architecture (1857), and veterinary science (1863) (Larson, 1977). As occupational groups created professional associations to promote specializations, a new profession, public lecturing, emerged to provide practical guidance to the aspiring middle class. By the 1840s, a corps of "professional" lecturers were serving perhaps 400,000 people weekly. They enjoyed "occupational identity and prestige, an income, and a public intellectual role" (Scott, 1980, p. 799).

From Cotton Mather onward, a tradition of willing volunteers and mutual responsibility had developed in adult education. If these volunteers were familiar with adult learning principles, identified in Thomas Pole's manual as early as 1814 (Verner, 1967), it was from experience rather than study. The concept of mutual improvement was the foundation of the volunteers' efforts. However, volunteer lecturers often had little extrinsic motivation or even opportunity to improve their teaching skills.

Adult education developed rapidly in the 1830s, and institutions in flourishing intellectual communities had talented volunteers who regularly gave their services. Inevitably, other institutions were unable to sustain their volunteer programs for very long. Nevertheless, in an era of growing literacy and improved communications, the public appetite for self-improvement seemed insatiable. Various institutions resorted to recommended lecturers outside the community, and market forces soon introduced payment for expenses plus a modest fee. Lecturers whose services were most in demand came to expect even higher fees. By the 1840s, supportive newspapers and magazines had legitimized the role of such "professionals" (Scott, 1983).

Institutions also expected more of lecturers. In 1826, Boston Mechanics' Institute sought those that spoke in plain and nontechnical language. Four years later, William C. Woodbridge, editor of the new *American Annals of Education,* concluded that the original reliance on well-intentioned volunteers was being supplanted. There was now a willingness to pay those deemed to have both subject competence and teaching skills.

Such incentives stimulated the professionalizing process.

New England educators in particular (Ferguson, 1965) believed that public lectures should be not only a demonstration of authority and competence (as judged by one's peers) but also a performance (measured by its effect on the emotions). While one could easily assess popularity, objective measures of competence were lacking, as were opportunities to cultivate competence (or even an adequate market for those deemed to possess it).

The absence of training opportunities did not deter ministers, schoolteachers, and college graduates from exploring career possibilities in adult education. Many ministers found in the lyceum an ideal secular platform for their views. Henry Barnard believed in public responsibility for adult education; he thought schoolteachers should be selected for their suitability for evening classes and study circles.

Many public lecturers were very popular. By 1856, Ralph Waldo Emerson was lecturing in Illinois, Wisconsin, Michigan, and Ohio and commenting on the ambitious cultural expectations he encountered. Even a lecturer as popular as Emerson "tried out most of his lectures on his fellow townsmen" before venturing on the lecture circuit (Bode, 1956, p. 189). Wendell Phillips received over 2,000 invitations to deliver his lecture on "the Lost Arts." Theodore Parker, the radical Unitarian minister from Boston, attracted an ever-growing public and "gave an average of forty to eighty lectures a season for ten years" (Struik, 1968, p. 271). Expectations called for "interesting and refreshing men and women of education and culture, and at the same time of pleasing, moving, and instructing those of feebler acquirements, or no acquirements at all" (Holland, 1865, p. 362). In the democracy of the West, "culture meant useful knowledge, and practical, provocative ideas" (Mead, 1951, p. 20). The delivery of those ideas was expected to involve visual aids, experiments, and/or demonstrations, and some oratorical flourish by an Eastern celebrity.

The growing organization of lecture tours, some with an international dimension, also encouraged professionalization (Keane, 1985a). Secretaries of mechanics' institutes and lyceums first arranged such tours on an informal basis; then, from 1842 to 1849, Holbrook coordinated many such arrangements with a lyceum bureau in New York. Improved communications soon made it easier to serve the growing demand for "self-improvement." By 1855, the Bryant Association of Sandusky, Ohio, began operation, the first of several commercial lecture bureaus. Such bureaus established registers of lecturers deemed "eminent," considering the sometimes conflicting factors of subject competence, teaching ability, and reputation. This credentialing process embraced ethical considerations in line with professionalization and also served to reinforce mainstream views on religion and the social order.

The sciences benefited greatly from the professionalizing process. The word *scientist* was first used in 1840 by Dr. William Whewell in his *Philosophy of the Inductive Sciences*, yet only six years later, Joseph Henry, head of the Smithsonian Institution, promoted professionalization in the sciences. Henry spoke scathingly, and with male chauvinism, of so-called "men of science." They "burn phosphorous in oxygen and exhibit a few experiments to a class of young ladies" (Miller, 1966, p. 195). He equated much public lecturing with charlatanism and contended that a professional association would mitigate the negative influences of incompetent lecturers (Haskell, 1977). Some argued that "university training [had] replaced self-improvement, the technical journal supplanted the gentleman's magazine, science left the parlor cabinet and moved into the lab" (Daniels, 1972, p. 101). Even as the new (1848) American Association for the Advancement of Science was professionalizing the field (Kohlstedt, 1976), mechanics' institutes and lyceums were helping to meet an increasing popular demand (Rossiter, 1976). As the 1860s approached, hobbyist volunteers contributed less and less to this popularization. Instead, new college scientists, balancing institutional obligations with extension commitments, rose to meet more of the demand (Bates, 1965). Some of these requests, which came from the new agricultural colleges established after 1840, were a source of chagrin to part-time, and largely self-educated, "experts" (Rossiter, 1976).

The Lowell Institute, inaugurated in Boston in 1839, was particularly influential in public lecturing. It had a $250,000 endowment to provide free general and specialist courses, the latter only open to women "when practicable" (Grattan, 1962, p. 41). The institute paid a two-thousand-dollar course fee to such people as Benjamin Silliman, Scottish geologist Charles Lyell, and Swiss zoologist Louis Agassiz. Some two thousand enrolled in Silliman's general course on geology, while Lyell's students embraced "the most affluent and eminent in the various learned professions to the humblest mechanics" (Lyell, 1845, Vol. 1, p. 250).

Even as the public lecture movement grew in popularity, the move to professionalize encountered resistance. Cynics disparaged such "star" lecturers as Ralph Waldo Emerson (Mead, 1951). The *Mechanics Mirror* asked, "Shall mere scientific men, and not operatives, be the high priests who shall explain the laws and teach the principles which direct our respective mechanical callings?" (Calvert, 1967, p. 36). That sense of alienation was coupled with a perception that "useful knowledge" for serious students was becoming less important. Instead, "professional" lecturers were simplifying their presentations to attract and entertain more profitable middle-class audiences (Rossiter, 1971).

Public lecturing provided a full-time occupation for some, but most lecturers combined it with another occupation. Satirist and poet Park Benjamin had decided as early as 1849 to adopt "the profession of lecturer, and intended to devote his whole time and attention to that profession" (Scott, 1980, p. 799). Benjamin Silliman, professor of chemistry and natural history at Yale, began public lecturing in 1831 and soon earned more than at the university. By 1835, he was considering asking for a leave of absence to devote himself full time to such work. More common during the 1840s was a four- or five-month lecturing season, with $50 to $100 plus expenses for each presentation. Some lecturers delivered "between 75 and 140 lectures each year, earning between $3,500 and $6,000" (Scott, 1983, p. 282). A few of the traveling lecturers enjoyed a full-time career in lecturing; most spent the remainder of the year in other occupations. There were lecturers who were active in the American Lyceum or in its regional groupings or who were researching or publishing in their basic discipline. However, most of them took a largely reactive role in adult education. Their jobs were complex and unstable, but the "professionals" had met some important needs of the aspiring, stratified publics, while largely avoiding general criticism.

Summary

The mechanics' institutes sought to supplement the apprenticeship education of skilled workers and transform the workers into innovators and inventors who accepted the new industrial morality. Middle-class human and material resources were provided, assuming a community of interests and excluding controversial issues. Established from coast to coast, the institutes developed an information network that included overseas institutes.

Necessarily experimental, the institutes soon realized the immensity of their task, and labor increasingly challenged the assumed community of interests. As students sought a broader curriculum, economic viability suggested serving a broader public. Contemporaries saw some of the resultant innovations as an abandonment of high ideals. Only two institutes survive in the United States, but some of the pioneer libraries, museums, and evening class programs were bequeathed to public bodies.

The lyceums sought to promote the public schools, and to provide an education program for the community in general. Some lyceums aimed to serve particular publics that were based on race, gender, religion, or occupation, but leadership remained largely in middle-class hands. A more widespread movement than the institutes, lyceums tended to have more informal and discursive programs, while continuing to exclude controversial issues. Spreading from the Northeast to the South, to the Midwest, and ultimately to England, their vitality was essentially local in origin. Optimistic plans for county, state, national, and eventually an international organization proved largely impractical, although informal contacts continued. The lyceums disseminated mostly mainstream (Northern) culture and values. While some controversial issues surfaced with the approach of the Civil War, the movement was already in decline as an educational force. As with the institutes, public bodies inherited some lyceum assets.

Adult education traditions included both learning from independent study and voluntarism with "friends educating friends." In the 1830s, the rise of a corps of "professional" lecturers challenged these traditions. Some college lecturers engaged in extension teaching, but many traveling lecturers earned often lucrative fees from the lyceums and mechanics' institutes. The public expected volunteers to be altruistic, ethical, and civic-minded; "professionals" were expected to be more competent in their subject and in their teaching ability, to have theatrical flair, and to use visual aids. Some new lecturers came from basic disciplines in the process of securing professional recognition. Nevertheless, their status as adult educators rested on public, not peer, approval and did not carry the autonomy normally given to members of recognized professions. Often mediating between the local and national, or even international, community, they primarily served the interests of the upwardly mobile publics.

7

Education and Labor

As a group, the elite of skilled workers seemed to epitomize the great potential for an educational investment by a republican society. By exploring this situation, we will identify some of the many conflicts of interest that arose during the slow expansion of educational opportunity.

Education's Role

Thomas Jefferson, who saw virtue in a republic of small farmers, had described craftsmen as "the panders of vice" (Rayback, 1959, p. 64). Others extolled this elite of skilled workers as "virtuous mechanics" who needed only the opportunities provided by democracy to show that "knowledge is power." From the ranks of skilled workers had come signatories of the Declaration of Independence, such as Benjamin Franklin, printer; George Walton, carpenter; and Roger Sherman, cordwainer. Expecting to progress almost routinely into the ranks of minor employers and so obtain the vote, they epitomized success. However, even as white male suffrage became the norm, labor realized that material success and upward mobility were becoming elusive in a changing society. Did adult education have a role to play in this context?

97

In the Jacksonian period, labor inherited ambivalent feelings toward formal adult education. To some, it seemed an intangible if not esoteric response to the immediate and brutal realities of the changing workplace. Accordingly, middle-class initiatives were often ignored by their targeted clientele, the skilled workers, as happened with the launching of Brooklyn Apprentices Library, New York, and with the Franklin Institute, Philadelphia.

Some skilled workers resented their exclusion from societies launched to serve middle-class intellectual interests. In 1826, the *Boston Newsletter and City Record* asked, "What literary advantages have the mass of our citizens derived from the Athenaeum? Who gets a peep within its lofty walls without a ten-dollar bill?" (Stephens and Roderick, 1984, p. 93). By 1832, over half of Boston's seventeen educational bodies had admitted mechanics and apprentices (Calvert, 1967). However, membership was often solely by election, as in the Western Academy of Natural Sciences in Cincinnati in 1835, where as late as 1856, mechanics' institute leaders contended that the scientific societies were exclusive. Workers' suspicion of middle-class motives heightened this resentment. Were the middle classes sponsoring a separate, "useful," and circumscribed form of adult education for a labor force that had yet to establish its own priorities?

Disunity and Dissent

Labor rejected the evangelical reformers' opinion that the workers' problem was sin, not lack of economic and educational opportunity, and that the antidote was sobriety and thrift. However, in proclaiming that fundamental social problems existed, labor's own prescriptions for change were as varied as its various constituents. Some looked to an idealized past and supported utopian communities; others sought to benefit from, or transform, the looming urban, industrial future. The labor movement was "composed not only of trade unions but of alleged political parties of working men [whose] leaders stood apart from the pursuit of the main chance (of material gain) and from its moralistic critics" (Pessen, 1967, p. vii). Some argue that radicalism was not conducive to opportunistic Americans in the Jacksonian period, that most laborers desired "not to achieve utopia or doctrinaire political goals, but improvement in the economic position of skilled journeymen" (Pessen, 1967, p. 51). This improvement was precisely what promoters claimed that the much publicized "useful knowledge" would stimulate. Workers had "no militant desire to acquire their own education as an essential, political weapon for wresting rights from a ruling class" (Thistlethwaite, 1967, p. 140).

Prior to about 1840, the life-styles of most skilled workers were barely affected by industrialization, although there were geographical and trade differences. Bruce Laurie (1973, 1979) shows that in Philadelphia, earlier work and leisure patterns continued to midcentury despite industrialization. Conversely, Howard Rock (1979) identifies cultural conflicts in many New York trades before 1820. Susan Hirsch (1978) shows that Newark underwent an abrupt change after the panic of 1837: the previous hierarchical dominance of the skilled workers evaporated and "within months, both the vestiges of mechanics' unity and the journeymen's unions were gone" (p. 88). In Cincinnati, the largest city in the West, "the age of the artisan" spanned the period 1788–1843. Here, "journeymen of the 1830s saw their world increasingly divided between those who steadfastly upheld the virtues and mysteries of the craft and those who abandoned tradition by venturing into new manufactories or working for degraded wholesale craft employers" (Ross, 1985, p. 40). Increasingly, aspiring skilled workers ceased to view "apprentice" and "journeyman" as transitional stages to "master." In 1836, New York journeymen tailors showed a lack of faith in such transition by striking.

In 1829, a year after the working men's movement began in Philadelphia, a committee of that city's workers concluded that social inequities were educatively based. They argued that "the original element of despotism is a monopoly of talent, which consigns the multitude to comparative ignorance, and secures the balance of knowledge on the side of the rich and the rulers" (Welter, 1975, p. 288). In 1830, the party reiterated a naive faith that "in obtaining an equal system of education, we will rid ourselves of every existing evil" (Walters, 1978, p. 185). It concluded that the current limited attainments of journeymen were less likely to benefit its cause than the knowledge possessed by business and professional people.

The potential value of education for workers was undermined by relative inaccessibility. Massachusetts labor leader Seth Luther (1836) asked how education could play a major role while many worked a thirteen-hour day (p. 17). Thomas Skidmore (1829), a New York labor leader soon excluded for his radicalism, suggested that the stress on "education as they call it" was misplaced, that this stress was "for the purpose of diverting the people from the possession" of basic material necessities (p. 369). At the same time, factionalism was already jeopardizing the influence of journeymen and enhancing the influence of employers in the New York City movement.

The views of some influential people—among them Henry Barnard, secretary for education in Connecticut and Rhode Island and later the first U.S. Commissioner of Education—seemed to give credence to Skidmore's suspicions. In Barnard's view, the goals of education included an acceptance of industrial capitalism and laissez-faire economics as well as a rejection of labor protest. Self-made Horace Mann, secretary for education in Massachusetts, was another influential proponent of individual perfectibility; he saw it as an alternative to political action and as a deterrent to the class conflict arising as a result of the uneven distribution of wealth.

Unsuccessful political action soon led to conflicts in the early labor movement. As early as 1830, "the disillusioned Owen (and Evans) now counseled mechanics to devote themselves to self-improvement instead of politics" (Pessen, 1967, p. 71). Curoe's pioneer research (1926) suggests labor's disillusionment with available education, as well as its conviction that education ought to play an important part in social reform. He concluded that these early labor organizations "hoped ultimately to develop under their own auspices the lectures, reading rooms, etc., which those from outside were offering them on their own terms" (pp. 44–45). Clearly, there was a recognition of the social control aspects of much of the adult education that was being provided. There was also a realization that labor would be unable to offset this in the immediate future.

Artisan Culture and Immigrants

For white males, at least, a working-class ideology, consciousness, and cultural life were evolving slowly from the links of workplace, neighborhood, and national origin. The trade unions played a limited role in this development. They were confined to skilled workers, excluded African Americans, and "several, such as the printers, hotel waiters, shoemakers, and tailors, excluded women as well" (Foner, 1974, p. 5). Thus, "artisan culture prevented men from perceiving the circumstances and accommodating the interests of women as workers" (Blewett, 1987, p. 34). Artisan culture similarly ignored the interests of women and minorities as learners. The early labor movement's educational ambitions were largely those of skilled, white, male workers, either native- or European-born. Learning was continually taking place in their social and religious lives, their neighborhoods, and the workplace. However, their commitment to a formal adult education provided by others proved tentative and often transitory. Southern workers were even less likely to participate; Laurie (1989) characterizes them as "poor, illiterate, and fresh from the countryside . . . quintessential preindustrial workers ignorant of the new 'rules of the game' and not avid to learn" (p. 32).

Besides their apprenticeship training, many workers had informal education in the workshops. In the early nineteenth century, the small shoemakers' workshops of New England "buzzed with opinion on political, social, and religious reform. It was even said that preachers in Randolph, Massachusetts, read drafts of sermons to area shoemakers in order to get pointers beforehand. New York stonecutter and sculptor John Frazee traced his tendency to think philosophically to shop talk" (Laurie, 1989, p. 37). Volunteer fire companies, taverns, saloons, and even city markets often served as opportunities for the exchange of news and opinions.

In this particularly didactic culture, these adults were, however, continually subject to the pervasive informal education provided by others in print, in the workplace, in church, in prison, in the hospital, and in a variety of community power bases. Thus, as the new industrial morality gained ground, it threatened workers' ambitions for self-improvement by eroding the independence associated with their craft knowledge and skills. Their reaction was to seek "as much autonomy and control as possible over their work lives and their leisure-time worlds" (Stephenson and Asher, 1986, p. 1). So while workers often eagerly sampled new educational endeavors, their continued participation was not guaranteed. Their disparate leaders, often eager to support education, had diverse and sometimes conflicting objectives, which varied from an investment in future generations to the development of class consciousness in the current generation. They also sought perfectibility, sociability, social justice, democracy, and self-esteem.

Among the ranks of the several hundred thousand members of the pre-1837 labor movement, adult education had remained at most a subsidiary reform objective. A latent suspicion of theoretical studies persisted and was seen among New York workers in the 1840s; the *Mechanics' Mirror* concluded that "no credence will be given to any scientific work, unless it comes from the workshop or studio of the practical mechanic" (Calvert, 1967, p. 36).

White males tended to monopolize the skilled trades, but increasing immigration saw the "ethnically homogeneous working class . . . become a polyglot group by the 1850s" (Laurie, 1989, p. 27). Responses to education proved to be equally diverse: immigrant groups from specific European localities often settled in equally specific American localities and frequently established their own cultural associations to sustain their traditional communal existence. Signs of acceptance by other immigrant cultures, or by the majority culture, such as membership in their institutions, varied. While some skilled immigrants found an acceptable American craft identity, many retained their European class identity, resulting in a social, economic, and cultural fragmentation.

The contrast between the Cornish and the Irish immigrant illustrates this point (Keane, 1974): previously settled Americans tended to regard the Cornish miners as "skilled" and "acceptable" but the Irish workers as "unskilled" and "unacceptable." The former had worked the Wisconsin lead mines in the 1820s; the Michigan iron and copper mines in the 1840s; and the gold, silver, and mercury mines of the Rockies at midcentury. The Cornish believed that "the mines depended on Cornishmen for their mine captains, bosses, shift-managers, foremen" (Rowse, 1969, p. 171). However, a

German traveler noted that "their mining experience and knowledge was always very limited, and they insisted on holding fast to their old methods brought from abroad. Moreover, they were ordinarily completely uneducated" (Rowe, 1974). The Cornish were clannish and had little formal schooling; their success seems to have come from often painfully acquired workplace skills and knowledge as well as occasional evening school attendance.

The Irish, with whom the Cornish often feuded (Rowse, 1969), came in large numbers after the 1846 famine in Ireland. Forsaking their traditional farmwork, they moved to the cities. The Cornish, on the other hand, frequently invested the profits of their mining in the purchase of farms. The Cornish were Methodist; the Irish, Catholic. In prosperous and labor-starved Cincinnati in 1825, the most populous city in the West, the 7 percent Irish population was the target of strong antagonism. The city had a Methodist church but no Catholic church, because "until 1822 they were prescribed from building any house of worship within the city limits" (Ross, 1985, p. 6). Religious intolerance intensified economic competition, with skilled workers often hostile to largely unskilled Irish labor, whom they believed clung to the preindustrial, traditional life-styles characteristic of the South. Critics charged that the Irish did not share the modern (Protestant) values of education, temperance, frugality, and efficiency upon which voluntary associations were based.

As the example of the immigrants illustrates, ethnicity, religion, neighborhood of residence, and gender might affect the degree to which workers participated in the community as well the relevance, for them, of "useful knowledge." Events in Cincinnati over three decades demonstrate the influence of such factors: in 1828, the establishment of the mechanics' institute reflected the assumed community of interests of the mainly native-born journeymen and minor employers. Conversely, the 1859 establishment of the city's Workingman's Hall reflected the separate social, economic, and cultural interests of the rising new German labor community (Ross, 1985). Possibly hoping to bridge such gulfs, in 1855 the mechanics' institute introduced a course in German, but the enrollment was small (Clopper, 1953). Class divergence was also apparent in that city in 1854, when the targeted membership largely ignored the institute's appeal for financial support, but the business and professional classes were able to raise money for their own exclusive societies. Clearly, industrialization and large-scale immigration were eroding the tenuous community of interests of masters and journeymen.

Some members feared that the employers who supported these ventures did so to control work, leisure, and education. The disaffected accordingly sought to develop a separate working-class culture. In New York, in 1841, the American Benevolent and Manual Labor Society began an intellectual cultivation of skilled workers, offering programs in modern foreign languages, bookkeeping, agriculture, and the mechanic arts. The objective was that "mechanics may be better qualified to meet the professional man in our halls of legislation and in other stations of society" (Calvert, 1967, p. 39).

The search for a separate working-class culture continued despite the ongoing rhetoric of upward mobility. In 1849, Aiken, observing the Lowell textile factories, concluded that "he who five years ago was working for wages, will now be found transacting business for himself, and a few years hence, will be likely to be found a hirer of the labor of others" (p. 16). Significantly, despite the many women workers at Lowell, this mobility was ascribed only to males. Even so, Laurie (1989) suggests that "more journeymen probably lived better in 1820 than in 1850" (p. 59). Many highly skilled Northern workers did improve their income levels in the prosperous 1850s, even though periodic recessions and an increasing division of labor had tempered earlier ambitions for upward mobility. Education still contributed to the skill and income that shaped status distinction, but the original enthusiasm had flagged (Hirsch, 1978). The National Labor Union convention of 1866 recognized not only the power of education but the power inherent in its control. It urged that "mechanics' institutes, lyceums, and reading rooms be established wherever practicable, and that the institutes be erected on land owned by the several labor associations" (Curoe, 1926, pp. 71–72).

Increasingly, more wide-ranging citizen concerns with social and ethnocultural issues superseded the early focus on economic inequalities, fragmenting hopes for a working-class culture. Among such divisive issues of Jacksonian reform were the temperance crusades, which made much use of education. Temperance promoters feared that leisure might lead to idleness or dissipation amid the saloons, gambling parlors, theaters, and racetracks. They advocated an adherence to society's new values of sobriety, self-discipline, and useful knowledge. The Presbyterian churches played a major part in this crusade in the decade between 1825 and 1835, as did manufacturers and merchants who were promoting the new industrial morality. With the coming of steam-powered machinery, there were also increased concerns for safety.

Advocates produced a multitude of publications and delivered sermons and public lectures, then formed the American Society for the Promotion of Temperance in 1826, with local and state organizations. Reformers also sought to contribute to the programs of the mechanics' institutes, lyceums, literary societies, debating clubs, library associations, and fraternal organizations. The middle class administrations of voluntary societies generally accepted such offers, but artisan members were ambivalent. Alcohol was a traditional release from a demanding life, and their societies and trade unions often met in free accommodation at the saloons. Philadelphia artisans liked neither the call for total abstinence nor the crusade's close identification with Presbyterianism (Laurie, 1974). The crusade was part of the middle-class reform agenda for aspiring skilled workers; after the commercial panic of 1837, a second crusade produced a series of temperance-beneficial societies. The reform agenda proclaimed common interests between employers and employees and ascribed such social ills as poverty to intemperance, ignorance, infidelity, idleness, and the competition of immigrant labor. The new moral code stressed work and useful knowledge and denigrated various kinds of recreation and leisure activities. Thus, in 1845, Philadelphia's minor employers and skilled workers founded the Order of United American Mechanics, fusing its temperance activities, mutual benefit provisions, and lecture program with a commitment to nativist policies.

Summary

Mechanics often sampled the formal adult education provision and inevitably absorbed much of the informal education being disseminated. However, labor's response remained ambivalent as it slowly developed its own cultural agenda, defined largely by skilled, white, native American male workers. Labor leaders saw adult education as a minor item in their reform agenda and exhibited some antipathy both to theoretical studies and to academics. By the 1850s, increased immigration reduced this workforce's homogeneity. It also heightened cultural and other differences between native Americans and immigrants, between skilled workers and the business and professional classes, and among different immigrant groups. Even among relatively privileged white males, such differences created increasingly complex responses to adult education.

An increasing number of social and ethnocultural issues also tempered any "rags to riches" belief in adult education. The temperance crusades, for example, drew a mixed response from workers jealous of their traditional forms of leisure and recreation. Such campaigns had less impact in the South, if only because temperance advocates might also be abolitionists and advocates of women's rights.

8

Developing the "True Woman"

The education of (white) women similarly became an issue in republican society. Fundamental questions of educational aims, scope, and societal recognition were to influence groups as diverse as public schoolteachers and Lowell textile workers. Responses to the questions suggest some paradoxes inherent in contemporary rhetoric.

Role Definitions

The need to educate women for the management of the household was a recurring theme in a (male) egalitarian republic. It assumed a continuing subordination of women, and it recognized the educative role of the mother and of those virtues deemed essential in a "true woman." Fostering these virtues seemed to require an education stressing religion and "polite accomplishments" (Rosenberg, 1982; Walter, 1986).

Women were expected to cultivate such virtues as modesty, innocence, piety, and domesticity, besides the "polite accomplishments" or "ornaments" noted by Jefferson. Conservative reformers such as Noah Webster stressed the "domestic value" of education, while Benjamin Rush emphasized its value to republican society.

Radical reformers such as Judith Sargent Murray and Sarah Pierce focused on the value to women themselves. In 1798, questioning women's ascribed status and roles, Murray wrote of education helping the development of independence and rational thought. In 1818, Pierce, principal of the academy at Litchfield, Connecticut, told her students that equality of intellect implied equality of educational goals and opportunities (Norton, 1980).

Social class, race, religion, and geographic region influenced the increase in facilities for women's education, and for most women the opportunities remained circumscribed. In 1787, Abigail Adams took advantage of her husband's appointment as ambassador to Britain to attend a course of science lectures in London, learning about electricity, magnetism, hydrostatics, optics, and pneumatics, and lamenting about the lectures she had missed. She also expressed delight with the "assemblage of ideas entirely new" (Levin, 1987, p. 237). Later, new seminaries and academies "for young ladies" enabled women to pursue formal education. The educational opportunities were more apparent in the North than in the South (Norton, 1980) and among white, Protestant women of the "well-to-do" classes and white, Catholic women of the middle and upper classes (Curti, 1959). Such education, even at the celebrated coeducational Oberlin College (1833), was based on ascribed roles of womanhood and motherhood rather than on aspirations for intellectual growth.

Independent study was significant to women, who "shaped their intellectual lives out of their own reading, their diary keeping, and their letter writing. Their study was squeezed into the domestic tasks their families—even the most supportive—required of them" (Kerber, 1988, p. 35). In 1805, twenty young women organized a self-improvement society, the Boston Gleaning Circle. At its weekly meetings, they discussed "any book favorable to the improvement of the mind . . . [in] divinity, history, geography, astronomy, travels, poetry, &c but novels and romances are absolutely excluded" (Kerber, 1980, p. 241). The exclusions represented a continuing attempt to direct education away from "unruly passion" and into civic virtue. The "improvement of the mind" was a topic addressed by many authors, who furnished study guides for their readers. When William Andrus Alcott (1849) published his *Letters to a Sis-*

ter, or Women's Mission, he emphasized self-education and identified the subjects worthy of attention.

The definition of women's role as mothers and homemakers circumscribed their opportunity for education and the nature of education available to them. Mercy Otis Warren, the lifelong correspondent of Abigail Adams, accepted the primacy of her domestic obligations, but nevertheless felt able to follow her literary interests. Sarah C. Edgarton (1843), writer and poet, was to proclaim that "woman is not necessarily born for marriage. She has the birthright of an independent existence" and anyhow, "she is but half-wedded who cannot enter into the intellectual sympathies of her companion" (pp. 94–95). Sarah Grimke (1838), daughter of a prosperous South Carolina planter, concluded that most women concentrated on developing their "external charms," oblivious to their educational inequalities: "They seldom think that men will be allured by intellectual acquirements, because they find that where any mental superiority exists, a woman is generally shunned" (pp. 46–48). Grimke left her privileged heritage to lecture on abolition and feminism.

Criticism of the status quo came also from Margaret Fuller Ossoli (1852), a teacher, critic, and essayist who joined the staff of Horace Greeley's *New York Tribune.* She argued that most women's education lacked breadth and that women lacked adequate opportunities to apply their learning in society. James Truslow Adams (1944) credited such "frustration and the desire for social advancement" with women forming their own literary circles in the nineteenth century. He even suggested that this was "the real beginning of the idea of adult education," even if "women did immense harm to American culture by feminizing and prettifying it" (p. 138). He thus recognized women's cultural influence but denigrated it by comparing it to the normative cultural standards established by (white, middle-class) men.

Despite the expansion of opportunities for women's education, its forms remained constrained by role definitions and assertions of women's limited intellectual abilities. The writings of Emma Hart Willard (1787–1870) and Catharine Beecher (1800–1878), who published some of the first American women's contributions to women's education (Burstyn, 1974; Lutz, [1929] 1964), promoted the republican values that channeled women's contributions into social roles complementary to the roles of men. Willard and Beecher did not seek to empower women to contest the male predominance in political or economic spheres; in fact, Catharine Beecher (1838) considered that education should promote in every adult and child a deference to social superiors. Only the roles of wife and mother justified educational provision. Great importance was attached to women as the moral guardians of the republic, an extension of the mother's role as educator of her children. Some writers also considered women's roles to include schoolteacher, physician, and even minister.

Women as Schoolteachers

Schoolteaching proved to be the first of the professionalizing occupations that women entered on a regular and substantial basis, staffing the growing number of common schools founded after 1830. Philosophically, this was a logical "expansion into the public realm of woman's role as republican mother" (Burstyn, 1990, p. 47). Pragmatically speaking, hiring women teachers at salaries lower than men's was a way of containing the cost of school expansion. With Horace Mann's promotion of the first state normal school at Lexington, Massachusetts, in 1839, some women gained entry to the new field of preservice professional education; tuition was free, although students had to pay for their maintenance and books during the three-year course. Initially, only twenty-one women enrolled; others, lacking financial resources, might enroll for the minimum of one year or continue their education part-time in addition to their teaching.

Such part-time education might take various forms: participation in teachers' institutes or conventions, attendance at lyceum or academy courses, or study of women's and literary magazines committed to educating women as teachers. Henry Barnard, in particular, committed himself to the continuing professional education of teachers, promoting readily available educational publications, site visits to other schools, supervision and accountability, teachers' associations, and teachers' institutes.

Increased literacy, as well as technical improvements in

printing and transportation, helped the growth of a market for women's magazines and for women as writers and editors. Such magazines reviewed textbooks and teaching methods, provided independent study guides, and identified the contributions of prominent educators and the work of teachers' institutes. They also publicized the need for continuing education and offered an ongoing critique of educational developments. In 1838, Sarah J. Hale, editor of the *Ladies Magazine,* argued that women made the best schoolteachers; she went on to campaign vigorously for federally supported state normal schools for women. Many women, unable to afford the expenses associated with tuition-free teacher education, also faced obstacles in continuing their education by other means. They received salaries that might only equal one-third the salary of male teachers and were obliged to board at different homes in the country districts. In 1841, Henry Barnard concluded that the factory and the workshop offered more inducements for women than did schoolteaching.

Despite the hardships, the systematic learning associated with schoolteaching often helped women enter more satisfying careers. Thus, 46 percent of the highest-achieving women born between 1790 and 1830 had taught school, as had over half of the African-American women listed in *Notable American Women* between 1790 and 1870 (Solomon, 1985). About one-quarter of all white, Massachusetts-born women seem to have spent some time as schoolteachers, mostly in their youth during the antebellum period. That these women were mostly single or widowed and typically spent only two and one-half years in this occupation suggests that many women considered schoolteaching to be a short-term occupation.

Women in the Health Sciences and Religion

Women's ascribed nurturing role led them into the health sciences. They had traditionally served as midwives since the colonial period, benefiting occasionally from training under the apprenticeship system. However, they rarely had access to any formal instruction in anatomy. Some women secured employment as nursing attendants and, in the late colonial period, occasionally received formal instruction for the role. In her diary (1785–1812), Martha Ballard of Hallowell, Maine, described an extension of her responsibilities as midwife: she now cared for the sick and laid out the dead (Ulrich, 1987).

Medical science was undergoing substantial changes, but that had little impact on women's preparation for related careers. As we have seen, male physicians made early attempts to escape from, or at least supplement, the limitations of apprenticeship training, but the early medical schools denied admittance to women, so they could not follow suit. Women necessarily continued to depend largely on existing ad hoc practical training, supplemented on occasion by independent study or public lectures. However, in 1847, Elizabeth Blackwell became the first woman to enter a chartered American medical school, in Geneva, New York. Blackwell had been a schoolteacher in Ohio, Kentucky, and in the Carolinas, and she had commenced her medical studies independently with a South Carolina physician in 1846 (Baker, 1952). Before her graduation in 1849, other women were already practicing medicine in New York but without certification. Lydia F. Fowler, who became an instructor in midwifery at a New York college before the Civil War, also benefited from a previous teaching role, having completed a very successful English lecture tour on the then-popular "science" of phrenology (Lovejoy, 1957). Around midcentury, the magazine editors broadened their public education campaign, championing women's right to enter dental schools and improved nursing education and instruction in physiology and anatomy for mothers.

In religion also, women had yet to obtain much recognition. In fact, the General Court had banished Anne Hutchinson, a colonial midwife, for heresy: she had lectured on theology to Puritan men and women in her Boston home. Women enjoyed more opportunity among the Quakers, since Quakers did not distinguish between clergy and laity. In 1776, Ann Lee, from Watervliet, New York, led a breakaway sect, the Shakers. However, women like Lee had largely prepared themselves for their roles without the benefit of the formal education that characterized many male ministers. It was thus an event when, in 1851, Antoinette B. Blackwell, a mother of six children, graduated in divinity from Oberlin College and was ordained two years later to serve a Congregational church in South Butler, New York. Her subsequent career as minister, author, lecturer, and worker for abolition and women's rights drew her into the more liberal Unitarian church.

The Lowell Experiment

Clearly, many women could not, or did not, aspire to such occupations as the ministry, medicine, and dentistry. For them, the education and life-style of the New England factory women were frequently hailed as an exemplar of social and economic improvement. Francis Cabot Lowell and his Boston associates sought to introduce cotton textile manufacture without the exploitation characteristic of factories in Britain, so they required female employees to reside in company-supervised boarding houses. Mills at Waltham, Massachusetts, introduced this system in 1815, and by 1823, an entire community had evolved around the mills in East Chelmsford (later renamed Lowell), Massachusetts. The system spread across New England, attracting mainly farmers' daughters, who sent home much of the money earned for minding the looms and spinning frames. They earned the then-high wage of just over three dollars weekly for a twelve- or thirteen-hour working day. Nearly half of that was deducted for room and board. These young women lived an onerous, circumscribed existence.

The Lawrence Company, for example, followed Puritan traditions. It required its employees to display "a laudable love of temperance and virtue, and [be] animated by a sense of their moral and social obligations" (Josephson, 1949, p. 72). With the workday ending as late as 7 P.M. or even 7:30 P.M., and a 10 P.M. curfew common, the boarders had few opportunities to develop relationships with outsiders. Instead, they lived and worked in close proximity, and their social life was carefully supervised. They "rested, talked, sewed, wrote letters, read books and magazines . . . found friends who accompanied them to shops, to lyceum lectures, to church and church-sponsored events" (Dublin, 1979, p. 173). Their patterns of speech and morality were also influenced in a factory workforce that was already particularly homogeneous in terms of gender, age, and ethnicity.

To complement the moral supervision that the boarding houses provided and the required church attendance, employers quickly promoted an educational program. They established a Lowell library in 1825, built a lyceum, and supported evening school classes. Soon, lectures were available in "the churches, the Lowell Lyceum, the Lowell Institute, the Mercantile Library Association, the mechanics' institutes, the Middlesex Mechanics' Association" (Bushman, 1981, p. 40). Many employees responded to these opportunities. "The works of contemporary writers such as Dickens, Irving, Poe, Tennyson, and Whittier grew as familiar to the operatives as they were to the most educated class in America at that time" (Josephson, 1949, p. 88). The boarding houses soon attracted the attentions of booksellers and other salespeople, and "phrenologists and charlatans of all kinds came too, offering their services at bargain prices or trying to sell tickets to lectures on every conceivable subject" (Josephson, 1949, p. 69). For the country women who flocked to Lowell, there were unheard-of opportunities to hear lectures by eminent speakers. Harriet Martineau, a popularizer of contemporary laissez-faire economics, attended Ralph Waldo Emerson's lecture on historical biography at Lowell Mechanics' Institute, where she noticed women operatives in the audience who were "all wakeful and interested, all well-dressed and ladylike" (Josephson, 1949, pp. 86–87).

One Lowell mill manager compared the support he received from "the most intelligent, best educated" workers in times of conflict, with the "passion and jealousy" of "the ignorant and uneducated" (Curti, 1959, p. 83). Education thus supported the new industrial morality, and mill owners encouraged such prominent visitors as Anthony Trollope and Charles Dickens to proclaim the merits of the Lowell experiment. The self-improvement circles in boarding houses and churches and the mentoring that influenced the manners, speech, and dress of new arrivals exemplified this commitment.

From the essays and stories written in a circle at the Second Universalist Church came the first issue of the *Lowell Offering* in October 1840. In April 1841, the *Operatives' Magazine* followed, from a circle at the First Congregational Church, and yet others appeared (Stearns, 1930). The *Operatives' Magazine* editor identified its objective: "to encourage the cultivation of the intellectual and moral energies of our operatives, by offering them a medium of communicating their thoughts upon moral, religious, and literary subjects, but not for the publication of nonsense" (Foner, 1977, p. 44). These literary contributions attracted a largely positive response from people as diverse as educational reformer Emma Willard, publisher Horace Greeley, and controversial preacher William Ellery Channing. Eventually, the male editors of both the *Lowell Offering* and the *Operatives Magazine* resigned in favor of women who were, or had been, textile workers. Harriet Farley, later editor of the former, responded to the transcendentalist Orestes A. Brownson's charge that factory work exploited women. She referred specifically to the "improvement circles, the lyceum and institute, the social religious meetings, the circulating and other libraries. . . . Our well filled churches and lecture halls, and the high character of our clergymen and lecturers, will testify that the state of intelligence and morals is not low" (Foner, 1977, p. 33). Farley was, in effect, rebutting Brownson's attack on the mill owners by defending the operatives!

Perhaps the most famous operative was Lucy Larcom, who began work in 1835, at the age of eleven, and remained until 1846. After her Lowell experience, she was graduated from Monticello Female Academy, Alton, Illinois, in 1852. She taught school in Massachusetts for some years, then became a writer. Larcom's (1890) recollections of life in Lowell were positive, and she noted the opportunities for study without criticizing them. She joined a self-improvement circle and the town library, attended evening classes and lyceum lectures, her objective being "to learn all I could, so that I should be fit to teach, or to write, as the way opened" (p. 161). She encountered a prohibition on taking books into the spinning mill; accordingly, "I made my window-seat into a small library of poetry, pasting its side all over with newspaper clippings" (pp. 175–176). The Lowell reform movements did not interest her; instead, she transferred from a relatively well-paid spinning position to a job in a cloth room that allowed her to read the classics while she worked. Some of her contemporaries followed this example. Six months' earnings was enough to finance a semester at a ladies' seminary.

Such educational endeavors need to be seen in the paternalistic context in which they operated. As Hannah Josephson (1949) showed, militant women workers were demonstrating against their conditions as early as 1834; indeed, by the following decade their British counterparts were working shorter hours and tending fewer looms (p. 281). Yet the *Lowell Offering* and the *Operatives' Magazine* contained little hint of dissatisfaction.

Sarah G. Bagley, a weaver, typified the operatives' evolving responses. She arrived at Lowell in 1836 and became a member of the Lowell Improvement Circle, a teacher at a free evening school, and a temperance advocate. Writing for the *Lowell Offering* on the "Pleasures of Factory Life," she noted the "benevolence of our agents and superintendents" and the abundant public lectures (Foner, 1977, p. 37). By 1845, after the journal rejected her critical articles, she became a founder and president of the Lowell Female Labor Reform Association. In that year, she also testified in Boston before a state legislative committee that was formed to hear petitions for a ten-hour working day. She argued that the existing system debarred able and conscientious women from using the available educational facilities.

After the demise of the *Lowell Offering* came publication of a series of journals edited by women factory workers. These "carried their share of genteel poetry, stories, and advice on general conduct," but also a "note of class consciousness was sounded in many forms, including poetry and definitions" (Foner, 1977, p. 75). Thus, in 1847, the *Voice of Industry* noted the provision of libraries and lectures, relating them to the thirteen-hour working day that "drains off the vital energy and unfits for study or reflection. They need amusement, relaxation, rest, and not mental exertion of any kind. . . . A few can and do thus avail themselves of these advantages, but the great mass are there to toil and toil only" (Foner, 1977, p. 93). Catharine Beecher (1846) visited the Lowell mills in 1845 and concluded that study time would have to be taken from the hours normally used for recreation and relaxation; she suggested that women would be better employed as schoolteachers, leaving factory work to men.

The Lowell educational program stimulated an interest in contemporary issues and brought country dwellers more into the mainstream of thought and manners. As market forces began to obstruct traditional paternalism, women's protests contributed to a working-class culture and consciousness previously formed solely by male experiences. The failure of the movement toward a ten-hour workday in the mid-forties and the slump of 1848 effectively ended this educational venture. However, some participants had derived enough confidence to enter those professionalizing occupations open to women. One writer concludes that their protests were "a direct consequence of the increasing opportunities offered them in these years. The Lowell mills both exploited and liberated women in ways unknown to the preindustrial economy" (Dublin, 1979, p. 185).

Achievements and Limitations

By the Civil War, the entry of women into some professionalizing occupations was an evident but nevertheless very limited step toward a goal of equal opportunity, since few of these occupations admitted women and women seldom gained access to preservice education. Generally, women had to continue their education while working. Although many men similarly continued their education, they had the expectation of higher salaries and better career prospects. Conversely, society expected women to leave the workforce upon marriage. It was thus more than a question of women's limited access to professional careers. Conservative influences stressing stereotyped roles inhibited the empowerment that professional education might have generated. Instead, one writer concludes that these professional women displayed a lack of creativity in failing to address wider issues and in pursuing their own independent intellectual development (Conway, 1974).

For some women, the denial of recognition was galling. In 1847, the *Voice of Industry* urged, "Give us an opportunity, time and means to cultivate our minds. Treat us as equals, and we will show you that we are not naturally more peevish, more fretful and idiotic than the other sex. In short, restore us to our rights, and we will prove ourselves intelligent, virtuous, and reasonable beings" (Foner, 1977, p. 313).

Participation in reform movements would enable some women to achieve the recognition that had eluded them. As women who formed auxiliaries of the American Anti-Slavery Society discovered, this participation often revealed educational inadequacies:

"there was not a woman capable of taking the chair and organizing the meeting in due order, and they had to call in a man to aid them" (Tyler, 1962, p. 445). Social customs were also uncovered: Susan B. Anthony was refused permission to address an 1852 convention of temperance societies in Albany, New York, because "ladies were there to listen, not to take part in the proceedings" (Tyler, 1962, p. 448). However, Lucretia Mott and Elizabeth Cady Stanton had already launched a movement to secure women's rights. In July 1848, they had convened a meeting in Seneca Falls, New York, and issued a Declaration of Sentiments modeled on the Declaration of Independence. Even those who disagreed with women's suffrage "agreed on the necessity of full liberal and professional education for women equal to that offered white men" (Solomon, 1985, p. 42). This quest for a liberal education was based on the concept of learning to think for oneself. It emphasized women's continuing search for an independent identity beyond the family, instead of the traditional complementary role.

Summary

Much attention was paid to the education of women in the new republic, but this was largely in order to fulfill ascribed status and roles. Such factors as social class, race, and geographic region were apparent in the proliferating seminaries and academies "for young ladies." Independent study proved very important for women, but there were limited outlets for applying their knowledge. Many women became schoolteachers, but most relied on part-time study rather than formal preservice education. Schoolteaching also provided an avenue to other careers. Part-time study or apprenticeship qualified some women as midwives or nursing assistants, but did not gain them certification as physicians. Around midcentury, many journals campaigned for women's entry to preservice professional programs, and an employer-supported educational program formed part of the highly acclaimed regimen of women workers in the Lowell mills. However, paternalism gave way to exploitation. The early empowerment of the dedicated few was evident, as was the later protest and critical interpretation of the many. Women proved more likely to achieve recognition from involvement in broader social movements than from participation in formal education, although the commitment to the latter was less divisive than it was to the former.

9

Education and Minorities

The dominant white society's self-interest dictated some early attention to the education of Native Americans and of African Americans, free and unfree. Among minorities themselves, there was also an early perception of education as an avenue to acceptance, if not advancement, in the larger society. Our exploration of minority education emphasizes the role of social control rather than the rhetoric of social progress.

Native Americans

The Continental Congress moved promptly in 1776 to secure Indian support against the British. It sent a minister and a blacksmith to the Delaware Indians and two teachers to the New York Indians. It also funded the education of some Indian students at the College of New Jersey (Princeton University) and at Dartmouth College. The investment proved worthwhile, for "the efforts of the missionaries and teachers bore slight but telling results in winning Indian support during the Revolution" (Adams, 1946, p. 28).

After the Revolutionary War, responsibility for Indian affairs was placed with General Henry Knox, Washington's secretary of war, who was committed to avoiding conflict and having treaties with the Indians. Accordingly, after 1791, missionaries joined the federal Indian agents responsible for developing vocational skills in agriculture and crafts in order to transform the Native American from a nomadic hunter into a "civilized" farmer, thereby opening the plains to white settlement. Knox reported that "the teaching of improved methods of agriculture would demand great knowledge and much time, for the procedure would differ from that commonly used to teach white farmers" (Adams, 1946, p. 30). Differences applied even to those tribes with an agricultural heritage, since females sometimes performed such work. Annual appropriations now financed the provision of farm animals and implements, and there was a variety of skilled tradespeople to teach farming, milling, blacksmithing, spinning, weaving, house building, and the "domestic arts."

Significantly, Knox commended missionary activities as cheaper than military intervention. He encouraged the Presbyterian, Congregational, and Dutch Reform churches to cooperate after their foundation in 1810 of the American Board of Commissioners for Foreign Missions. Beyond schooling for the children, the missionaries provided, for the adults, instruction in religion, English, domestic economy, and agriculture. Starting in 1819, Congress made annual appropriations to the Civilization Fund to promote missionary programs of literacy and vocational education. In the following year, Indian treaties began to include specific cash annuities for Indian education.

Beginning in 1816, the Presbyterians and Moravians were the most active among the Cherokees. By 1828, the Cherokees had established their own printing press, using a phonetic alphabet designed earlier by George Guess, a mixed-blood Cherokee known as Sequoyah (Viola, 1990). Impressed with the reading skills of whites, Sequoyah embarked on a study program, assigning eighty-five characters, representing the essential sounds of his own language, to a syllabary (Foster, 1979; Moreland and Goldenstein, 1985). Other Cherokees and eventually missionary teachers also used the syllabary, and it enabled thousands to read and write their own language. Soon, the Cherokees were publishing a newspaper, the *Cherokee Phoenix*, religious texts and a Bible, and even their own constitution. They established a legal code, a court, and a bicameral legislature, while adopting a settled farming existence. The newspaper furnished information on local, national, and international events, included contributions on literature, on natural history, and on agricultural improvements, and received much recognition in its short life.

A system of informal adult education developed through the medium of the Cherokee language, and, with Cherokees as teachers, contributed to the tribe's social, economic, and political progress. By the time of the Indian Removal Act (May 1830), their changed status was evident, reflected in stock raising, intensive agriculture, intermarriage with whites, the ownership of African-American slaves, and the ability of many to "read and write English and keep track of money" (Young, 1987, p. 80). However, such development led neither to a continuing toleration of a divergent culture nor to its speedy assimilation into the majority culture. Instead, federal policy dictated the removal of Indians, whether literate or not, to west of the Mississippi. This drew mixed reaction from the missionaries. Later generations, such as the family of broadcaster Edward R. Murrow, remembered the Indian Removal Act long afterward. A forebear, Andy Murrow, "one quarter Cherokee, had been eighteen when his mother's people were uprooted under the removal order that sent the southern tribes on a death march" (Sperber, 1987, p. 2).

Government and missionary endeavor continued to present cultural images that conflicted with the realities of life on the frontier, particularly noticeable after the removal of the eastern tribes in the 1830s. A variety of Christian denominations also contributed to the confusion experienced by the Indians whom they had converted. The Baptists were active in the Southeast, the Methodists in the Southeast and the Pacific Northwest, the Anglicans in Minnesota and the Dakotas, and the Catholics in the Great Lakes and the Far West as far down as California. Members of the various tribes might differ radically from one another—from "civilized," English-speaking Protestant Indian farmers to hostile hunters to Spanish-speaking Catholics—but all of them faced the onslaught of white settlement.

Intertribal contact and intermarriage sometimes generated complicated relationships and issues. Thus, there was the common Scottish ancestry of both Methodist John Ross, "principal chief of the Cherokee from 1828 to 1866, and his antagonist, Andrew Jackson" (Young, 1987, p. 76). Among the Choctaws of Mississippi, mixed bloods aspiring to leadership challenged the decision of the full-blooded chiefs to move from their tribal lands to Arkansas and replace them with mixed bloods. Like the Cherokees, these Choctaws had hoped to retain their ancestral homelands by becoming "civilized," but federal officers preferred to negotiate with traditional chiefs.

The appointment of a commissioner of Indian Affairs in 1832 renewed federal interest in Indian education, mainly in children's schooling but partly in adult vocational education. The latter often took place on farms, with white instructors under government or missionary supervision. Indians who participated displayed no lack of aptitude or skill, as the new reservations in eastern Oklahoma showed: graduates of Cherokee tribal schools might attend eastern colleges or the Cherokee Female Seminary (1851) at Tahlequah. However, the conflicts resulting from white expansion in the decades preceding the Civil War created an unstable climate for Indian–white relations. Soon after its establishment in 1849, the Department of the Interior noted such difficulties, concluding that Indian "educational progress could not be commensurate with the expenditure of energy and money" (Adams, 1946, p. 44). The "civilizing mission" of transforming nomadic hunters into yeoman farmers had been an integral part of public policy, but this report was a belated admission that a republican article of faith might not be realized.

By the Civil War, Indian–white relations had generally proceeded through the first three of the four traditional stages of majority–minority relations: from initial contact to competition to accommodation (in some cases). But the proclaimed goal of general assimilation had not been achieved (Park, 1950). Had Jeffersonian philanthropy succeeded in "civilizing" the Indians, Sheehan (1974) hypothesizes, it might have led to "the disappearance of an entire race" (p. 278). But the "old ways" of family, peers, religion, custom, economy, and tribal government had not disappeared. While clearly under siege, they remained as educative forces in the face of the "new ways" of literacy, Christianity, and farming.

African Americans

In the idealism of the early republic, many free blacks, both male and female, aspired to equal opportunity, and slaves aspired to eventual emancipation. White society did not extend its "true womanhood" philosophy to include black women, and the "race uplift" philosophy did not distinguish between the education of black men and women. It is therefore appropriate to consider the education of male and female African Americans simultaneously, although male and female family roles, even among slaves, were not equal (Farnham, 1987). The unequal family roles should be kept in mind when considering differences between North and South, free and slave, and provision by others and by blacks themselves.

Mutual improvement or benevolent societies were founded by African Americans in the late eighteenth century in both North and South, the latter usually in secret (Berlin, 1974). Such societies were primarily concerned with sickness and poverty but also with the general well-being of black communities. They perceived education as an important component of well-being, and black women and men both participated. Thus, "free black men and women" established the African Union Society of Newport, Rhode Island, in 1780 "to promote the welfare of the colored community" (Perkins, 1988, p. 67). Similar aims characterized the Perseverance Benevolent and Mutual Aid Association of New Orleans of 1783, the Free African Society of Philadelphia of 1787, the Boston African Society of 1796, and the Benevolent Daughters of Philadelphia of 1796 (Ballard, 1984; Curry, 1981).

Later, in antebellum United States, "the black churches served as the most far-reaching agencies of black adult education" (Ihle, 1990, p. 15). African Americans in the South usually remained members of white churches. In the early 1800s, blacks in the North increasingly established independent churches, which took on broad social responsibilities (Sternett, 1975; Webber, 1978).

There was also a clear educational role in the early abolition societies and in the African-American–held national conventions, begun in 1794. In 1798, the national convention concluded that popular acceptance of equality was a prerequisite for emancipation. This decision made education "the primary object of all the abolition societies" (Jordan, 1968, p. 361). Education was often on the agenda of the later African-American conventions, held first in Philadelphia in 1830 and then regularly until the Civil War (Franklin and Moss, 1988). White supporters joined African Americans at the first convention in 1830 to propose raising funds to establish a black college, while delegates at the 1847 convention sought access to white colleges.

The commercial and technical education of African Americans was also encouraged. In the decades leading to the Civil War, African Americans in the North established a variety of benevolent, temperance, and literary societies (Porter, 1969) and a number of largely short-lived newspapers (Dann, 1971; Bullock, 1981). Numerous "phoenix" societies promoted the improvement of "morals, literature, and the mechanic arts," among them the New York Phoenix Society of 1833, which provided a library and reading room, a lecture program, and discussion groups. The Gilbert Lyceum (1841) of Philadelphia admitted both men and women to its lecture program (Ihle, 1990). Elsewhere, African Americans joined in the general cultural awakening preceding the Civil War, epitomized by the growing proliferation of societies, such as the California Academy of Natural Sciences, the Historical Society, and the Negro San Francisco Atheneum in San Francisco in 1853 (Lotchin, 1974). There were also the contributions of the African-American women who became evangelists: some "traveled the Mid-Atlantic region, preaching at the revivals and camp meetings popular during the first half of the nineteenth century" (Burstyn, 1990, p. 47).

Among white reformers, prosperous Bostonian lawyer James Sullivan noted in 1795 that education had created prejudice against African Americans in the minds of whites. He concluded that the only way to eradicate slavery was to educate slaves, a view Jordan (1968) describes as "the most eloquent and prophetic plea for Negro education" (p. 355). Such pleas often met with indifference or opposition, but the Quakers proved particularly persistent, since education was an integral part of their abolitionist efforts, and they encountered an enthusiastic response from potential students when establishing adult evening schools in Philadelphia and New York in 1815–16 (Verner, 1967). A Philadelphia evening school for

African-American (male) students increased its enrollment from 112 to 374 by the fifth meeting; a separate evening school for African-American female students soon opened. In New York City, the Quaker enrollment of African-American male students increased from 50 to 120 by the third meeting. Such schools sought to enable students to read the Bible, since sin was held to be the consequence of illiteracy. Coolie Verner (1967) terms these Quaker promoters the "originators of adult education" (p. 3). African-American women had fewer opportunities, even with the now-proliferating women's seminaries. Oberlin College, Ohio, began admitting African-American students in 1833. When Prudence Crandall, Quaker principal of Canterbury Female Academy, Connecticut, enrolled the first African-American student in 1832, she was ostracized by the townsfolk (Strane, 1990).

Those improvements in educational access that did appear have been criticized as "scattered, ephemeral, and, on the whole, unsuccessful" (Jordan, 1968, p. 354). In the South, there was predictably less progress. Here, three factors influenced the slaves: the pedagogy imposed by their owners, the pedagogy within their own peer groups or family relationships, and the efforts of reformers.

Slave owners were concerned with skill training, with the socialization of the slave system, and to some extent with salvation. The growing plantation economy was increasingly self-sufficient. Slaves were taught the skills to produce its food, clothing, equipment, and houses. Such skills might also increase the slave's value if subsequently sold. The owners clearly derived most of the economic benefits of skill training, whether by apprenticeship or more informal means. However, the slaves also tended to prize such training for its status and relative freedom (Albanese, 1976). But white journeymen pressured slave owners not to train slaves for skilled employment. In 1791, for example, the Baltimore Carpenters' Society resolved to admit to membership "only those employers who refused to use slaves, or accept slaves as apprentices" (Laurie, 1989, p. 50). The planters nevertheless combated restrictions that white journeymen sought to enforce and continued to provide skill training to southern blacks. "In most Southern cities free Negro artisans were essential to supply the needs of the community. In Charleston, there were free Blacks in highly skilled occupations—carpenters, tailors, shoemakers, cabinetmakers, masons, and butchers" (Foner, 1974, p. 8).

Foner (1974) estimates that "in a number of Northern cities between 1790 and 1820 a large proportion, perhaps most, of the skilled craftsmen were Blacks" (p. 5). Both New Jersey and New York, in the same period, required that young African Americans, either apprentices or slaves, must be taught to read (Jordan, 1968). However, employers gave little support even to free African Americans in the North, who were increasingly excluded from the skilled trades. Laurie (1989) says, "Racial violence helped destroy what remained of a black artisan class in both regions by the 1850s. Only in Charleston did free black artisans hold their own" (p. 62).

The teachings of some white and African-American evangelical ministers integrated both socialization and salvation, and their preaching proclaimed scriptural support for the institution of slavery (Mathews, 1977; Sternett, 1975). Accordingly, the slaveholders lost some of their earlier diffidence toward religion and instead tended to perceive it as a potential means of social control. Whether from self-interest or genuine concern for their slaves' salvation, some slaveholders even insisted on religious instruction and participation.

The owners' concern for their own salvation doubtless influenced one particular development: "the wills of many owners contained provisions for the education of their slaves and occasionally for their manumission" (Bullock, 1967, p. 6). However, even freed slaves in the antebellum South could seldom get an education without an ongoing struggle (Berlin, 1974), although many did manage to obtain at least the basics. In 1820 Baltimore, some two hundred African Americans enrolled in an adult evening school. Five years later the program of some day and evening schools included Latin and French (Franklin and Moss, 1988), but educational limitations continued to hinder the economic progress of African Americans. There was however "a larger number of free colored planters" in Louisiana in the 1850s (Olmstead, 1856), and "a few [blacks] entered more highly skilled occupations or started businesses" in the South during the 1840s and 1850s (Schweninger, 1990, p. 43). Meanwhile, some slave owners needed literate slaves to do various business tasks on the plantation (Webber, 1978).

Literacy attracted the most controversy. Levine (1977) estimates that only 7 percent of adult African Americans were literate at the time of emancipation. He concludes that "along with spatial mobility, literacy was one of the chief symbols of the former slaves' new status, one of the manifest signs that they were no longer chattels" (p. 155). Both races perceived that such education would enable African Americans to enter the world of their white masters. Conversely, the masters' perception of African-American oral culture as essentially inferior or peculiar to that race may have helped the survival of that tradition in an otherwise hostile environment. Accordingly, with some support from whites and freed slaves, literacy was to develop slowly among the slaves, particularly in urban areas. Such support "would have come to naught, had the slaves not responded to the opportunity and had they not used their acquired skill to teach others" (Genovese, 1976, p. 564).

Slave revolts led by Gabriel Prosser in Henrico County, Virginia (1800), by Denmark Vesey in Charleston (1822), and by Nat Turner in Southampton County, Virginia (1831) increased white hostility to the education of African Americans. That Prosser was a blacksmith, Vesey a free black carpenter, and Turner a carpenter before he became a preacher suggested a link between rebellion and learning.

Slave owners promoted the oral teaching of religion and the demonstration of useful skills while they sought to exclude a literacy that might provide an avenue for abolitionist opinions. However, the North and the South, influenced by economic changes and by the former's abolition of slavery by the 1830s, were developing different outlooks, one result of which was the growth of a northern middle class that wanted to reform the South's "peculiar institution."

Reaction to abolitionist agitation resulted in a more rigorous enforcement of "Slave Codes," the various regulations that had developed to govern the relations between the races. In 1831, Virginia prohibited teaching slaves and free African Americans. However, in 1842, Virginia permitted the education of a particular slave so that he could tutor a blind white youth. Such exemptions were granted only under stringent conditions, despite common assertions that African Americans lacked intellectual abilities and found religion no more than an enjoyable diversion. However, by midcentury, a legal prohibition was not the greatest obstacle, rather the "social ostracism which faced slaves, and owners who taught their slaves" (Gainey, 1986, p. 108).

Frances Wright, a highly controversial radical, decided to apply Robert Owen's cooperative ideas to the education of slaves, preparatory to emancipation. Her contention was that "until equality be planted in the mind, in the habits, in the manners, in the feelings, think not it can ever be in the condition" (Pessen, 1967, p. 185). With the advice of George Flower, founder of the English colony in Illinois, she planned and in 1825 introduced Nashoba, a model plantation in Tennessee. She entrusted its supervision to an overseer, who was also responsible for teaching vocational skills to the slaves to prepare them for employment. Meanwhile, at New Harmony, she lectured on social reform and was criticized for supporting miscegenation and condemning organized religion and marriage. By 1828, Nashoba had not yet prospered, there was little educational activity and critics were denouncing it as a "free love colony." Accordingly, Wright canceled the experiment, emancipated the slaves, and resettled them in Haiti. Unlike Owen's utopian schemes, this venture, with its indifferent leadership and overly ambitious objectives, contributed little to an educational heritage.

Meanwhile, some slaves met in "hush harbors," secret congregations that combined their aspirations for freedom with traditional storytelling and the singing of spirituals. "On any given evening slaves might transcend their temporal situation by singing their sacred songs of hope, attempt to control it by putting into practice one or more of their varied store of folk beliefs, and understand it and its immediate imperatives by reciting some of their tales" (Levine, 1977, p. 134). Such meetings helped the slave culture survive, even in the absence of literacy. These clandestine gatherings were sometimes a venue for the teaching of literacy: "Once slaves learned the basic subjects, many of them took control of the educational process and began to teach fellow slaves" (Whiteaker, 1990, p. 8).

Frederick Douglass was such a teacher. Born in Talbot County, Maryland, in 1818, the son of an African-American slave mother and a white father, Douglass was taught to read by the wife of a slave-owning family with help from some poor whites in exchange for food. Later, he passed on his knowledge to other slaves. In 1836, his master hired him to a shipbuilder to be taught the trade of ship's caulker. Relegated instead to casual labor, he was beaten by white apprentices during a strike; his master then placed him with another shipbuilder. This time he learned enough of the craft to earn some money. In 1838, he escaped to the North and settled in New Bedford, Massachusetts. Though he hoped to find work as a caulker, he was again relegated to casual work. By 1841, he was speaking at meetings of the American Anti-Slavery Society on Nantucket Island, alongside William Lloyd Garrison and Wendell Phillips. Later, he went on to achieve fame as a reformer, largely by virtue of his impressive platform oratory (Quarles, 1948; McFeely, 1990). His own experience led him to appeal to employers "to give Blacks an opportunity to become apprentices and to work at trades once they had acquired skills" (Foner, 1974, pp. 7, 11). To promote this objective, he accepted the vice presidency of the American League of Colored Laborers (1850), which aimed to promote agricultural, commercial, and industrial education.

As an articulate fugitive slave, Douglass dramatized the success stories of the age (Douglass, 1962). He contended that slavery's physical constraints were a lesser handicap than the state of mind they engendered. Eschewing the education for social control that slave owners generally provided, Douglass and others sought a liberating education, showing that African Americans could develop intellectually and contribute to the broader agenda of reform. Douglas attended the 1848 Seneca Falls Convention on Women's Rights and spoke in favor of giving women the franchise; in Britain, he spoke in favor of working-class suffrage. This commitment to Enlightenment values was much publicized on the lecture circuit. Similarly, before the Civil War, other African Americans had attended college at Amherst, Bowdoin, Franklin, Oberlin, Rutland, and the Harvard Medical School (Franklin and Moss, 1988). The very success of the few highlighted the restrictions faced by the many.

On November 7, 1861, the South Atlantic Blockading Squadron captured the town of Port Royal, South Carolina, liberating ten thousand illiterate slaves. The garrison commander, Brigadier General Thomas W. Sherman, wanted to educate the freed slaves, so he recommended that Washington dispatch superintendents and instructors. The education program that was organized became a prototype for programs created during the Reconstruction period. Rose (1964) calls the Port Royal experiment a rehearsal for reconstruction. Under federal supervision, freedmen's aid societies in New York, Boston, and Philadelphia supplied teachers for an educational experiment involving children and adults in sabbath schools. William T. Richardson, a member of the American Missionary Association, then initiated separate adult evening schools and introduced a basic education program. Rachal (1986) says, "Black education stepped forward, and thousands of adults acquired some rudimentary skills through study in their cabins, plantation schools, evening schools, and army camps" (p. 20).

Summary

Soon after independence, missionaries and federal Indian agents quickly deployed to mobilize Indian support against the British. Instructors were sent to "civilize" the Indians by teaching "useful skills," settled farming, and Christianity. Sequoyah and the Cherokees developed a written culture, and, like the Choctaws, a settled agricultural existence. Nevertheless, they were all deported west with the eastern tribes. Government instructors on the Oklahoma reservations continued the "civilizing mission," and some Native American students entered eastern colleges. However, Native American educational influences persisted and combated assimilation.

Beyond its role in community societies, adult education was important for African Americans in the North, in churches and black conventions, in phoenix societies, lyceums, and African-American newspapers. African Americans also supported Quaker evening schools. Such provision developed an awareness of the black heritage and of the few opportunities for advancement. In 1833, Oberlin College, Ohio, became the first college to regularly enroll African Americans. In the South, slave owners promoted both the demonstration of useful skills and the oral teaching of religion among their slaves, but only as means to further slaveholders' needs. Some free African Americans managed nevertheless to obtain an education, enter skilled trades, or even purchase their

own plantations. But they faced continuing hostility that was pro-
voked by slave revolts and abolitionist efforts. Fanny Wright's
attempt to teach vocational skills to slaves failed. Meanwhile, in
"hush harbors," slaves preserved their oral culture and, as did Frederick Douglass, shared their literacy skills. In an 1861 "rehearsal for
reconstruction" at Port Royal Sound, South Carolina, some ten
thousand freed slaves had the opportunity to become literate, although here, as with plantation education, social control rather
than black emancipation may have been the goal.

PART THREE

Adult Education in an Era of Modernization

10

Preparing for Civic and Work Life

In the half-century from the end of the Civil War to the eve of World War I, educative institutions and learning opportunities for adults proliferated. Knowles (1977) believes that the multiplication of adult education institutions was the period's dominant theme (p. 74). Motives for diffusing knowledge and culture were diverse and included the desire for commercial gain, an intrinsic belief in the value of a liberal education, and a conviction that knowledge, diffused to all segments of the population, would propel civilization forward. In the economic sphere, educational opportunities expanded and changed as scientific agriculture and industrialization rendered obsolete the old forms of informal learning and craft training. Leaders used adult education to fashion the civic culture and to shape the agricultural and industrial workforce.

Lecturing, Chautauqua, and University Extension

Three national systems diffused knowledge and culture through organized adult education activities: the public lecture movement, which survived the Civil War in community-based lyceums; the Chautauqua Institution, providing a liberal college education for lay persons; and university extension, connecting the public to the scientific research produced by universities.

Education by Lecture

In 1868, James Redpath, an abolitionist reformer and journalist, furthered the professionalization of lecturing by organizing the Boston Lyceum Bureau as a booking office for lecturers, who would pay him 10 percent of their fee (Oliver, 1965). Lecture bureau managers such as Redpath had a keen sense of what audiences wanted, and they recognized that only through a variety of events, including entertainment, could the lecture lyceum survive. Lecturing as a movement began to decline in the 1870s because of the economic depression, the loss of gifted orators, and the increased emphasis on entertainment. In the 1890s, lectures regained popularity when prosperity returned and progressive reformers brought issues to the public (McBath, 1980). By the early 1900s, more than 150 lecture bureaus were in operation, and the 6 largest booked three thousand dates each winter.

Until early in the twentieth century, the public platform was a primary instrument for communication and "nationalization of American culture" (McBath, 1980, p. 321). As an agency of intellectual, cultural, and political thought, the lecture platform helped diffuse and popularize knowledge. Lecturers bridged the gap between the cultural and intellectual life of urban centers and that of rural communities and small towns, thus reducing country dwellers' sense of isolation and connecting them, however briefly, to public issues. In American communities, the public platform was a democratic institution in which all could participate regardless of literacy skills or station in life. In the protest movements, lecturing became a powerful tool for reformers, who used rhetoric to express their discontent and to make their voices heard in a system that had ignored them. Orators became the philosophers of these social movements and through rhetoric defined the problems associated with industrialization, urban disruption of traditional rural life, and disenfranchisement. Ordinary people had the capacity to learn, they believed; persuasion and education would effect change (Gunderson, 1980).

Chautauqua Innovations

In August of 1874, the most innovative venture in popular education for adults—the chautauqua—began inauspiciously as a two-week summer institute for Sunday school teachers at Fair Point, New York. In 1876, the founders, Sunday school advocates John Vincent, a Methodist pastor and later bishop, and Lewis Miller, an Ohio inventor, expanded and diversified the Chautauqua Institution program to create a liberal college experience for adults. Chautauqua rose in prominence as an educational and cultural center just as increased leisure time—including vacations—became available to the middle class. At the summer residential program, the middle class found a wide range of cultural opportunities and the latest in religious and secular thought. National leaders contributed to Chautauqua's programs in civic, cultural, and scholarly life. Richard T. Ely, Jane Addams, Jacob Riis, and others expressed progressive ideas for resolving the conflicts in American life. In English Bible study, William Rainey Harper initiated critical analysis of the scriptures, and when he was criticized by conservative clergymen, founder Vincent defended Harper's right to do this (Morrison, 1974).

In 1878, Vincent extended opportunities for self-education with the Chautauqua Literary and Scientific Circle (CLSC). The CLSC provided a systematic plan for study through home reading, featuring a book club and study circles in local communities. Through the CLSC organ *The Chautauquan* plus the local circles, chautauqua permeated the villages and small towns of America (Morrison, 1974). Managing the CLSC was a mammoth task; from shortly after its formation until her death in 1917, Kate Kimball was the "mother superior of the CLSC" (Morrison, 1974, p. 65).

Vincent's philosophy anticipated many of the arguments for adult education that would be made in the post–World War I period (Vincent, [1886] 1971). Vincent asserted that adulthood was the best time for intellectual improvement, and that education could occur at any age and place, not just in relation to school, teachers, and examinations. Throughout life, he said, educational influences were at work: persons learned through their experiences, and the crisis events of life were particularly important as occasions of learning. Chautauqua offered respite from daily duties, a chance for refreshment, for intellectual stimulation, and to acquire morality and spirituality. With his belief in the sacredness of all knowledge, in self-culture, and in the universal right to knowledge, Vincent insisted that continued learning in adulthood was a religious obligation (Stubblefield, 1981b).

Chautauqua brought together the sacred and secular as "a cultural response to a changing world" in which science challenged religious authority, labor was in conflict, women's roles were in question, and the heterogeneous nation was rapidly growing (Trachtenberg, 1984). Vincent envisioned the home as the center of learning, with chautauqua ideas spreading to local circles and networks of friends and organizations. Chautauqua believed that citizenship was "aligned to the idea of a cultured life" (Trachtenberg, 1984, p. 11), but it failed ultimately because social problems required more than a cultural solution.

The chautauqua idea immediately spread, and in 1876, independent chautauquas that imitated the New York Chautauqua were founded by religious leaders, businessmen, and educators concerned with providing cultural improvement and moral uplift to their communities. Almost three hundred of these independent chautauquas were organized in all but five states and in three countries, closely aligned with religion, particularly Methodist (Gluck, 1984).

Then Keith Vawter, a Lyceum Bureau operator, invented the tent or "circuit" chautauqua that traveled from town to town. The first venture, launched in 1904, lost money, but in 1907, a circuit of 33 towns proved successful. By 1910 when Vawter had streamlined the procedure, the circuit chautauquas spread rapidly (McCown, 1984; Morrison, 1974): having a chautauqua became a matter of community pride, and community leaders willingly underwrote the costs. The circuit chautauquas reached their peak after World War I. In 1920, twenty-one companies operated ninety-three circuits in the United States and Canada and presented programs in 8,580 towns to audiences that numbered 35,449,750. Chautauqua had great educational value, particularly in the political and social discussion generated by platform speakers for temperance, suffrage, labor reform, and progressive reform. In 1930, the last chautauqua circuit made the rounds (McCown, 1984).

American Model of University Extension

Herbert Baxter Adams, professor of history at Johns Hopkins University and an activist for popular education, first called attention to the English university extension model and its potential application in the United States in an 1885 report to the commissioner of education. Then, in a speech at the 1887 convention of the American Library Association, he inspired the first American lecture programs based on the English model. Early sponsors of university extension were independent associations and societies rather than universities themselves. The largest and most important independent society to promote a systematic extension system was the American Society for the Extension of University Teaching, organized in Philadelphia in 1890. A national conference sponsored by the society in 1891 revealed considerable extension activities and organizational sponsorships (Woytanowitz, 1974). Ultimately, the private and state universities, with their superior resources, would prevail over chautauqua and the independent societies.

Extension began to develop as a separate field of educational activity in universities. In 1885, the University of Wisconsin developed the "short course" and the farmers' institute, followed shortly by programs for mechanics, lecture courses, and a summer school for teachers. President Thomas C. Chamberlin believed that the university should serve mechanics as well as farmers, offer cultural as well as practical courses, and assist local associations in their educational efforts in industry, the professions, or general culture. In New York, Melvil Dewey's advocacy resulted in an 1891 legislative appropriation of tax monies for a University of the State of New York extension.

A year later, under the presidency of William Rainey Harper, the University of Chicago opened, offering the university proper, university publications, and university extension, which included lecture courses, off-campus university courses, correspondence studies, and library extension. Harper and other university professors, who had learned at the Chautauqua Institution how to marry scholarly activities to public service, regarded extension as the "secular counterpart of evangelism"; its mission, they believed, was to "bring culture to the uncultured" just as the traveling circuit riders once brought religion to the frontier (Storr, 1966, p. 196).

The English model of university extension—lectures by university professors at off-campus locations—flourished from 1892 to 1899 and then declined. In the first decade of the twentieth century, extension revived and developed in its distinctly American form, finding its role as the handmaiden to the modern American research university—which itself accompanied industrialization and the development of a unified national economy (Diner, 1980). Professional scholars and researchers replaced the old college teacher, and these new academic professionals, believing that knowledge was the key to progress and being committed to public service, sought to remake the social order according to the tenets of their professions. Modern life had grown too complex to rely for guidance on conventional wisdom and experience, and the expert professor was now in demand, "serving on governmental boards and commissions, testifying before legislative committees, offering advice to the public on child rearing, decoration, sports, civic improvements, military preparedness, foreign policy, food preparation, health, morals, and religion" (Harris, 1979). This outreach fell under the rubric of general welfare work, which Louis R. Reber (1914, p. 43), dean of extension at the University of Wisconsin, described as "based upon the theory that there is a large field of human interests, specifically social in their nature, which is not covered by any other public educational agency."

In 1915, the organization of the National University Extension Association in Madison, Wisconsin, "represented the victory of the service conception of extension over the English model" (Woytanowitz, 1974, p. 152). Under the leadership of President Charles Van Hise, the University of Wisconsin pioneered the "new" university extension known as the "Wisconsin Idea." In 1907, Dean Reber had made the division successful by offering popular services and by playing the role of "broker" in the distribution of the benefits of modern science (Curti and Carstensen, 1949; Woytanowitz, 1974). The modern university, Van Hise (1915) explained in a conference address, had integrated its three central functions of culture, vocation, and research into one dominant idea—service. Carrying knowledge to the people was one aspect of the service mission of the university, Van Hise argued, and the university was the proper center for extending knowledge to the masses. Van Hise based his ideas of service on Lester Ward's *Applied Sociology:* talent could be found among all classes of people, Ward asserted, and developing the talent of all would result in material and social progress. A perfectly organized society would help ordinary persons develop their potential, he wrote. While Van Hise doubted that this could be accomplished, it should nevertheless be extension's aim, he said, "to assist the ordinary individual as well as the man of talent" (Van Hise, 1915, p. 24). "This then is the purpose of University Extension," Van Hise concluded, "to carry light and opportunity to every human being in all parts of the nation: this is the only adequate ideal of service for the university" (p. 24).

Informal Learning

After the Civil War, both the public library and the publishing industry expanded greatly because of the rise of a mass audience for books, magazines, and journals. The expansion of common schooling had raised the education level and reading was now popular (Cole, 1979). Modern museums, established in this period, educated the masses through object display, and world fairs became popular as a new form of mass learning and entertainment.

The Media

Magazines expanded in number and in the range of coverage. In 1892, the Chicago *Graphic* noted, "Every field of human thought has been entered and as the field has broadened new magazines have arisen to occupy the territory, and the magazine has become not only a school of literature but of science, art and politics as well" (Tebbel, 1974, p. 259). Magazines such as the *North American Review*, the leading journal of ideas, published the views of pundits on the problems of the emerging industrial society. In the 1890s, the new ten-cent magazine served a public watchdog function, creating a mass audience for general magazines by virtue of writing style, illustrations, and coverage of foreign and domestic events. *McClures,* founded in 1893, achieved success when it began "muckraking" in 1902, exposing corruption in corporations and government (Tebbel, 1974).

Between 1875 and 1893, publishers capitalized on the popularity of paperback books by issuing paperbound "libraries." Readers were also attracted to book clubs, such as the Funk & Wagnalls' Standard Library series, which sent subscribers a book every two weeks. There was also a developing readership for good literature as mass-market publishing disseminated the classics. Good writers attracted so much attention that they suddenly had fan clubs and were considered celebrities (Tebbel, 1974). Also popular were books by freelance intellectuals who analyzed the problems of American society after the widespread labor violence and unrest of the 1880s. Henry George's *Progress and Poverty* (1879), Edward Bellamy's *Looking Backward* (1888), and others demonstrated "the existence of a vast market for social thought" (Haskell, 1977, p. 199). Clubs were formed to discuss the ideas of George and Bellamy; Bellamy clubs spread across the Midwest.

Public Libraries

From the end of the Civil War to the entry of the United States into World War I, public, tax-supported libraries replaced the ad hoc, private mechanics', mercantile, or social libraries. This emerging public library system sought to define a social mission and attract readers. In the 1870s and 1880s, librarians chose collections to interest artisans and merchants and to teach talented members of the lower class the values of the higher classes (DuMont, 1977). By the 1890s, this reformative goal shifted to an educational goal—to promote the reading of good literature—as librarians sought mass support; then the educational goal gave way to an emphasis on reading as recreation (including fiction), which gave library users free choice (Garrison, 1979).

Public libraries proliferated and gained public acceptance through the professionalization efforts of librarians, through philanthropic support, and through the libraries' participation in Americanization and progressive reform programs. In 1876, a major U.S. Bureau of Education publication on public libraries—Melvil Dewey's decimal classification and subject index—and the formation of the American Library Association gave public libraries visibility, a knowledge classification system, and a voice. The new association did not adopt a statement of objectives, but librarians clearly believed in the library's educational purpose and shared responsibility with the public school for the education of the people (DuMont, 1977).

In the late 1880s, Andrew Carnegie's philanthropy, which exceeded all other donations to libraries, spurred the greatest period of library growth. From 1886 to 1917, Carnegie's $41 million built public libraries in 1,420 towns and cities in the United States, and the Carnegie Trust also supported libraries in Canada and Britain. Carnegie's library philanthropy was based on the ideology of the self-made man and the precepts of social control. Carnegie believed that reading aided individual self-improvement, and as immigrants and workers gained greater knowledge of economic and social matters, they would be content with their positions (Mickelson, 1975).

About 1890, rural Americans migrating to the cities, and city-dwelling southern and eastern European immigrants, became a new clientele for public libraries. In response, public libraries emerged in the city, and librarians guided the newcomers toward middle-class values. Perceiving social consequences in the Americanization crusade, librarians attracted immigrants by providing books in the immigrants' own languages and by advertising their services, giving lectures on American life in foreign languages, and teaching English (Garrison, 1979). In many cities, the public library became a community center, organizing clubs, offering lectures and classes, and providing space for group meetings (Garrison, 1979). State libraries took books to small villages and rural areas and placed them in post offices, homes, and schools. Around 1900, librarians used book lists, book displays, and talks on books to stimulate adults to read (Lee, 1966).

Museums and World Fairs

In the late nineteenth and early twentieth centuries, museums provided a new institutional form for displaying and teaching the vastly extended knowledge about the material world and for restoring a sense of historical continuity, which had been threatened by discovery of other cultures, by industrialization, and by immigration. Museums presented culture, Harris (1990) notes, as "agreed-upon values and standards which could be applied to judgment, to history, to civilization itself" (p. 137). Museum founders aspired to influence public taste, "increasing knowledge, expanding experience, and shaping preference" (Harris, 1990, p. 57). John Cotton

Dana, founder of the Newark Museum in 1909, expressed the social philosophy of the museum as educational institution: a museum, he said, promoted learning by evoking curiosity and questions to ultimately "help the members of the community to become happier, wiser, and more effective human beings" (Alexander, 1979, p. 13).

The American Museum of Natural History of New York City (1869) and others became centers of research to add to human knowledge of the natural world. Museum exhibitions provided education, and Darwin's theory of the evolution of the human species provided rationale for studying the development of the natural world (Alexander, 1979). American history museums received support from historical societies, and in 1876 half of the seventy-six historical societies had museums. Historic houses preservation projects, such as the preservation of Mount Vernon beginning in 1860, made museums out of historic houses for historical and patriotic purposes (Alexander, 1979). The great fine arts museums educated through exhibitions and organized learning experiences; in 1905, for example, the Metropolitan Museum of Art in New York City appointed a supervisor for education and offered lectures, lantern slide collections, and publications for adults, while in 1907, the Boston Museum of Fine Arts appointed a docent to conduct one-hour interpretive tours.

Fairs, too, displayed objects for educational purposes. Agricultural societies and mechanics' institutes had earlier made significant educational use of fairs, but international exhibitions, or world fairs, as they were called in the United States, created a new, powerful social institution that gathered together huge crowds to be entertained and educated. At the exhibitions, government, commercial enterprises, scholars, and private associations "presented their view of the world to the masses" (Greenhalgh, 1988, p. 27). The American tradition began with the Philadelphia Centennial Exposition in 1876, and the exhibits of machinery and industrial and agricultural inventions found a permanent home in the Smithsonian National Museum Building, which was completed in 1881. From 1876 to the eve of World War I, at least eleven world fairs were held in the United States. Visitors used "expositions as adult education courses" (Harris, 1979, p. 436). Exposition organizers created specific themes to demonstrate the march of progress in the humanities and sciences. Expositions also offered lectures and scholarly meetings. The World Congress Auxiliary at the World's Columbian Exposition in Chicago in 1893 created twenty departments representing "intellectual and social categories through which progress might be discerned and further problems identified" (Trachtenberg, 1982, p. 214). Separate congresses for literature, history, art, philosophy, science, temperance, religion, and woman's progress attracted 700,000 persons in five months.

World fairs that focused on progress faced issues of equality and democracy. Women used the world fairs as a forum to express discontent with their role in American society (Greenhalgh, 1988). At the 1893 Columbian Exposition, women presented themselves as the originators of human industry and as man's equal, but women's buildings at later fairs discarded the sociopolitical focus in favor of women's traditional role as homemaker. Fairs, when not ignoring African Americans, displayed them in cultural terms: fairs in the South, for example, showed how the African-American population had been integrated into southern economy. Native Americans, presented first as immoral savages, were later treated as an enemy defying American standards and progress. The Buffalo Pan-American World's Fair displayed the culture of countries controlled by the United States—Cuba, Puerto Rico, Alaska, Hawaii, and the Philippines.

Agriculture

After the Civil War, the search for a means to disseminate scientific knowledge to farmers began with a circuit of itinerant lecturers or "farmers' institutes," the "first popular technique for directly reaching the mass of ordinary farmers" (Scott, 1970, pp. 58–59). Administered by the department of agriculture in some states and by the agricultural college or experiment station in others, by 1900 "the adult farmers' school" was accepted as part of the education of rural adults. At the same time, innovations were developing: women's clubs and institutes, educational trains with exhibits and lecturers, demonstrations used in lectures, movable schools, short courses, and farmers' institutes for young people. By 1914, over seven thousand institutes were held annually, employing over one thousand lecturers, and attendance ranged from two and one-half to over three million (Moss and Lass, 1988). The institute method accomplished much but could not ensure that farmers would turn knowledge into practice. The institutes, Scott (1970, p. 137) notes, "were a transitional stage in the evolution of a teaching method for the countryside."

In 1887, the federal government had made the experiment station a national institution through the Hatch Act, which granted each state $15,000 per year. Agricultural experiment stations assumed an important role in agricultural education, becoming in effect "general bureaus of information" (Rosenberg, 1976, p. 158). Station scientists responded to farmers' questions, wrote bulletins, gave demonstrations, and conducted lecture tours.

But the turning point came in 1902, when the USDA launched a campaign to improve agriculture in the South and appointed Seaman Knapp as a special agent (Scott, 1970). In 1903, Knapp's success with the Porter demonstration farm in Terrell, Texas, established the community demonstration run by the farmer himself as an effective teaching method. Observing a successful farmer in the community trying a new farming method helped other farmers overcome their reluctance toward innovation. Knapp hesitated at first to include African Americans, but in 1904 he accepted them as demonstrators and cooperators. In 1906, he began cooperation with Tuskegee Institute, and Thomas M. Campbell was hired as the first African-American agent in Knapp's program. Knapp's counterpart in the North and West was William J. Spillman, who in 1905 became the director of the USDA's Office of Farm Management. Demonstration work expanded with financial support from the General Education Board; in 1906 W. C. Stallings of Smith County, Texas, became the first county agent, supported by both local and federal monies. Other support for agents to work directly with farmers came from the Office of Farm Management, farm organizations, and grants from Julius Rosenwald of Sears, Roebuck and Company. In 1911, Spillman began to coordinate these various efforts.

Support for a federally financed nationwide agricultural extension system came from several organizations, including the Association of American Agricultural Colleges and Experiment Stations, the 1909 report of the Commission on Country Life created by President Theodore Roosevelt, and the National Soil Fertility League, an organization of business interests. Congress worked out how such a program should be organized, administered, and financed. Agreement was reached on several essential matters: that federal appropriations were necessary, that agricultural extension should be administered by the agriculture colleges, and that extension projects financed by federal funds must be agreed upon by the college involved and the USDA. On May 8, 1914, President Woodrow Wilson signed the Smith-Lever Act, which created the Cooperative Extension Service.

The Cooperative Extension Service proved successful in creating partnerships at three levels of government, in disseminating knowledge from the land-grant universities to farmers and their families in local communities, and in administering federal programs during the national emergencies of World War I, the Depression, and World War II. Such a successful model would later attract the attention of others who advocated similar programs for engineering, labor, and science and technology extension—none of which, however, attracted sufficient support to create a system of adult education modeled after the Cooperative Extension Service.

The Industrial Workforce

The industrialization process that began in the United States well before the Civil War had by the 1890s radically transformed the American social structure and the culture of work (Gutman, 1976). In the 1870s and 1880s, the industrial workplace changed when new, rational procedures were installed to increase productivity, distribution, and inventory. Knowledge became very important in the productive system, with engineers replacing artisans (Trachtenberg, 1982), accompanied by increased specialization and fragmentation into smaller areas of technique and learning. Management took control of knowledge that once belonged to workers.

Education for Work

In response to these changing conditions, new forms of education for work evolved. Vocational education addressed the deficiency of schools in preparing youth for industrial jobs (Jacoby, 1985; Lazerson and Grubb, 1974a). The vocational education movement marked the shift from reliance on natural resources to reliance on human resources and a skilled workforce (Lazerson and Grubb, 1974a). In 1906, several interest groups founded the National Society for the Promotion of Industrial Education to gain support for a public system of vocational education. After a favorable report from the Commission on National Aid to Vocational Education, Congress passed the Smith-Hughes Act in 1917 and created the Federal Board for Vocational Education to administer the Act (Barlow, 1967). The Smith-Hughes Act supported trade, industrial and agricultural education and home economics in schools, and part-time instruction for persons over fourteen. In 1919, 86 percent of all students in federally funded vocational schools were part-time and in 1924, 92 percent (Lazerson and Grubb, 1974a).

Other adults received training and education through private trade schools, correspondence study, and in-plant apprenticeship programs. Founded in 1881, the New York Trade School, the first of the private trade schools, admitted persons over seventeen (Barlow, 1967; Nelson, 1975). The first textile school, the Philadelphia Textile School, established in 1882–83, was the prototype for schools established in the late nineteenth century in New England and the southern states. Correspondence study offered by commercial organizations was available for those unable to attend school; courses such as mine safety by Thomas J. Foster, editor of *Mining Herald* of Shenandoah, Pennsylvania, proved to be popular. The International Correspondence School of Scranton, Pennsylvania, established in 1891, became the largest and best known of the correspondence schools, enrolling over two million students between 1891 and 1920, and hundreds of other schools were soon formed. Knowles (1977, p. 40) concludes "that the commercial correspondence schools had brought systematic learning opportunities to more adults by World War I than had any previous institutional form of adult education." Many schools exploited students for the sake of profit, failing to provide the education they advertised. The National Home Study Council, organized in 1926, developed standards for commercial correspondence schools.

Larger companies established new apprenticeship programs

because informal methods of recruitment had failed to attract skilled workers capable of handling advanced technology. In the 1870s, the first apprenticeship programs were introduced that rotated apprentices among different jobs and required academic courses related to shop work. Through these educational programs, employers also sought to teach the virtues of hard work, loyalty, and respect for authority (Nelson, 1975). General Electric initiated the apprentice supervisor, an employee assigned to oversee apprentices, and in 1904, Magnus W. Alexander, the apprentice supervisor at the General Electric plant in Lynn, Massachusetts, created a separate training department (Nelson, 1975). The new apprenticeship program became popular, and in 1913, the National Association of Corporation Schools institutionalized the movement.

Systematic management, begun in the 1880s by managers and engineers to alleviate traditional shop management shortcomings, became "scientific" management when Frederick W. Taylor invented the rate-setting method based on time study. This scientific management—the best-known feature of the new factory system—took hold between Taylor's retirement in 1901 and his death in 1905 and provided a way for managers to gain control over workers. It reversed worker autonomy by establishing the process of conducting specific tasks and by prescribing the number of piecework products to be produced in a specific time. Neither Taylor nor his disciples had much expertise or interest in training, apprenticeship, or vocational education. It was left to others to connect Taylor's ideas about "the science" of each person's work—to the practice of education (Neumann, 1979).

The Human Element

Industrialization in the United States changed the nature of work, the culture of the workplace, and the way of life. Workers did not take these transformations in stride. In the late 1890s, industry and social reformers responded to labor unrest, strikes, and radical political ideas by forming the industrial welfare movement, which brought progressive humanitarian reform into the workplace. Welfare work was part of a trend toward dealing with the human element of manufacturing, management, and work relations (Korman,

1967). A wide range of activities addressed such concerns as work conditions, the family, community life, and culture. Welfare programs included profit-sharing, recreation, training and education, libraries, reading rooms, music groups, theaters, gardening and other types of clubs, gymnasiums, cafeterias, and day care centers.

A new position, the "welfare secretary" or manager, was created to administer these programs; these managers—settlement house workers, teachers, ministers, and physicians—applied their reform interests to the workplace. Many were women, and this new position permitted them to enter "the all-male realm of management in large industries and businesses," a world previously closed to them (Kryder, 1985, p. 15). Pioneering welfare managers who headed first corporate programs were Lena Harvey of National Cash Register of Dayton, Ohio, Gertrude Becks of McCormick Harvester Machine Company (later International Harvester) of Chicago, and the Reverend Samuel Marquis of Ford Motor Company.

To achieve social control was a clear goal of these programs. At the Ford Motor Company, worker participation in the "Five Dollar Day" profit-sharing plan initiated in 1914 required not only high productivity but "good" family life and good character as certified by "advisers" who visited workers' homes. At the national level, the League of Social Service, the Welfare Department of the National Civic Federation, and the Industrial Department of the YMCA led industrial welfare activities, seeking to bring harmony to the workplace (Nelson, 1975; Jacoby, 1985).

Industrial welfare was initially voluntary, but the passage of protective labor legislation required employees to teach workers fundamentals of safety and sanitation. In 1883, protective legislation was pioneered in Wisconsin with the establishment of the Wisconsin Bureau of Labor and Industrial Statistics. The safety movement began in 1906–1907 with the founding of the American Museum of Safety by William Tolman, "the first major safety propaganda organization" (Nelson, 1975, p. 32), but it was the Triangle Shirtwaist Factory fire in 1911 in New York City that brought safety problems to national attention. The National Safety Council, organized in 1912, promoted safety education programs for the workforce, and after World War I, the safety movement spread as workmen's compensation legislation compelled managers to examine the benefits of accident prevention.

Summary

As educational and informal learning agencies proliferated, diffusing culture, information, and knowledge, adults began to understand and respond to an expanding and changing society and economy. Moralists, social reformers and critics, and civic and political leaders became educators by way of the public platform and through books, magazines, and newspapers. The public library, museums, and world fairs reached the masses by providing informal learning opportunities. Chautauqua and university extension— new adult education institutions—pioneered a systematic program for the dissemination of liberal culture and the application of scientific knowledge to vocational groups and the general public.

A more sophisticated system for disseminating scientific agriculture to ordinary farmers based on the demonstration method and the county agent—the Cooperative Extension Service—replaced the system of itinerant lecturers called the farmers' institutes. Machine production and management control of the work process created a new culture of work and prompted attention to the development of human resources through apprenticeship and other forms of vocational education. Corporations responded to undisciplined and untrained immigrants and migrants from rural areas and to widespread labor unrest through education, training, and social and recreational programs known as the industrial welfare movement.

11

Challenging the Limits to Advancement and Mobility

Some initiatives in adult education addressed changes in social conditions and unresolved issues of social justice. In this time of social upheaval, Americans searched for new understanding and the means to control the consequences of industrialization, urbanization, and mass immigration. Groups whose spheres of activity had been restricted—women, industrial workers, farmers, African Americans, and Native Americans—created alternative knowledge and educative organizations to break free from these constraints.

"The Politics of Domesticity"

What was considered "one of the basic social conflicts of the nineteenth century," the debate over the role of women, turned upon women's desire to determine their own spheres of activities, hitherto limited by men to the moral and cultural arenas (Scott and Scott, 1975). According to American political rhetoric, all persons were equal, but popular belief held that women were inferior to men. As society became industrial and urban, home was less often the center of intellectual and social life, and women whose activities were restricted to the home were left out of the intellectual and cultural mainstream. More women were working outside the home now, but in terms of the planning and development of society, they were less influential than men. Middle-class women had more leisure time as well, and they began to challenge the prevailing notion of gender-specific spheres. Self-improvement and self-education were by-products of the many organizations established by women. Scott and Scott (1975) note that "all the voluntary associations of whatever kind served as training schools in which members learned how to organize and conduct projects, developed skill in public speaking, and articulated a body of interests which women shared" (p. 21).

The Woman's Club Movement

The woman's club movement began almost simultaneously in 1868 in Boston and New York City. Members of the New England Woman's Club of Boston were mainly reformers whose work in social movements had given them an alternative vision of America and the skills to enlarge women's sphere of activities (Blair, 1980). When the New York Press Club excluded women from a dinner given for Charles Dickens, who was in America on a lecture tour, feminist journalist Jane Cunningham Croly responded by organizing Sorosis; the philosopher and "the single most important figure in the woman's club movement," Croly espoused a "domestic feminism" ideology, in which women engaged in improving society, but without the militancy of the suffragists (Blair, 1980).

From the 1870s through the 1890s, women organized literary clubs, many inspired by Sorosis, the New England Woman's Club, or the Association for the Advancement of Women (AAW). The clubs emphasized cultural appreciation and though often called "colleges" or "universities," they did not have college standards. The women's clubs counteracted the isolation of women confined to home, created a sisterhood free of male dominance, and taught women respect for their own domain. Club activities helped women acquire skills in studying, writing, speaking, and organizing. Gradually, they moved beyond self-improvement to confront serious problems and to establish scholarships, build clubhouses, and study social issues. Through the clubs, women learned how to effect change (Blair, 1980).

Croly proposed an alternative to the militant women's suffrage movement: a women's legislature to deal with women's issues, with legislative bodies for each community. In October 1873, Sorosis organized the Association for the Advancement of Women (AAW), whose purpose was to improve the status of women. The AAW Congress met in a different city each year and built programs based on a belief in women's moral obligation to improve society. In 1897, the last congress met in Springfield, Massachusetts. With the organization of the General Federation of Women's Clubs in 1890, the AAW was no longer needed (Blair, 1980).

By the early 1880s, higher education opportunities for women had produced many college-educated women who had no financial need to work and did not want to teach, but who wanted to do something useful. In January 1882, sixty-five women met in Boston to organize the Association of Collegiate Alumnae. Any woman college graduate was eligible for membership. Regional branches were soon formed, and in 1921, the association became the American Association of University Women (AAUW) (Talbot and Rosenberry, 1931).

Women's Rights

Women's hope to be given the vote after the Civil War was not realized. The women's movement then split over several issues and in 1869 formed separate organizations. Elizabeth Cady Stanton and Susan B. Anthony organized the National Woman Suffrage Association to work for national enfranchisement and to directly attack the prevailing ideology of woman's status. Lucy Stone and Elizabeth Blackwell organized the American Woman Suffrage Association to support enfranchisement state by state and to work within a framework of gentility.

As the movement philosopher, Stanton upheld the natural rights of women and the republican principle that all persons are created equal. If her challenge to woman's traditional subordinate role gained acceptance, it would generate a revolution in social relationships. She attacked the biological argument that men and women have different natures, the theological argument that God created women to be ruled by men, and the sociological argument that the family unit must be represented publicly by the husband (Campbell, 1987).

Women suffragists brought their cause to other women, to men, and to legislatures through a variety of educational and communication channels. Stone, Anthony, Stanton, and other women suffrage leaders were orators, and they became well known on the lecture platform. Suffragist newspapers publicized their activities, arguments for suffrage positions, and strategies for achieving suffrage goals. In educating women for suffrage, conventions played an important role, too: committees reported, resolutions were discussed, speeches were made to inspire and agitate, and letters from absent friends were read; exhibitions presented the suffragist case (McCurdy, 1980). The week-long celebration of the World Congress of Representative Women at the 1893 Chicago World Fair attracted almost 150,000 people. Suffragists also attempted to persuade as well as to educate: leaders testified before state and federal legislative committees, submitted petitions, and organized campaigns to win the vote (McCurdy, 1980).

Social Reform

Suffrage was not women's only concern. In 1874, the Woman's Christian Temperance Union (WCTU) gave women a national voice in political and social issues, a grass-roots organization to solve social problems, and an agency for changing their role in American society (Bordin, 1981). Until 1900, the WCTU was the leading temperance organization and the leading women's organization in the United States. Historian Carl Degler (1984) calls it "a school on a national scale for the education of women in social affairs and the need for social reform" (p. 393).

The WCTU grew out of the women's crusade that began in Hillsboro, Ohio, in December 1873. The next summer at Chautauqua, women discussed forming a national organization, and in November 1874 in Cleveland, Ohio, the WCTU held its first national convention. By the 1870s and 1880s, a large number of middle- and upper-middle-class women had sufficient education and enough leisure time to support a mass movement. A multifaceted program attracted women with varying goals and interests from many segments of society (Bordin, 1981).

In the 1870s, the WCTU concentrated on the moral persuasion and evangelical methods used in the crusades, on education in the Sunday schools and public schools, and on publicity through newspapers and the publication of literature. Frances Willard, president from 1879 to her death in 1898, brought a new militancy, and the WCTU became a major force for social reform. Willard convinced the membership to adopt a "do everything" policy and to commit to "militant feminism, equal rights, and full participation in the political process" (Bordin, 1981, p. 116). By 1896, twenty-five of the thirty-nine WCTU national departments dealt wholly or in large part with such nontemperance issues as prison reform, children, labor, working conditions for women, and the health hazards of smoking. The WCTU's greatest assets were the strong networks of local community units with autonomy to select and initiate projects. A task force of professional organizers had responsibility for organizing new units by coming to a community, giving a lecture on temperance, and, with luck, drawing a large crowd, then issuing a call for a meeting of interested women the next day to form a local union (Bordin, 1981). Organizers also kept old units functioning.

The Rhetoric of Dissent

The industrial revolution that began before the Civil War brought technological advances to agriculture as well as to manufacturing. New farm implements, such as the reaper, brought farmers into contact with distant manufacturers. New urban markets, made more accessible by the railroad, required new efforts at distribution. As historian Thomas Woods (1991) notes, "Technological agricultural knowledge began to spread in the mid-nineteenth century and gradually began to replace traditional agricultural wisdom" (p. 19). Prior to land-grant universities and extension agents, the agricultural press and agricultural societies served the educational needs of farmers. Farmers, as a class, also began to recognize their own interests: they saw a need for political activity as they confronted the monopolistic capitalism of the banks, who set the interest rates; the railroads, which fixed transportation costs; and the middlemen, who established prices for products (Buck, 1913). Farmers also began to decline in status with the fading of the Jeffersonian vision of the yeoman farmer as the backbone of democracy (Woods, 1991).

Farmers

The National Grange of the Patrons of Husbandry, founded in 1867 by Oliver Hudson Kelley and several other colleagues in the U.S. Department of Agriculture, sought to advance agriculture through education, to improve the living and working conditions of farmers and their families, to make them more knowledgeable about farming methods, and to overcome their isolation. In the mid 1850s, Kelley had organized the Benton County Agricultural Society in the Minnesota Territory; it became the prototype for the Grange. His skills as an organizer and writer attracted farmers to the organization, and local and state granges began to form. Beyond its educational and social purposes, Kelley wanted the Grange to engage in nonpartisan political activity, so he promoted cooperatives to enhance the farmers' economic power. Kelley's views did not prevail, and by 1875, his power to influence the direction of the National Grange had waned.

The Grange experienced its greatest growth in the financial panic and depression in 1873, when farmers turned to politics to remedy their economic ills. By January 1874, almost nine thousand granges, with a total membership of 643,125, had been organized in twenty-four states (Woods, 1991). In January 1875, the grange began to decline but revived again in the late 1880s (Buck, 1913).

The Grange's greatest contribution to farm life was as a social and educational institution at the local, state, and national level. Local granges conducted most of the educational activities, each one appointing one officer to be the lecturer who prepared programs for each meeting. Members were trained in public speaking and parliamentary procedure. Leaders at all levels emphasized reading, and some granges organized libraries and reading clubs. Grange news and opinions were communicated through state newspapers and the national monthly, *Grange Record,* which began publication in 1877. State and national conventions were educational activities and brought men and women together from across the state and nation to share ideas. The Grange admitted women to full membership but did not officially support women's suffrage.

At the height of the Grange's political involvement in 1874–75, local "farmers' alliances" were established in New York, Kansas, and Texas. State and multistate coalitions were formed, merging in 1889 to form the Farmers' and Laborers' Union of America, popularly known as the National Farmers Alliance and Industrial Union or the Southern Alliance. In 1880 in the Northwest, a new organization emerged: the Northwestern Alliance, which, unlike the Southern Alliance, was political from the beginning.

The Southern Alliance, considered a school, had an educational purpose (Mitchell, 1987). Charles Macune of Texas, the principal educational theorist for the alliance, portrayed America as a two-class society (the producing class and the nonproducing class), identified the importance of farmers, and taught that farmers and other common people had responsibility for preserving democracy. In getting farmers to accept this role, lecturers were the key. Working at the suballiance, state, and national organizational level, they encouraged farmers to overcome their deference to Democratic party officials and businessmen, to understand their relationship to other farmers, and to recognize that their condition derived from the dominion of capitalism and not solely from their personal actions. Periodic assemblies—rallies, meetings, and camps—brought farmers together and created a sense of group identity. Lectures helped to compensate for the low literacy levels of many farmers.

Creating a formal pedagogy to educate for political action, Charles Macune founded the *National Economist* in 1888 as the educational journal of the alliance and its organizational core. It was published weekly and became the text used in suballiance meetings. The state alliances and the Colored Farmers' Alliance published other papers, providing an inexpensive, efficient method of disseminating information and putting farmers in control of the sources of knowledge, which until then had been controlled by the major newspapers. Edward Bellamy's *Looking Backward: 2000–1887,* published in 1887, provided the intellectual inspiration for the alliance and populist leaders who promoted Bellamy's ideas among members (McHugh, 1978). *"Looking Backward,"* McHugh (1978, p. 64) said, "captured the agrarian imagination primarily because it described the outlines of a futuristic social vision" and "articulated the utopic American commonwealth that nationwide Populist victories would allegedly occasion."

The alliance did not succeed in creating a suballiance of producers or in enlisting professional and business persons and northern industrial workers, and in fact it had little understanding of industrial conditions. It also remained a white organization, the racial issue being too deeply embedded in the southern way of life to permit a racially mixed organization (African Americans could attend alliance rallies, but they could not be members). In 1886, African Americans organized a parallel alliance, the Colored Farmers' Alliance and Cooperative Union, and by 1891 the Colored Farmers' Alliance was the largest African-American organization, with more than one million members in twelve state organizations. The Southern Farmers' Alliance had more success challenging the traditional gentility of southern women and in articulating a new role for women based on education and economic self-sufficiency (Jeffrey, 1987)—it put women on equal footing with men, permitting them to study, write, and speak on the general issues of economics, politics, and education.

In the 1890s, alliance leaders turned from education to political action in order to achieve their goals. Unsuccessful in two national presidential elections, the southern agrarian reform movement waned. Though the Farmers' Alliance continued into the twentieth century, by the mid 1890s, its importance as an educational institution had diminished.

Working People

The Grange and the Farmers' Alliance had their urban, industrial counterpart in the Noble Order of the Knights of Labor, organized as a secret fraternal order in Philadelphia in 1869. After labor demonstrated its strength in the 1877 strikes of the railroad workers and coal miners, the Knights became a national union, gaining prominence under the leadership of Terence Powderly, who became the Grand Master Workman in 1879. Formed by craftsmen, the Knights worked for greater labor solidarity and opened membership to all workers of any race, color, or nationality, including African Americans and women. African Americans sometimes joined locals with whites and sometimes organized their own locals; by 1886, approximately sixty thousand African Americans were members. For women, membership in the Knights represented a challenge to the idea of separate spheres because the Knights regarded women as producers regardless of where they worked. Women were officially admitted in 1881, and by 1887, about sixty-five thousand women had joined (Fink, 1983).

The Knights and other unions in the labor movement were built on eighteenth-century republican ideas of equal rights, the relation between work and self-worth, and family-centered households. Powderly saw the Knights as an educational organization to awaken working, producing citizens and to equip them to obtain their rights. National officers went into the field to explain principles of the organization, economic problems of workers, and union structure. State assemblies created their own programs by appointing state organizers and lecturers, and local assemblies created educational programs for their members (McLaurin, 1978). Because the locals were a mixed assembly with diverse membership and because many members had little in common, the Knights could not, as did the suballiances of the Farmers' Alliance, "act as a schoolroom which forged its members into a cohesive unit" (McLaurin, 1978, p. 119).

The Knights educated through lecturers and the press. In the mid 1880s, John O'Keefe was appointed permanent southern lecturer, and Leonora M. Barry, the only woman to hold national office, was appointed general investigator for women's work and became, in her educational work, a popular lecturer (Levine, 1983). The Knights' national paper, the *Journal of United Labor,* read in the South as well as the North, provided information about the order's activities, taught Knight principles, and reported general information about organized labor.

The Knights also engaged in economic action (principally by organizing cooperatives, about one hundred by the mid 1880s) and political action. In 1883, they engaged in strikes, which greatly increased membership. When the Haymarket riot of May 4, 1886, raised the specter of labor radicalism, the Knights experienced a rapid decline in membership. Proponents of trade unionism challenged the Knights' reform unionism and in 1886 organized the American Federation of Labor (AFL), which soon became the dominant labor organization. AFL president Samuel Gompers regarded unions as the means for workers to get their share of an expanding capitalism, through alliances with the state and corporations. However, Gompers eschewed the growing workers' education movement, believing its agenda to be too radical. Because of the AFL's opposition, workers' education grew outside the boundaries of organized labor until the 1920s.

Origins of Workers' Education

Leaders in the workers' education movement found models for workers' education in England and Scandinavia (Altenbaugh and Paulston, 1980; Hansome, 1941). Workers' education found support from well-known educators such as Charles Beard, who believed in the value of education especially designed for workers. Social reform–minded middle-class women supported workers' education as a means to advance the interests of working women, and socialists promoted a broad-based educational program centered on the role of workers in social change and on their cultural advancement (Rogin and Rachlin, 1968). The workers' education movement had no coordinating institution, and the various participants in the movement were divided by differing theories and pragmatic interests (Roydhouse, 1984).

Socialists

From 1900 on, the socialists promoted workers' education, disseminating socialist theory and practices on a national scale through study circles, lyceums, discussions and classes, papers, pamphlets, books, and periodicals. Finnish immigrants with socialist beliefs founded the Work People's College (1903–1940), the first labor college in the United States. In the middle of the first decade of the twentieth century, Thomas E. Will operated the American Socialist College at Wichita, Kansas, and Walter Thomas Mills, the College of Social Science at Kansas City (Hansome, 1941). In 1906, the Rand School of Social Science (1906–1956) opened in New York City (Cornell, 1976), springing from an idea conceived by Mrs. Carrie Rand, who was influenced by her son-in-law, George Herron, a Christian socialist and reformer. A full-day program was initiated in 1911, followed by great expansion in the 1915–1916 school year.

Socialists found a receptive audience for their organizational and educational activities among working people in the southwest region (Green, 1978). Party intellectuals and propagandists carried out their activities through the press and through summer encampments. By 1912, over sixty thousand salesmen had been enlisted to sell subscriptions to the *Appeal to Reason,* the largest and most important of the socialist weekly newspapers; leaders also organized local chapters and conducted educational meetings (Green, 1978). Summer encampments brought together isolated farmers, workers, and their families in an educational forum. The most important encampment, the Grand Saline in East Texas, began in 1904 and continued for the following thirteen summers.

Initiative of Women

Concern over the plight of women in the industrial workforce resulted in new organizations to address their specific problems. The British Women's Trade Union League provided the model for the National Women's Trade Union League organized at the 1903 AFL convention. Margaret Dreir Robins, president of the national and the Chicago branch from 1907 until her retirement in 1924, played an active role in the League's efforts to organize women into unions, secure protective legislation, and provide education (Kirby, 1987; Payne, 1988).

The league focused its organizing efforts on unskilled, immigrant women (those whom the AFL refused to organize) because it believed that women were a permanent, not temporary, part of the workforce. The league was a cross-class organization, and women workers served on the executive committee in equal numbers to the middle-class female reformers and supporters. In the tradition of the Knights of Labor, Robins sought through unions to create a new kind of associational life that would transform human relationships. She regarded union membership as an educational process in which women would learn to think, see themselves as part of an association, and act with communal intent, not as isolated individuals. Robins called the union "the greatest school of democracy, the great school and university of the working people" (Payne, 1988, p. 82).

In 1914, the League organized the Training School for Women Organizers, "the first residential workers' education program established in the United States" (Jacoby, 1984, p. 6). The year-long, full-time study program trained women as union organizers. Courses related to labor issues and field work and included administrative work in unions as well as organizing. Due to financial problems, the school was discontinued in 1926, but it provided a model for women workers' education schools in the 1920s and helped women enter into union leadership. Forty-four women attended the training school, and thirty-three served the labor movement in some way.

From its inception in 1858, the Young Women's Christian Association (YWCA) had been concerned with working women. In 1904, Florence Simms became the first YWCA national industrial secretary, and she led the transformation of the YWCA from social services for poor women to studying "industrial capitalism and demanding far-reaching economic and social reforms" (Frederickson, 1984, p. 77). In 1908, the industrial group became an autonomous department in the national organization and began to address issues of working conditions, wages, health, and protective legislation. Simms led the department to develop industrial clubs in the factories, laundries, stores, and mills where women worked; these clubs were self-governing units led by the local membership. The number of industrial clubs increased from 375 in 1914 to more than 800 in 1918.

At the national level, the International Ladies Garment Workers Union (ILGWU) was a pioneer in workers' education (Wong, 1984). Juliet Poyntz's innovative educational programming as education director of Local 25 in New York City provided the model for the ILGWU programs. Poyntz organized workers' education programs at public school sites that she called Unity Centers. In 1916, the ILGWU initiated its own education program with Poyntz as part-time director and expanded the number of Unity Centers at public schools. Poyntz created recreational centers called

Unity Houses and established a Workers' University at Washington Irving High School in New York City. She resigned in late 1918, but by then she had established the basic foundation for the ILGWU's educational program, along with cofounder Fannia Cohn, who in 1916 became the first woman to be elected vice-president of the ILGWU and in 1917 was appointed organizing secretary of the General Education Committee.

The strength of the ILGWU's educational programs grew out of Poyntz's and Cohn's ideas, which would later be called "social unionism": a trade union that educated its members would be an instrument for creating a new social order. Poyntz and Cohn created, in effect, a community in which union members could learn, with Romey Unity Centers situated in the public schools. Aside from the benefits of individual education and knowledge, the workers' education program that these women developed had the goal of strengthening the union. The program's motto, "Knowledge is power," was identical to the motto of the mechanics' institutes of the 1820s. The Unity Centers offered courses "in labor problems, economics, American history and government, literature, and psychology" in order to help members form sound judgments and create a new and better social order (Wong, 1984, p. 41).

African-American Adults

Reconstruction began during the Civil War, when army and voluntary agencies came in contact with slaves, but the North did not plan adequately for the transition from slavery to freedom. In March 1865, Congress created the Bureau of Refugees, Freedmen, and Abandoned Lands as the principal agency of postwar reconstruction and placed it under the jurisdiction of the War Department. Known popularly as the Freedmen's Bureau, the legislation that established the bureau was vague and did not mention education. This permitted its commissioner, General Oliver D. Howard, to shape the bureau in his own way.

Freedmen's Aid Societies

In carrying out its educational work, the bureau selected voluntary societies to provide the actual services, especially evangelical societies and in particular the American Missionary Association, a Congregationalist society. The educational work of the various Freedmen's Aid Societies grew rapidly. By 1866, northern funds supported more than 1,400 teachers and 975 schools, increasing by the end of the decade to over 2,500 teachers and over 2,000 schools. From 1862 to 1872, fifty-one societies were conducting freedmen's education.

Both the religious and secular societies defined education broadly to include literacy skills, moral instruction, and higher education for some. Believing that slavery had retarded African-American development, both groups regarded the central educational challenge as one of character building and elevated moral training and affective learning, not intellectual achievement (Butchart, 1980). The educational program of the Freedmen's Aid Societies included northern-type common schools for children during the day and for adults in the evening. In addition to school activities, out-of-school and self-help programs were organized to instill in adults self-control and to change aspects of African-American culture that whites considered inferior. Temperance self-help associations, called "Bands of Hope" or "Cold Water Societies," were organized (Jones, 1980). To elevate home life, teachers made visits to instruct women in home economics and organized special classes that combined sewing prayer, and discussion (Jones, 1980).

African Americans needed no help, however, to recognize that independence could be secured through the ability to read the newspapers, the Bible, and labor contracts, and to correspond with relatives. They organized their own schools and supported education through public schools. By 1867, the Freedmen's Bureau required African Americans to pay for a large proportion of their schools, offering as a rationale that the financial burden would teach them self-sufficiency. The freedmen acquiesced (Butchart, 1980).

In the late 1860s and early 1870s, the federal government and voluntary societies began retrenchment. In 1872, Congress disbanded the Freedmen's Bureau. Northern women found the South less attractive, and denominational societies turned their attention to higher education for African Americans. The withdrawal of federal troops in 1877 ended the attempt of northern republicans to remold southern society. Southern states then disenfranchised African Americans, instituting segregation by law.

Racial Pride and Self-Help

African Americans were thrust back on their own resources; their economic and political advancement would rest on their own achievements. Booker T. Washington, head of Tuskegee Institute, became the principal architect of the African-American response to segregation. Washington had formed his philosophy under the tutelage of Samuel Armstrong, founder of Hampton Institute, who believed that African Americans would gain equal rights only when they made whites see they deserved it due to their progress in education, labor, money management, and family life. Through industrial education as practiced at Hampton, their character would be formed, and they would acquire useful skills for their subservient role in a white-controlled society (Anderson, 1988).

Washington came into national leadership during the birth of the New South. To raise money for Tuskegee and other African-American colleges, he appealed to southern whites and to northern philanthropists, focusing on the importance of economics and education, not civil rights, in order to avoid alienating them. Washington developed a national reputation for oratory and through his rhetoric articulated the philosophy of self-help (Olson, 1987). His speech at the Cotton States and International Exposition at Atlanta in September 1895, which brought him to national attention, called on whites to work with African Americans in building a new South and on African Americans to recognize that they had to begin at the bottom, doing physical work.

Agencies and Other Resources

African-American adult education was most often conducted as part of a larger program offered by educational and social self-help agencies. In a segregated and discriminatory society, African Americans were forced to resort to their resources and to create their own institutions. The African-American church, the first and most important of these, became the center for social life, preserving African culture, providing development of leadership skills and experience in self-reliance, teaching social values, and supporting elementary, higher, and adult education. The church, Higginbotham (1993) notes, served a mediating function between the black community and the white institutions, providing a public sphere in which African Americans could express themselves and develop "a black collective will and identity" (p. 9). Denominations created their own publishing houses to write and distribute educational materials. Local churches also engaged in benevolent and social work and occasionally sponsored industrial education classes and lecture bureaus (Meier, 1966). By 1906, the National Baptist Convention of the U.S.A. had over two million members and had become the third-largest religious body after the Roman Catholic church and the Methodist Episcopal churches (Higginbotham, 1993).

Various other local and national organizations also provided educational opportunities for adults (Franklin, 1978): mutual benefit associations, secret fraternal orders, the YMCA, the YWCA, literary clubs, and newspapers. The economic and social problems of African Americans who migrated to northern and southern cities prompted the founding of the National Urban League in 1911. In 1910, some African Americans, influenced by Washington's belief in the power of economic and educational gains, joined forces with white settlement workers to organize the National Association for the Advancement of Colored People (NAACP). A new African American was emerging, distinguished by independence, racial pride, and the desire to improve his status (Meier, 1966).

Native Americans

After the Civil War, President Grant's new policy assigned Indians to the reservations and subjected them to the authority of the Bureau of Indian Affairs (BIA). In 1871, the federal government took control of Indian education, centralized it under a special agency of the BIA (Berkhofer, 1978), mandated that the English language be used in the schools, and placed emphasis on industrial and domestic training (Prucha, 1986). The Dawes General Allotment Act of 1887 gave Indians homestead acreage, freeing them from dependency on the federal government; it also promoted assimilation into white society. Not many Native Americans became independent farmers, though, and the federal subsidies continued.

Under the assimilation policy, BIA agents began to teach Indians how to farm (Bolt, 1987). The 1880 *Instructions to Indian Agents* stated that the chief duty of an agent "is to induce his Indians to labor in civilized pursuits" (Prucha, 1986, p. 243). Agents taught Indians how to learn by doing and not just by watching others; agents then assisted Indians in cultivating their own farms, a continuation of federal policy initiated after the War of Independence. The home, too, was considered important, and the BIA believed that to convert women to this new economy would be easier than trying to convert men. The BIA instructed Indian women in homemaking and in 1891 appointed women teachers for the task. The BIA believed that mothers who received training would not undo at home what their daughters had learned in school. In the 1890s, the YMCA and the YWCA began to work with Native Americans as well.

The "Indian problem" was an active concern of whites with humanitarian and evangelical motives (Bolt, 1987). The Women's National Indian Association, organized in 1879, drew support from Baptists and other church groups for its missionary work, schools, and health care. To disseminate its message, it published a monthly journal called *The Indian's Friend*. A second reform group that was organized in 1882, the Indian Rights Association, created networks in several cities. In 1883, the Lake Mohonk Conference of Friends of the Indian met each summer at the resort's hotel in New York state; the Conference featured formal papers and discussions and developed planks for a platform, which they disseminated through an annual report that was widely publicized.

In 1911, Indians organized the Society of American Indians, the first pan-Indian political association, to pursue their own educational and reform agenda (Bolt, 1987). Like white and black reform groups of the progressive period, the society membership comprised the better-educated middle classes with the desire to help the less fortunate. Headquartered in Washington, D.C., the society lobbied and worked for reform in Indian administration. Its educational and informational work included publication of a quarterly journal, distribution of propaganda, and endorsements of education at both the public school and adult level. The society tried to establish community centers to reach its constituents but lacked sufficient resources; nevertheless, it proved that Native American leaders could work effectively within both the white and the Indian systems.

The Society of American Indians encouraged celebration of American Indian Day to foster self-help and pride and to "offset the exploitative Wild West Shows" (Bolt, 1987, p. 291), prevalent particularly in the late nineteenth century, with such promoters as the famous William F. "Buffalo Bill" Cody. White reformers believed that the Wild West shows competed with the attempts to provide American education for Indians and to educate whites about Indians (Prucha, 1984), that the shows communicated the wrong image of Indians to the white community. Conversely, they felt, glorifying the Indians' savage past was not the right way to bring Indians into civilization.

Summary

Many groups used education to improve their status in American society. In voluntary associations, women organized to challenge the male belief in separate spheres, develop their own capabilities for learning and cooperative action, and connect with the outside world through study and through the suffrage, temperance, and reform movements.

Scientific research, industrialization, and corporate domination left farmers and industrial workers disadvantaged and powerless. The Grange and Farmers' Alliance served as schools for farmers, and the Knights of Labor served as a school for industrial workers, to make them aware of their interests as a class and to challenge corporate domination. Socialist workers' education programs challenged capitalism, and both working- and middle-class women promoted social reform through education sponsored by national associations and labor unions.

Education of African-American adults advanced initially through education for freedmen provided by the Freedmen's Bureau and northern missionary societies. Then, African Americans, by their own efforts, built on a philosophy of self-help and racial pride to create their own educational institutions. The Bureau of Indian Affairs taught farming and homemaking to Native American adults living on the reservations. White organizations turned their humanitarian and evangelical interests to the study and promotion of solutions to the Indian problem, and Indians promoted reform and education through the Society of American Indians.

•

12

Supporting the New Industrial and Urban Order

Industrialization and urbanization significantly altered American life in the last quarter of the nineteenth century and the first two decades of the twentieth. As Carl Degler (1984) describes: "In the years between 1880 and 1915, industrialization and urbanization, like two gigantic hands touching the spinning clay on a potter's wheel, refashioned the contours of American society; institutions with a long lineage and stability like the Church and the home were shaken and altered. To an American who was alive in 1870, the world of forty years later lost many of its familiar bench marks" (p. 368).

The adverse conditions of city life, factory, and immigration inspired "progressivism," which began first as a local and state response in the 1890s and then grew into a national reform movement. Although quite diverse in their political agendas, progressive reformers agreed that people are responsible for each other and for establishing new social organizations to create a more humane society. New forms of adult education were explored.

Urban, Industrial, and Immigrant Society

From the 1880s to the beginning of World War I, a new wave of immigrants from the peasant population of eastern and southern

Europe settled in American cities (Degler, 1984). Another great migration of both African Americans and whites—from rural areas in New England and the South to urban areas—swelled the populations of cities. These movements coincided with the industrialization of the nation and resulted in new, technically specialized organizations requiring new and diverse skills. However, traditional educative agencies had few resources for responding to the needs of these dislocated populations.

The Settlement Movement

In England, Americans discovered the settlement house, a social and educational answer to the problems of urban and industrial life (Davis, 1967). After Stanton Coit established the first settlement house in the United States in 1886, the idea spread so rapidly that by 1910 there were over four hundred. College-educated women seeking to apply Christian values to the larger world but not wanting a career in teaching found new career opportunities in the settlement movement. In 1889, Jane Addams and Ellen Gates Starr opened Chicago's Hull House, the most famous settlement house in the United States (Addams, [1910] 1961; Lagemann, 1985).

Education quickly emerged as a major component of settlement house work. From an initial interest in giving university culture to working persons, settlement workers soon were providing kindergarten and day care, homemaking and child care classes, English language classes, lectures and discussion, vocational training, clubs, and museums and art galleries. Thus, settlements became the testing ground of progressive education ideas for adults and children, or, in the words of one worker, "the kindergarten for adults" (Davis, 1967, p. 44). Jane Addams (1899), an admirer of William James and associate of John Dewey, fashioned a unique educational role for the settlements as agencies that applied knowledge to the conduct of life. Settlements were like national bureaus that collected and analyzed data, interpreted situations, and then enlisted various persons and groups to lobby for legal remedies or to form national organizations. Settlement workers led the efforts to organize the National Association for the Advancement of Colored People, the

National Consumers League, the National Child Labor Committee, and the National Women's Trade Union League.

Community Centers, People's Institutes, and Forums

Social settlements were pioneers in the community approach to providing social and educational services, but other models soon appeared. The social center movement, utilizing public schools and recreational centers, began in Rochester, New York, in 1907, under the direction of Edward J. Ward, a Presbyterian minister experienced in providing educational and recreational services (Stevens, 1972). Ward became the leader in focusing national attention on schools as social centers. Moving to the University of Wisconsin's Extension Department in 1909, he organized the Wisconsin Bureau of Civic and Social Center Development. In 1911, the bureau sponsored a national conference to consider schools as social centers. Conference participants endorsed the role of the community center as "a basic institutional agency for reform" (Gibson, 1986, p. 188). As an outgrowth of the conference, the National Community Center Association was organized in 1916.

Ideologically, the community center sought to control the leisure time of workers and immigrants. Organizationally, it became a recreation, civic, and educational magnet for children and adults (Glueck, 1927; Stevens, 1972; Ward, 1913). Recreational activities proved more popular than civic activities, but the school as a civic center became a polling place in many communities and a community forum for discussion of civic issues, and through civic clubs it offered political socialization for adults and Americanization for immigrants.

In New York City, three nationally known institutions worked as part of a larger national reform movement to elevate the cultural life of the working class and immigrants. Cooper Union, founded before the Civil War by industrialist and philanthropist Peter Cooper, grew into a major educational and lecture center. Charles Sprague Smith left a professorship at Columbia University to bring high culture to the masses by organizing the People's Institute in 1897. The New York City Free Lecture System (1889–1928), under the direction of Henry M. Leipziger, addressed the educational needs of immigrants (Grattan, 1955), and Leipziger is credited with bringing the term *adult education* into popular use (Stubblefield and Rachal, 1992). Cooper Union's Sunday evening lecture program provided the model for George Coleman of the Boston Baptist Social Union, who led the community-based lecture program of the Ford Hall Forum in Boston. The Ford Hall Foundation, founded in 1914, provided national leadership in promoting the value of public forums and in assisting local communities (Lurie, 1930).

Club Women and Reform

In the 1890s, Protestant white women turned club efforts away from culture, and Jewish women expanded from activities within the synagogue to social reform. African-American women organized to promote uplift and social reform. In 1890, the General Federation of Women's Clubs appealed to women to use their unique understanding of community and social problems to effect reform. Membership in this national organization numbered 160,000 (white) women in 1896 (Degler, 1980). The federation endorsed women's suffrage in 1914. On race and suffrage issues, the federation sought to avoid offense, eventually in 1902 admitting black women (Blair, 1980). In 1904 under the presidency of Ellen Martin Henrotin, the federation began a total reform effort, establishing committees to investigate and suggest solutions in civil service, industrial conditions, child labor, civics, and such public health concerns as tuberculosis.

American-born Jewish women also began to redefine their role outside the home, focusing their attention on the public sphere by establishing the National Council of Jewish Women in 1893 (Toll, 1989). Many were already active in women's clubs. Like Jane Addams and other young Protestant women, young Jewish women sought to be socially useful and found inspiration in the settlement movement. An invitation to hold a Jewish Women's Congress as part of the World Parliament of Religions at the Columbian Exposition in Chicago in 1893 inspired Jewish women to play a broader role in the Jewish religious community and in secular society. The council, notes its historian, Faith Rogow (1993), enabled Jewish women to develop a public voice, to participate in the larger progressive social reform movement, and to bring social reform concerns into the Jewish community.

In the two decades before World War I, it was the African-American women's clubs that best illustrated the self-help and racial solidarity philosophy. The greatest development came after the organization of the General Federation of Women's Clubs in 1890. Black women's clubs emerged in major cities between 1890 and 1895, and in 1896, the National Federation of Afro-American Women and the Colored Women's League of Washington, D.C., merged to form the National Association of Colored Women, with Margaret Murray Washington, Booker T. Washington's third wife, as president. It remained the major national organization of black women until 1935, when it was succeeded by the National Council of Negro Women (Moses, 1978). As a self-help organization, the association worked for the uplift of black people through prison reform, orphanages, legal services, antilynching activities, temperance, labor reform, and suffrage.

Immigrant Communities

Neither the humane Americanization efforts of settlement workers nor the harsh Americanization efforts of patriotic societies, public schools, and nativists influenced many of the immigrants because efforts to teach immigrants the English language for work and citizenship overlooked their need for education in their native language, traditions, and culture (Seller, 1978). A variety of ethnic-specific immigrant organizations and media, Seller (1978) notes, provided education, and immigrants participated because they identified with these agencies. Learning occurred formally in educational institutions such as the Hungarian Free Lyceum in New York City and the Polish University in Chicago and in noneducational organizations, and informally in natural gathering places. Boarding houses, coffee shops, saloons, immigrant organizations, fraternal organizations, unions, churches, the theater, and the language presses—all these provided educational opportunities. Ethnic papers carried news, commentary and opinion, and cultural features, and in order to read the papers many immigrants became literate. In 1920, the foreign language press readership ranged between 7.6 and 10 million (Seller, 1978).

Reorientation of Religious Communities

The social, economic, and intellectual transformation occurring in the post–Civil War era profoundly affected the three major religious communities in the United States. For Protestants, the Sunday School movement, a principal agency of mission advance in the antebellum period, revived after the Civil War to reach out to unaffiliated children and adults. It was so successful that Ahlstrom (1972, p. 742) concludes that "the Sunday Schools did produce a pious and knowledgeable laity on a scale unequaled anywhere in Christendom." For half a century after the Civil War, the YMCA and the YWCA, both transported from England prior to the Civil War, led the way for Protestant intervention with immigrants, industrial workers, African Americans, Native Americans, military personnel, and business and professional people (Ahlstrom, 1972; Gaustad, 1990).

Liberal theology produced new educational approaches to deal with scientific challenges to traditional theology. A liberal consensus emphasizing human freedom and capacity for altruism and social progress found expression in "a revised estimate of the purpose and power of religious education" (Ahlstrom, 1972, p. 781). The psychology of religion, new learning theory, and progressive educational ideas provided the intellectual underpinnings of this new approach to religious education, which was promoted by the Religious Education Association, founded in 1903. The YMCA and the YWCA, under the influence of this religious education movement, were testing fields for educational and social programs to build character through group methods (Hopkins, 1951; Sims, 1936).

As a submovement within liberalism, the social gospel movement addressed the problems of urban poverty and industrialization through the institutional church and through dissemination of its ideas to middle-class Protestants. Churches adopting the institutional model kept their buildings open throughout the week and provided facilities and social and educational programs similar to settlement house programs. By 1894, there were enough churches with these programs to create an Open and Institutional Church League (Schlesinger, 1978). Sermons, lectures, magazines, novels, and interdenominational congresses challenged Protestants to respond to poverty. Charles M. Sheldon's *In His Steps* (1897) became a best-seller, and the Chautauqua summer assembly provided a lecture platform for advocates of progressive Christianity. Several Protestant denominations created agencies to deal with the labor issue, and in 1908, delegates from thirty-three denominations organized the Federal Council of Churches to focus on social issues.

From 1820 to 1920, Catholic immigration created a diverse church, and the local parish became a center for preserving immigrants' language and culture. A Catholic configuration of educative institutions that began to appear in the early 1800s expanded between the end of the post-Civil War era and World War I (Dolan, 1985). For children, school was the primary educative institution, but for adults, educative agencies included the family, in which women had the primary educational responsibility; the press; the church, through preaching and the parish library; the Catholic summer school, patterned after Chautauqua; and men's fraternities, of which the Knights of Columbus (1882) was the most famous and successful. The devotional confraternity, the most important parish society of the nineteenth century, experienced a dramatic rise in the 1860s, and other parish societies, increasing in number after 1880, began to serve social, recreational, charitable, and educational goals as well as religious ones. By the 1890s, religious reading had become a nationwide movement with its own organization and journal, the *Catholic Reading Circle Review;* there were more than two hundred fifty reading circles, with a total of ten thousand members (Dolan, 1985). In 1901, the progressive American Federation of Catholic Societies was organized to foster Catholic interests, one of which was to educate Catholics on social questions through "lectures, pamphlets, and books" (Dolan, 1985, p. 342).

A wave of German Jewish immigrants arrived between the 1820s and the 1870s and assimilated into American life, establishing synagogues and their own charitable and cultural organizations (Herberg, 1960). In the 1880s, a massive immigration of Jews from eastern Europe presented a major adult education challenge. Most settled in New York City's Lower East Side. The Yiddish-speaking East European Jews made the Yiddish vernacular "an agent of enlightenment and Americanization" to "bring folk divorced from the mainstream of western civilization into conversation with their times" (Rischin, 1977). Yiddish became the major means of communication through periodicals, the daily press, and romantic fiction. The Yiddish theater, the lecture platform, formal societies, and the coffee house or "Jewish saloon" became agencies of Jewish intellectual and cultural life. Jewish labor organizations created their own institutions that served as agencies for adult education (Howe, 1976; Rischin, 1977). They had faith in the power of knowledge, their quest guided by the ideal of the "self-educated worker." Howe (1976) describes their experience: "Learning in its own right, learning for the sake of future generations, learning for the social revolution, learning in behalf of Jewish renewal—all melted into one upsurge of self-discovery" (pp. 245-246).

Americanized German Jews fostered the Americanization of the East European Jews through the Hebrew Institute, organized in 1889 and renamed the Educational Alliance in 1893. It combined public forum, day-care, recreation, vocational and citizenship training, and a reading room with Eastern European language newspapers. English was the alliance's official language; courses could not be taught in Yiddish until the first decade of the twentieth century (Rischin, 1977).

In 1898, Thomas Davidson gave a lecture series at the Educational Alliance to Jewish male and female laborers. The lectures being well-received, Davidson continued formal classes until his death in 1900. Correspondence between Davidson and his students was compiled and published in *The Education of the Wage-Earners* (1904). Sociologist Lewis Feuer (1987) calls this book "the story of the greatest experiment in adult education that was ever carried out in the United States" (p. 289). Davidson showed this second generation of Jews a path between rejecting their parents' heritage and embracing Marxist ideology and secularism. Students led by Morris Cohen continued Davidson's work in the Breadwinner's College (1900-1917).

Expertise and the Family

Industrialization, urbanization, and immigration had consequences for the family. One response was the Society for the Study of Child Nature in New York City, organized by Felix Adler in 1888 for upper-middle-class mothers who wanted information from experts, not just from writers. In 1897, a broader movement resulted when mothers' clubs from around the country founded the National Congress of Mothers (Ehrenreich and English, 1978), renamed the National Congress of Parents and Teachers in 1924. The National Congress approached the crisis of the family and child rearing as an educational and reform task. G. Stanley Hall, the leader of the child–study movement in the late nineteenth century, became the "intellectual patron saint" of the congress, which institutionalized and disseminated Hall's theories on psychology and science into the public sphere (Schlossman, 1976, p. 445). The National Congress derived the definition and goals of parent education from progressive reform ideas that emphasized the moral obligation of women to cultivate their role as mothers and to engage in social reforms to improve the well-being of children (Schlossman, 1976).

Progressive parent education as developed by the National Congress involved a combination of self-instruction and group instruction. These middle-class women believed in the importance of parent education for all classes of society, and they took education to the poor, though on middle-class terms. Through home visits and mothers' clubs, they disseminated their knowledge of psychology and medicine to the poor. So that mothers could take action against social injustice and promote legislation, they studied the social and political matters that influenced the home. The Overstreets (1949), early historians of the Parent Teachers Association, called the National Congress a new adult education movement based on the principle of learning by doing. As a lay organization, the National Congress of Mothers learned from the knowledge produced by experts, but they interpreted and applied the knowledge to serve their own social and political goals.

In contrast, the domestic science movement reversed the roles and subordinated women to the experts. In 1899, leaders in the domestic science movement began the first of ten conferences at Lake Placid, New York, to define the field; in 1908, these efforts culminated in the formation of the American Home Economics Association and a new discipline eventually called *home economics.* Domestic science experts advanced the idea of housekeeping as a full-time profession and as an adventure in new knowledge. The germ theory of disease, first known to the public in the 1890s, became the scientific foundation of this field and transformed housecleaning into a crusade for sanitary conditions. Advocates of efficiency in homemaking found an important impetus to this movement in Frederick W. Taylor's scientific management approach in industry. They also found support in the women's movement because it appeared to elevate the status of homemakers and provided a rationale for higher education for women (Ehrenreich and English, 1978). The domestic science movement and home economics, the discipline it spawned, were part of the culture of professionalism that emerged in the late nineteenth century (Matthews, 1987). Home economists categorized as many household tasks as possible and set standards for them. In presenting themselves as experts, they taught housewives to distrust their own tastes and to doubt their own competence in child rearing.

The Americanism Era

Industrialization, urbanization, immigration, and the closing of the frontier evoked a variety of responses, but many believed that America needed an ideology to strengthen unity. They found this ideology in "Americanism." In the presidential campaign of 1916, the chief issues were the war and war preparedness. Candidates called for 100 percent Americanism and for nationalizing America. Those who found hyphenated Americans a threat denounced immigrant communities and their foreign language newspapers, cultural traditions, political activities, and ties to the old country (McClymer, 1980). In the Americanism era, adult education became an instrument of national purpose, an agency for character building, cultural conformity, and opinion formation. In retrospect, as we shall see, this era would prove to be a watershed for adult education in America.

The Military and Social Betterment

In 1914, the preparedness movement advocated military discipline and training in a nonmilitary context as a character-building tool (Borden, 1989). Opponents argued that civic virtues should remain the province of civilians and not be made the responsibility of a centralized, hierarchical, and highly developed caste system, but their arguments did not prevail. The first official action to implement the nonmilitary aspects of training came with Section 27 of the National Defense Act of 1916, which called for soldiers to receive both military training and education to prepare for jobs in civilian life. The programs were to be voluntary and did not provide for civilian teachers.

Upon declaration of war in April 1917, the army confronted the enormous task of classification, training, and morale maintenance, aided by psychologists at their own request. In August 1917, the secretary of war established the Committee of Classification of Personnel in the Army. Dr. Walter Scott Dill organized classification and Dr. Robert M. Yerkes, intelligence testing. The personnel committee prepared a new classification of occupations and offered training in personnel management. Yerkes and his colleagues developed a standard test to determine mental competence and administered a program that tested almost two million men and ranked them on a scale from A to E. The Alpha and Beta exams Yerkes devised were "the first mass-produced written tests of intelligence" (Gould, 1981, p. 195). The army used the results of the tests to classify the recruits and to identify those to be trained as officers, to be assigned to trade skills, or to be discharged.

Linking the military with higher education institutions and with the technical and trade schools offering relevant skill training for draftees became the task of the Committee on Education and Special Training, established by the War Department. C. R. Dooley, manager of the educational department of Westinghouse Electric and Manufacturing Company, was appointed educational director of vocational instruction. In all, the committee trained 130,000 men—110,000 of whom became soldiers—by the time armistice was signed on November 11, 1919.

For illiterate and non-English-speaking draftees, the War Department in July 1918 established schools to teach English with a four-month compulsory course. The army adapted the YMCA's English-language program, adding courses in citizenship, American history, geography, and government. The army had 107 development battalions and by February 1919, almost twenty-five thousand illiterate and non–English-speaking troops had received training (Borden, 1989).

Education programs also addressed moral behavior and provided activities for leisure time. Progressive reformers brought their religious, moral, reform, and scientific approach to the problems of temperance and venereal disease. The Commission on Training Camp Activities, established to direct these programs, also started vocational schools, systemwide educational centers directed by the Y to teach general knowledge, and clubhouses built and administered by the Y. By 1918, over 100,000 men were enrolled. The American Library Association (ALA) provided reading material to servicemen, forming the Library War Service of the ALA in October 1917, raising five million dollars, and distributing ten million books and magazines. Maintaining their roles as moral guardians, librarians collaborated with wartime censorship, and in the summer of 1918, the ALA complied with the War Department's order not to stock certain books in the camp libraries (Garrison, 1979). All army vocational courses incorporated citizenship materials that extolled the merits of capitalism and the sins of workers who loaf on the job (Borden, 1989). The Committee on Education and Special Training required each contract school to teach a war issues course so that soldiers would understand why America entered the war.

The Committee on Camp Training Activities was responsible for educational activities in Europe, but the programs were operated by a YMCA education commission, chaired by John Erskine, an English professor at Columbia University, until the army assumed control in December 1918. Educational activities proved popular, and by the armistice, France had six hundred organizers, and three-fourths of the two million men had registered for courses. Soldiers also enrolled in English and French technical schools and universities. Because the demand exceeded the space, the army organized the Allied Expeditionary Forces University at Beaune, France, and an agricultural school at Allery. The university had a short life:

classes were offered between March 15 and May 29, 1919, and the University closed on June 7 (Rohfeld, 1989).

Immigrants

Americanization efforts intensified as the United States prepared to enter the war. With Frances Kellor as the leading spokesperson, the Committee for Immigrants in America, organized in 1914, and the National Americanization Committee, organized in 1915, aggressively spearheaded an Americanization policy through industry and the federal government. In 1917, the committee subsidized the Immigration Committee of the U.S. Chamber of Commerce, and the National Americanization Committee became the voice of the business and professional communities. Kellor urged that industrial welfare programs include an Americanization emphasis and require attendance at educational programs. From 1916 to 1918, Kellor and her supporters campaigned for Americanization to be a part of "humanizing efforts being carried on by industrial organizations" (Korman, 1967, p. 153). Among industrialists, Henry Ford became one of the most ardent supporters of Americanization.

During the war, the National Americanization Committee subsidized the Division of Immigrant Education in the Bureau of Education and became in effect a partner with the Bureau of Education to control Americanization policy (McClymer, 1980). The committee staff received appointments as special collaborators to the bureau, and Kellor became a special adviser to the commissioner to supervise the new agency, the War Work Extension.

Among federal agencies concerned about the cultural and political loyalty of the foreign born, the Bureau of Naturalization took the lead by declaring citizenship training a part of national security and moving to place it under the public schools (McClymer, 1982). Prior to 1916, few public school systems had programs for adult immigrants, but by 1921, thirty-one states had Americanization laws. In spite of considerable activity, the public school night programs enrolled fewer than 2 percent of the approximately fourteen million nonnaturalized immigrants that were above compulsory school age (Seller, 1978). Although educators claimed education as the weapon in the Americanization struggle, they did not develop material, a method, a philosophy, or a consensus about what to teach. Even after the war, there were few established principles or procedures, and McClymer (1982) concludes that no scientific pedagogy emerged from the Americanization experience.

Civilian Thinking

President Wilson created the Committee on Public Information to provide the public with information and to secure support for the war. George Creel, appointed chair, supported progressive reform and advocated military training as a way to make better citizens. Creel brought hundreds of like-minded men and women to work on the committee. As Vaughn (1980, p. 37) describes it, it "was thus an organization composed of liberal, reform-minded journalists and intellectuals—some of the most forward-looking members of American society." They saw the committee as a federal educational agency and means of social reform. Through the literature, produced mainly by the Division of Civic and Educational Publications, the committee presented the war to the American people as a battle to preserve democracy and justified American intervention as an extension and reaffirmation of America's missionary tradition to extend America's democratic ideals to the world (Vaughn, 1980).

The Committee on Public Information used all media and included all segments of American society in its educative and propaganda efforts (Vaughn, 1980), especially focusing on the working class, women, and new immigrants. Through articles and stories in the feature sections of Sunday papers, expositions and exhibits, cartoons, and film, the committee spread the war story. News was disseminated from various government agencies. Foreign-language newspapers were reviewed for violations and committee pamphlets were translated into foreign languages for immigrants. Through the work of two hundred to three hundred scholars, the Division of Civic and Educational Publications produced, among other publications, the pamphlets in the Red, White, and Blue Information Series and the War Information Series, which sold millions of copies. The Division of Four-Minute Men sent local volunteers to speak in the movie theaters between films for a maximum of four minutes. At the war's end, the Four-Minute Men had 74,500 speakers. The speaking division sent prominent people to speak as representatives of the government and organized a war conference in each state to arouse the citizenry for the war effort. Under the auspices of the National Council of Defense, state and local councils of defense were organized to provide information about and promote the war effort. These councils, President Wilson believed, could help unite the country.

Efforts to shape civilian thinking about the war turned repressive, and demonstrating loyalty to the government became the new focus of reform idealism. Through federal laws and executive orders, government agencies and civilian groups severely restricted free public speech and the free exchange of ideas in books, periodicals, and newspapers. The federal government, under the Espionage and Sedition Acts, prosecuted almost twenty-two hundred people and convicted over a thousand including socialist leader Eugene Debs. The postal service censored mail entering the United States as well as printed material entering and leaving the country.

The war brought government into adult education to promote propaganda and cultural conformity and to restrict the free flow of ideas and information through its coercive powers. Educators—public school teachers, university professors, and public librarians—were made agents of the state.

The War's Effects

The war proved to have several consequences for adult education. Community and educational agencies became prominent and clearly demonstrated their own importance, thus strengthening the institutional base of adult education. The newly formed Cooperative Extension Service demonstrated its value and brought together local programs with a common objective and a national purpose (Rasmussen, 1989). University extension received federal support through the Division of Educational Extension in the Department of the Interior's Bureau of Education. The division was a clearinghouse for university extension directors and also served as a "cooperative agency for adult education" in division projects with other federal agencies and national voluntary associations (Bittner, 1920). The wartime Americanization programs of the public schools made adult education a legitimate activity, and the Smith–Hughes Act of 1917 provided resources. A successful experience during the war prompted library leaders to propose the Enlarged Program (later called "Books for Everybody") to extend library services to six million rural Americans and provide self-study courses to promote general adult education. Community centers demonstrated their importance in promoting effective use of community resources and marshaling citizen participation.

Government power that supported adult education in the interest of the national good turned against adult education in the interest of suppressing supposed disloyalty. In the "Red Scare" that swept the country between 1919 and 1920, the New York state legislature created a committee, chaired by Clayton Riley Lusk, freshman Republican senator, to investigate charges against persons alleged to have spread German propaganda during the war (McClymer, 1980). Lusk made adult education an object of investigation, turning attention first to the Rand School for Social Science, a socialist-affiliated school, and then to the United Neighborhood Houses (UNH), an organization of New York City settlement houses. In 1921, state legislation gave New York control over the curricula of its public and private educational agencies for adults and children (except for religious schools). Under this act, the UNH was required to apply for a license for each of the approximately four thousand clubs or classes it operated. The UNH complied, but the Rand School challenged the constitutionality of the act by refusing to get the permission of the Board of Regents. The law remained in effect until its repeal in 1923.

The army experience left an uncertain legacy for adult education. Critics charged that the army intelligence tests measured educational levels and cultural experiences, not innate intelligence. Refusing to listen to criticism, Yerkes and his colleagues used the test findings to generalize about the American population at large. They claimed, for example, that the average mental age of the white American male was slightly above the moron level, that African Americans were intellectually inferior to whites, and that immigrants from Nordic countries were superior to those from southern and eastern Europe (Gould, 1981). C. C. Brigham translated these "facts" into a blueprint for social action in his 1923 book, *A Study of American Intelligence.* Six years later, Gould (1981) writes, he acknowledged that the tests had measured knowledge of American culture rather than innate intelligence.

These "scientific" interpretations provided arguments for racial segregation, for denying African Americans access to higher education, and for restricting immigration from southern and eastern Europe. They also cast doubt on the American people's ability to benefit from adult education or to function effectively in social and civic affairs without guidance from experts. Many untoward conditions in American life, these interpreters believed, could be explained by the average mental age, and efforts to change these conditions through education or employment would be fruitless (Gould, 1981).

However, the wartime experience demonstrated that adult males could be trained and educated and that they were motivated toward—and had the intellectual ability to benefit from—general education. Many leaders of the postwar adult education movement were trained through their army experience (Rohfeld, 1989). Secretary of War Newton Baker sought to continue the army's educational program into peacetime, and in civilian life, he ardently supported adult education. As president of the Carnegie Corporation, Frederick P. Keppel, third assistant secretary of war, played the key role in organizing the American Association for Adult Education.

Summary

Settlement houses, community centers, and public and private educational agencies—urban organizations focused on neighborhoods—sought to elevate the cultural life of immigrants and workers, assist their adjustment to urban society, and engage them in the civic process. White, Jewish, and African-American club women promoted social reform through study, advocacy, and action. Immigrant organizations helped specific ethnic groups learn their native languages, traditions, and culture. Catholic and Jewish adult education efforts responded to a massive immigration that swelled their ranks, while Protestants reached adults through the Sunday school, the YMCA and YWCA, and the institutional church. In the National Congress of Mothers, middle-class women evaluated and adapted expert knowledge and extended parent education to all classes of society. The domestic science movement attempted to elevate the homemaker's role to a profession.

In the war effort, adult education played an important role. The army incorporated elements of a vast school as men were tested, classified, and trained; taught moral principles; and in general educated. The war focused attention on the "immigrant problem," and private associations, industry, and government promoted the cultural conformity of immigrants. Universities, community centers, and public libraries provided valuable services in adult education and gained increased recognition for their role in adult education. Many political and educational leaders found in their war experience a training ground for leadership in the adult education movement of the 1920s. But the war also taught another, more ominous lesson—about the power of the state to deny the very basics of adult education: intellectual freedom, free speech, and the right to hold unpopular ideas.

PART FOUR

The Nation Amid
Crisis and Recovery

13

Ordering Knowledge
for the American Public

Prescriptions to remedy the educational deficiencies of adults came as the United States began the postwar period. In 1919, Glenn Frank, formerly a platform lecturer, then editor of the *Century,* later president of the University of Wisconsin, called for the revitalization of public lecturing, a powerful educational force in American life since before the Civil War. He envisioned lecturers as teachers, giving the average American citizen a base of general knowledge, connecting the specialist and the layperson, pioneering new intellectual and social trails, and interpreting issues of concern. However, the conditions that would have permitted such a profession to flourish in American society had already passed. A more highly educated middle class, new knowledge, new occupations, new leisure, and new media demanded new means for diffusing knowledge and culture to the public.

Educational Domain

In the 1920s, the Carnegie Corporation of New York initiated a major campaign on behalf of adult education; in 1926, it culminated in the organization of the American Association for Adult Education (AAAE). Andrew Carnegie had organized the Carnegie

Corporation in 1911 for the general purpose of promoting and diffusing knowledge among the people. Under the leadership of Henry Pritchett and Elihu Root, the Carnegie Corporation identified urgent national problems that could be addressed through education (Lagemann, 1989). The emergence of an interdependent society—increasingly more complex and difficult to manage—gave rise to experts in various fields and the use of this expert knowledge to inform policy. Pritchett and Root believed that the general public needed to be informed, that "a public intelligence" must be developed. James Harvey Robinson (1924) agreed, calling for "the humanizing of scientific knowledge" so that the general public would be able to make informed decisions.

Prior to its excursion into adult education, the Carnegie Corporation commissioned several studies, one of which, the *Americanization Studies: The Acculturation of Immigrant Groups into American Society,* resulted in ten books on the process through which the foreign born were transformed into American citizens. A second study, William S. Learned's *The American Public Library and the Diffusion of Knowledge* (1924), analyzed knowledge diffusion and provided the rationale for Carnegie's activities in adult education. Learned called for the library to become a "community intelligence center," to be directed by a new kind of library personnel who had expertise in specific areas and knew the specific needs and interests of adults in the community.

Several factors drove the Carnegie Corporation initiatives in adult education. Anticipating that leisure time and demand for postschool education for adults would increase, the trustees wanted to develop educational opportunities outside the educational system, opportunities that were well organized, regularly scheduled, and noncommercial. In schools and universities, the young people would learn basic skills; through various other forms, adults would have access to information. The Carnegie Corporation regarded adult education as "a means of diffusion which would restore to individuals the power to make decisions about their lives" (Rose, 1989b, p. 142).

In 1924, Carnegie Corporation trustees directed their new president, Frederick Keppel, to begin a program of adult education. Keppel knew about the wartime programs of the Commission on

Training Camp Activities, but perhaps his most important influence was an English publication, *The Way Out,* a collection of essays by representatives of the Workers' Education Association. These essays called for an experiment in liberal education that would offer advanced study to the working class, a kind of adult education they believed would result in social stability (Lagemann, 1989). Keppel called together an advisory council of leading adult educators from various fields, commissioned several studies of adult education, and finally convened several regional conferences. As a result, the AAAE was formed in 1926. The Carnegie idea of diffusing knowledge through adult education was not clearly communicated to the delegates, however (Rose, 1989b). The focus shifted from individuals to institutions and methods, from learning outside the classroom to classroom learning, although interest in noninstitutional learning—through library, radio, and film—remained.

The AAAE, technically an independent organization, had to meet the demands of the different institutions that provided support, especially the Carnegie Corporation, which provided administrative support. The selection of Morse Cartwright, Keppel's administrative assistant, as AAAE's executive director ensured close cooperation, especially as the AAAE's executive committee took on the task of screening requests to the Carnegie Corporation for adult education funding.

Through the AAAE, the Carnegie Corporation initiated research, experimental projects, demonstrations, and institutional and special-population studies that would lead to improved practice in adult education. The AAAE disseminated ideas through annual conferences and through the *The Journal of Adult Education.* It brought together educators, civic leaders, and intellectuals and promoted use of the term *adult education* to give a name to the scattered impulses for individual self-improvement, community betterment, and the diffusion of knowledge. These efforts led to a recognition of a new level of education that was more than schooling, an education for adults in their life roles. Its sponsorship of Edward L. Thorndike's research, published as *Adult Learning* and *Adult Interests,* gave scientific evidence of the ability of adults to learn and of the ongoing interests that would motivate them to do so. AAAE's sponsorship of doctoral studies in adult education at

Teachers College, Columbia University, introduced adult education as a field of university study and began the professionalization of the leadership of adult education.

These achievements notwithstanding, the AAAE greatly circumscribed the boundaries of adult education by exclusive focus on liberal education. Its leaders held that adult education in a democracy must create informed citizens, promote tolerance and understanding of differences, and maintain social stability. This concept of education's role and of the existing social structure precluded any support for a type of adult education that would address conditions related to class or ethnicity. Nor did the adult education experiment achieve its intended goals. Lagemann (1987) concludes: "The efforts floundered partly because Keppel was interested in innovation as highly diverse experimentation rather than as the more deliberate (and implicitly highly directive) fostering of desirable social trends and partly because the 1930s depression spawned many nonschool educational programs in addition to and different from those encouraged by the Corporation" (pp. 213-214).

Some scholars would later claim that the adult education movement of the interwar period espoused a social reform agenda that soon faded in response to professional concerns (Cotton, 1968). It is true that several key AAAE leaders—liberal social scientists Charles Beard, Eduard Lindeman, and Harry Overstreet among others—held social reconstructionist views and involved themselves in the workers' education movement and other liberal causes. In reality, social reconstructionists' views on class or race never became part of the AAAE agenda, nor did the AAAE go beyond the claim that the health of democracy depended on a citizenry informed through adult education. In its early years, the AAAE appeared to be impartial by refusing to associate adult education with any social causes or special groups. In the economic and political crisis of the Depression with its New Deal emergency education relief programs, the AAAE through Morse Cartwright rejected both the concept of adult education for liberal social action and the idea that the federal government had any constructive role in adult education (Jones, 1991; Stubblefield, 1988).

In the interwar period, the AAAE remained the dominant organization for the advancement of general adult education. In

1924, an organization created by the National Education Association—the NEA's Department of Adult Education—provided a complement to the AAAE's liberal education emphasis and later competed with it for members. Initially restricting its membership, the department was open only to teachers and administrators who were under the auspices of public schools. As public school adult educators began to work with other educative agencies within communities, the department opened its membership in 1938 to anyone working educationally with adults (Luke, 1992). In the early 1940s, several adult educators with little or no experience in public schools achieved leadership positions. These new leaders, particularly Leland Bradford, who would become one of the founders of the National Training Laboratories, began to envision a new national organization that would more adequately serve the needs of the entire field. In 1951, both organizations dissolved to form the Adult Education Association of the U.S.A.

Media, Culture, and Learning

In the 1920s and 1930s, it became a major educational task to connect the more highly educated public with the new professional understanding of the world. Social scientists produced different bodies of knowledge in order to understand and explain changes in the social order, but this new knowledge—specialized, complex, and often contradictory to common sense—was not easily disseminated to the lay public (Susman, 1984). In the 1920s, a more highly educated and urbanized America formed a mass market for publications (Tebbel, 1978), and in the new consumer culture, there was new leisure time for educational opportunities at the adult level (Susman, 1984).

Books and the Popularization of Culture

Popularization became one means to disseminate knowledge to the lay public. In the 1920s, books providing "outline" knowledge began to appear. The pecuniary interest of commercial publishers was met by "an honest urge on the part of the public to get a package of easily digested culture" (Tebbel, 1978, p. 34). These books addressed common concerns about civilization and its progress (Susman, 1984). Most important, they answered the need to understand the meaning of human history itself; H. G. Wells's *The Outline of History* was the most significant of these, becoming a best-seller in 1921 and continuing to sell to the present.

During the Depression, the public turned to books on how to succeed. Self-help books, ignoring the assaults on capitalism, taught Americans how to be successful through personality development. Dale Carnegie's *How to Win Friends and Influence People,* the most widely sold of this genre, prescribed success through adjustment to the social order and helping other people feel important (Susman, 1984); it sold 750,000 in its first year and 3,250,000 by 1948.

The American search for culture through books was facilitated by hardcover reprints, which extended access to a larger public; the paperback book revolution; and the introduction of large-scale book clubs. In 1925, Random House bought the Modern Library and reprinted hard cover classics, and in 1921, E. Haldeman-Julius established "the cheapest of all mass market lines," the Little Blue Books, which became "an American institution" (Tebbel, 1978, p. 6). By selling books for a nickel and advertising in newspapers, Haldeman-Julius sold three hundred million books by his death in 1951. The most important breakthrough in paperbacks occurred in 1939 when Robert F. de Graff and others introduced twenty-five-cent Pocket Books, creating a new class of book buyers: service workers and middle-class professionals. The modern book club concept, which began in 1926 with the formation of the Book-of-the-Month Club and the Literary Guild, proved popular.

Magazines for the Educated

Time, The New Yorker, and *Reader's Digest,* creations of the 1920s, were the most important representatives of a new magazine genre that dealt with "facts," and they came at a turning point in the intellectual life of the nation. As Marquis (1986) notes: "For the last time, an educated person could comprehend the latest in science and medicine, art and literature, music, engineering, sociology, psychology, politics, and world affairs before most of these disciplines shattered into arcane subspecialties, guarded by the specialist's jargon" (p. 109). Henry Luce, an innovator in mass media communication, founded *Time* magazine as an educational institution to provide facts to readers; he modeled the structure of the magazine after the structure of a university, and dividing it into departments. By 1934, *Time* had a circulation of half a million and by 1937, 650,000. Its readers were college educated people, leaders in various walks of life, and opinion makers (Marquis, 1986).

"Sight and Sound" Media

Technological advances were now broadening cultural communication from the print medium to the medium of "sight and sound." In the 1920s and 1930s, radio matured "as a full-fledged medium of communication," and was soon used for informal learning (Marquis, 1986, p. 27). Through radio, millions of small-town and rural residents had access to good music, an opportunity previously reserved for the elite. The soap opera—a new dramatic genre created for radio—appeared in 1931, and by 1937, there were thirty-one soap operas on radio. Though often derided, soap operas served an educational function for housewives by helping them realize that others shared their problems, by showing them how others responded to and resolved conflict, and by reinforcing their values (Susman, 1984). By 1939, radio had supplanted the newspaper as "the preferred source of news" (Perrett, 1985, p. 138). Luce started *The March of Time* on CBS radio in 1931, reporting the news to millions of listeners weekly. Radio gave Americans access to the world, aided in the shift of public opinion away from isolationism, and enabled Americans to hear their leaders. President Franklin D. Roosevelt used the radio to share national values.

　　Photography and film also changed cultural communication. The photograph reached out to nonreaders; *Life* magazine, founded in 1936, invented the "picture essay." Luce's *The March of Time* newsreel let theater audiences see and experience events in a new way, and in the 1930s, the documentary emerged as a distinctive genre, capable of exploring an event or situation in detail.

　　Marquis (1986) assesses the impact of the mass media on the learning of the American public: "But whatever their formal education, the mass media offered Americans the richest menu of informal learning in human history. Within the framework of entertainment, the new channels of communication provided consumers with vivid lessons in manners, morals, hygiene, nutrition, fashion, childrearing, sports, interpersonal relations, community resources, history, nature, science and technology. The mass media presented their huge audiences with both a window and a mirror: a panoramic view of the great world outside and also a vivid and appealing reflection of themselves as members of one great audience and even as consumers of the same brands of toothpaste and toilet paper" (p. 6).

Agencies to Diffuse Culture and Knowledge

A national system of educational agencies for formal and informal learning that had formed before World War I now adapted to the changing circumstances of the 1920s and 1930s. Through universities, public schools, libraries, museums, and exhibitions, many Americans had access to knowledge. Restrictions still applied to African Americans and to adults with insufficient literacy skills, who for the first time became the object of national attention.

University Activities

Before the war, the efforts of university extensions to reach all the people of the state had been divided into general extension and cooperative extension, but the two divisions grew unevenly. The Cooperative Extension Service developed as a unique experiment in American education. Operated as part of each state's land-grant university, this cooperative venture between the federal, state, and local governments provided a tax base with which to address the educational needs of the agricultural population through the efforts of a full-time instructional staff of county agents serving farmers, homemakers, and youth (Houle, 1959). When World War I began, the service became an agency in support of the war effort, but after the war, it returned to its educational function (Rasmussen, 1989). In the 1920s, it gained a powerful national ally with the organization of the American Farm Bureau Federation. Representing the farm bloc, the federation lobbied Congress for extension funding.

The USDA established a national administrative support system for state and local extension programs.

Confronted with the farm depression of the 1920s, the federation and the USDA promoted farmers' cooperatives to market products under the leadership of county agents. In addition to handling that crisis, extension promoted more efficient production, assisted farmers to adopt new technologies, and advocated a total farm management approach. Women farmers also contributed directly to farm productivity as well as managing the household and rearing children, and the development of home economics and nutrition as new professional fields greatly strengthened extension's work with families. An institutional structure developed under the rubric of 4-H that expanded the original canning and gardening clubs into a comprehensive youth program operating through both extension and school clubs. By 1930, extension had developed a philosophy and method to undergird its work as a voluntary educational program whose goal was to effect change and whose success depended on meeting the needs of the people.

General extension served both rural and urban populations, but its development and operation differed considerably from cooperative extension. Houle (1959) observes that general extension depended on fees, had less autonomy within the university structure, had a diffuse population to serve, drew on the university curricula, relied on traditional methodologies, and depended on part-time instructional staff with outside careers. General extension grew unevenly among universities because each institution was autonomous.

The National University Extension Association gave leadership to the development of general extension among the major state and private universities, promoted the professionalization of university extension, and sought to establish itself as an elitist institutional organization (Drazek and Associates, 1965; Edelson, n.d.; Rohfeld, 1990). First, it defined extension as the sole provider of organized instruction in which the adult gave systematic attention to analysis, application, and synthesis; this role differed from that of agencies that promoted informal and nonsequential learning. Second, the association maintained that in cooperative relationships with nonuniversity organizations, universities would be dominant. Spencer Miller, Jr., secretary of the Workers' Education

Bureau, pleaded for universities to support workers' education but not to coopt it. Richard R. Price, in the president's address at the 1924 conference, replied that university extension would maintain the same policy for workers' education that it did for other groups: the university would be in control. Third, the association developed a nomenclature for extension units and standards for extension courses. Fourth, it restricted membership to schools that had university-level instruction, which meant the large state and major private universities, thus excluding normal schools and teachers' colleges (Edelson, n.d.).

University extension expanded in several directions in the 1930s. Within communities, universities established branches and extension centers for bachelor's degree studies. In 1936, the University of Minnesota dedicated the first residential conference center. The Depression prompted universities to expand their offerings to include community development, providing as part of this effort educational activities in Civilian Conservation Corps camps and WPA programs. The University of Minnesota received a Carnegie Corporation grant to study the abilities of extension students, with the intention of strengthening the status of extension in the university structure. In addition, the association initiated discussion of proper credit for learning no matter what the educational structure (Drazek and Associates, 1965). In the 1920s, the radio offered great promise for linking the university with the public, and by 1928, sixty-five colleges and universities were using radio. But time on commercial stations became scarce, and universities found that operating their own stations was expensive. By 1940, it was clear that the educational promise of radio would not be realized (Portman, 1978). Universities reached the nonresident adult student through credit and noncredit correspondence courses. After World War I, the University of Wisconsin, among others, added new courses for returning veterans, homemaking and civic education courses for women, who now had the vote, and courses for teachers (Rose, 1991).

Evening colleges sponsored by municipal universities also provided educational opportunities for adults, though their activities have been less publicized than those of state and private universities. By 1925, eleven evening colleges had been chartered, most

by privately endowed or church-sponsored colleges and universities
(Dyer, 1956). They provided college education close to home and
met the growing needs of business and industry for specially trained
workers. In 1930, Cleveland College, which had been organized in
1925 in affiliation with Western Reserve University, enrolled over
seven thousand students in 559 classes. These students comprised
every social and occupational class in Cleveland. A full-time day
college and Division of Informal Adult Education were later added;
the division offered short courses on parent education and health
and general education courses on art, literature, and music. In 1939,
evening college deans who had been active in the Association of
Urban Universities (founded in 1915) created their own organization, the Association of University Evening Colleges. Thus began
a second phase of development marked by a greater identification
of the evening college's mission, administration, and relationship
with the larger university (Dyer, 1956).

A unique university experiment in adult education for the
educated began in 1919 when the New School for Social Research
in New York City was established by distinguished social scientists
of Columbia University and editors of the liberal *New Republic*
magazine. Founded to promote social science research and adult
education in a university setting but unconstrained by bureaucracy,
the New School aspired to be an agency for social reconstruction.
The founders could not, however, agree on social goals. Charles
Beard and James Harvey Robinson were popular lecturers, but others such as Thorstein Veblen did not appreciate adult classes or hold
lecturing in high esteem. In 1923, adult education rather than social
science research and social change became the main focus of the
New School; it later became a degree-granting university (Rutkoff
and Scott, 1986; Stubblefield, 1988).

Public Schools

At the beginning of the 1920s, public schools offered programs for
adults in academic subjects, Americanization, and vocational education, later adding avocational and personal improvement courses.
Annual enrollments in the mid-twenties varied from 200,000 to
1,000,000. In the 1920s, some states changed the title of the director

of Immigrant Education or Vocational Education to director of
Adult Education, but the number of states offering financial aid
increased very slowly—twenty-one by 1935, only seven of which
went to programs other than Americanization and literacy education (Knowles, 1977).

The human side of the public school system's role in adult
education is revealed in the example of Emily Griffith and the Opportunity School of Denver, Colorado. The school, an adult, industrial, and vocational school, opened in the fall of 1916 as part of the
Denver public school system. Griffith, who served as principal until
1933, combined social work services with education, provided counseling, gave money to the hungry and homeless, and found jobs for
clients. With almost twenty-four hundred students the first year, the
school charged only for the cost of materials, enrolled persons of all
ages, and had no educational prerequisites. Both individual and
group instruction were available, and adults who had an immediate
need to learn could begin at any time during the year (Bluemel,
1970).

The National Education Association (NEA) organized the
Department of the Wider Use of Schoolhouses (1915-1922) and the
Department of Immigrant Education (1921-1924), which became
the Department of Adult Education in 1924 (Wesley, 1957). Beginning in 1926, when the NEA organized a Commission on Coordination in Adult Education, and throughout the 1930s, the NEA
Department of Adult Education coordinated with the public
schools to implement adult education under both public and private auspices at the national, state, and local levels. The department
also extended membership beyond puolic school teachers and administrators of adult programs to educators in other public institutions, such as libraries (Knowles, 1977).

Before the war, the community school was expected to become the center for education, recreation, and civic life, but this did
not materialize as the number of school centers decreased between
1916-1923. During the Depression, the community school movement revitalized around the idea of community schools as agents of
social reconstruction. Leaders promoting this idea argued that the
local community "should be thought of as a school in which both
adults and children learn through study and action" and that "all

life is educative" (Everett, 1938, pp. v, 435–462). The eventual model for the post–World War II period was the Flint Community School Program, which began in 1935 in Flint, Michigan.

Modern Literacy Campaigns

Until the late nineteenth century, literacy had been important for religious understanding, economic mobility, and community membership as well as for being a social virtue in itself. By the late nineteenth and early twentieth centuries, however, illiteracy came to be regarded as a social problem (Rose, 1990). Americanization programs used literacy to inculcate social values. The 1910 national census documented a high rate of illiteracy, which hindered economic modernization in the South. World War I focused national attention on the problem when draft registration revealed the high rate of illiteracy.

Literacy campaigns began in the South at the state level. In 1911, Cora Wilson Stewart, superintendent of schools in Rowan County, Kentucky, initiated a southern literacy campaign with the "Moonlight Schools," the first adult literacy schools. Her efforts across the state led the Kentucky state legislature to create the Kentucky Illiteracy Commission in 1914, and Stewart soon became a national leader in literacy (Nelms, 1984). In 1914, Will Lou Gray, a South Carolina club woman, began a program of literacy classes with volunteer teachers. The state government assumed more responsibility; in 1917, it established the South Carolina Illiteracy Commission, and in 1919, it made literacy education a function of the state Department of Education, with Will Lou Gray as supervisor of adults schools (Akenson and Neufeldt, 1990). In Alabama, African-American leaders took the initiative in raising monies to secure matching state funds when local authorities failed to do so. Philanthropic organizations such as Slater, Phelp-Stokes, and Rosenwald made donations, and the African-American supervisors, who were funded by the Jeanes Foundation, recruited and taught African-American adults. In the average southern county, African-American illiteracy was reduced by 12.3 percent between 1910 and 1930, but the reduction can be attributed to the higher school attendance rates as well as to the literacy campaigns (Akenson and Neufeldt, 1990).

National literacy campaigns began in 1924 with the National Illiteracy Conference in Washington, D.C. This conference resulted in the first National Illiteracy Crusade, but without goals or resources, the effort served only to create public awareness of the problem. In the rhetoric of the campaign, President Calvin Coolidge called illiteracy a threat to the American way of life, associating it with poverty and crime. A second literacy initiative began in November 1929 when President Herbert Hoover appointed another advisory committee on National Illiteracy; its goal was to make five million adults literate within three months, before the completion of the 1930 census. The motive was apparently political, because Hoover appropriated no federal monies. In December 1929, the campaign was launched with Native Americans, African Americans, and immigrants added to the target populations (Quigley, 1991).

Libraries, Museums, and Exhibitions

In the 1920s, public library leaders' search for a significant social role for the library led them to adult education. As Garrison (1979) notes: "By 1920 the public library had assumed much of its modern form. The early vision of the public library as an intellectual center and of the librarian as a major educational figure in the community was unrealized. The public library survived as a peripheral cultural and intellectual institution" (pp. 222–223). The American Library Association's interest in adult education began in 1924 at its annual conference, at which it created a Commission on the Library and Adult Education, receiving support from the Carnegie Corporation. The commission's report was published in 1926 as *Libraries and Adult Education,* becoming the fifth book in the Carnegie-sponsored Studies in Adult Education series. The commission disbanded to be replaced by the Board on the Library and Adult Education. The ALA promoted further dissemination of library adult education in a periodical on *Adult Education and the Library* (1925–1931). Public libraries initiated new library services for adults, including the Reader's Advisor Service, and these advisers became the first library representatives to take part in adult education (Knowles, 1977). With Carnegie support, the ALA initiated the Reading with a Purpose courses in 1925, and by 1931, fifty-four courses had been published.

The ALA and Carnegie sponsored studies on reading habits of adults, notably *The Reading Interests and Habits of Adults* by William S. Gray and *What People Want to Read* by Douglas Waples and Ralph Tyler (Knowles, 1977). The partnership between Carnegie and the ALA rested on their philosophical agreement that adult education strengthened democracy and that liberal adult education was the kind of adult education needed. Advocates such as Alvin Johnson called the library "the people's university." Nevertheless, library professionals did not all agree that the library should become an agency of adult education, and by the early 1930s, the enthusiasm had begun to wane (Rachal, 1990).

In the upheavals of the interwar period, the cultural importance of museums grew as art museums emphasized their educational role (Harris, 1990). In the Depression, people turned to the museum as an inexpensive form of entertainment and for relief from the grimness of day-to-day life. As great numbers of Americans visited art museums, the museums' educational value for the general public became apparent, and both the Rockefeller Foundation and the Carnegie Corporation began to regard museums as "part of a system of out-of-school education" (Newsom and Silver, 1978, p. 15.) By 1930, the United States had 167 art museums, which meant that every city with a population of at least 250,000 had one or more art museums (Marquis, 1986). When the Museum of Modern Art in New York City (MOMA) opened in November 1929, MOMA's trustees and director regarded it as as an educational institution. In 1931, MOMA began sending exhibits around the country, attracting large crowds (Marquis, 1986).

In 1924, the American Association of Museums initiated museum audience research, hiring Edward S. Robinson to conduct "carefully controlled time-and-motion studies of museum visitors" (Alexander, 1979, p. 165). Robinson and his associates timed how long visitors spent at each exhibit and observed how they moved past exhibits. They discovered that each exhibit competed with other exhibits and that the design of the exhibit affected the number of visitors it attracted.

Both private philanthropy and the federal government supported museum education. Preservation projects created outdoor museums; colonial Williamsburg was established in 1926 with the sponsorship of John D. Rockefeller, Jr. In 1929, Greenfield Village at Dearborn, Michigan, moved historic buildings to a new location, creating the indoor Henry Ford Museum (Alexander, 1979). Under the auspices of the National Park Service, organized in 1916, Yellowstone National Park took the lead in developing an educational component. The American Association of Museums constructed museums and roadside exhibits in Yellowstone with a grant from the Laura Spelman Rockefeller Memorial. In 1929, the National Park Service organized the Committee on the Study of Educational Problems in National Parks to examine the educational role of parks and in 1930 created the Branch of Education in its Washington office (Sharp, 1987).

In the interwar period, expositions were no longer such powerful educational and cultural forces. Americans were less certain about the possibility of organizing the products of scholarly research in the natural and social sciences and the humanities into a coherent understanding of the world. The worldwide economic depression, World War I, and the rise of facism in Europe made people apprehensive of the idea of progress (Harris, 1990). The 1933 Chicago World's Fair called "A Century of Progress," assessed America's achievements in the fields of literary criticism and social science, and commentators analyzed this crisis of confidence (Susman, 1984). The era of exhibitions of national and international significance came to an end with the 1939–40 New York World's Fair and the San Francisco Golden Gate International Exposition. The San Francisco exposition sought to meet the goals of the New Deal by restoring faith in the American economic system, with corporate sponsors envisioning a commercial link between the United States and countries of the Pacific. The New York Fair, whose theme was "The World of Tomorrow," promised to show the way to a better and more enlightened life in the midst of ill health and poverty and challenged the belief systems of Nazi Germany and Russian communism by portraying the superiority of America's "scientifically materialist society" (Marquis, 1986, p. 202). Both fairs closed as financial and cultural disasters (Perrett, 1985).

The Workplace as School

By 1920, a blueprint for modern education in the workplace had emerged. Contemporary surveys by Kelly (1920) and Morris (1921) showed a philosophy, curriculum, methods, delivery system, and organizational structure. Kelly's 1920 *Training Industrial Workers,* claimed by John Brewer (1920) to be "the first comprehensive book on the subject of education in industry" (p. viii), sets forth an educational creed for industry and a rationale for training. Every industrial worker needs training, and the employee, the employer, and the public have an interest in meeting this need. Without training, employees cannot achieve their highest potential, productivity suffers, and economic and social progress are retarded (Kelly, 1920). A well-balanced training program included the components of retraining, training for promotion and transfers, improving the efficiency of older workers, and, most important, preparing young workers for entering the workforce.

The modern corporation required training both in technical skills and in higher intellectual skills. Morris's analysis (1921) of the products of Westinghouse Electric and Manufacturing Company, a major manufacturing company recognized for its exemplary training program, showed that in addition to skills "an immense amount of initiating intelligence must be constantly introduced in inventing and improving both the products and also their means of production" (p. 3). Engineers, specialized technicians, and mechanics exercised independence in control of machines, for which the Education Department provided training for these "differentiations of productive skill and intelligence" (p. 3).

Corporations addressed their training needs with in-house and out-of-house programs. In-house programs included apprenticeship training, supervisory training, and on-the-job training. Industry established formal schools such as the Ford Motor Company Trade School in 1916, the Westinghouse Technical Night School, and the General Motors Institute of Technology. Outside programs included evening schools for general education. Joint programs were also created. The American Banking Institute, established in 1900 and composed of autonomous chapters, offered courses for bank employees. The Insurance Institute of America, formed in

1909, began educational programs in 1924. Correspondence study remained popular and was reportedly the most widely used method for learning trades (Steinmetz, 1976).

Training as an occupational specialization emerged before the end of World War I. The first national conference of personnel managers, held in 1916, was followed in 1918 by the organization of the National Association of Employment Managers (Jacoby, 1985). In 1922, the National Association of Corporation Schools and the National Association of Employment Managers (training was a major concern for the latter group) merged to become the National Personnel Association, and a year later, it became the American Management Association (Peffer, 1932).

Industry applied to its educational programs lessons learned during wartime, individualizing instruction, focusing on mastery, modularizing courses, emphasizing outcomes, and developing curriculum on the basis of job analysis (Neumann, 1979). After the war, the leaders who had developed and administered wartime training for soldiers now used their military experience, stressing performance tests in education, applying army training methods and performance tests to apprenticeship training, and establishing specifications for acceptable performance. Charles R. Allen's synthesis of wartime training methods (*The Instructor, the Man, and the Job,* 1921) gained recognition as a "classic text" (Neumann, 1979).

In 1914, Charles R. Allen, a pioneer in analyzing tasks and breaking jobs down to component parts, developed the conference method for training foremen. In the interwar period, both management and supervisors began to realize that employees could judge the value of training and that if courses did not appeal to students, they had to be discontinued. New viewpoints toward training emerged, and to address the unique setting of the work organization as a training site, new teaching methods developed that did not have a "counterpart in institutional education" (Cooper, 1942, p. v). One of these, developed especially for employee education, was "the rehearsal-conference method of training," preferred when participants had experience to draw upon for discussion. In the conference method, employees developed standards of practice for specific operations; this participative learning enlisted the employee's cooperation, sold the employee on the program, and increased the possibility that the training would transfer to the job (Cooper, 1942).

New programs were also developed to train supervisors and managers. The foremen's club movement grew out of the Dayton, Ohio, YMCA-sponsored class for foremen during the war and spread rapidly within Dayton as well as to other parts of the country. Between 1923 and 1936, Purdue University trained ten thousand foremen from 616 companies in eighty-seven cities (Graebner, 1987, p. 79). In 1925, the National Association of Foremen was organized, and between 1918 and the 1930s, the profession developed guiding rules and principles. The educational method that was applied to foremen training became more sophisticated. A democratic system of education, drawn from progressive education and the new social psychology, used small groups, group discussion, and leaders. Between 1930 and 1933, foremen training was drastically curtailed, but it revived after 1933. Foremen's clubs also came back after 1933 "to promote a sense of cohesion and loyalty to management through social activities and lectures" (Jacoby, 1985, p. 230). In 1938, the Y's leadership manual sought to instill in the foreman a sense of responsibility for creating a group spirit in factories. Once workers understood their responsibilities in the workplace, they would then transfer that larger learning to the community. In this way, the foremen's clubs participated in democratic social engineering.

Summary

From 1926 to 1941, the American Association for Adult Education, with generous support from the Carnegie Corporation, advanced the idea of adult education as a new educational domain, creating awareness among leaders in many fields of endeavor and within the public at large about the importance of continuing learning in the changing world of the 1920s and 1930s. As an agency of informal learning, the print media addressed the needs of a more highly educated public for knowledge through popularization methods and magazines of "facts," and the new media of radio, film, and photography brought information and culture through "sight and sound."

Before World War I, such educational and cultural institutions as university general extension and cooperative extension, public schools, public libraries, museums, and exhibitions had begun to form a national system of formal and informal learning for adults. After the war, these institutions stabilized, expanded, or adapted their programs in eras of prosperity and depression to address needs for work-related, cultural, and personal development. In the 1920s, it was clear that the productivity of the modern corporation required a system of instruction. Training expanded, instructional methods unique to industry were adapted or developed, and the training function was addressed by a national organization.

14

Education's Role
in Addressing
Unfinished Agendas

A system of adult education took shape in the interwar period. Its prominent feature, as described in the previous chapter, was the development of institutional forms of adult education for knowledge dissemination to the general public and for the training of workers. The commercial media and economic and educational institutions all used adult education to promote a socially and economically conservative agenda, an approach supported by the leaders of the American Association for Adult Education, who believed the social purpose of adult education was the education of individual citizens. Another theory of adult education, however, sought to reconcile conflicts among racial, religious, and economic groups; to redress inequities; and to advance the cause of marginalized citizens.

Social Conflict

In the interwar period, the American faith in the power of education to resolve social problems found expression in several initiatives. The Inquiry, an ambitious organization designed to eliminate social conflict through social education, was created by some members of the National Conference on the Christian Way who believed that education was a better way to resolve conflict than was the application of Christian principles. Founded and led by Bruno Lasker and financed by philanthropy, the Inquiry (1923–1933) conducted research and created experimental programs in social conflict resolution. Participants in Inquiry projects shared a common interest in making conflict manageable. Graebner (1987, p. 53) describes their assumptions and methods: "If prejudice was socially conditioned, it could be socially eliminated. The tools were those of democratic social engineering: groups, discussions, conferences, panels, inquiry, participation, leadership." The Inquiry brought together leaders in the group process movement who were committed to democratic social engineering, and they applied tools of democratic social engineering to conflicts of class, business, race relations, religion, international affairs, and communities. The Inquiry produced literature, manuals, and methods to be used in small group programs; existing institutions were encouraged to create these programs through clubs and conferences. Many were Protestant religious organizations; others were settlement houses, women's clubs, child study groups, and social work organizations. Inquiry leaders sought tangible results in their programs and debated whether their efforts were education or propaganda and whether the leader should simply help the group or should also provide specific guidance.

The Inquiry fell beyond the definition of adult education offered by the AAAE, but for Eduard C. Lindeman, a consultant to The Inquiry and later author of the classic *The Meaning of Adult Education* (1926), this project exemplified his view of adult education as social education. Social education, Lindeman (1933) wrote in his evaluation of the project, produces "socialized individuals" who can "function constructively in collective fashion" (p. 172). Education that rejects social methods becomes irrelevant in a society where collectives dominate. Though the Inquiry folded after a decade, its pioneering conference method demonstrated how education becomes socially important when it goes beyond the acquisition of knowledge to the application of knowledge to problem solving in real-life situations.

An equally ambitious but more narrowly focused project, organized and directed by southern white women, was the Association of Southern Women for the Prevention of Lynching (ASWPL) (Hall, 1974). The belief that only through the leadership of white women could lynching be prevented grew out of meetings between the educated, middle-class women of both races in the Woman's Committee of the Commission on Interracial Cooperation. The commission responded in 1930 by creating the ASWPL as an independent agency with Jessie Daniel Ames of Texas as director. Ames brought experience with the woman's suffrage movement, the League of Women Voters, and the Woman's Committee. She organized state and local branches of the ASWPL to work with women's organizations in Protestant churches (particularly Methodist), YWCAs, and elsewhere. The ASWPL attracted forty-three thousand local women supporters who were distinguished by "a hunger for knowledge of an outside world to which they were increasingly linked and participation in a network of missionary societies that exposed them to changing social ideas couched in the language of evangelical reform" (Hall, 1974, p. 191).

Ames and the ASWPL attacked the problem of lynching through education. As the first task, they challenged white racism, the southern preoccupation with rape, and the code of chivalry imposed upon southern white women. Lynching, they taught, had more to do with maintaining the caste system than with interracial sexual relations. As a second educational strategy, they collected precise information about lynching through investigative reporting and through antilynching protests. A third strategy brought the message of law and order to the South through speakers, literature, and theater, making the campaign "a political education in a patriarchal world" (Hall, 1974, p. 221).

Both the Inquiry and the ASWPL represent intensive, short-term, educational interventions in social and racial conflict. Neither of the organizations survived in the institutional structure of adult education. An independent organization, created in 1920 to help women participate as citizens, fared better.

Women as Citizens

Women won their hard-fought battle for suffrage with the ratification of the Nineteenth Amendment to the Constitution. To equip women to participate as citizens, the National American Woman's Suffrage Association organized the League of Women Voters as an independent organization in 1920 (Black, 1989). Participation in the suffrage movement had been an educational and empowering experience, as women learned about democracy, how to manage their associations, and how to work with men, and they applied these skills to the newly organized league (Black, 1989). The league's education of its members began immediately in a two-week school for political education conducted by the University of Chicago and throughout the year in similar three- to seven-day schools. A nine-month correspondence course published in *The Woman Citizen* informed women about the realities of government and politics.

The league began by incorporating Carrie Catt's interests in civic education, women's legal rights, and social feminist legislation. Catt was a suffrage leader who, during her second presidency (1916–1920) of the National American Woman's Suffrage Association, led the campaign that resulted in passage of the woman's suffrage amendment. As a woman's organization, the league gave women a voice for their own particular interests, but at the same time it equipped them to work with men as equals. In the next two decades, the league and its political and educational agenda developed slowly. The league had adopted a nonpartisan policy in order to have something to offer every public official, but it trained women for participation in public life and encouraged members to engage in partisan politics and run for public office. Members' interests determined the programs at the national conventions and state leagues, and until the early 1930s, the annual convention—in which the programs and goals for the next year were decided—served as a vehicle of civic training for women. Study came before action. Brumbaugh (1946) characterized the league's philosophy as a blending of democratic values and the method of science: gather data about a problem, draw conclusions, and test them.

This early emphasis on the civic education of new women voters soon expanded to encompass the need of the whole electorate for continuous study of political problems, as the league began to think of "its own membership as a nucleus of effort to guide disinterested political thought and activism" (Brumbaugh, 1946, p. 52). But in 1934, the league took a decided shift of direction, turning from civic education to action, becoming a pressure group to lobby for good government. The national board curtailed local league participation and assumed authority to establish the League's projects and to decide which measures should be objects for legislative action.

African Americans

African Americans entered the 1920s with an established educational ecology comprising institutions that they had organized and directed as well as white agencies, such as the YMCA and YWCA, that offered educational opportunities for African Americans. In 1935, the educational work of African-American women was further strengthened by the establishment of the National Council of Negro Women, with Mary McLeod Bethune as the first president. The council coordinated twenty national and ninety-five local organizations with a membership of 850,000 African-American women (Ware, 1982).

Within the African-American community, differing views about the relation of black people to the white culture resulted in sharply divergent philosophies and programs of adult education. As an advocate of ethnic identity and pride, Marcus Garvey challenged the integrationist and moral persuasion approach chosen by the NAACP and the National Urban League. In 1918, Garvey organized the Universal Negro Improvement Association (UNIA) as a fraternal organization and the African Communities League as a stock company owned by the association to operate business enterprises promoting racial consciousness and pride through economic success. Garvey fostered adult education through the UNIA, an organization Colin (1988) describes as the "largest African-American liberation and adult education movement in the history of this country" and "the most influential" (pp. 154–155). The UNIA fostered racial identity and pride and through its programs attempted to overcome the effects of colonization and develop ethnic independence, identity, and pride. White adult educators sought to eradicate racial references, but Garvey wanted to educate African Americans about their race and develop ethnic consciousness.

The UNIA developed ethnic consciousness and trained its

leaders at several levels and through various formats (Colin, 1988). At the grass-roots level, local branches were organized and by 1926 the 814 branches in the United States and the 215 international branches had an estimated membership of about 600,000 (Colin, 1988, p. 156). Each local branch shaped its own rituals and practices for the mandated weekly meetings, which usually began with prayers and songs followed by inspirational talks and musical entertainment. At the national level, the UNIA–African Communities League Civil Services Board, the Booker T. Washington University in New York City, the Correspondence Course for African Philosophy, and the School of African Philosophy were established to train UNIA leaders. UNIA males between eighteen and fifty-five found occupational and leadership opportunities in the Universal African Legions, and Liberty Hall in New York City served as a lyceum for its members, offering weekly meetings and lectures. At the international level, the Second and Third International Conventions of the Negro People of the World brought participants into the larger Pan-Africanism movement.

Another group of African-American intellectuals, community leaders, and educators who did not espouse Garvey's separatist policies established an alliance with the white establishment leaders of the adult education movement to define an adult education philosophy and program for blacks. Alain Locke, professor of philosophy at Howard University, reportedly was the first African-American intellectual to recognize the potential of the adult education movement for the economic and cultural advancement of African Americans (Holmes, 1965). Locke's editorship of a 1925 issue of *Survey Graphic*, later expanded into a book called *The New Negro*, brought to national attention a distinctive African-American culture as demonstrated in the Harlem Renaissance. Locke's long-term association with the Carnegie Corporation and the American Association for Adult Education began when he was a delegate to the first Carnegie Corporation–sponsored conference on adult education in 1924, continued when he was an adviser to Keppel and the AAAE, and concluded when he became the first African-American president of the AAAE in 1945–46 (Lagemann, 1989).

In several ways, the Carnegie Corporation and the AAAE sought to strengthen adult education within the African-American community. The AAAE funded an experimental adult education program offered by libraries in Atlanta and Harlem, sponsored four conferences on "Adult Education and the Negro" at leading African-American colleges, and supported the Associates in Negro Folk Education. Between 1936 and 1941, the Associates, with Locke as editor, published the *Bronze Booklets,* a series on Negro history and cultural contributions, intended as reading courses. The Associates also commissioned W.E.B. DuBois to address "The Negro and Social Reconstruction," but the Carnegie Corporation and the Associates' publication committee found the DuBois manuscript unacceptable. Locke's correspondence with DuBois offers no specific reasons for rejecting the manuscript, but scholars suggest that it may have been because of DuBois's prosegregationist views and his criticisms of the New Deal (Marable, 1982).

By several actions, the Carnegie Corporation and the AAAE reinforced the segregated and inferior status of African Americans in American society. They required that whites have administrative control of the library project, and they imposed a liberal education model on adult education programs under their sponsorship. African-American intellectuals such as Ira De A. Reid (1936) and Alain Locke (1989), while acknowledging that the different races and classes of society needed liberal education, argued for special programs to address the unique problems of African Americans as an economically and culturally disadvantaged group. In particular, they believed that black people could experience social transformation through education only if they derived inspiration and pride from knowledge of their distinctive cultural heritage.

Parent Education

African Americans, however, were not the only group to be singled out as an object of attention from a philanthropic foundation. In the 1920s, the parent education movement became a testing ground for the belief in the "popularization of scientific knowledge as the key to social betterment" (Schlossman, 1983, p. 16). This belief guided the thought and work of Lawrence K. Frank, an officer at the Laura Spelman Rockefeller Memorial Foundation (LSRM), who led the parent education movement of the 1920s. As the key to social progress, the application of science had to begin with young children, but developing healthy and intelligent children meant teaching their parents. This could be done, for Frank believed that parenthood could become a "totally learned behavior" (Schlossman, 1983, p. 25).

Frank and the LSRM sought to gain support for child development and parent education through grants to certain universities to conduct scientific research and to train practitioners. To enhance the prestige of child development research, Frank wanted women's colleges and their graduates to expand the definition of liberal education to include child development. Efforts also were made to persuade the American Association of University Women (AAUW) to take leadership in a national parent education movement and to include the study of scientific literature on child development in the educational programs of the local chapters. A national movement for parent education required local organizations at the grass-roots level.

Frank found in the Child Study Association of America a model of parent education, for the association was committed to scientific research and publishing and held lectures and regular meetings. In 1925, the association, sponsored by an LSRM grant, organized two formal meetings that put "parent education on the nation's intellectual map" (Schlossman, 1983, p. 17). A meeting restricted to parent education scholars and practitioners created an identity for this new field of practice. A public conference that attracted several thousands publicized parent education and resulted in an important publication, *Concerning Parents*. The movement gained further impetus in the mid 1920s with the formation of the National Council of Parent Education and the founding of a mass parent education magazine, *Parents' Magazine*. Between 1923 and 1929, the LSRM spent over seven million dollars to promote "standardized, expert-controlled child raising" (Ehrenreich and English, 1978, p. 207) and helped stimulate the work of seventy-five major parent education organizations. By the end of the 1920s, "the movement had become one of the most widely discussed and visible new forces on the educational scene" (Schlossman, 1983, p. 18).

The Depression's Challenge to Capitalism

The Depression undermined the population's belief in capitalism, raising issues that elicited educational and community organizing strategies. One such response was the establishment in 1934 of the School of Social Studies in San Francisco. Founder Alexander Meiklejohn, his wife Helen, and John Walker Powell regarded the school as a national experiment in adult education to see how the control of the city's cultural life, traditionally dominated by a few families, could be broadened and how class divisions could be addressed (Powell, 1942; Stubblefield, 1988). Opening in the aftermath of a bitter and divisive strike by the longshoremen and overtly addressing the abuses of capitalism, the school tried to help citizens understand the social and economic situation and plan intelligent responses to the changes in the economic system that the founders believed would soon occur. To accomplish its goals, the school adapted the book discussion group format to engage the participants in a study of the author as thinker, mind-at-work solving a social problem. Thus participants developed the critical thinking skills they needed to perform the duties of citizens but also struggled toward mental maturity. The school drew upon every field of knowledge dealing with society's concerns in order to help students translate knowledge into intelligence. The pedagogy derived from a basic theorem that adult education deals with adults as thinking agents who are able to implement their own purposes and who are concerned with the meaning of their actions (Stubblefield, 1988, p. 106).

For all its social concern, the learning activities of the School of Social Studies remained in the classroom and focused on individual change. The Communist Party of the United States of America, however, engaged in direct grass-roots political education through community organizing (Fisher, 1984); after the Wall Street crash, a vital party-led community movement quickly arose, organizing the unemployed to march in cities to demand relief. Although the Communist Party subordinated the councils to the purposes of the larger national organization, the local councils did address local needs. The party's efforts to organize the black community for racial cooperation and equality brought whites and blacks into one organization working for similar goals—under black leadership, a unique occurrence in 1930s America. The Women's Commission addressed the Communist party agenda for women through the *Working Woman* and a woman's column in the *Daily Worker*. At the local level, the party addressed issues of everyday concern to women, such as free milk for children, and protested eviction for nonpayment of rent. About the party's community organizing efforts, Fisher (1984) concludes: "Community organizing as practiced by the CPUSA was successful because it emphasized organizational discipline, defined local issues in a national and international context, linked community struggles with those in the workplace, developed alliances between black and white workers, and offered a thorough political analysis of the problems community people faced" (p. 44).

The Catholic Worker Movement, founded in late 1932 by Peter Maurin and Dorothy Day, offered a cultural critique of American capitalism and sought to establish a Christian social order based on traditional Catholicism. Members volunteered in acts of mercy through houses of hospitality that served the urban poor. By 1985, there were over ninety Catholic Worker houses of hospitality and farms across the country; many had found unique ministries in prisons and among refugees. The Catholic Workers permitted members to express their own opinions even if they differed from the Catholic church's position, and it also permitted leadership by women of whom Dorothy Day, its cofounder and leader, was the best-known but not the only example.

The Catholic Workers placed education at the heart of their critique. Hospitality houses became "learning centers where theory was tested in praxis" (O'Gorman and Coy, 1988, p. 243). These peace advocates found practical expression for their ideals in the houses where residents learned and practiced nonviolence to guests. Roundtable discussions in the houses brought together all elements of the community; scholars, the middle class, and workers shared equally in working out the program for social reconstruction. The *Catholic Worker*, distinguished from other religious newspapers by the infusion of traditional Catholicism into issues of social justice, disseminated the Catholic Workers' message to the public. In its pages, Dorothy Day practiced advocacy journalism. By refusing paid advertising, she remained uncompromised, emphasizing pacificism and calling for radical social reconstruction based on the New Testament gospels, of which the residents' houses were a prime example.

Saul Alinsky promoted a nonideological community-organizing process in 1939 with the establishment of the Back of the Yards Neighborhood Council of Chicago (Fisher, 1984). Through the council, Alinsky brought priests together with CIO union organizers, merchants, and neighborhood residents to work on community problems with a "conflict" approach: mobilizing power against the established interests of factory owners and others to gain concessions for working people. What Alinsky called "popular education" occupied a place of central importance in community organizing (Alinsky, 1969). Education begins when representatives from different segments of the community are brought into a people's organization and through their relationship develop understanding of one another as individuals, and the educational process continues as they define social issues and learn that their personal problems are often common problems. Education thrives when "the community climate [is] receptive to learning and education" (Fisher, 1984, p. 159); this requires identifying a problem or need and then helping the community analyze it and find a solution.

Workers' Education for Collective Action

Workers' education expanded after World War I as "the vanguard of a new movement dedicated to the creation of an economically and socially just society" (Wong, 1984, p. 39). Not all participants in the workers' education movement espoused revolutionary change: some wanted to address the inequities and injustice imposed on women and blacks, counter the domination of factory owners, or provide educational opportunities to the disadvantaged. But workers' education evolved as a distinct form of adult education concerned with collective action and with encouraging students to serve the labor movement and society. With its emphasis on working-class interests and collective action for workers, workers' education differed from the conception of adult education that evolved in this period under the aegis of the AAAE—focused on serving individuals in their efforts at self-improvement and culture. Several initiatives conducted independently or cooperatively comprised the workers' education movement in the 1920s and 1930s.

Workers' Education Bureau

When the AFL declined to take national responsibility for workers' education, others organized the Workers' Education Bureau (WEB) in 1921 (Altenbaugh, 1990). Modeled after the Workers' Education Association of England, the WEB served as a clearinghouse for workers' education. It gained support from outside the labor movement, particularly for its publication program, which insisted that workers need to be citizens. Between 1926 and 1940, the Carnegie Corporation gave the WEB a total of $140,250. Several intellectuals active in the adult education movement served on the publication committee, including Charles A. Beard, Eduard C. Lindeman, James Harvey Robinson, and Everett Dean Martin. The Workers' Bookshelf popularized art, literature, natural science, and social science in a series of short books to help workers understand problems of industrial society and to satisfy their cultural hunger. When the AFL leadership recognized the potential of worker's education for strengthening the labor movement—and the threat it posed as a progressive opposition to the AFL—the AFL gained control of the WEB board and limited its work to education and research. Restricted from dealing with trade union policy issues, the WEB lost its voice for social reform. It served as the educational arm of the AFL until 1954, when it was reorganized as the AFL Department of Education.

Women Workers' Education

Women, who were now entering the industrial work force in greater numbers, created their own organizations for education. By far the most important and far reaching of these, and the one most influential on women's workers' education, was the YMCA's Industrial Department. Its workers' education programs reached more working women than the educational efforts of any other contemporary organization (Frederickson, 1984). Established in 1904, the department expanded during the war as it focused attention on the working conditions of women and greatly extended its work in the South among black women. It also promoted social reform preceded by education to analyze social and industrial issues. Lucy Carner, who succeeded Florence Simms in 1923 as the department secretary, attached great educational importance to the learning that occurred as women managed local clubs, departments, and regional and national organizations. Between 1920 and 1940, fifteen thousand working women had attended the department-sponsored annual summer conferences on social and industrial issues.

Summer schools for women workers became important agencies for education, and of these schools, the Bryn Mawr Summer School (1921-1938) became the model for others established in the interwar period (Heller, 1984). With Hilda Smith as director, the summer school served women from eighteen to thirty-two who had an elementary education and two years of industrial experience; African Americans were admitted in 1926. The program offered liberal studies derived from John Dewey and theories of progressive education. A radicalized curriculum and student activism made the school unwelcome at Bryn Mawr, and in 1940, it relocated as the Hudson Shore Labor School. Participants in Heller's forty- to sixty-year follow-up study (1984) reported that their eight-week experience had promoted their personal development, increased their knowledge, and brought them into contact with other races, classes, and ideologies. Several became active in union affairs and a few became national union leaders.

In 1928, the summer schools organized the Affiliated Schools for Women Workers, with Hilda Smith as director, to serve as coordinator and clearinghouse (Roydhouse, 1984). Eleanor Coit replaced Hilda Smith as director in 1932. Reorganized as the American Labor Education Services (ALES) in 1939, it served a coordinating function for workers' education for men and women. The ALES upheld freedom of discussion in its programs, avoiding taking sides with either the AFL or the CIO. The Fund for Adult Education allowed the ALES to continue its work until Coit's retirement in 1962, when it disbanded. Roydhouse (1984) writes, "ALES historian Doris Brody believes that the tension between the commitment to freedom of discussion and the increasing political conservatism of organized labor created conflict and eroded the ability of the ALES to foster workers' education" (p. 202).

Labor Colleges

Labor colleges developed as independent educational agencies, an alternative to the trade union colleges sponsored by local trade unions and workers' education sponsored by universities. Their development was a reaction to the AFL's refusal to support alternative education sympathetic to the working class, its rules against democratic participation in the labor movement, and its exclusion of women, blacks, and unskilled and industrial workers (Altenbaugh, 1980, 1990). Leaders in the labor colleges, seeking to create a cooperative society with few social distinctions, educated the working-class leaders to work for a new social order. Organized by liberal intellectuals and union activists, the labor-college leaders modeled their program on universities that offered demanding intellectual study, but they grounded their college's ideology in the labor movement and used a progressive pedagogy. The best-known of these colleges, the Brookwood Labor College near Katonah, New York, opened in 1921 with great expectations but closed in 1937 amidst charges of radicalism, its economic support dwindling. Other well-known labor colleges experienced the same problems and had short lives: the Work People's College (1903–1941) in Duluth, Minnesota, and Commonwealth College (1923–1940) in Mena, Arkansas.

The Highlander Folk School, which Myles Horton founded in 1932 at Monteagle, Tennessee, played an important role in educating union leaders and members in the southern labor movement in the 1930s and 1940s. Highlander, however, was not a labor college; Horton had modeled it partially after the Grundtvigian folk school in Denmark, a residential school that sought to awaken in young adults a sense of their unique abilities and responsibilities to the larger community (Glen, 1988; Horton, 1989). Highlander served the southern Appalachian people in their struggle for social and economic justice through education; it later gained its greatest visibility in the civil rights movement of the 1950s and 1960s.

Adult Religious Education

Knowles's historical study in 1977 evaluates the growth of adult education by the extent to which adult education had become a differentiated activity in institutions. Using this criterion, he claims that churches in the 1920s and 1930s lagged behind other institutions. His perspective, while understandable, obscures how religious institutions actually educated adults and how adult religious education took shape within the context of a larger educational plan to transform the social order. The prewar educational configurations established by Protestants, Catholics, and Jews changed in the face of new social conditions. In the 1920s, Protestant hegemony lessened as evidenced in the failure of Prohibition, the weakening of sabbath observance, and the new attitudes toward recreation and leisure. Churches could no longer direct public opinion and were less able to discipline their own members (Ahlstrom, 1972). Both the Catholic and Jewish communities had experienced tremendous growth through immigration, but the end of massive immigration of ethnic groups in the 1920s permitted the religious groups to redirect the energies expended on meeting immigrant needs toward meeting the educational needs of those establishing a permanent place in American society.

In the 1920s, Protestant conservatives began to push an anti-science agenda, focusing on evolution, which was contradictory to their interpretation of the Bible. They fought to keep the teaching of evolution out of the public schools and churches. Issues of scholarship, science, and the role of the church in society found expression in adult religious education. In the interwar period, the Protestant Sunday school became less a movement than a church program, but from the 1920s to the 1950s, it remained the church's major adult education activity, the International Uniform lesson series its primary curriculum (Stokes, 1977). The Sunday school had by then developed as a lay-led institution with its own curriculum, organizational structure, and liturgy and with conversion as its central purpose (Lynn and Wright, 1980). In 1945, the National Association of Evangelicals organized the National Sunday School Association to give leadership to this educational ministry.

Liberals envisioned a broader church role in adult education, so the International Council of Religious Education organized the United Christian Adult Movement in 1936 to unify Protestant efforts (Knowles, 1977). The Learning for Life program initiated weekday and weeknight programs, with courses organized around such areas of adult experience as the Bible, family life, church outreach, community issues, and social problems. This new adult education emphasis made use of study groups, the Sunday evening forum, men's and women's clubs, radio discussion groups, and arts and crafts programs (Johnson, 1936).

Interdenominational and parachurch organizations shaped the thinking of laity and clergy about social problems and the role of churches. In 1908, Protestant social concerns found expression in the Federal Council of Churches, but other interdenominational organizations also addressed a broad range of problems that engaged both clergy and laity in study and action (Ahlstrom, 1972). In 1918, the Interchurch World Movement organized as a cooperative evangelical effort for education to assist churches in planning, training personnel, and fund-raising for the postwar Protestant mission, but the movement's vision exceeded its resources and it disbanded in the early 1920s. In the Depression, interdenominational groups formed to revive the social gospel emphasis. After 1928, the Fellowship of Reconciliation focused on social and economic matters, calling attention to class struggles and denouncing the treatment of African Americans, and in 1936, the United Council for Christian Democracy organized to coordinate denominational and church efforts in social justice. Conservative denominations such as Methodists and Baptists formed organizations to protect the status quo and individualism. Frank Buchman mounted another conservative effort to change individuals by organizing Moral Re-Armament.

Catholics used many forms to educate adults, but they did not make adult education a differentiated activity as did Protestants with their Sunday School movement and general adult education programs (Dolan, 1985; Elias, 1982). Through the efforts of Bishop Edwin O'Hara, in 1935, American bishops approved a United States office of the Confraternity of Christian Doctrine to give leadership to the religious education of youth and adults, offering adult study clubs, correspondence courses, and training for lay catechists. The

National Catholic Welfare Conference, organized in 1919, promoted the "broad religious, educational, and social interests of Catholics" and established lay organizations such as the National Conference of Catholic Men and the National Conference of Catholic Women (Elias, 1982, p. 140). The conference's Social Action Department used conferences, summer institutes, and labor schools to educate priests and the laity about the social principles of Catholicism, particularly as they related to industrial problems. In the 1930s and 1940s, the Catholic Action movement engaged lay members, especially the more college-educated and professional, in activities organized around special interests rather than on programs centered on the parish. Concern about family life led to new organizations. In 1943, a married couples' retreat program, the Cana Conference, focused on developing personal responsibility and attitudes; this approach proved so successful that by 1950, 75 percent of the dioceses sponsored them.

In the American Jewish community, the synagogue, community centers, and national Jewish organizations provided the major sponsorship of adult education. Broadly speaking, adult education sought to create a Jewish identity and loyalty and promote liberal learning. These purposes found different expressions in the three branches of Judaism. The Orthodox emphasized Jewish traditions and the Reform, Jewish culture and history; the Conservative balanced both emphases (Elias, 1982). A new institutional form emerged in the 1920s—the synagogue-center. Its philosophy recognized no separation of religious and secular knowledge and sought to bring all human faculties under the purview of the synagogue by sponsoring social, recreational, and educational activities. Many Jews were attracted to these activities (Raphael, 1984). The Congregational Institute of Jewish Studies developed a program of adult studies conducted in synagogues or community centers that featured weekly meetings with small-group study on a specific topic followed by a lecture series. Prominent among the large national organizations that used adult education as part of their program were B'nai B'rith, the National Council of Jewish Women, the American Jewish Committee, and the American Jewish Congress. Institutes of Judaism, a program organized by B'nai B'rith, featured retreats for adults to study with Jewish scholars.

Summary

An ambitious program of social education and action research, the Inquiry, attempted to solve religious, racial, economic, and international conflicts, and an educational campaign by the Association of Southern Women for the Prevention of Lynching sought to end the lynching of African Americans. Women suffragists organized the League of Women Voters to prepare women for their newly secured right to participate in the political process. Some African Americans addressed educational needs through ethnic identity and pride as taught by Marcus Garvey, while others worked with the white establishment to create a philosophy and program appropriate for African Americans as a disenfranchised and disadvantaged minority. Popularization of scientific knowledge about child development became the basis for a national parent education movement.

The Depression evoked several educational approaches: the study of social problems, political education in the context of community organizing, and the formation of a new Catholic lay organization. Workers' education received support and coordination from the Workers' Education Bureau; women created programs for women workers through the YWCA and summer schools; and social reformers created labor colleges to support the ideology of the labor movement. The interwar period brought new conditions for the major religious groups; Protestant hegemony weakened and the Catholic and Jewish communities confronted the end of immigration. Religious groups responded with new activities in the church, parish, and synagogue, new formats of learning for special groups and specific subject matter, and by the expansion of national organizations.

15

Educational Responses
to National Emergencies

Gradually, the federal government was drawn into adult education. Shortly before World War I, responding partly to pressure from interest groups, the government created ongoing programs for adults in agricultural, vocational, and home economics education. During the war, the government supported "Americanization" programs to make immigrants more fully committed to the American way of life. Before a decade of prosperity had passed, an economic depression produced massive unemployment, and the federal government created large-scale adult education programs as part of an overall jobs program. Even while the New Deal continued, America's entry into World War II demanded new adult education programs for the military and civilian workforce in support of the war effort.

The New Deal

Of the many domains of American life into which the New Deal entered, it was welcomed by education, particularly adult education, as an energizing force. Praised by some and criticized by others, the New Deal intervention into adult education engaged segments of the adult population in systematic study for the first time. It also generated debates about the control of adult education and its social purposes.

Outside the System

The New Deal program in education began in April 1933 when Congress appropriated $500,000,000 for distribution to the states for welfare, with the other half for use by a new agency, the Federal Emergency Relief Administration (Kornbluh, 1987; Maskin, 1973; Tyack, Lowe, and Hansot, 1984). Harry Hopkins, its administrator, created the Emergency Education Division. The emergency educational programs Hopkins envisioned excluded federal support for local public education programs. Hence the federal programs addressed the two areas of education neglected by the public schools: nursery school education and adult education. Many New Deal reformers wanted to redistribute wealth and opportunity and achieve social justice, but they questioned the ability of the educational establishment to respond to the present social crisis. Indeed, the alternative plans submitted by the National Education Association did not guarantee that funding would reach the poor (Tyack, Lowe, and Hansot, 1984).

An Enlarged Adult Education Program

The educational philosophy and programming initiatives of the New Deal were derivative and eclectic, drawn from previous attempts to address societal dislocations. Social engineering as an educational practice had long been established. Hopkins wanted to reduce the threats to democracy posed by the poor and foreign-born and native-born illiterates whom he believed were open to radical influences from abroad and were easy prey to propaganda. The reduced work week and employment allowed leisure time that needed to be converted from idle to constructive time. But Hopkins also believed in education for individual enlightenment for adults to examine social, political, and economic issues, which in turn would lead to greater participation in government and community life. To preserve democracy, citizens needed, in Kornbluh's words (1987, p. 29), "language literacy" and "social literacy." Lewis R.

Alderman, an adult education specialist whom Hopkins appointed as director of the Emergency Education Program in the U.S. Office of Education, shared Hopkins's views (Maskin, 1973).

This New Deal program for adults provided a variety of opportunities for segments of society that did not generally participate in systematic learning experiences. "General adult education" had the largest enrollment; by 1937, 200,000 people were enrolled in twenty thousand general education classes to study the social sciences and humanities, public affairs, parliamentary procedure, and real estate. About 25 percent of the program's students were in literacy education classes, which Hopkins had authorized as the first emergency program. Through innovative classes, illiterates learned to read newspapers and write letters, and teachers addressed life needs and prepared pamphlets in nutrition, child care, and basic health. Estimates are that approximately 1,300,000 persons learned to read and write in New Deal classes. African-American leaders made sure that African Americans were included in the program. The job of promoting federal government activities was assigned to Ambrose Caliver, a Ph.D. graduate from Teachers College, Columbia University, who had been appointed by President Hoover in 1930 to be the U.S. Office of Education specialist in Negro education (Maskin, 1973).

The smallest segment of the program, workers' education, also proved to be the most controversial and was viewed with suspicion by New Deal administrators and organized labor. In 1933, Hilda Smith, director of the Bryn Mawr Summer School for Women Workers, was appointed educational specialist in charge of workers' education. At its peak in December 1936, the workers' education program enrolled sixty-five thousand in three thousand classes with a thousand instructors in thirty-three states (Kornbluh, 1987). Smith's programs, which treated concerns of wage earners as a class, met with opposition from relief administrators and public school administrators. They believed a special workers' education program would lead to agitation and class consciousness, as did the AFL, which only wanted to prepare union leaders. In 1939, the opposition won, and the project became the Workers' Service Program, a community service project, which removed it from the WPA program administrative supervision.

One of Smith's most important contributions to the educational relief programs was her leadership in establishing and administering teacher training programs for practitioners in workers' education and other Emergency Education Program activities. Kornbluh (1987, p. 60) calls them "the first federally funded teacher-training program in this country." Teacher training began in 1934 with the establishment of sixteen centers on college campuses, which implemented Smith's philosophy of using education to help people solve social and economic problems. The centers operated as laboratories where trainees worked democratically and in groups to develop their own philosophy of education, learned methods for teaching adults, and learned to understand the life experience of workers.

A new initiative for the federal government, far reaching in its scope, was the public forum program initiated and administered by John Studebaker when he became U.S. Commissioner of Education in 1934 (Graebner, 1987; Studebaker, 1935). While superintendent of the Des Moines, Iowa, public schools in 1933, Studebaker had initiated a public forum program with a grant from the Carnegie Corporation through the AAAE. Before leaving Des Moines, Studebaker wrote *The American Way,* a philosophy of the public forum that guided his New Deal efforts. Under the sponsorship of the New Deal, the idea of the public forum was widely adopted; by 1937, 1,500 projects had been initiated or associated with this demonstration project. Studebaker sincerely believed that radical and alien ideas would be thoroughly discredited in a public exchange of opinion. The forum arrangement, however, did not permit the free and open exchange of ideas, for Studebaker did not believe that the average citizen could understand the complexities of modern life. Thus, forum leaders not only selected the topics and speakers but also manipulated the discussion sessions to discredit ideas that challenged the American system (Graebner, 1987).

Youth and Young Adults

Authorized in March 1933, the Civilian Conservation Corps (CCC) enrolled unmarried youth between the ages of eighteen and twenty-five. Few had held jobs. Enrollees had on the average completed eighth or ninth grade in school, and many had dropped out of school. Their families were on relief, and many came from broken homes (Salmond, 1967; Tyack, Lowe, and Hansot, 1984). A civilian, Robert Fechner, was appointed administrator of the program; the army, assisted by the Forest Service and the National Park Service, controlled its operations. By the end of the year, plans for an educational program had been made, and Clarence S. Marsh, director of the evening session at the University of Buffalo, was appointed director although the program remained subordinate to the army and to Fechner. Fechner refused to let Marsh enlarge the program to focus on social education and fearing any hint of radical ideas banned one of the books in a series that the Office of Education had commissioned in order to teach corpsmen about the Depression and unemployment. Productive adults, Fechner and the army leaders believed, were shaped through the disciplines of hard work, obedience, and cleanliness (Tyack, Lowe, and Hansot, 1984). In spite of these limitations, the educational program did help many become literate, gain a high school diploma, and continue on to college; it gave them civilian job skills and provided a second chance for education (Salmond, 1967).

The CCC admitted only men. Though Hilda Smith urged the administration to create similar camps for unemployed women, it was Eleanor Roosevelt who secured the creation of "she-she-she" camps (so called because they resembled the CCC camps for men). Smith, basing the residential program on her workers' education model, described the program as "a social laboratory in which it is hoped that the girls will acquire the skills, poise, a knowledge of resources and experience in self-government and democratic procedures" (Kornbluh, 1984, p. 269). Operated by the state relief agencies, the camps served between eight thousand and ten thousand women from 1934 to 1937 in over one-hundred centers, with programs lasting from six to eight weeks (Kornbluh, 1984). The program did not have the full support of New Deal administrators, and the reduced relief funds in 1937 provided a reason to disband the "she-she-she" camps.

President Roosevelt created by executive order the National Youth Administration (NYA) within the WPA to serve sixteen- to twenty-four-year-olds (Tyack, Lowe, and Hansot, 1984). The director, Aubrey Williams, a social worker and minister, brought an understanding of relief and education that was different from the Fechner-army CCC approach. Williams wanted to help those at the bottom, and through the state directors, he kept the operation of the NYA close to the local communities. He enrolled black students and hired black staff; the prominent black woman leader Mary McLeod Bethune headed the Division of Negro Affairs in the NYA central office. Community projects, resident centers, and vocational training were developed for out-of-school youth, enrolling 2,677,000, of whom 45 percent were female. In these training centers, young people earned minimum wages, produced goods, and learned skills transferable to the private sector.

The TVA

Created in 1933, the Tennessee Valley Authority (TVA) expanded an electrification project into "a social enterprise aimed at a total regional resource development" (Robbins, 1972, p. 79). TVA leaders recognized the value of education in reshaping the Tennessee Valley because people needed to learn how to change their environment. Formal educational programs for employee training were developed in TVA field offices. The most important of these programs operated in TVA's training section within the Personnel Department, but other divisions also operated programs. Each of the planning divisions initiated educational efforts, including community development, demonstration farms, and library programs. Robbins (1972) judges the TVA to be successful as a social enterprise because it recognized that workers and families needed skills and knowledge to be more self-sufficient, it minimized the consequences of dislocation by bringing community residents together to discuss plans, and it helped community residents understand that the changes made by machines were part of a larger plan for community and regional improvement. As admirable as their activities were, the TVA was not entirely successful in reaching either blacks or whites at the lower end of the socioeconomic scale (Robbins, 1972). Though its public policy was nondiscrimination, the TVA nonetheless held the color line for African Americans, operating within prevailing patterns of segregation.

The Democratization of Culture

The creation of the Works Progress Administration in 1935, as well as increased relief appropriations, provided support for four new federal cultural projects known as Federal One: the Federal Art Project, the Federal Music Project, the Federal Writers' Project, and the Federal Theatre Project. Harry Hopkins wanted to use cultural projects for social reform—to make people aware of their lives and "to bring together artist and people and to use the uplifting power of art to enrich the lives of ordinary citizens" (Matthews, 1975, p. 319). The Writers' Project produced more than a thousand publications that depicted the American scene. The life history project recorded the lives of ordinary people of various ethnic groups and included slave narratives. The 378 books and pamphlets produced as a tour guide to states, cities, and places of interest were "a road map for the cultural rediscovery of America" (Matthews, 1975, p. 335). The Fine Arts Project under the direction of Holger Cahill provided a staff of qualified artists for 103 community art centers in small towns and through these fostered art appreciation and engaged participants in creating art projects.

Federal Theatre Project director Hallie Flanagan sought to create a national public theater and between 1935 and 1939 produced over twelve hundred varied stage shows. Flanagan made the Federal Theatre an instrument of reform, confronting problems of American life and standing "against reaction, against prejudice, against racial, religious, and political intolerance" (Flanagan, 1985, p. 367). The Living Newspaper provided the clearest example of theater as education in using a documentary style to show the lives of ordinary people, in presenting evidence of social problems in dramatic form, and in dealing creatively with controversial issues. *Spirochete* told the story of syphilis, and it proved to be one of several public events that brought the disease to public consciousness, resulting in the Wassermann test to detect syphilis in couples applying for a marriage license (Gysel, 1989). Charges that communists had infiltrated the Federal Theatre created a political issue, giving the theater a role in the politics of culture. In 1939, Congress abolished the Federal Theatre Project after an investigation by the House Committee to Investigate Un-American Activities under Chairman Martin Dies.

Opponents of the New Deal found in the Federal Theatre a highly visible target to express their reaction to the New Deal "spending policy, the liberal attitude toward labor, aliens, and members of minority parties" (Flanagan, [1940] 1985, p. 347).

African Americans and Native Americans

For African-American adults, the New Deal was a mixed blessing. Programs in the arts and theater for African Americans were neither numerous nor well-funded. National Youth Administration programs for African Americans "reinforced traditional socioeconomic patterns" (Smith, 1988, p. 240) by training young men for jobs available in local communities and young women for domestic work. African Americans were appointed as state and local directors, and African Americans comprised 13 percent of the out-of-school program participants and 10 percent of those in the student work programs. Patterns of segregation were maintained in WPA classes and the CCC camps. However, the Farm Security Administration that replaced the Resettlement Administration in 1937 aided African Americans through its loan program and through its educational program, which introduced new production and marketing methods.

In large northern cities, the WPA introduced progressive programs into African-American communities and turned ghetto schools into centers of activity for the African-American community. By the end of the 1930s, almost 100,000 northern African Americans had participated in the Emergency Education Program. Its programs brought into the ghettos for the first time such topics as literacy, workers' education, Negro history, nursery education, and parent education. The WPA leaders, believing in the importance of strong community-based organizations, aided African-American social welfare institutions. Programs in Harlem and Chicago were marked by conflicts with conservatives, charges of discrimination, and constant threat of curtailment of funds but were progressive, the first programs to recognize the educational needs of northern and southern African Americans (Maskin, 1973).

The 1920s marked an important shift in the policy toward Native Americans. In 1924, Congress granted citizenship to all Indians who lived in the territorial United States. Informed by the anthropological concepts of culture and cultural pluralism, scientists and scholars began to attribute the Indian problem to economic and social conditions, not individual character, and to respect the importance of Indian culture. The reorganization of Indian Services began in 1928, after the publication of the Meriam Report, a study that called for professional involvement to bring work with Native Americans up to date in such areas as community development, education, and vocational training (Berkhofer, 1978). The New Deal brought a new era of reform in Indian administration. John Collier, commissioner of Indian Affairs from 1933 to 1945, advanced a far-reaching agenda for Native American reform that sought the ultimate integration of Indians into white society while preserving their culture. Many of these reforms were incorporated into the Indian Reorganization Act passed by Congress in 1934. While this act did not provide for formal adult education, existing voluntary classes for literacy and agricultural extension were continued. Other activities addressed educational needs: CCC programs, health, expansion of home extension and 4-H, and construction of "chapter houses" to serve as social and community centers. School programs resulted in decreased illiteracy in the 1930s, but no systematic program to counter adult illiteracy was developed (Adams, 1946).

New Deal Intervention

The New Deal interventions greatly exceeded previous federal initiatives in adult education in terms of the groups served and the range of subject matter included. The very scope and the social reform aims of many of these programs generated significant concerns about the federal role in adult education. Established institutions in particular objected to both the social reform aims and the creation of new agencies to implement them. The National Education Association argued for placing adult education under the auspices of the public school system. The AAAE questioned the appropriateness of a governmental role at all, arguing that adult education should be under private auspices and not subject to control by government (Stubblefield, 1988). The AFL argued for directing workers' education toward the functional goal of union management. Other conservative groups regarded adult education as an agency to inculcate a work ethic and develop skills for employment in an industrial society.

Among such social reformers as Hopkins, Smith, and Williams, a broader conception of adult education as social education prevailed. Rejecting education as a means to shape individuals to serve institutional purposes, they believed adults had the ability to understand the problems of American society and the skills to discuss and implement decisions. If culture were made available to ordinary citizens—through the creative works of artists, writers, and playwrights—it would uplift and enrich them. However inadequately and briefly, the New Deal offered new educational opportunities to the working class, African Americans, and Native Americans. Unemployed women received little attention, their right to work and their importance to the workforce as yet unrecognized.

Civilians and the Military

Following America's entrance into the war in 1941, the New Deal educational programs were dismantled. The CCC was discontinued in 1942, the WPA and NYA in 1943. Both the CCC and the NYA had provided training for the war, but enrollment dropped as young men entered the military or defense industries. The NYA had the support of businessmen because it provided trained labor. It had opposition, however, from organized education, which argued that a federally operated educational agency worked against state control of education, and from others who regarded the NYA under Aubrey Williams as a radical agency (Polenberg, 1972). In the face of wartime education and training needs, disagreements over the federal government's role in education, which had marked the Depression years, abated. The armed forces engaged millions of Americans in compulsory training for military functions and in voluntary education for the pursuit of individual interests and intellectual stimulation in leisure time. Americans were also mobilized for education and training not just as armed services personnel but also as industrial workers and patriotic citizens.

The Home Front

Wars are fought not only with troops and weapons, but also with ideals and public opinion. Historian Merle Curti (1964) claims that unlike the divisiveness created by World War I, "no war had been fought with as much unanimity as World War II" (p. 732). Public opinion, however, was not left to chance. In October 1941, President Roosevelt created the Office of Facts and Figures and appointed Archibald MacLeish, a poet of national reputation, to head the agency. Believing in the capacity of an informed citizenry to make enlightened decisions once they had the facts, MacLeish used the office as a public forum to provide information. In June 1942, the Office of War Information (OWI), under the direction of journalist, author, and radio commentator Elmer Davis, replaced the Office of Facts and Figures (Winkler, 1978). Davis advanced an information-reporting role instead of an educational role for the office, but the military's refusal to provide information made his efforts more difficult, and some viewed the OWI as "the president's publicity bureau" (Winkler, 1978, p. 53).

Both the educational and reportorial functions were lost when the domestic branch of the OWI was reorganized in 1943. It curtailed the production of pamphlets and replaced serious discussion of war issues with advertising techniques. After this, Blum (1976, p. 45) concludes, "the OWI contributed little to a civilian people, who in most cases and at most times were fighting the war on imagination alone." With some exceptions, advertisers, writers, and playwrights depicted the enemy as without humanity, and against whom revenge should be taken (Blum, 1976).

Training Needs of Civilian Workers

The wartime demands on American industries required more workers trained in science and engineering, more rapid training for skilled positions, and orientation and training for new women and minority factory workers. Civilian manpower needs were anticipated in June 1940 when Congress made its first appropriation for national defense training. Both the federal government and private industry took initiative to train the civilian work force. The War

Manpower Commission, created in April 1942, established policies and regulations to meet the needs of industry and agriculture. Within the commission, the Bureau of Training coordinated the work of the Apprenticeship Training Service, the Training Within Industry Service, and the War Training Programs of the U.S. Office of Education (Grace, 1948). Industry initiated a massive training program to deal with labor shortages. At the request of the commission, industry projected manpower needs for both the present and the future, described the jobs according to standard terms taken from the *Dictionary of Occupational Titles,* conducted a job analysis, created a structure of classifying jobs, and broke skilled jobs down into smaller steps to permit easier and faster learning (Jacoby, 1985). An expanded Civil Service Commission training program prepared qualified civilian employees for the War Department, the Navy Department, and the Merchant Marines, and a program operated independently by the War Department trained three million people (Grace, 1948).

A special wartime college experience for civilians was offered through the Engineering, Science and Management War Training Program sponsored by the Department of Education and offered in 250 colleges. In 1942–43, 800,000 men and women took college courses to promote productivity. The courses lasted from three to six months and were usually coordinated by extension and engineering divisions.

Discrimination against women and African Americans carried over into the defense industry training programs. Women did not become a significant part of these programs until the spring of 1942, when Congress approved a supplemental training appropriation and prohibited discrimination on the grounds of gender or race. Even then, training for women was scarce until February 1942, when the War Production Board extended training for women to equal that of men. Participation in these programs helped women gain skills but, more important, self-confidence (Foner, 1980). In another action, the U.S. Office of Education issued a declaration prohibiting discrimination in defense training programs, and the Office of Production Management established a Negro employment and training branch to facilitate African Americans' training in defense industries (Franklin and Moss, 1988).

The war highlighted once again the importance of management and supervision in industry. During the war, there was more training in human relations skills for foremen. Dale Carnegie–type courses proliferated in order to help foremen maintain discipline and persuasively counteract the influence of the union steward. Training became more sophisticated, using behavioral techniques such as sociodrama, sociometry, and role playing. Through the Training Within Industry program, the federal government enrolled a half million foremen in its own foremen training program. It was hoped that supervisors who understood the needs of workers would reduce the number of grievances filed and thereby increase production (Jacoby, 1985). The need for managers was greater than could be accommodated in the emergency training programs developed during the war, so at the request of the federal government, the Harvard Business School created a series of three-month courses for sales personnel who had management and supervisory positions. This began the short-term, advanced management course program at Harvard Business School that was to become popular after the war (Urwick, 1954).

Armed Services Personnel

The United States built an armed forces of about twelve million people, and Grace (1948) claimed that those who entered the services were the best that America had to offer. Of the more than seven million army trainees, 10 percent had one to four years of college, over 25 percent had four years of high school, and almost a third had one to three years of high school (Grace, 1948). Yet the Selective Service rejected 676,000 men because they had not completed four years of schooling (Curti, 1964). The Depression had sharply reduced the financial resources of public schools and colleges. "The war," observes Perrett (1985) in his popular account of this period, "had exposed all the deficiencies in American education" (p. 375).

Applying the best civilian thinking about curriculum, the armed forces launched a massive training program to produce combat personnel and occupational specialists to operate the services (Grace, 1948). Military education focused on training and indoctrination rather than on general subjects, and it differed from civilian education in that the military had financial resources, selected the students, and exercised twenty-four-hour control over their lives. But even with unlimited authority, the services valued the needs and morale of the personnel (Grace, 1948). The armed services trained for specific jobs to enable a person to perform alone or work as a member of a team. As Grace (1948) observed: "Time did not permit the development of the well-rounded individual or even of the all-around soldier. Speed, specialization, and standardization were the imperatives" (p. 21).

The army and navy used colleges for special training in the Navy V-12 program and the Army Specialized Training Program, which, along with similar programs, accelerated college education, expanded science and technology courses, and introduced new methods of instruction. In making college education available based on ability and not on social status, the program had the unintended sociological consequence of democratizing higher education. Because of their experience, many trainees returned to college after the war (Keefer, 1988).

Millions had been taught to read and write by the WPA in the 1930s, yet the Selective Service found one in every five adults functionally illiterate. The army moved quickly to address the illiteracy problem; in July 1941, it established a special training unit at each replacement training center and developed functional training materials related to the individual's army experience. Using methods similar to civilian programs, the literacy programs taught reading and arithmetic skills at the fourth-grade level, used everyday language for communication with officers and enlisted men, and explained why the United States was at war. After June 1943, 302,838 were assigned to the special training units, and 254,272 successfully completed the program. Of those, 79 percent took sixty days or less to meet the standards (Houle, Burr, Hamilton, and Yale, 1947).

About one million African-American men and women served in the armed services during the war, about a half-million overseas. Women were accepted in the Women's Auxiliary Corps, and men were trained as aviation pilots. The navy had the worst discrimination record—not until 1942 were African Americans permitted to enlist for general service, at which time they were trained at a separate unit at the Great Lakes Naval Training Station. Recruits who showed promise received additional training at Hampton Institute (Franklin and Moss, 1988).

Leisure and Patriotic Uses of Education

Education for nonmilitary purposes explained to armed services personnel the reasons for participating in the war, provided information about the progress of the war, and offered opportunities to become more effective through off-duty, voluntary study (Grace, 1948). In the army, an information and education philosophy and program gradually grew out of an initial emphasis on morale, welfare, and recreation. In the winter of 1942, plans for nonmilitary education made it analogous to civilian education: students would have freedom to choose courses of study, and motivation would come from their initiative and interest (Houle, Burr, Hamilton, and Yale, 1947).

      Recreational and educational activities for armed services personnel in their off-duty leisure time were well and carefully developed. Social science techniques were used to study motivation, adjustments, and attitudes. As Curti (1964) concludes, "Never in peacetime had the knowledge social scientists made available been used in attacking the problems of group association and morale in so direct and constructive a way" (p. 742). Research conducted by the research branch of the Information and Education Division became the basis for formulating policy, planning programs, and measuring their effectiveness. A monthly publication, *What the Soldier Thinks,* made research reports available to all levels of the War Department, including the unit information-education officer. The Information and Education Division made its chief contribution to the morale of soldiers in the production and distribution of the *Why We Fight* film series under the direction of Frank Capra (a successful Hollywood filmmaker known for such films as *Mr. Smith Goes to Washington*); in 1942, all military personnel were mandated to see the series. Culbert (1983) notes the "extraordinary similarities between the concept and practice of information, orientation, and propaganda" (p. 175). Not intended to be objective, *Why We Fight* evoked loyalty and incited patriotic fervor.

For off-duty education and overall development of servicemen, the armed services made extensive use of several programs. Correspondence study overcame obstacles of time and distance and enabled individuals to pursue their own interests. The army conducted the largest correspondence program in the war through the Army Institute, which in 1942 became the United States Armed Forces Institute at Madison, Wisconsin. Books became more accessible as a result of the Victory Book campaigns and the publication of special editions for use by the armed forces. Locally organized evening classes for soldiers began first in the United States and then were extended to Europe and the Pacific. A foreign-language program gave troops the skills to manage prisoners of war and work with the nationals of allied and hostile countries. Discussion groups addressed issues of "personal, community, national, or international importance" (Houle, Burr, Hamilton, and Yale, 1947, p. 111). The army provided news and information in the *Yank* and *Stars and Stripes* newspapers, and the Armed Forces Radio Service broadcast worldwide.

To aid the transition of service personnel to civilian life, the army established the Army Education Program. Specialized vocational courses trained soldiers for employment or further study and provided information about employment opportunities. Through general courses, soldiers updated their knowledge about American life. Instruction ranged from literacy and general education at elementary and secondary levels through technical training to college level courses. Approximately half a million soldiers participated in programs offered in the Mediterranean and European theaters of operation.

Consequences of the War

Fearful of the untoward consequences of a massive influx of new workers into the economy, the President, Congress, the American Legion, and the American Council on Education considered early in the war how to reintegrate veterans into American society. On June 22, 1944, President Roosevelt signed into law the Servicemen's Readjustment Act, popularly known as the "GI Bill of Rights." The GI Bill supported forms of education that ranged from adult literacy classes, high school completion, college, and professional schools to vocational training (Olson, 1974). Blum (1976) notes that war taught a lesson not learned in peace: "The war had demonstrated, alike in the armed services and in private industry, the advantages of training and education, which Americans regularly listed as opportunities they cherished for themselves and their children" (p. 25).

Some civilian education leaders recognized the importance of the World War II programs in training and education and saw possible implications for adaptation in peacetime. The American Council on Education, with funding from the Carnegie Corporation and the General Education Board and the approval of the secretaries of the War and Navy, sponsored a two-year study by the Commission on Implications of Armed Services Educational Programs. Headed by Alonzo Grace, the commission produced nine monographs on different aspects of military educational programs as well as Grace's summary report, *Educational Lessons from Wartime Training*. Grace (1948) gave positive marks to the wartime programs but also noted the differing opinions regarding applications to civilian education. Those who saw and appreciated such potential valued wartime's educational efficiency and control and considered it a model that could revolutionize civilian education. But a system of training fell far short of being a system of education for free persons (Grace, 1948).

The adult education community found the off-duty, voluntary programs—developed by the army and navy—those that could be properly classified as adult education—to be a case study of great importance to the emerging status of adult education as a field of practice and study. As Houle, Burr, Hamilton, and Yale (1948) observed, "In the future it is likely that the Army and Navy off-duty programs will be considered to have been among the first of the large-scale adult educational activities" (p. 227). Houle, the author of this section, acknowledges the difficulty of applying the experience of the military in wartime to peacetime civilian programs. Nevertheless, both military and civilian adult educators made decisions about program objectives, administration, instructional materials, staff services, guiding and counseling students, recruiting students, program evaluation, financing, and physical facilities

(Houle, Burr, Hamilton, and Yale, 1948). Houle juxtaposed his knowledge of adult education theory and practice with his study of military education to frame a set of operating principles for adult education as an emerging endeavor. Houle's ideas regarding method included these principles: adults will learn a task better if the immediate steps of the task and the larger goal are both explained. Presenting basic theory will aid in the learning of specific skills. Students need to understand how the instruction fits into the larger context of their lives. Four decades later, these operating principles remain relevant, and they may mark the turning point in the postwar efforts of adult educators to refine the principles and theory of adult education.

The war experience also affected higher education. In anticipation of a great influx of veterans into higher education after the war, the American Council on Education recommended establishing an accreditation program to assess the knowledge and skills acquired through U.S. Armed Forces Institute correspondence courses and to assist military personnel to assess the educational significance of military experiences. Accordingly, the University of Chicago developed end-of-course tests, examinations to determine proficiency in subject matter, and examinations to determine returning veterans' level for their future schooling. In 1944, the American Council on Education published *A Guide to the Evaluation of Military Experiences in the Armed Services,* a handbook for civilian educators describing military courses and recommendations for credit (Houle, Burr, Hamilton, and Yale, 1947; Rohfeld, 1990; Rose, 1989a). Accreditation was important for higher education officials and veterans alike because it accelerated veterans' progress in postwar higher education.

Summary

In the New Deal, the federal government intervened in adult education in a massive and unprecedented way. Segments of the adult population previously unreached by education engaged in systematic instruction and informal learning through structured programs for literacy, homemaking, and vocational education, and through cultural projects, regional development, and youth programs. Workers' education and the Federal Theatre Project, which were openly critical of American society, were among the programs that drew charges of communist infiltration. The interest groups of public education and labor unions sought to gain control of aspects of the program, while the AAAE cautioned against any federal involvement in the dissemination of knowledge to the public.

Industrial production in support of the war effort and military action required a massive training and educational effort to equip industrial workers, specialists in military occupations, and combat personnel. In the military, training for specific functions received priority, but the military provided opportunities for continuing study. Procedures for accrediting military training were developed, and the implications of military education for civilian education were studied.

PART FIVE

America at the Peak of World Power

16

Entering the Age
of Adult Education

In the half-century since World War II, the United States entered the age of adult education. A rising educational level and the emergence of the postindustrial society made continuing education the norm of adult life. The educative agencies for adults—media, libraries, museums, colleges and universities, and public schools—continued their essential social function of disseminating knowledge while responding to broader national agendas of anticommunism, economic competitiveness, and the War on Poverty. Television became a new agency for informal adult learning. Continuing education for work performance, and workplace sponsorship of education, became central features of the postwar period.

Connections Between Past and Present

In the age of adult education, the media, libraries, and museums remained important agencies of informal learning. Television soon touched the lives of most Americans, becoming a pervasive though unacknowledged educator. New library activities ranged from aiding new readers to supporting adult college students in independent study programs. Museums actively reached out to the adult public through object displays, major exhibitions that attracted large audiences, and continuing education.

Television

As radio and motion pictures altered the landscape of informal adult learning in the interwar period, so did commercial television in the postwar period. By the mid 1950s, 66 percent of all American homes had television sets. Television quickly became a major source of entertainment and news, for Americans invested more time and attention in television than in any other communication medium (Chafe, 1991; Lacy, 1978). Americans found in early television a reinforcement of "the conservative, celebratory values of the dominant culture": situation comedies portrayed male dominance and female subservience as the road to happiness (Chafe, 1991). Later situation comedies and dramas brought incest, homosexual relations, interracial marriages, and war into the immediacy of the living room for family and public discussion (Meyerowitz, 1985). Television also enabled persons of widely different backgrounds to share a common experience. Alex Haley's novel *Roots* galvanized the nation as a television miniseries in 1977; through its depiction of the African origins of the African-American experience, black people came to understand and take pride in their heritage, and white Americans were forced to confront the cruelty of slavery.

The commercial television industry's distinction between education and entertainment underestimated television's educational role. Schiller (1989) observes that television "is now one of the most influential, largely unacknowledged educators in the country" (p. 106), and "for a large part of the population, TV is the teacher, though the lessons transmitted rarely are recognized as such" (p. 107). In fact, the lessons are disguised in an entertainment format so that products may be marketed.

An alternative to market-driven commercial television was provided by the Public Broadcasting Act of 1967. To oversee noncommercial broadcasting, a nonprofit Corporation for Public Broadcasting was organized. The corporation then established the Public Broadcasting Service in 1969 and National Public Radio in 1970. The Public Broadcasting Act followed an established federal legislative pattern in giving organizational structure and direction to a system already in place. As early as 1951, educators and educational broadcasters, supported by funding from the Ford Foundation and its subsidiary, the Fund for Adult Education, began working for educational broadcasting policies and programming (Blakely, 1979).

The report of the Carnegie Commission on Educational Television (1967) was the basis for the Public Broadcasting Act. The commission rejected the idea of a national educational television system that provided educational programming. It recommended, instead, the creation of a "public" broadcasting system—public in the sense of being free of the constraints of commercial television— to provide cultural and informational programming (Blakely, 1979).

Libraries

In the 1920s and 1930s, the American Library Association, in alliance with the American Association for Adult Education, organized its work with adults around the emerging concept of adult education. After World War II, library professionals adopted the broader concept of adult services. In 1957, the ALA established the Adult Services Division, and the adult education goal became secondary to recreational and informational services (Heim, 1990; Van Fleet, 1990). In the 1970s, professional librarians began to consider the implications of a life-span education paradigm, popularly referred to as lifelong learning. However, the concept of lifelong learning has yet to prove more effective in defining an educational mission than the concept of adult education was in the 1920s and 1930s (Van Fleet, 1990).

As the public library sought to rationalize its mission around emerging educational concepts, it also responded to national needs in the Cold War and the War on Poverty. The library initiated such projects as the Great Issues Program in 1948 and the American Heritage Project in 1951 to help Americans understand global politics in the Cold War. In the War on Poverty, libraries provided services to disadvantaged adults with limited reading ability and offered federally funded outreach programs through the Library Services and Construction Act, Community Action Programs, and

VISTA (Lacy, 1978). The emergence, in the late 1960s and early 1970s, of an older, more diverse college student body and expanded nontraditional higher education programs brought the library into a cooperative arrangement with the College Entrance Examination Board to help adults prepare for the College-Level Examination Program and gain credit for independent study (Van Fleet, 1990).

America's entrance into the information age and concerns about a national system of library and information services once again challenged the public library to redefine its role. The Library Services Acts of 1958 extended federal government support to libraries. The National Advisory Commission on Libraries, appointed by President Johnson, recommended adoption of a national policy to provide adequate library services (Lacy 1978). In support of this policy, Congress created a National Commission on Libraries and Information Science. In November 1979, the White House Conference on Library and Information Services addressed issues directly related to adult education. The conference recognized that information needs "are a constant, persistent by-product of life in modern society," but a preconference study showed that libraries were only slowly making the transition from providing reading material to offering information (Chen, 1982, p. 80). Information seekers neither sought help from the library with any frequency nor regarded it as the best source of information. Without change, public libraries face "extinction in the postindustrial and information-rich society" (pp. 92–93).

Preserving the Past

The 1960s witnessed a museum boom: "a new museum was founded every 3.3 days" (Glasser, 1989, p. 188). In the early 1960s, museum adult education programs expanded as museums recognized affluent and educated adults as a source of income and a supporting constituency (Solinger, 1989). Museum attendance also expanded, attributed in part to more college-educated people in the population who had been exposed to the arts, to government support for art, to a period of extended prosperity, and to more leisure time. The social movements of the 1960s challenged the museum as well as other cultural institutions to be more responsive to minority and ethnic concerns, and by 1979, more than 100 ethnic minority museums had been created (Alexander, 1979).

A new seriousness characterized the adult education work of the museum community as the museum directed greater attention to education, to the educator, to the visitor as learner, to the environment as educative, and to the museum as a provider of continuing education. The American Association of Museums organized the Standing Professional Committee in 1973 to represent workers in museum education, and the committee sponsored the 1976 "Learning Theories Seminars" and published *The Museum and the Visitor* (Collins, 1981). In the 1970s and 1980s, new research related adult learning theory to adults as museum visitors and showed how museums offer learning opportunities (Carr, 1989; Gunther, 1989). A major initiative in advancing museum education was the Smithsonian Institution Kellogg Project, which began in 1982 and was extended through 1988, sponsored by the W. K. Kellogg Foundation (Solinger, 1989). The project conducted a national colloquia with twelve participating museums to identify museum issues. These museums, which ranged in type from the Museum of Science in Boston to the Children's Museum of Indianapolis to the Cherokee National Museum of Tahlequah, Oklahoma, agreed to develop demonstration projects for the community. Professionals from over two hundred museums participated in six regional and topical workshops and a ten-day residency program at the Smithsonian on adult learning in museums.

Agencies of the Emerging Learning Society

An emerging learning society challenged colleges and universities, the Cooperative Extension Service, community colleges, and public schools to redefine their missions and structures to serve the needs of a growing adult constituency. As education became a lifelong activity, educational programs became, for adult learners, a consumer product to be purchased and, for institutional providers, a commodity for mass marketing. Changing societal conditions, rising educational levels and expectations, increasing continuing education needs of an emerging postindustrial society, and changing demographics created an unsettled environment for traditional education agencies.

Universities

Universities confronted a student body nontraditional in age, attendance patterns, and learning orientation. Students were increasingly adult and part-time; they arranged educational activities around family, community, and career responsibilities; and they entered or reentered higher education to further career goals. Between 1966 and the mid 1980s, the number of part-time students increased 150 percent (Sparks, 1985). In the 1970s, colleges and universities responded by creating alternative structures and delivery systems for degree programs for adults who needed to study part-time or off-campus (Houle, 1974). Weekend colleges served adult students when facilities were not used by traditional-age students and when adults had time. Adult degree programs, pioneered in the early 1950s by Columbia University, Brooklyn College, and the University of Oklahoma, recognized the differences between adults and youth as learners. The development of the College Proficiency Examination Program and the College-Level Examination Program—tests to assess academic achievement—led to the assessment degree, which measured competencies gained through forms of study other than courses. Founded in 1974, the Cooperative Assessment of Experiential Learning, now the Council for Adult and Experiential Learning, has provided leadership for this new movement in higher education.

Universities encountered another growing student body, the ten million adults who enrolled annually for noncredit programs (Sparks, 1985). University residential centers for continuing education became popular in the 1950s, stimulated by the Kellogg Foundation's funding of nine centers (Rohfeld, 1990). Continuing education became increasingly important for career enhancement and civic participation. This expansion of noncredit programs presented universities with a problem of accountability, standardization, and record keeping. Work on a solution to this problem began in 1968 at a conference of national professional and education associations and federal agencies. In 1971, a new measuring unit called the Continuing Education Unit was created for reporting university continuing education activities (Kaplan and Veri, 1974).

Many adults needed assistance with their educational decisions and in gaining access to university programs. In the early 1970s, a new concept called educational brokering responded to this need (Hefferman, 1981). Educational brokering centers brought together several education functions previously isolated, namely, providing information about higher education opportunities, assessing academic and occupational skills, helping to form educational plans, making referrals to educational and social services, and advocating on behalf of adult learners when educational institutions erected barriers (Barton, 1982). The National Center for Educational Brokering, established in 1976, provided national coordination.

Innovations in outreach extended beyond individual learners to encompass the community as a sphere of university service. One model of community development focused on citizen participation. The University of Montana, with funding from the Rockefeller Foundation, conducted one of the earlier efforts, known as the Montana Study, from 1944 to 1947 (Counter, 1989). Citizens in ten Montana communities participated in the project. Meeting weekly for ten weeks, they used a study guide to learn about their community, and then each community group recommended ways to improve. These study groups were educational in that citizens learned about their communities and about how to conduct research and produce recommendations from data. Another model combined citizen participation and the delivery of services. In 1968, Tuskegee Institute created the Human Resources Development Center to address problems of the Alabama Black Belt region. The center developed and implemented programs that ranged from community education to manpower training to community food and nutrition. Through solicitation of foundation funding and formation of national advisory councils, Tuskegee focused national attention on the region. Local citizens participated in identifying needed programs and monitoring the delivery of services through advisory councils.

Universities explored another outreach mechanism, urban extension, with leadership from the Ford Foundation. From 1959 to the 1960s, the foundation funded eight university programs and two nonacademic institutional programs through its urban research, education and extension grants (Perkins, 1978). In creating this program, the foundation anticipated that the federal government would actively promote and fund projects in support of the university urban extension approach. Federal support did not materialize, however. Instead of funding a university urban extension program similar to the Cooperative Extension Service for agriculture, the federal government chose to entice the universities into community services through Title I of the Higher Education Act of 1965. Title I provided funds for projects through a competitive proposal process and required that universities match a percentage of the budget. Funding levels were limited, and the availability of funds, contingent on congressional action, was never certain. In 1981, Title I funding ended. The act also established the National Advisory Council on Extension and Continuing Education. The council had no power to act beyond making recommendations, and in 1987, it was abolished. The program did not in any way represent a full-scale assault on urban problems, nor did it receive much legislative or executive support (Rohfeld, 1990). Its success would have to be judged by the impact of university programs on local communities.

Collaborative relationships between universities, business, industry, and labor unions have resulted in cooperative arrangements, new program development, and delivery of on-site credit and noncredit courses and academic degrees (Charner and Rolzinski, 1987; Stack and Hutton, 1980). The Business Development and Training Center at the Great Valley Corporate Center in Malvern, Pennsylvania, organized in the early 1980s, serves as a brokering agency between the education and training needs of corporations in this high-tech field and postsecondary institutions. Boston College formed an educational partnership with several labor unions in Massachusetts, assisting them, through an emphasis on self-management, with problems related to industrial dislocation and structural changes.

Two vastly different initiatives with somewhat similar concerns sought to redirect the university from its vocational and research orientation to a liberal learning orientation and to challenge the university's monopoly on knowledge. The quasi-independent Center for the Study of Liberal Education for Adults was established in 1951 through the initiative of the Association of University Evening Colleges, with funding by the Fund for Adult Education (Dyer, 1956; Whipple, 1967). The center worked with the association to articulate the philosophy and rationale of the evening college and to rethink its mission in the context of liberal education. However, by 1955, the center had embarked on a broader and more ambitious agenda that addressed the meaning of liberal education for adults. When the Fund for Adult Education disbanded in 1961, the center continued its work with a final grant from the fund, but unable to secure substantial and dependable funding, it disbanded in the late 1960s.

In the Cold War, the center's call for a humane, liberal education seemed irrelevant in the face of the prevailing American belief that survival would come by "science and its handmaiden, technical 'know-how'" (Whipple, 1967, p. 26). A new form and philosophy of university education, born out of the student civil rights movement and the student free speech movement in the 1960s, had more staying power as an adult education innovation (Draves, 1980). The free university at first offered an alternative to the lockstep curriculum of universities, and it engaged students in social and political critique. With its disengagement from the campus to serve the community at large in the early 1970s, the free university entered the lifelong learning community—a movement in its nascency—and was recognized as an adult education institution. The free universities found their student body in the baby boomers who had completed college in the 1960s and now wanted career and personal development. The free university movement created an alternative institution to challenge the university's monopoly on knowledge; in time, however, that alternative institution became just another, though innovative, educational service provider.

The Extension Service Mission

After the war, the Cooperative Extension Service redirected its efforts away from administering emergency programs—a task that it had assumed almost from its formation in 1914 until the end of the war in 1945—and toward its original educational role. The 1948 national extension report called for an expanded concept of education that went beyond providing information: to help people think, to broaden subject matter, and to provide service to new audiences. Extension continued to serve its mainstream clientele, the middle-class farm community, but in the 1950s, it also began to address social problems through rural development programs, leadership training, and county-level councils. Using the grants-in-aid made available in the War on Poverty, extension expanded its formula-funded mainstream programs to serve the disadvantaged and urban poor. A pilot program culminated in the national Expanded Food and Nutrition Education Program in 1968.

In the 1970s and 1980s, Congress expanded extension's program emphasis even as extension's traditional rural population base was declining. Having gained legitimacy because of "the uniqueness of its informal educational program to help people develop their own potentials," extension's legitimacy nevertheless came to be questioned (Warner and Christenson, 1984). The 1977 Food and Agriculture Act mandated an evaluation of the social and economic consequences of extension's programs, and other evaluation studies followed. The Reagan administration threatened extension's continued operation. In response, extension sought focus and legitimacy in an issues-oriented program supported by centers of excellence to conduct research and develop programmatic responses.

Community Colleges

The junior college had become part of the higher education system prior to World War II but not part of the adult education system (Brint and Karabel, 1989). After the war, the junior college's mission and student body greatly expanded as it evolved to a community college. Its acceptance as part of the higher education system was supported by a report from President Truman's Commission on Higher Education. The commission called for equality of opportunity in education and the expansion of higher education. It envisioned a key role for the junior college in providing terminal training for "semiprofessional workers" for which four years of college was not required (Brint and Karabel, 1989). The commission recommended replacing the term *junior* with *community* and redirecting the community college toward meeting local needs.

Community colleges soon became the fastest-growing segment of higher education, and by the 1960s, community colleges had evolved as major providers of adult education at the community level, reaching out to various publics and institutions of the community through programs that were variously titled but often known as community education services (Cohen and Brawer, 1989). These services greatly expanded in the 1970s, only to be curtailed in the 1980s because of funding. Even with declines in funding, enrollment in noncredit activities in the 1980s ranged from three to four million annually (Cohen and Brawer, 1989). Not bound by credit hour or state funding regulations, community education employed flexible delivery systems, designed programs for special groups, entered into cooperative sponsorship with other organizations, and made facilities available to community groups.

In the 1970s, the community college began to define a more precise identity as a higher education institution in relation to the community and workplace. Edmund J. Gleazer, Jr., president of the American Association of Community and Junior Colleges, believed the community college should be the learning center of the community, developing programs to address the community's needs. Community colleges also began to develop stronger linkages to business and industry by offering subsidized skills training and customized training, often delivered on-site (Brint and Karabel, 1989). Strategies to position the community college as a lifelong learning center and as a provider of training for business and industry remained problematic for many (Brint and Karabel, 1989; Cohen and Brawer, 1989). These strategies, critics argued, compromised the mission of the community college as a higher education institution offering academic and occupational programs; its purpose was to engage students in rigorous study and development of broad skills, not to extend beyond the perceived needs of the community or to accommodate the training needs of an employer.

Adult Education Through Public Schools

As the United States entered the 1950s, only one-third of all school districts offered adult education programs, and these were mainly in urban areas, financed most often by local district funds rather than by state funds, and limited to vocational education. As public

school adult education administrators began to consider community needs, the curriculum expanded to include "activities in the
arts, sciences, public affairs, and the humanities, specifically designed to foster and develop economic, political, and cultural liter-
acies" (Luke, 1960, p. 346). The Fund for Adult Education provided
funds to hire state directors in six states, to train them to provide
general and liberal education, and to train local directors of adult
education (Luke, 1960). In the War on Poverty, public schools,
along with community colleges in some states, became the providers
of adult basic education and high school completion programs
through adult high schools, competency-based programs, and the
General Education Development (GED) program.

In the 1960s, a broader role for the public schools was envisioned in the emerging concept of community education, a role that
the Charles Stewart Mott Foundation supported through doctoral
fellowships and community education centers in universities and
state departments of education. Community schools grew rapidly
and by 1978 numbered almost six thousand. At the state level, the
community education concept gained support, as indicated in legislation for community education (DeLargy, 1989). In the late 1960s
and early 1970s, an expanded concept of community education,
incorporating a community development focus, retained the public
school as the base of operations but emphasized a process that identified all the educational needs of the community and planned how
to address those needs (Decker, 1972). The community education
concept remained in dispute among public school educators, who
questioned whether solving community problems was part of the
public school function.

Education for and About Work

Clark's observation (1966) that historians might characterize this
period as "the first age in which massive amounts of money were
spent to educate people after they started to work" (p. v) surely was
confirmed in the years that followed. Work-related education and
training for adults became widespread in institutions and occupations in the public, for-profit, and independent sectors in which
goods, services, and information were produced and distributed.

Large-scale education and training operations now prevailed in the professions, the military, government, business and industry, and labor unions.

The Armed Forces

Modern military education began with mobilization for World War II and accelerated in the postwar period (Maloy, Gager, and Sullivan, 1976). The armed forces pioneered early in "recurrent education" or "lifelong education," providing education and training at different stages in a service person's career. They differed from civilian organizations in their power to compel participation or provide strong inducements. Education in the armed forces served the dual purpose of equipping service personnel to perform their duties better and preparing them for the civilian workforce when discharged.

To equip personnel for service requirements, the armed forces established an educational system that parallels the civilian system. It provided education and training for occupational specialties, technical equipment operation, administration and supply, and professional services. Tuition-assisted, off-duty education programs at civilian education institutions, taught on and off base, made college-level education available to thousands. The United States Armed Forces Institute, established in 1942, offered correspondence courses, the GED testing program, the College-Level Examination Program, and, through the American Council on Education, an evaluation of service training for college-level equivalency. The armed forces were brought into the War on Poverty in 1966 through "Project 100,000," a program to remedy educational deficiencies, in which men with educational deficiencies were accepted into the service and then participated in special adult basic education and GED programs (Brodsky, 1970).

Voluntary military education received greater support in 1970, when service in the armed forces became voluntary. In 1974, the Defense Activity for Nontraditional Education Support replaced the United States Armed Forces Institute. Several initiatives provided more flexible transfer options for service personnel, among these the Community College of the Air Force (1972), which combined training in air force technical schools with voluntary education courses, resulting in an associate of applied science degree. The Servicemembers Opportunity College created a consortium of 438 member colleges that accept credits taken from other schools. Civilian colleges also deliver programs on military installations (Veeman and Singer, 1989).

Continuing Professional Education

The 1960s marked a turning point in the continuing education of professionals, ushering in what Houle (1983) describes as the second era in continuing professional education. Until then, responsibility for staying up to date in one's field of specialization rested with the individual. In this situation, continuing education was a "mindset" in that each patient presented a unique intellectual challenge for continuing learning (Caplan, 1983). In the 1960s, the public-at-large and the government questioned the adequacy of individual self-direction and began to call for monitoring performance. This second era of continuing professional education centered on helping laggards achieve acceptable standards of practice (Houle, 1983). Many states made continuing education mandatory for relicensure of physicians, lawyers, nurses, certified public accountants, real estate brokers, and many others. Expectations were high that continuing education would result in more competent practice, but a more balanced appraisal held that a professional's continuing education occurs as part of the total system of practice, not just through short-term courses (Caplan, 1983).

The knowledge explosion stimulated the growth and acceptance of continuing professional education, but other important factors were the growing acceptance of lifelong learning hastened by the increase of specialization after World War II and the recognition that adult learning differs from the learning of children in significant ways (Caplan, 1983). Continuing professional education evolves as attention is given to high standards for practitioners, to the professionalization process and the purposes of the professions in society, and to an understanding of the dynamics of continuing learning among professions (Cervero, 1989; Houle, 1980, 1983). Comparative studies of professional continuing education have shown similarities across the professions in the learning and educational task and similarities to the broader field of adult education (Houle, 1980).

Workplace Education

The educational and training system that expanded to support the war effort continued to expand in the postwar period. In their survey of classrooms in the factory, Clark and Sloan (1958) observe that corporate education programs had "almost burst into existence during the past ten years" (p. 25) as business and industry began to create their own education programs. By the mid 1960s, certain patterns of development in work-related education were observable (Lusterman, 1977; Risley, 1960). The explosion of knowledge had altered the nature of work, and the increasing complexity of jobs required that workers at all levels be continually educated and trained. The more an industry invested in research and development, the more it had to invest in education and training: the creation of new products or processes required changes in the manufacturing procedures and the training of workers and technicians to manage these procedures.

Programs developed by corporations provided training for job-related functions, and by 1960, distinct programs were operating for line workers, foremen and supervisors, managers, and technical and professional personnel. Corporate programs also included education for higher intellectual achievement: liberal education, human relations training, economic education, reading skills, creative thinking, and public speaking. Some corporations offered general education for personal development to employees and their families (Risley, 1960). Many corporations made major investments in more sophisticated and advanced levels of human resource development by building their own training facilities. Xerox's Learning Center in Leesburg, Virginia, is the largest but not the only one (Eurich, 1985). Eighteen corporate educational institutions offer academic degrees, and one of these, the National Technological University, offers all courses by telecommunication. The use of telecommunication and computers transcended the limitations of time and place that made knowledge inaccessible to many (Eurich, 1985).

In the 1950s, new ways of thinking about organizations found

expression in a new system of training called organization development (OD). OD as a process for understanding and changing human
systems derived from the earlier developments of academic and corporate researchers in laboratory training, survey and action research,
and feedback techniques (French, 1985). A variety of interventions
soon evolved to facilitate human relationships, to modify the tech-
nostructure, and to enhance the management of human resources
(Huse and Cummings, 1985). Team building, quality of worklife,
and career development and planning programs were among the
most popular and widely adopted of these interventions.

Information on the exact number of employees receiving
training, on the number of companies providing it, and on the cost
of training is not reliable (Eurich, 1990). Estimates on the number
of employees in training range from 14 to 35.5 million workers; the
higher estimate places about one-third of the workforce in training.
In spite of the expenditures and the development of corporate learning systems, Census Bureau data indicate that in the mid 1980s,
employers provided formal job training to only 10 percent of their
employees and formal training for upgrading skills to only 11 percent (Carnevale, Gainer, and Villet, 1990). Unevenly distributed,
training opportunities are concentrated in large companies and
more often in high-tech and manufacturing companies; the 48 percent of the workforce employed in small companies are less likely
to receive training. Training is also unequally distributed across job
classifications: management, professionals, and technicians receive
most of the training, clerical workers receive the least. Only recently
have programs in workplace literacy been initiated to address the
needs of those lacking basic skills (Eurich, 1990).

Corporate education and training systems do not exist in
isolation from the larger social and economic conditions that are
related to education. The War on Poverty made clear the importance of economics for individual and social well-being: individuals
cannot advance without jobs, and they contribute to society only if
they are economically productive. President Johnson's 1968 State of
the Union address called upon the private sector to provide training
for work, and the National Alliance of Businessmen was formed
that year to marshal business support. In the 1960s, differently prepared employees entered the workforce, including adults with low

levels of literacy and other educational disadvantages. The private-public relationship was further strengthened through the Comprehensive Employment Training Act and its successor, the Job Training Partnership Act, which give employers considerable input into decisions about government-sponsored training.

In the 1970s and 1980s, the fears about the perceived inability of the United States to compete in a global economic sphere turned concern about the capabilities of workers into a national crisis. Public education bore the brunt of the criticism for its putative failure to prepare youth for work. In spite of the outcry, human resource development remains a loosely coupled system comprising corporations, government, and educational institutions whose training and education programs overlap but are not integrated. Corporations meet some of their human resource development needs through in-house programs, but other needs are met through linkages with community colleges and universities and through programs offered by public schools, vocational training schools, proprietary schools, community-based organizations, and associations (Carnevale, Gainer, and Villet, 1990; Eurich, 1985).

Every new organizational function requires specialized personnel for its management, and long before the present expansion in training, the professionalization process began. In 1942, the state organizations of training directors formed the American Society of Training Directors, renamed the American Society for Training and Development (ASTD) in 1945. The training field expanded rapidly and ASTD became the flagship organization for trainers. From a membership of almost four thousand in 1959 and six thousand in 1967, ASTD's membership increased to fifty thousand national and local memberships by 1989 (Watkins, 1989). The professionalization process moved slowly but gained momentum as the field of training expanded into human resource development. By 1970, the concept of human resource development (HRD) began to replace training and development as the central concept and broadened the function to include consultation and organizational problem solving. Developments in the 1980s included a 1983 ASTD study that identified areas of practice and competencies needed for training and development functions; expanded the concept of human resource development into the three domains of training and development, organization development, and career development; explored certification programs for HRD practitioners; and developed models for graduate professional programs. In 1989, Watkins (p. 42) observed that "the training of trainers is itself a massive educational undertaking" as only 8 percent of trainers had degrees in HRD.

Labor Education

Postwar labor education moved markedly away from the social and economic reform aims, multiagency sponsorship, and alliance with liberal intellectuals that characterized the 1920s and 1930s. Narrowing its functions, labor education focused on helping trade unions meet their organizational and personnel needs and working in partnership with corporations to secure economic benefits for union members. In this redefinition of function, labor education became institutionalized within trade unions and universities (Denker, 1981).

Greater involvement of colleges and universities produced a near revolutionary change in labor education (Freeman and Brickner, 1990). University labor studies grew out of industrial relations study programs that began in major private and state universities in the 1930s and 1940s (Denker, 1981). Labor education leaders believed that labor and management had different goals, and that labor education should therefore establish an identity separate from industrial relations. In 1945, at the American Labor Education Service Conference, labor education leaders began the process of creating a separate institutional identity in the university for labor education. Unions were identified as the clientele of labor education studies programs, which would address the need of unions for trained personnel to direct specialized services (Denker, 1981).

To provide leadership for labor studies programs, labor studies professors and others organized the University Labor Education Association, which became the University and College Labor Education Association in the mid 1970s in recognition of the greater involvement of community colleges. Colleges and universities initiated long-term certificate programs and noncredit, liberal arts collaborative programs such as Cornell University's "liberal-arts-for-labor program" (Barton, 1982). Degree-granting programs soon followed: in 1965, the University of Massachusetts offered the first master's degree in labor studies and in 1967, Rutgers the first bachelor's degree. (Rutgers later developed a master's and doctor of education degree.) About forty-seven colleges now offer a concentration or major in labor studies. Community colleges also began offering two-year associate degree programs in labor studies, and by 1977, the number had grown to about forty.

Unions also actively negotiated education and training for their members (Levine and Hutton, 1980) and served as prime contractors for Department of Labor training programs that served 265,000 individuals with awards totaling $185 million. Unions have included apprenticeship and on-the-job training in collective bargain agreements. In 1964, the United Auto Workers negotiated the first tuition refund programs with the three major automobile manufacturers. By 1978, unions had negotiated twenty-one educational trust funds in which employers contribute to a fund managed by a board of trustees. Education became a service, along with legal services, health, and counseling, that is negotiated as part of the contract. The growth of public employee unions in the 1960s stimulated the spread of this new welfare service model. Many union members were women and people of color who held dead-end jobs and needed assistance in job advancement (Aronowitz, 1990). As a striking example of this phenomenon, District Council 7 of the American Federation of State, County, and Municipal Employees negotiated with New York City in 1969 to establish an educational fund. The union then organized its own college as an undergraduate division of the College of New Rochelle.

Women unionists, long denied places in the union structure, found support in the women's movement to advocate for women's concerns (Wertheimer, 1981). Some unions created a special department or enlarged existing departments to address these issues, and university labor studies programs gave greater attention to women's concerns. The United Auto Workers and the International Union of Electrical Workers led in initiating programs for women (Johnson and Komer, 1981). The Electrical Workers began its work in 1957 by sponsoring the National Women's Conference, and in 1972, it created a women's department in the Social Action Department to serve as a liaison between the national, district, and local unions.

The Coalition of Labor Union Women, organized in 1974 to secure the collective interests of women, provided education on such subjects as how to campaign for union office and how to deal with sexual harassment.

At the national level, the AFL-CIO conducts education through its Department of Education; others, such as the Department of Social Security and the Department of Community Services, conduct education related to their functions. The AFL-CIO established the George Meany Labor Studies Center in Silver Spring, Maryland, to provide training for the staffs of national unions associated with the AFL-CIO. Through the School for Adult and Experiential Learning of Antioch University in Yellow Springs, Ohio, the center offers an external bachelor's degree.

Education, however, has not become a priority for trade unions. U.S. Department of Labor data of the early 1970s showed that there were 175 national and international unions in the United States with about 21 million members. Of these trade unions, only about 25 percent had established an education department (Mackenzie, 1976).

Summary

The new "sight and sound" medium of commercial television replaced radio as the most popular medium of informal learning; public radio and television provided alternative programming but reached a more limited audience. Public libraries struggled to find a compelling educational direction and to adapt to the new information age, while museums aggressively promoted their educational role. The knowledge explosion, Great Society programs, global economic competition, and the emerging postindustrial society called for new responses from educational agencies and economic institutions to train skilled workers and provide continuing education. Universities, community colleges, and public schools offered new programs for new clients through both traditional and innovative delivery systems. Education became continuing, pervasive, and increasingly central to the mission of the professions, the military, government, business and industry, and labor unions.

17

Adult Education's Critical and Conserving Functions

From the end of the war in 1945 until the early 1990s when the Soviet Union dissolved, the perceived threat of communism and America's world leadership role dominated American political, economic, and social concerns. So strong was the commitment to anticommunism that any criticism of the American way of life appeared unpatriotic. Economic interests overrode other concerns as "the safeguarding of the environment, the use of nuclear energy, public versus private sector interests, etc., received short shrift" (Schiller, 1989, p. 25). Yet many Americans questioned and challenged assumptions about American social structure and foreign policy decisions. Rachel Carson's *Silent Spring* alerted the public to the danger of pesticides, and Ralph Nader's *Unsafe at Any Speed* warned of unsafe consumer products. Around the issues of civil rights, the women's movement, the environment, consumer rights, nuclear energy, and the Vietnam war, citizen concerns escalated into organized movements that combined social criticism, informal adult learning, and action.

Challenges to the Hierarchies

The civil rights, women's rights, and community organizing movements challenged the prevailing hierarchies of race, gender, and class in postwar America. This challenge required movement leaders and participants to overcome their own longstanding acquiescence to subordination perpetuated through socialization and maintained by laws. Leaders used many strategies to achieve movement goals, but processes of informal learning, as in earlier democratic social movements, informed and empowered participants to appreciate their own worth, the validity of their cause, and their abilities to change the system.

The Civil Rights Movement

On December 1, 1955, in Montgomery, Alabama, Rosa Parks's arrest for refusing to sit in the back of the bus sparked the Montgomery protest and set in motion the modern civil rights movement. African Americans organized the Montgomery Improvement Association to direct the protest and chose the Rev. Martin Luther King, Jr., as president. King and the other leaders confronted two critical educational tasks in turning the passive masses into protestors with a strategy. The Fellowship of Reconciliation assisted King and others in the Montgomery protest to understand and use nonviolence. The fellowship and the Congress of Racial Equality had acquired both theoretical and practical knowledge of nonviolent protest and had used it in direct action. Rev. Glenn E. Smiley of the fellowship came to Montgomery early in the protest and taught the masses, King, Ralph Abernathy, and other leaders who knew little about nonviolence. During this period, King accepted nonviolence as the way. In the weekly mass meetings, participants were trained in nonviolence as the strategy of social change, literature on nonviolence was distributed, and participants learned through role play how to anticipate and respond to hostile behavior. Leaders from other cities came to Montgomery to learn strategies of nonviolence and of mass protest movements. From the Montgomery movement emerged the concept of the "nonviolent workshop" and a team of persons expert in strategies of nonviolence who traveled to the South to places where protest was emerging (Morris, 1984).

A second education task centered on turning passive people into protestors. This called for a fundamental change in how African Americans understood their relationship to white society. In the face of social and economic oppression, the African-American church had taught them to be passive. From this theology, however, King and others derived a latent protest message that became the theological justification for protest: religion should stop being indifferent to social conditions and become a militant force in society (Morris, 1984).

Other educational support came from outside the African-American community through the Highlander Folk School's civil rights movement leadership training and creation of the Citizenship School Program (Glen, 1988; Horton, 1989; Morris, 1984; Tjerandsen, 1980). In the 1950s, Highlander brought African Americans and white southern leaders together in integrated meetings. Participants from both races identified problems in the community. Of particular concern to the Highlander staff was helping African Americans understand that only they could end the oppression. Rosa Parks was a participant in one of these workshops. Highlander also reached out to black and white college students with weekend workshops beginning in 1954. In February 1960, African-American students at North Carolina A&T College in Greensboro sparked a massive protest when they attempted to eat at a lunch counter. At the seventh workshop for college students held at Highlander the following April, Horton and others led the African-American students to articulate their philosophy, their attitudes toward nonviolence, and their social goals. The Student Nonviolent Coordinating Committee (SNCC), a student organization proposed at the workshop, was created two weeks later in a meeting called by the Southern Christian Leadership Conference (SCLC).

Another Highlander project that proved central to the civil rights movement was the Community Leadership Training Program on Johns Island, South Carolina, led by residents Esau Jenkins and Septima Clark; it resulted in the establishment of the Citizenship School Program there. African Americans who had achieved respect in the community but were not certified as public school teachers were selected to teach. School leaders believed that the ability to relate to adults and to use innovative methods was more important than formal training. Literacy skills were taught using subject matter chosen to alert African Americans to their political obligations.

The program spread to other states. Highlander, antici- pating that segregationist opposition would force its closing, transferred the Citizenship School Program to the SCLC, organized in 1957 to give political direction to black churches enlisted in the civil rights movement. The SCLC secured funding from the Mar- shall Field Foundation, renaming it the Citizenship Education Pro- gram, and used the Citizenship Education Program as the educational base to create a mass protest movement to obtain the right to vote. The SCLC organized schools and training programs in which teachers learned not only how to teach people to read and write but also how to protest and challenge power and its distribu- tion in the community. When teachers returned to their commun- ities, they taught African Americans how to work for their rights in a democracy.

Women's Rights

Women reformers coalesced around women's issues in 1961 when President Kennedy established the Presidential Commission on the Status of Women, which became "perhaps the most important land- mark on the way to greater political influence and a new feminist consciousness for the reformers" (Wandersee, 1988, p. 16). In 1963, Betty Friedan's *The Feminine Mystique* provided the catalyst for the women's movement. Friedan called for women unfulfilled by home and family to create a life of their own. Women disappointed with the commission and inspired by Friedan's work formed a separate organization for women. Incorporated in 1966 with tremendous growth during the late 1960s and early 1970s, the National Orga- nization for Women (NOW) provided national leadership for the women's movement. Task forces studied and developed national policy on such issues as "poverty, minority women and women's rights, labor unions and working women, the image of women, textbooks, marriage and divorce, employment, sports, child care, and sexuality and lesbianism . . . " (Wandersee, 1988, p. 47). In lo- cal chapters, women organized task forces to meet their own agendas.

NOW reformers pursued a political, activist course through demonstrations, a nationwide Strike for Equality on the fiftieth anniversary of the passage of the Nineteenth Amendment, and annual conventions. In 1977, the First National Women's Conference held in Houston adopted a twenty-six-plank national plan; the main plank called for adoption of the Equal Rights Amendment (ERA), which at that time enjoyed national and bipartisan political support.

Another wing of the women's movement known as cultural or "radical" feminism located the source of women's oppression in the patriarchal system. Early in the movement, a powerful educational process emerged to enable women to examine their oppression. The first consciousness-raising group reportedly grew out of a radical women's group in New York. After the women shared their experience at the First National Women's Liberation Conference in November 1968, consciousness-raising groups mushroomed (Hart, 1990). The process appears simple in its explanation, but in operation it became an instrument of personal liberation, a research method, and the basis for theory building. Several principles governed the methods used in consciousness-raising groups: women shared personal experiences in a group context—important in order to validate the subjective experiences—and then used these experiences to understand female oppression in a larger sociopolitical context.

Several gender-related issues concerned with women's control of their bodies became the focus for study, organization, and action. Women created their own educational programs, rape crisis centers, and health collectives. Rape emerged as an issue in the 1970s, and Susan Brownmiller's *Against Our Will: Men, Women, and Rape* offered a feminist interpretation of rape. Rape crisis centers, of which about four hundred existed by the mid 1970s, used education as a central strategy, and political education and consciousness raising were at the heart of the educational effort. The Boston Women's Health Book Collective began as a course in which women at first shared their experiences but then conducted research on their own bodies. In 1970, *Women and Their Bodies: A Course* resulted; a revised edition published in 1973 as *Our Bodies, Ourselves* became a best-seller and a textbook for the self-education of women. Under successive revisions as the women's movement matured, *Our Bodies, Ourselves* moved away from "objective" medical knowledge to interpretations derived from "a woman-centered culture" (Kahn, 1990, p. 122).

The liberal and radical feminist challenge to traditional knowledge about women brought a counter movement by the New Right, which reasserted traditional beliefs about male-female relationships, birth control, abortion, and the ERA. Phyllis Schlafly led the fight against the ERA, creating the National Committee to Stop ERA and the *Eagle Forum Newsletter* and linking the ERA with lesbianism and abortion. In 1973, the Supreme Court's decision on *Roe* v. *Wade* struck down laws against abortion, and several single-issue groups formed in opposition to promote antiabortion legislation. Some branches of the antiabortion movement opposed the feminist movement positions not just about the fetus, but about relationships between men and women, issues concerning family and children, women's employment, and the ERA.

Informal Political Education for Social Change

Community organizing entailed a process of informal political education in which persons learned to identify their own interests, to collect information, to confront the community and political power structure, and to collaborate to attain results. A major force in community organizing was Saul Alinsky and his Industrial Areas Foundation (IAF). In 1947, Alinsky organized the Community Service Organization (CSO) in California. In 1953, the Schwarzhaupt Foundation awarded the CSO a grant to intensify its efforts to address discrimination against Mexican Americans. A coordinator was hired and local units were organized through house meetings. In the first projects, English and citizenship education were taught and voter registration drives were organized. Learning occurred as part of action projects, and leaders were trained informally by organizers in relation to their functions rather than in formal leadership meetings. A three-year grant, beginning in 1955, funded an educational program led by experienced community organizers; it focused on helping members learn to think about issues in a broader social, economic, and political context (Tjerandsen, 1980).

Cesar Chavez, a CSO organizer and later a member of the national board, used the CSO model as he organized the United

Farm Workers Union. Believing that the CSO had become dominated by middle-class interests, Chavez adopted many of its features for the union, including house meetings for organizing; programs built on the social, economic, and political interests of workers; service centers; and workers' control of the program (Tjerandsen, 1980).

After Alinsky's death in 1972, the IAF began to connect its organizing efforts with community institutions through a process called "value-based organizing" (Boyte, 1989, p. 81). The IAF came to regard the community organizations they created as "schools of public life," "self-funded citizen organizations where people learn the arts and skills of a politics far more multidimensional than voting" (Boyte, 1989, p. 81). In major community organizing projects such as COPS in San Antonio, BUILD in Baltimore, EBC in New York City, and UNO in Los Angeles, IAF created these schools of public life, which returned power to citizens unable due to their lack of skills and of knowledge about public affairs to influence the political process.

These social movements challenging the hierarchies of race, gender, and class used educational processes to overcome the passivity of the disenfranchised, to inform them about societal structures, and to develop their skills for action. Even though this form of education might properly be called civic education, it did not fit the traditional pattern of civic education, which accepted rather than challenged social structures.

Civic and Community Life

From the late 1940s to 1980, adult education theorists, working within and on behalf of the social system, refined and expanded a programmatic theory of community development as a form of adult education. In the 1940s, they also began to formulate a philosophy of citizenship for community development education, articulating a vocation of citizenship and defining the competencies required of citizens in a democracy (Stubblefield, 1981a). Adult education theorists were only one of the groups interested in adult civic education.

Adult civic education took many forms, ranging from study discussion groups to community action. This "mainstream" civic education involved primarily the well-educated, white, middle class, whose study of foreign and domestic issues was expected to produce the well-informed citizen. Metropolitan and regional citizen leagues promoted research and education on policy issues as well as open public discussion (Oliver, 1983). The Twin Cities Citizens League of Minneapolis-St. Paul, founded in 1952, grew to three thousand dues-paying members and four hundred organizational members. The league at first sponsored public forums, later engaged in direct action to secure school improvement, and now helps set the agenda of public issues to be discussed, conducts research, and holds public forums.

The Cold War demonstrated the complexity of foreign affairs as a topic of study. In 1918, the Foreign Policy Association had been created as a membership organization to work for United States membership in the League of Nations. In 1955 after the Korean War, it created the Great Decisions program. Issues were selected in early summer, materials produced and made available in January for discussions held in February and March. Community organizations such as women's clubs, libraries, and senior centers sponsored the discussions; other major sponsors include seventy World Affairs Councils affiliated with the association (Oliver, 1983).

In the 1950s, the Ford Foundation created several semi-independent subsidiaries to develop and implement programs related to national and international concerns, including education (Sutton, 1987). As an associate director of the foundation, Robert Hutchins, formerly president of the University of Chicago and founder of the Great Books Foundation, developed the educational programs. The foundation created the Fund for Adult Education and provided 47.4 million over a ten-year period (1951–1961) for its activities. Focusing exclusively on liberal adult education rather than on the entire field of adult education, the fund exercised considerable influence on adult liberal education. Among the first to recognize the educational potential of television, fund officers provided grants for early developmental work in the educational uses of this new medium. Of particular interest to the fund was the development of liberal education for business and union leaders, assisted through grants to both business and labor organizations. From 1951 to 1961, the fund provided for the research and programmatic efforts of the Center for the Study of Liberal Education for Adults. Operating as a "think-tank" in adult liberal education, the center's publications remain an enduring legacy of the fund. The fund's generous support of the Adult Education Association of the U.S.A. is responsible for such innovative projects as the *Adult Leadership* magazine, but, as Chapter Eighteen shows, the fund's insistence that projects be oriented toward liberal education diverted the association's attention from the interests of the larger field of adult education.

The fund also developed and implemented its own experimental discussion projects (Fund for Adult Education, 1961). To anchor programs in local communities, it initiated a test cities program in twelve cities that in turn experimented with different ways of delivering liberal adult education through newly created councils or universities. Fearful that the threats posed by Soviet achievements in space would challenge the American way of life, in 1958 the fund turned attention to what it called "education for public responsibility," providing grants to national organizations to conduct conferences, presenting an awards program in 1959 and 1960 for the best speeches and articles about public responsibility, and producing mass media projects on television and radio. In the late 1950s, the Ford Foundation reconsidered the feasibility of operating programs through semi-independent subsidiaries. In 1961, the fund made final long-term grants to several organizations and programs it had been supporting, then disbanded.

Under the auspices of the federal and state governments, the National Endowment for the Humanities (NEH) established state humanities councils to promote discussion of public policy and to bring academics into contact with citizens. For the 1976 bicentennial, the NEH sponsored the American Issues Forum to promote a national discussion of issues through one thousand forums across the country, which were attended by an estimated 100,000 persons; the NEH also sponsored a series of programs on public television and radio and courses published lesson by lesson in newspapers. In 1977–78, the NEH sponsored more than twelve hundred National Energy Forums, which were coordinated by four hundred community colleges in ten regions and conducted by local community leaders and organizations.

To provide a domestic counterpart to the Foreign Policy Association, fourteen national organizations and foundations organized the Domestic Policy Association. In 1981, the Domestic Policy Association, with major sponsorship from the Kettering Foundation, initiated the National Issues Forum. The forum sought to bridge the gap between the policy maker and the citizen, to inform the citizen, and to influence public policy. Meaningful participation by citizens in policy decision making requires that they have the ability to make good judgments about policy options (Yankelovich, 1991). Along with Kettering, the Public Agenda Foundation and Brown University's Center for Foreign Policy Development have moved beyond the traditional lecture-discussion or study-discussion to develop methods to assist citizens in working through their own ambivalences and values to reach an informed judgment. David Matthews of Kettering used the term "choicework" to describe the process of "working through" and resolution (Yankelovich, 1991, p. 246). A key methodological task was to build a bridge between expert opinion and public opinion. The National Issues Forum achieves this by preparing three special books each year. Experts translate technical data and theoretical ideas into language that nonspecialists can understand. In community forums or smaller study circles, participants use an iterative process to work through their differences over issues. At the conclusion of these discussions, participants complete opinion questionnaires, which are relayed to policy makers.

In the 1970s, Americans emulated forms of Scandinavian folk education and the study circle. The Folk Education Association of America was founded in the mid 1970s to advance nonformal learning programs in the format of folk schools, study circles, and community-based programs (Spicer, 1991). Folk education assisted individuals and groups in community problem solving, in redressing social injustice, and in personal growth. The Swedish study circle idea was brought to the United States in 1978 by Norman Kurland of the New York State Board of Education. The New York State Study Circle Consortium disseminated the concept and offered study circles to help people learn for the sake of learning or engage in community problem solving. The Study Circles Resource Center, organized in 1988 as a national clearinghouse and resource center, provides materials on study circles. Among the organizations using this method is the International Union of the Bricklayers and Allied Craftsmen. In 1986, the union initiated a study circle program as the centerpiece of a member education program in order to gain greater member participation in union affairs and relevant social issues (Oliver, 1987).

Values for Adult Living

Movements for adult education formed around perceived threats to, or dysfunctional features of, American society. Three of these combined content, method, and social purpose to promote skills for democracy, to develop human potential, and to foster the values of western civilization.

Resocializing Roles

The interests of social scientists and adult educators combined in 1946 to create a new social practice known as laboratory training. Kurt Lewin, "the intellectual father of NTL," the National Training Laboratory in Group Development (Hirsch, 1987, p. 114), Ronald Lippitt, Leland Bradford, and Kenneth Benne derived the principles of laboratory training from their earlier theoretical work in group dynamics, leadership styles, and the work conference as a group problem-solving process (Benne, 1964). They first implemented these principles in 1946 at a workshop at State Teachers College in New Britain, Connecticut, to promote research about groups and to train leaders to comply with the Fair Employment Practices Act in local communities. At the workshop, the staff recognized that examining "here and now" events—processing the interactions in the group meetings—could be a powerful tool for reeducation. A second workshop held in 1947 in Bethel, Maine, incorporated this new insight. The NTL of the National Education Association was organized, administered as a program in the National Education Association's Division of Adult Education.

NTL's initial efforts focused on leadership development and group dynamics research and their uses for social change. The founders regarded the two educational innovations of "T-group" (training group) and laboratory education as "a venture in adult education" (Bradford, Gibb, and Benne, 1964, p. 4). Adults were, they believed, poorly prepared to cope with the changes wrought by physical sciences and technology. Through laboratory training, adults would gain new behavioral skills to handle changes in social structures and a new understanding of the group as the link between the individual and larger social structures. The laboratory method incorporated the perspectives of different disciplines, but at its core it remained a method of reeducation and planned change for human systems (Benne, 1975).

In the 1950s, NTL began to move away from the focus on social issues and political responsibility to organizational development and personal growth. It developed a new constituency of business and corporate clients who wanted to use organizational development to serve their business interests, a move that many believe took NTL into bureaucratic structures that were undemocratic and hierarchical and in support of corporative practices of "racism, sexism, and class exploitation" (Hirsch, 1987, pp. 48–49). An emphasis on personal growth was incorporated into laboratory training by the Western Training Lab, an NTL regional laboratory in California. The NTL summer programs at Bethel soon included personal growth groups, which became known as "sensitivity training" and found a ready audience in a society that was mobile, affluent, and secular. It rapidly became a movement concerned with "the need for new forms of self-expression and interpersonal relations" (Back, 1972, p. 32).

Achieving Potential

Sensitivity training as a kind of laboratory training formed part of the human potential movement that began in the 1960s and flourished in the 1970s and 1980s. Abraham Maslow and other "Third Force" psychologists who believed in the almost unlimited potential for "self-actualization" provided the intellectual leadership. Michael Murphy and Richard Price founded Esalen Institute as a place where the best of Western and Eastern culture could come together, and in the summer of 1962, Esalen began its summer Human Potentiality series, a term they learned from Aldous Huxley. In 1963, the three main features of Esalen's program were established: encounter groups, gestalt therapy, and body awareness. Esalen became the "cultural midwife," a meeting place of ideas and a center for developing new therapies (Anderson, 1983). By the early 1970s, Esalen had developed a nationwide reputation and the human potential movement was under way (Anderson, 1983). But what kind of movement was it?

George Brown, professor of education at the University of California, Santa Barbara, interpreted Esalen's work not as psychotherapy, as some had argued, but as "adult 'compensatory' education" (Anderson, 1983, p. 190). Adults came to Esalen and to the other growth centers to learn what they had failed to learn as children and youth: to integrate the body and mind and to get in touch with their feelings.

In the 1970s, ideas generated by the movement, combined with marketing, transformed the human potential movement into marketplace psychology, which "took off as a mass cultural phenomenon on its own" (Ehrenreich and English, 1978, pp. 302–303). The core idea of marketplace psychology is that individuals are responsible only for their own feelings, and relationships become a product to be developed, used, and discarded when they are no longer useful. Baby boomers entering their twenties in the 1970s became the mass audience for the personal growth industry, and they turned to self-help best-sellers such as *I'm OK—You're OK, How to Be Your Own Best Friend,* and *What Color Is Your Parachute?* for guidance to adult life. While some books were popular treatments of established therapies, an antiscientific and antiintellectual bias characterized marketplace psychology. Anyone could become an expert, and no scientific evidence was needed to establish the validity of the new therapies—for self-esteem, friendships, or sexual relationships—that were introduced to the American public. Popular psychology's "most revolutionary message was for women" (Ehrenreich and English, 1978, p. 297), and it addressed the new status of women, who were moving out of stable family relationships into a singles culture and a competitive economic environment. The message was that marketplace values were universal and applied to women. The values of love and caring had

no place. Assertiveness training became the new therapy for social-
izing women into less passive roles.

Sharing in the Great Conversation

Mortimer Adler and Robert Hutchins adapted the ancient idea of
education through book reading as a new form of adult education
in their Great Books reading program, which gained widespread
dissemination in the late 1940s and 1950s. In the 1920s, Mortimer
Adler brought the idea of the great books to the University of Chicago's President Hutchins; it was based on his experience in John
Erskine's general honors course at Columbia University and on his
work with an adult education model at the People's Institute in
New York City. In 1947, the Great Books idea began to spread, and
in less than a year, more than forty-three thousand persons in three
hundred cities were members of Great Books clubs. The movement
flourished through the 1950s and began to decline in the 1960s.
Adults had turned to Great Books clubs after the war as a "quest
for permanence and meaning in a world rendered transient and
confusing by the Second World War" (Rubin, 1992, p. 191).

    Adler and Hutchins made the great books the basis for a new
general education program, but they also quickly extended the idea
beyond the university into a program of adult education (Adler,
1977). Adler originally brought the idea, structured as a systematic
educational plan for adults, to the American public with the 1940
publication of *How to Read a Book*. Adler and Hutchins gained
favorable publicity when they organized and led a great books discussion with Chicago businessmen and their wives. A program conducted by the University College of the University of Chicago and
the Chicago Public Library demonstrated the feasibility of laypeo-
ple leading great books discussion groups. Traveling around the
country between 1945 and 1947, Adler spread the idea. The Great
Books Foundation, organized in 1947, made reprint editions of the
great books available for discussion groups and directed the network of Great Books clubs that began to form in 1946. In 1952, the
foundation published *Great Books of the Western World* in fifty-
four volumes; a two-volume *Syntopicon* provided an index to show
the unity of the ideas contained in the great books.

The Great Books clubs represented a humanistic education rooted in philosophy and metaphysics, and they connected adults to a tradition. As an adult education program, the Great Books clubs had shortcomings: a lay person led the discussion, and participants read the books without benefit of contextual materials. The popularity of the program diminished as the role of humanities in education diminished with the emergence of the postindustrial society. The critical and analytical skills that the humanists had claimed as their own were now employed in practical activities. Adherence to humanistic values seemed to require a commitment to self-discipline and a willingness to sacrifice for a cause. Such values had no place in a period dominated by the search for self-fulfillment and psychological discovery (Allen, 1983).

The Aging Society

Education about aging and education for older adults are dimensions of a larger social policy that has relegated older adults to the private sphere. "The coming of an aging society is a new historical event," writes Harry R. Moody (1988, p. 1), and American society has been ill prepared to deal with it. Industrial society made it possible for more Americans to reach old age but also segmented the human life course into the stages of youth, adulthood, and old age.

Interest in education for the older population emerged in the 1950s. A new field of university study and social practice called educational gerontology developed in response to the increasing proportion of the population sixty-five and older. It reflected concern for quality of life for older adults, recognition that this group has potential, and awareness of the need for trained personnel in gerontology (Peterson, 1985). Educators in the field of adult and continuing education were among the first to recognize the growth potential of older adults. The Adult Education Association of the U.S.A. organized a section on education for the aging and aged in 1951 and began a publication program that Peterson (1983, p. 28) credits with providing "much of our knowledge of activities before 1970." Howard Y. McClusky, professor of adult education at the University of Michigan, had a great impact on the development of the field, particularly through his paper on the educational needs of the older population, delivered at the 1971 White House Conference on Aging. In 1976, a new journal, *Educational Gerontology*, became the principal instrument for disseminating research and practices about education for aging and aged.

Programmatically, education for aging and older adults can be characterized as diverse in supporting philosophy, content, and institutional delivery systems. The Older Americans Act of 1965, since reauthorized several times, provided for federal, state, and local sharing for education, training, and research for older adults. In the 1970s, community colleges began offering programs for older adults under grants from the Administration on Aging in the Department of Health, Education, and Welfare. A new summer residential educational program housed on university campuses and resort centers, the Elderhostel, began in 1975 and has continued to grow and expand and is now considered an adult educational movement, demonstrating that older adults will commit time and money to serious study of liberal arts and civic education directed toward self-actualization. Universities such as Fordham and Harvard have established programs for older adults; other programs, such as Society Expeditions in Seattle and the University of Pittsburgh's Institute of Shipboard Education, combine travel and learning. Organized in 1971, Earthwatch matches amateur volunteers with scientific expeditions. Elders interested in education are retiring to college towns so they can have access to intellectual and cultural centers (Dychtwald and Flower, 1989).

Adult Religious Education and New Social Realities

During World War II, the interest of Americans in their religious heritage intensified, building after the war to a religious revival that continued until the 1960s. An increase in church affiliation and participation in the institutional life of churches and synagogues marked this resurgence, as church affiliation grew from 50 percent of the American people in 1950 to 69 percent in 1960 before declining to about 62 percent in 1970 (Ahlstrom, 1972).

Americans seeking security turned to renewed forms of revivalism and religion for peace of mind. Billy Graham became the most widely known spokesman for conservative evangelism and, through the Billy Graham Evangelistic Association (1950), used the mass media—"advertising, television, radio, paperback books, and cinema"—to disseminate his message (Ahlstrom, 1972, p. 957). To the insecure, religious best-sellers brought the message of religion as peace of mind (Ahlstrom, 1972). A Reform rabbi, Joshua Loth Liebman, applied Freudian psychology to problems of modern life in a book that became a best-seller, *Peace of Mind* (1946). Norman Vincent Peale, the most popular of the peace-of-mind inspirationalists, reached millions through *Guide to Confident Living* (1948) and *The Power of Positive Thinking* (1952).

In the flush of the postwar religious revival and its aftermath, Protestants, Catholics, and Jews reached their adult constituencies through a variety of educational activities, distinct programs for adults and activities used by church organizations and interest groups to support specific missions. In the 1950s, in their educational programs, Protestants began to use group techniques developed in the fields of adult education and group dynamics (Miller, 1960). The Department of Administration and Leadership of the National Council of Churches started the "Protestant Laboratory on Group Development" at Green Lake, Wisconsin, to train leaders in principles of laboratory learning. During five years of research in the local churches of several denominations, Paul Bergevin and John McKinley developed an intensive group training and program planning institute called the Indiana Plan for Adult Religious Education. Through the institute format, adults explored the meaning of their religious faith, assessed their growth in communication skills and personal development, learned how to conduct group discussions, and developed strategies for applying their new skills to other groups in the church and community. For these achievements, observers of Protestant adult religious education called the Indiana Plan one of the most important innovations of the 1950s (Kathan, 1977; Miller, 1960; Stokes, 1970). In 1958 and 1961, workshops on the Christian education of adults held at the University of Pittsburgh brought together denominational leaders and secular educationists to examine research, adult education methods, and programmatic assumptions.

Among evangelical Protestants, the Sunday school remained the prominent agency of adult education. Leadership for the evan-

gelical emphasis came from the National Association of Evangel-
icals-sponsored National Sunday School Association in 1945,
renamed the National Christian Education Association in 1980. Organized to revitalize a declining Sunday school and to counter liberal theology, the association developed a new uniform lesson series
focused on the Bible and the evangelical emphasis.

The adult education programs of mainstream Protestant denominations advanced along several lines. In the 1960s, adult education was no longer just Bible study for adults but was used as a
means of church renewal through small-group study of theology
and culture. Several denominations produced study materials especially for adults, and churches found new methods of outreach:
Bible study on commuter trains, coffee houses for the unaffiliated,
study of the religious implications of drama, and action-reflection
on social issues. The Paulist Press and the National Council of
Churches created guidelines for "living room dialogues," in which
small groups of persons of different denominations met to develop
mutual understanding. In the 1970s, greater attention was directed
toward meeting life-span needs. Research on adult development
revealed new opportunities for study related to sexuality, vocation,
and the aging process, and programming addressed the needs of
subgroups within the church: singles, women, never-marrieds, single parents, homosexuals, and the physically and mentally handicapped (Stokes, 1970, 1977).

Catholic adult education was conducted through the numerous Catholic organizations that incorporated an educational purpose: special group ministries, adult education centers, and parish
programs. Postwar Catholics "believed that all segments of American society needed the benefits of a Catholic influence" (Dolan,
1985, p. 391). They became aggressive in outreach through study
groups for non-Catholics and the media. Bishop Fulton J. Sheen's
"Life is Worth Living" broadcast from 1951 to 1957 reached an
audience of thirty million. In 1950, the lay-led Christian Family
Movement focused on the family in relation to society; by 1958, it
had a membership of thirty thousand couples, representing a shift
from the central place of the parish to "special-interest apostolates
with national organizations" (Dolan, 1985, p. 396). An experimental liberal education program to assist adults with concerns about
faith began in 1955 with the founding of the Catholic Adult Edu-

cation Center in Chicago; by 1969, the program had expanded from five local centers to twelve. Each center employed a coordinator trained in adult religious education who worked with several parishes. The idea spread to other parts of the country, but the centers ceased to be needed as parishes began to operate their own adult education programs (Stokes, 1970). At the national level, the National Catholic Adult Education Association was organized in 1958, but lack of support reduced it to a department of the National Catholic Education Association in 1972. The establishment of a Division of Adult Education by the United States Catholic Conference in 1970 marked a transition in Catholic adult education as more parish directors of religious education began to work with adults and more directors were appointed for adult religious education (Elias, 1982, pp. 140-144).

The Second Vatican Council (1962-1965) elevated adult education to a new level of importance in the Catholic church. New educational programs were needed to help Catholics learn a new liturgy, a more participative form of governance, a new emphasis on language of scripture and existential theology, and a greater personal responsibility in applying moral codes to themselves and to their own situations (Schaefer, 1977). A more inclusive view of education, going beyond a narrow focus on schools and children to include adults, resulted in new educative agencies. Training adults to teach the young became an important way of educating adults in the church. Short-term learning communities were created to help adults deal with affective levels of knowledge for marriage relationships, spiritual renewal, divorce, and bereavement. Justice and peace offices established around the country prepared curricula and offered workshops to help individuals become responsible for human needs. In the 1970s, 160 of the 167 dioceses in the United States had a "diocesan director" of adult education (Schaefer, 1977).

In the aftermath of the war, adult Jewish education—education for Jewish identity, heritage, values, and contemporary interests—became an important part of the Jewish community (Cohen, 1967, 1977). In the 1950s, national Jewish organizations began "specialized adult Jewish education programs" (Cohen, 1967, p. 108), and by 1964, twenty such organizations had specialized programs. B'nai B'rith, the American Jewish Congress, and the American Jewish Committee organized departments and committees for Jewish adult education programs after the war. Influenced by the field of general adult education, they belonged to the Council of National Organizations of the Adult Education Association, a national coordinating agency for volunteer organizations engaged in adult education (Cohen, 1967). This interest culminated in 1965, when eighteen national organizations convened the First National Conference on Adult Religious Education. In addition to national organizations, the three thousand synagogues in the United States claimed some form of adult Jewish education, and the four thousand Young Men's Hebrew Associations and Jewish community centers, with a total of two million members, sponsored programs.

Summary

The civil rights movement used informal learning processes to teach a strategy for protest, to foster literacy skills, and to promote citizenship education. The social reform wing of the women's rights movement pursued an activist agenda through task forces, demonstrations, and conferences, while feminists used consciousness-raising groups, and other study and action programs addressed gender-related issues regarding control of women's bodies. New processes for reeducation in adulthood were fostered through the laboratory learning and human potential movement, and the Great Books movement offered an education in the values of Western civilization.

Education for citizenship took the forms of informal political education to challenge the power structure, mainstream civic education to create the well-informed citizen, and folk education for personal and social empowerment. The older adult population became a new client group for educators, who generated programs for training, liberal education, and recreational learning. Among the three major religious groups, Protestants continued to use the Sunday school but created new forms and programs to address social issues, adult development needs, and the needs of subgroups in their adult constituency; with the impetus of the Second Vatican Council, adult education achieved new importance among Catholics; and the Jewish communities fostered Jewish identity, heritage, and interests through heightened attention to adult education.

18

Crafting a National Agenda
for Adult Education

Efforts to bring organizational, conceptual, and policy coherence to the numerous educational activities of adults began in the progressive era in the late nineteenth century. In the 1920s and 1930s, the Carnegie Corporation and the American Association for Adult Education sought to foster conceptual coherence by popularizing the term *adult education*. The Americanization movement, the emergency educational programs of the New Deal, and the World War II military and civilian educational programs demonstrated that large-scale adult education activities were feasible. These programs also demonstrated that educational interventions into the lives of adults could be used to advance federal policy goals.

In the post-World War II period, as in earlier periods, institutions and agencies, all with different agendas, sought to give direction to adult education. The organizations included professional associations, philanthropic foundations, educational testing services, the federal government, and corporations. Major efforts centered around organizational, conceptual, and policy concerns: what organizational structure, if any, could bring the various segments of the field into a cooperative relation? What concept could best fit the changing nature and role of the education of adults and perhaps become a rallying point for coordinated national planning? How should public resources be allocated and how should such decisions be made? The 1980s would end without definitive answers.

Unifying the Forces

Collaboration among major adult education organizations began in April 1946, when the first national conference of adult education national organizations was held in Detroit. Participating organizations were the AAAE, the Department of Adult Education of the National Education Association, the Adult Education Board of the American Library Association, the Educational Film Library Association, and the National University Extension Association (Knowles, 1977). Conference participants identified several national policy issues related to postwar readjustment that transcended the special interests of the separate associations—namely, the educational tasks related to returning veterans, conversion to a peacetime economy, social and technological changes, and the international situation.

Collaboration continued after the conference through the creation of the Joint Committee for the Study of Adult Education Policies, Principles, and Practices, comprising representatives of the five organizations that had sponsored the Detroit conference. The committee met in October 1946 to determine its function and identify major problems that could form the agenda for collaborative work among the cooperating organizations (Knowles, 1977). Some problems pertained to programmatic and operational concerns shared by the cooperating organizations, but others touched more deeply on the problems of American life: developing competent citizens, creating awareness of the need for continued learning, clarifying the relation between general adult education and vocational education, and addressing the special needs of the illiterate, handicapped, and foreign born. The Joint Committee changed its name to the Joint Commission for the Study of Adult Education and enlarged its representation, but it considered itself only a temporary organization with the purposes of promoting cooperation among agencies, encouraging research, and defining common policies. The commission's recommendation that the AAAE and the National

Education Association's Department of Adult Education combine to form a national organization set that merger in motion.

Forming a National Organization

In the early 1940s, leaders of the two organizations had considered collaborative activities but reached no agreements. By the late 1940s, both organizations had changed considerably. Without Carnegie Corporation support, the AAAE was moribund, having failed to adjust to its changing financial situation, to the changing conditions of adult education, and to the request of members for a more democratic governance structure. The Department of Adult Education had, on the other hand, enlarged its membership base to include personnel in nonpublic school institutions, involved members in national and regional meetings, covered a wide spectrum of topics in the *Adult Education Bulletin,* and permitted nonpublic school adult educators to assume leadership positions. In 1947, the National Training Laboratories, a pioneer in the application of group dynamics to adult education, had affiliated with the National Education Association's Department of Adult Education. When negotiations began in 1949, the association represented not only the traditional public school constituency but a nonpublic school constituency as well (Luke, 1992; Stubblefield, 1990).

Planning for a new national organization began in December 1949, culminating in the founding of the Adult Education Association of the U.S.A. (AEA) in May 1951 at Columbus, Ohio, and the first national conference, held in October 1951 in Los Angeles. The planners had left many matters undecided, including how to finance the association, until the functions had been identified. Events, however, did not permit an evolutionary development. At the organizational meeting, representatives of the Ford Foundation's newly organized Fund for Adult Education appeared with the offer of grants. Created to support liberal adult education, the fund brought money for programmatic and administrative support and a conception of adult education that emphasized liberal education. Conflicts over adult education as liberal education, applied group dynamics, or community development would divide the association and make its goal of giving direction to the field of adult education difficult, if not impossible.

Leaders of the new association wanted to unify the profession of adult education, with the AEA serving other organizations engaged in adult education. But the AEA also believed that an adult education movement had to be built from the community level up, not from the national level down. Adult education in its many varieties could not be an effective instrument for social progress if the national organization functioned as a professional society or interagency planning council. Rather, the leaders regarded adult education as a popular movement that needed organizational expression. Operationally, that meant strengthening community adult education by establishing programs, and a communications network among them, in every community. A market for adult education at the grass-roots level would result. At the community level, the public school system was clearly the principal agency, and in support of this effort, the Fund for Adult Education gave grants to create positions for state directors of adult education and to strengthen the ability of the public schools to promote liberal education, including strengthening the relationships among city, county, state, and regional organizations. With this funding, the AEA created the Area Organization and Conference Project (1952–1955). Based on surveys and fact-finding conferences, the project recommended that frequent fact-finding conferences among agencies and the appointment of AEA field consultants would facilitate interagency collaboration.

Beyond these obvious constituencies, the AEA reached out, through *Adult Leadership,* a magazine liberally supported by the fund, to a variety of institutions and organizations that worked with adults but did not identify their work as adult education: executives and supervisors in workplaces (who used adult education to achieve their goals) and leaders in voluntary organizations (who developed educational programs). Focusing on a specific theme each issue, the magazine disseminated the educational methods of the applied group dynamics movement on topics such as program development and implementation, working with small groups, social change, and community development. The magazine found an audience, but few subscribers committed themselves to the broader field of adult education by joining the AEA.

The AEA had assumed that there were many professionals and nonprofessionals representing various specializations who would welcome an opportunity to participate in the common fellowship of the AEA, through which they could promote common goals and gain new competencies. They would, in effect, come to regard their work as a social practice and not just as an institutional operation. A mass recruitment effort among selected populations of adult educators resulted in a membership of over thirteen thousand by 1955. When mass recruitment drives were discontinued, membership fell to 3,500 in 1961 (Knowles, 1962, p. 223).

A major task entailed carving out a unique position for the AEA among the other national adult education organizations. The AEA asserted that because of its focus on a general concept of adult education and not on a specific segment, it could provide leadership in promoting a common philosophy, research, interassociational communication, and policies. Mechanisms for interassociational cooperation remained undeveloped, with the exception of the Council of National Organizations and the National Association of Public School Adult Educators, both bound to the AEA, at least partially, as recipients of Fund for Adult Education grants channelled through the AEA.

The organization of the National Association of Public School Adult Educators in 1952 demonstrates the difficulty of serving the professional interests of adult educators in an institutional setting through a general membership organization concerned with the total field. Public school administrators, disappointed previously with the applied group dynamics emphasis of Leland Bradford, quickly came to believe that the AEA would not address their interests in the practical matters of administration and teaching (Luke, 1992). Their fears were reinforced with *Adult Leadership* magazine's group dynamics focus. Organized under the auspices of the NEA, the association remained an affiliate; while cooperating in AEA projects, it began to hold a separate national convention and and to promote the interests of public schools in adult education.

By 1954, Malcolm Knowles, the executive director of AEA, framed the idea of an adult education movement in practical terms and articulated achievable goals (Stubblefield, 1990)—for example, engaging all workers in adult education in a common fellowship and making the local community the focus of adult education (which we have already discussed). Some goals addressed status issues: securing acceptance of adult education as the fourth level of the national educational system and increasing research in adult education to produce as much knowledge about adult learning and behavior as already existed about children. Another goal was to make educational opportunities for socially required competencies available to everyone at public expense.

In 1958, having decided that the AEA had neither achieved its goal of becoming *the* national organization for the field nor was capable of doing so, the fund discontinued grants for general support and special projects. The AEA, like its predecessor, the AAAE, could not continue its ambitious agenda without foundation support; it became dependent on members, not on a professional staff, to carry out its activities. In 1958, as yet unaware of its vulnerability, the AEA rejected an opportunity to merge with the then-smaller American Society for Training and Development (Luke, 1992). The society, an organization for workplace education, became the largest adult education organization in the country. The AEA continued operation until 1982, when it merged with the National Association for Public Continuing and Adult Education (the former National Association of Public School Adult Educators organization) to form the American Association for Adult and Continuing Education (AAACE). Since 1958, the AEA/AAACE membership has hovered between three thousand and thirty-five hundred.

The AEA's failure to become the prime national organization in the field does not diminish its achievements and continuing contribution through AAACE. Among its important achievements was the creation of a scholarly apparatus for graduate education and the dissemination of research. The AEA's Commission of Professors of Adult Education developed the conceptual base for graduate professional study in *Adult Education: Outlines of an Emerging Field of University Study* (Jensen, Liveright, and Hallenbeck, 1964), and through its annual meetings it nourished the development of adult education professors. The AEA/AAACE established and continues to publish the only research journal in the field, *Adult Education*, now the *Adult Education Quarterly*. A comprehensive perspective on adult education is kept before the public, educational professionals, and policy makers through the Handbook series published each decade. In 1959, the National Seminar on Adult Education Research evolved into the Adult Education Research Conference, which continues to meet annually.

Direction Through a Coalition

Following the AEA's diminished role, a coalition of adult education organizations assumed responsibility for creating a national agenda for adult education. Communication among national adult education organizations began in 1961 when Syracuse University convened a meeting, attended by seventeen organizations, for consultation on its newly developed program on adult education materials. Discovering that they really knew little about each other, the participants established an organization known by various names but most often called the Committee of Adult Education Organizations. Some thirty-four organizations participated in the meetings, which were held from 1961 to 1969. The meetings culminated in 1969, when twenty of the adult education organizations participated in the Galaxy Conference in December 1969 in Washington, D.C. Eight held their annual conference, and others held official meetings. To promote agreement on the tasks of adult education, delegates to the conference approved a resolution called "Imperatives for Action" (Charters, 1971).

The "Imperatives for Action," prepared by representatives of the organizations a month earlier at the Wingspread Conference, called for creating a system of lifelong learning to empower adults to make wise choices in their role as decision makers (Charters, 1971). Opportunities for learning, said the report, should be so widespread that lifelong learning would became "an all pervasive influence" (Charters, 1971, p. 49). Pragmatically, the delegates recognized that their goals could not be achieved without political action, which required that the Coalition of Adult Education Organizations be strengthened. The goals to reduce the educational deficiencies of adults and to increase educational opportunities for undereducated adults reflect the influence of the War on Poverty.

Other goals, calling for financial support, federal government leadership, and organizational cooperation, addressed institutional needs and continued the earlier call of the AEA to make adult education an equal partner with other levels of education.

The bicentennial year, 1976, provided the occasion for the second Wingspread Conference, sponsored by the Coalition of Adult Education Organizations with funding from the W. K. Kellogg Foundation. Intending at first to update the 1969 Imperatives for Action statement, coalition planners upon further reflection decided that the emerging conception of adult education as one part of a lifelong learning process and as a force for social change had rendered the 1969 imperatives out of date. The new "Imperatives for Action" statement, approved at the 1976 conference, regarded adulthood as a time of change and development and the societal context of adult life as complex and in flux. The undereducated, the poor, the aging, women, and minorities needed easier access. Participants also recognized that work and education should be linked more effectively. In contrast to the 1969 imperatives, the 1976 report made the needs of learners, not those of institutions, the focus of planning. Learners should use educational resources, educational opportunities should become more accessible, and information and counseling assistance should be readily available. Other needs, addressed in previous studies, remained: expanding public awareness about learning opportunities and resources, increasing public and private financial support, enlarging the scope of research, and improving coordination of human and organizational resources ("Imperatives for Policy and Action in Lifelong Learning," 1976).

Having produced a new "Imperatives for Action," the coalition could not decide what to do with the report. Some members proposed seeking a second grant from Kellogg to disseminate the report in regional conferences. This project, they argued, would give the member organizations an opportunity to work on a common goal so they could seek unity. Working through grass-roots meetings would create a national dialogue on lifelong learning. The Adult Education Association, the National University Extension Association, and the Association of University Evening Colleges, perhaps afraid that the coalition if engaged in such action would become a competing organization, objected. The coalition desisted, but had it chosen to take the report to local communities and adult education organizations, it would have invited practitioners, community leaders, adult learners, and citizens to participate in the policy process. That grass-roots participation in the policy process would have influenced the direction of the evolving learning society remains doubtful. Nevertheless, an opportunity was lost.

Attracting Government Attention

Nothing resembling a comprehensive federal government policy on adult education would emerge in the almost half-century following the war. Federal initiatives in adult education after World War II began with modest interventions, escalated into a massive intervention in the Great Society education programs, but gradually diminished as a conservative agenda displaced the social reform impulse.

Early Initiatives

The Servicemen's Readjustment Act of 1944, popularly known as the GI Bill, provided educational benefits that in seven years resulted in the enrollment of nearly eight million returning veterans in higher education, public schools, and vocational schools. In addition to stemming the influx of veterans into the job market, the benefits opened higher education to the masses, providing financial support for all, regardless of family origin and economic circumstances (Ravitch, 1983). The more than two million veterans who attended colleges and universities broke the age barrier and also demonstrated that adult students had academic ability and scholarly intent. The educational benefits also produced skilled workers, professionals, and managers for the growing economy (Chafe, 1991; Perrett, 1985).

   In a second initiative, the President's Commission on Higher Education, appointed in 1946 by Truman at the request of the American Council on Education, published *Higher Education for American Democracy* in 1948 to address the role of higher education in meeting the manpower needs of the postwar period. The report noted that the impact of science, technology, and industrialization required that higher education be made available for everyone who had the ability, and the commission believed that the American people had ability. Almost half of the population, the commission estimated, could complete fourteen years of education, and one-third or more could complete advanced professional or liberal education degrees. Such optimism stands in marked contrast to the pessimism over the mental ability of the average adult that dominated in the post–World War I period. In expanding higher education opportunities, the commission called for redefining the role of two-year colleges to move beyond serving as adjuncts to universities or as "junior" colleges or extensions of high schools to become community colleges addressing the needs of local communities (Ravitch, 1983).

Expansion of adult and higher education opportunities soon reached its limits, however, when Congress considered creating a Labor Extension Service within the Department of Labor (Bowman, 1979). The idea for a federally sponsored labor education program grew out of the desire of labor education leaders to continue the work that had begun in the Workers' Service Program of the WPA. The National Committee for the Extension of Labor Education was established in 1945 to promote the creation of a labor extension service in the Department of Labor. A Labor Extension Act drafted in 1947 received bipartisan congressional support in both houses and support from all organized labor. Disagreements soon surfaced among the principal organizational sponsors over issues of administration, control, and the role of federal government in labor education. Accusations of subversive activities in the University of Michigan labor education program at the 1948 House hearings raised questions about the potentially subversive aspects of workers' education. Though the charges were not true, the fear remained, and the program at Michigan was closed. When Congress adjourned in the fall of 1950 without taking action on the bill, the National Committee disbanded for lack of funds and discontinued efforts to secure a labor education extension program.

Expanding the Federal Role

In the early 1960s, the Kennedy administration made a modest commitment to job training programs in the passage of the 1961 Area

Redevelopment Act and the 1962 Manpower Development Training Act. But massive federal intervention awaited President Lyndon Johnson's declaration of the War on Poverty in 1964. The "war" brought together the issues of race and poverty and used adult education as an instrument for social amelioration. Earlier, Michael Harrington's *The Other America* (1962) brought poverty to America's attention and shattered both the myth that America was a classless society and the belief among social scientists that economic prosperity would eradicate poverty. About fifty million persons in America were poor; among them were "the aged, the unskilled, the women heading households with small children, and others who were bound to be bypassed no matter how much economic growth occurred, because of the way that the system distributed income" (Murray, 1984, p. 28). African Americans constituted a large percentage of the poor, and they had not shared in the economic prosperity of post-World War II America. In the changing American economy, the poor could no longer advance through manual or semiskilled jobs. New employment opportunities created by increased production were closed to them because they lacked "education or training in technological skills" (Chafe, 1991, p. 237).

Planners of the War on Poverty chose to target individuals and the conditions that held them in poverty rather than deficiencies in the social and economic structure, and education played a major role. The Economic Opportunity Act of 1964—the centerpiece of the War on Poverty—addressed poverty through community action, manpower development, and literacy programs. Taking ideas from earlier federal and foundation community programs for juvenile delinquency, the Community Action Program focused primarily on poor urban African Americans, making them participants in the planning and management of their own local community programs. Programs were implemented through the local Community Action Agencies whose task was "to sponsor neighborhood self-help projects, promote social action, mobilize local resources, and coordinate local programs" (Fisher, 1984, p. 111). Southern and urban politicians objected to not having control over the monies and to the idea of blacks and the poor having control. Legislation passed between 1966 and 1968 began to restrict the activities of the local Community Action Agencies, and President Nixon's New Federalism, which replaced grants-in-aid with block grants, brought an end to the War on Poverty (Fisher, 1984).

To treat the illiteracy problem, the Economic Opportunity Act established the Adult Basic Education Program, which moved to the Office of Education with the passage of the Adult Education Act of 1966. This program provided appropriations to the states to conduct adult basic and secondary-level programs for persons eighteen years and older; it also provided for staff development and demonstration projects. The Reagan administration wanted greater state and private voluntary responsibility for literacy and a lesser role for the federal government. This program survived, however, and remains as the principal federal program—three million adults served in 1988—for adult basic education and high school completion (Beder, 1991). The definition of literacy that guided policy was reduced to literacy for functional role performance. The report of the Adult Performance Level project in 1975 provided the basis for a competency-based curriculum organized around the broad functional areas adults need in order to function adequately in society.

To bring the poor into the economy, the Economic Opportunity Act mandated training programs for the unemployed and those with low income. After the initial development of programs, federal policy for training began to shift toward consolidation, decentralization, and greater corporate involvement (Hamilton, 1990). In 1967, all the programs for depressed rural and urban areas administered by the Department of Labor were brought together in the Concentrated Employment Program. These included the Manpower Development Training Act, Neighborhood Youth Corps, Operation Mainstream, New Careers, Comprehensive Work and Training, Work Incentive, and JOBS. The Comprehensive Employment Training Act of 1973 (CETA) signaled a shift toward the decentralization of training to increase the responsibility of states and localities. Further decentralization occurred when the Job Training Partnership Act of 1982 replaced CETA. The job training programs became the responsibility of state governors, and business and industry joined the state as partners. The 1985 funding exceeded $3.5 billion.

In the mid 1960s, the conflict over the Vietnam war polarized the nation. The United States proved unequal to the twin tasks of eradicating poverty and establishing social justice and winning the war against communism abroad (Hodgson, 1978). With the assassinations of Martin Luther King and Robert Kennedy and the divisions over the war in Vietnam, the dominance of the reform movement ended. When Nixon was elected in 1968, political conservatism returned and remained until the 1990s. This ended the potential of the American social reform movements "to transform American society and to alter fundamental values of the dominant culture" (Chafe, 1991, p. viii).

Toward a Cooperative Relationship

Accompanying the initiatives for programs for the poor came greater federal participation in general adult education. Legislation created national advisory councils in adult education, continuing and extension education, and community education, all of which were disbanded in the 1980s. Two services established in the U.S. Office of Education greatly facilitated the gathering of statistics about adult education participation, programs, and resources: established in 1965, the National Center for Education Statistics began to collect data about participants and programs, and the Educational Resources Information Center created the Clearinghouse on Adult, Career, and Vocational Education, first at Syracuse University, then at Northern Illinois University, and later at Ohio State University.

In the late 1960s, the U.S. Office of Education addressed policy issues regarding general adult education by commissioning the Center for the Study of Liberal Education for Adults to survey the field of adult education and to make recommendations for action. A. A. Liveright's report (1968) paralleled earlier positions of the adult education community in calling for strengthening a national system of adult education that required both practitioner action and federal government leadership. His recommendations applied to the existing policy and administrative structure of adult education at the governmental and institutional level. At the commissioning of the study in 1966, Liveright along with others had anticipated growing federal involvement in adult education, but by the report's publication in 1968, the federal government had become preoccu-

pied with financing the war in Vietnam and combating racial unrest in the cities. The report had to be privately printed because the
Office of Education lacked money.

From Adult Education to Lifelong Learning

In the 1970s, a new vocabulary was introduced into policy considerations. Lifelong learning replaced adult education as the organizing concept. The term *lifelong learning* was the uniquely American
variation of a rethinking of educational policy that occurred in
UNESCO, the Council of Europe, and the Organization for Economic Cooperation and Development. Each organization's agenda
for educational policy reform differed, each developed a different
master concept for planning, and each master concept stimulated
reform. UNESCO adopted the term *lifelong education*; the Council
of Europe, the term *permanent education*; the Organization for Economic Organization and Cooperation, the term *recurrent education. Learning To Be,* the 1972 report of the International Commission on the Development of Education chaired by Edgar Faure,
brought this reconceptionalization of education policy to a wider
audience of educators, policy makers, and interested citizens. The
world created by science and technology, the commission concluded, required extending education throughout the lifespan and
creating a new pedagogy to encompass continual learning in adulthood. The commission called for lifelong learning to be adopted as
the master concept for planning.

Policy makers in the United States used these ideas in discussions about policy but neither adopted the master concepts nor used
them as the basis for creating an agenda for national policy reform.
A further restriction applied as well, for Americans erroneously
used the term *lifelong learning* as a synonym for adult education.
Using the term *lifelong learning,* the federal government, higher
education institutions and their national associations, national testing corporations, and foundations sought to create a national
agenda. Enthusiasts claimed that lifelong learning entailed a new
societal arrangement called the "learning society." However, Norman Kurland (1976), a staff member of the State Education Department of New York and a leader in lifelong learning reform,

describes a more modest agenda: "What should evolve . . . might best be thought of, not as a lifelong learning 'system,' but as a broad array of services in support of lifelong learning" (p. 10).

When then-Senator Walter Mondale introduced the Lifelong Learning Act as an amendment to the 1976 Higher Education Act, the educational community saw this as an opportunity to secure federal support for adult education and orchestrated a lobbying campaign to secure passage of the bill (Stewart, 1978). Leaders of the national adult education organizations, who would later prevent the dissemination of the Coalition of Adult Education Organizations' Second Wingspread "Imperatives for Action," had no reservations about the federal government taking a leadership role. The victory proved hollow: Congress authorized no appropriations, limiting implementation to instructing the assistant commissioner of education to submit a report by January 1, 1978. The language of the act provided a broad mandate for significant federal action, but the report of the Lifelong Learning Project, *Lifelong Learning and Public Policy* (1978), was only suggestive, singling out workers, urban youth, women, and older adults as groups with special needs that called for policy decisions. In reality, the term *lifelong learning* sounded more like a slogan than a description of a substantive concept. The whole process contained a major flaw, as Penelope L. Richardson (1979), the project coordinator, later noted: "In short, though the phrase 'lifelong education' is more likely to make the heart leap up than 'adult education,' inherently it has no particular theory of societal or individual good, and it offers no guidelines for policy makers or decision makers at any level" (p. 97).

Three other reports, issued in 1978 and 1979, projected the shape of a learning society. The Exxon Education Foundation funded projects conducted by the College Entrance Examination Board and the Educational Testing Service. The College Board's *Future Directions for a Learning Society* (1978) reported on several studies related to implementing more research, serving adults in transition, and creating more effective linkages between higher education institutions and adult learners. The project was later incorporated as a program within the College Board. The Educational Testing Service study (Peterson and Associates, 1979) on lifelong learning in America sought to map the field of postsecondary learning for program planners and directors, policy makers, and analysts. The report concluded that lifelong learning could best be implemented at the local level through a coordinating organization the authors called a Community Lifelong Learning Council. The National Institute for Education and the Ford Foundation funded a project on Financing Learning Opportunities for Adults (Windham, Kurland, and Levinsohn, 1978), which examined how to finance a lifelong learning policy, which was the most critical issue and the one on which policy floundered.

Several motives existed, some partly self-serving and self-protective. Educational institutions wanted to compensate for the declining student market (in the traditional age range) and to gather wider support by enlarging the umbrella of organized education to include museums, libraries, and community agencies. They also recognized that the educational system as it presently operated did not adequately address pressing problems such as the deficiencies in the early education of a larger number of adults—the 1977 census report estimated that one in five adults was functionally illiterate. A second problem was how to restructure the relationship between work and education. Under the proposed lifelong system, persons would be permitted to leave secondary and postsecondary education to enter the world of work and then return to education. Such a system would address the dropout problem. Youth who were not stimulated by school would be permitted to leave; when, in their work experience, they had acquired their own reasons for learning, they would return to formal education ready to learn. A system that permitted adults to alternate between education and work would provide for workforce retraining and education. A third problem was how to deal with the complexity of a modern society that required continuing learning, particularly in fields in which lateral job changes were commonplace and work more demanding.

The term *lifelong learning*—like *adult education*—proved too vague an idea for policy formation, but it did signal a shift in the locus of responsibility for learning in the adult years. Formerly, adults pursued education as a personal interest, but the changing requirements for continuing education had made learning in the adult years a matter of public interest. As such, considerable responsibility for leadership and finances belonged to government at the federal, state, and local levels. The federal government did not lack involvement in lifelong learning—it sponsored hundreds of lifelong learning programs. But federal activities lacked coordination (Hartle and Kutner, 1979). Unfortunately for advocates of systematic planning for lifelong learning, escalating national interest coincided with diminished federal resources in the late 1970s and with diminished federal responsibility for social needs under Reagan in the 1980s.

Adult Education and the Postindustrial Society

A new rallying point for policy considerations derived from a societal transformation variously known as the postindustrial society, the knowledge economy, and the service economy. Another factor was the diminished economic strength of the United States in the world economy (Moses, 1971). A new agenda formed around the crisis in workforce preparation, and corporations discussed ways to resolve this crisis. Public education came under severe attack, and a 1980 study declared that deficiencies in public education had put the nation at risk in the international economic market. However, the workforce crisis was not only a public education crisis but an adult learning crisis as well.

The transformation that became so apparent to the various segments of American society in the 1980s had been recognized and described as early as the 1950s by several observers of American commercial and social life (Bell, 1976; Clark, 1964; Drucker, 1978; Machlup, 1962; Toffler, 1971). They observed that work had shifted from goods-producing industries to service- and knowledge-producing industries. An economy driven by knowledge and technology made continuing education a condition for maintaining occupational competence. Changes in the economic exchanges affect all other domains of society and require continuing learning for maintaining parental, technical, social, cultural, and political competence. Such a society continually pushes individuals to the brink of "obsolescence and disorientation" (Clark, 1964, p. 15). "Ours is an educative society," writes Burton Clark in 1964, "and we are undoubtedly on the threshold of an age of adult education" (p. 16).

A society in transition raises new questions concerning

which domains of human activity will gain "social legitimation for adult learning," and as the United States entered the 1990s, attention was clearly focused on the economy (U.S. Department of Health, Education, and Welfare, 1972, p. 45). Other aspects of the postindustrial society were also domains of adult learning that received varying degrees of social recognition and transformation into public policy: quality of life, control of human behavior and genetic manipulation by science and technology, alternative lifestyles and the nature of the family, citizen participation in a society dominated by large organizations and experts, the meaning of work, the definition of literacy, and global interdependence. An industrial society regarded adult education as a social service to be distributed, but the postindustrial society regarded learning as a mode of adaptation for individuals and groups and "the key capital-forming industry of the postindustrial economy" (Choate, 1984, p. xi).

Summary

In the 1950s, the adult education community and segments of the philanthropic community sought to shape the field of adult education, establish it as an educational domain, and give it direction. In the 1960s, the federal government used adult education in the service of distributive social justice to address a crisis in race and class through the War on Poverty. In the 1970s, the education and philanthropic communities sought to gain recognition of lifelong learning as a master concept for planning and organizing services in support of adult learning. A transition to the postindustrial society made continuing learning an imperative and opened new discussion about bringing more domains of adult learning under the purview of adult education. In the 1980s, the workforce crisis became the catalyst for educational action.

Conclusion

Becoming Responsive to the Needs of All Learners

Forms of adult education are, in reality, social innovations through which an individual, organization, or government seeks to accomplish certain purposes. This book has presented a historical reconnaissance of the many events, activities, and actors that comprised this domain from the precolonizing period to the late twentieth century. While bound by the constraints of space, our approach has been first to complement earlier and more limited treatments of the colonial and antebellum period and second to bring coherence to the "adult educational jumble" (Adams, 1944, p. 128) of the late nineteenth and twentieth centuries. We have sought to widen the context of important issues and to recognize the strength of much revisionist criticism of earlier accounts. As current interest in the field produces more informed monographs, it will be possible to frame and answer even more questions.

One recurring issue that we have addressed is the issue of educational opportunity. America is considered the "land of opportunity" and its citizens have an often unbridled faith in education, but nevertheless, some people have failed to realize their ambitions. Dissatisfaction prompted many social reform movements and produced questions on the ideology and control of education. Since education had apparently furthered the careers of some individuals, why and how were others excluded from its benefits? Was education more an instrument for the stratification of opportunity than for its promotion? Such questions remain with us, hence the value of historical insights in contributing to their in-depth study and resolution.

Admittedly, this reconnaissance is more descriptive of events, activities, and the people involved than explanatory of causes. Nonetheless, understanding such a diffuse social phenomenon as adult education begins with a description of occurrences, which provides the basis for a preliminary mapping of adult education in American life. Running through this narrative are two themes that appear contradictory but in reality reflect a long-standing and still unresolved tension. In many respects, adult education continually became a more open and expansive system; at the same time, however, the social realities of race, gender, class, ethnicity, and religion restricted access to these opportunities.

An Open and Expanding System

The English transplanted to the colonies both a hierarchical social system and an activist educational system of home, school, church, print, and associations. Relatively few information systems existed, however, and many of these were accessible only to those with social status. After 1790, learning and public information systems became widespread and available to the many and not just the few (Brown, 1989). Access to public information and education became a necessary response to a government based on an informed citizenry and to a new "social hierarchy based on achievement rather than heredity" (Brown, 1989, p. 293). Public opinion emerged, with individuals voicing their thoughts on art, politics, religion, and the economy. These various forms of expression competed in an open society (Bailyn, 1977).

In commercial expansion, individuals found opportunity for success through hard work and initiative. The belief that success could be achieved in this new, open social and economic system gave rise to the myth of the self-made man. The conviction that individuals were responsible for their own success gave rise to the ideology of self-improvement and of educative systems to disseminate "useful knowledge" and to foster "self-culture." The individual's role in a socially, economically, and politically competitive society determined what knowledge was necessary, and educative systems expanded in response. The impetus for more information was supplied not just by technology but by the rise of individualism (Brown, 1989).

Individualism had limitations, and a rich and varied associational life emerged to enable individuals to pursue interests they shared in common but could only achieve by collective action. Between the spheres dominated by government and business there was a third sphere in which action depended upon the organized efforts of individuals and groups. By the time of de Tocqueville's visit to the United States in the 1830s, voluntary associations were extensive and embedded in American life. Through these associations, adults could act for themselves and for others who lacked resources or who were judged to need the guidance of the dominant culture. Some associations sought to advance a specifically educational agenda, but others used education to support the creation of utopian communities or to advance reform. Americans energetically set about to promote education, reform the prison system, care for the poor and disabled, and advocate temperance, peace, rights of women, and abolition (Tyler, [1944] 1962). The first half of the nineteenth century set the pattern for an adult education in which voluntary associations built around study and action promoted selected causes.

Forms of adult education evolved in response to changing conditions. Increases in scientific knowledge and technological applications brought change in work processes and workplace culture. Apprenticeship in an artisan culture yielded to formal vocational education in the industrial economy, and the knowledge economy would extend education for work throughout the adult years. Knowledge about the natural sciences and the social sciences changed how persons understood themselves, their relationship to others, and their place in the cosmos. The great experiments of the early and mid-nineteenth century—the lyceum, the mechanics' institutes, and the lecture movement—spread general knowledge and culture, as did the chautauquas, university extension, and world fairs of the late nineteenth and early twentieth centuries. In the second decade of the twentieth century, federal legislation created a national system of agricultural education through the Cooperative

Extension Service and vocational education for adults through the public schools. An expanded university extension system and urban evening colleges made higher education more accessible, and the explosion of community colleges after the second world war brought higher education within commuting distance for most adults. Access to knowledge became less dependent on one's range of social relationships and more available through the mass media of newspapers, magazines, and books that informed about current affairs and provided materials for self-education. The "sight and sound" culture of radio, motion pictures, and television supplemented the print media and further democratized access. Before we can judge the potential of new electronic telecommunications for providing universal access, questions of control and cost must be answered.

Americans learned because there was knowledge to master, technology to adapt, and life's uncertainties to be resolved. They also learned because of an ideology of self-improvement that spoke to the importance of learning and the promise of education for advancement. In several periods of knowledge expansion and social dislocation—the era of Jacksonian democracy, the progressive reform era, the 1920s, and the immediate post–World War II period— the era was an intensification of adult learning and education.

A pluralistic society generated differentiated systems of education and information diffusion. Certain visionaries however identified certain knowledge, values, and ideas that they believed should be held in common by all. Their efforts grew into national movements, taking form in lyceums and lectures, chautauquas, university extension, forums, and Great Books. Toward the end of the nineteenth century, the idea of adult education as a specific form or level of education appeared. Beginning in the 1920s, national organizations and coalitions of national organizations sought to gain support for, and give direction to, these differentiated systems. Arguments for adult education centered on various interpretations of the role of education under a democratic form of government, in a democratic associational life, and in a capitalistic economy. Eventually, education to enhance the productive activities of adults gained national ascendancy.

Paradox and Promise

In a democratic and putative classless society, there would seem to be little disagreement about the rights of all citizens to have access to knowledge. In reality, many factors circumscribed access to education and thus diminished social and occupational mobility. In the colonial majority culture, the assumption was that one received an education deemed appropriate to one's place in society—a place circumscribed by such considerations as social class, gender, religion, race, and ethnicity. With independence had come the expectation that all this was to change. However, the proclaimed egalitarianism of the new nation was to prove hollow when applied to adult education, with paradoxical commitments to cultural independence, progress, and the maintenance of the status quo. Such policies would continue, since educational opportunities were determined by one's "station in life." Education deemed suitable for women, Native Americans, African Americans, workers, and immigrants were intended to keep these groups in their subservient relationship to the majority culture.

Unwilling to accept such limitations, these groups created alternative educative systems to challenge both their ascribed station and the rationale used by the majority culture to restrict their access to civic and economic rights. Therefore, in addition to official educative systems for self-improvement and productive skills, a new form of adult education emerged, which sometimes compensated for the shortcomings of the education offered by the majority culture and at other times challenged the dominant culture's denigrating ideology of gender, race, ethnicity, and class. Many had to find educational opportunities not in the mainstream institutions of culture, education, and work, but in associations they organized themselves or with the assistance of reformers. These democratic social movements gave birth to new educational forms that nourished the liberatory and educational aspirations of women, African Americans, Native Americans, workers, farmers, and immigrants. The new social and education history of the post–World War II era has recognized the legitimacy of their protests and the central role of education in their efforts; until recently, this tradition of adult education lay submerged.

In the last quarter of the nineteenth century, the forces of industrialization, urbanization, immigration, and migration transformed American society and ushered in a new era of adult education to ameliorate the dislocations these new forces created. The ameliorative uses of adult education—prominent in progressive reform ideology—found expression in the new institutions of university extension, settlement houses and social centers, national women's clubs, and organizations for Americanization. A signal shift in adult education occurred with the emergence of the "new" social sciences, expert professors, and the research university. Professional knowledge challenged the conventional and traditional knowledge that governed many domains of human life, and experts claimed superior ability to teach proper performance of social roles previously learned through emulation of experienced practitioners.

Americans used adult education to advance national agendas through short-term interventions, but these were not part of a long-range plan of national support. In the Americanization movement of 1915–1924, a pervasive fear of immigrants and foreign ideas left little faith in amelioration, and adult education became coercive and propagandist to manipulate public opinion. Twice the federal government intervened with national adult education programs in times of social dislocation but without formulating a long-term public policy. In the New Deal, millions of Americans previously unserved by adult education programs benefited from the emergency education relief effort. Subsidized programs in general and vocational education for adults with limited resources—the poor, African Americans, Native Americans, workers—contributed to their personal welfare and to the nation's. Similarly, the 1960s War on Poverty attacked the problems of poverty and race through education but did not address the structural causes. Once again, Americans demonstrated their faith in expert knowledge and education as the central components of social reform. In the War on Poverty, however, the broad-based vocational, cultural, and educational programs of the New Deal gave way to a more narrow focus on literacy and vocational training. In the 1970s and 1980s, the educational requirements of an information society, global economic competition, and continuing poverty raised new questions about the adequacy of education provided at all age levels. Particularly vulnerable in this society are the unskilled and semiskilled, the illiterate, and the undereducated. Limited resources—their own and those provided by government—restrict their opportunities for education and training. Persons in the resource-rich corporations and military, particularly technical workers and managers, find more adequate provision.

Adult education in the United States has been and remains a diverse activity. Many interpretations of its history are possible, depending on the vantage point from which one begins. Adult education emerged not as a form of a definable system such as schooling or higher education but in the form of definable educative systems. These educative systems ranged from the relatively simple systems created by individuals to pursue learning goals to the more complex organizational systems of family, religious and educational institutions, voluntary and cultural organizations, racial and ethnic groups, and the workplace. Estimates can only be made of the largely unrecorded efforts of persons, individually and in small groups, who have sought to improve themselves or society through educative activities pursued independently. These efforts encompassed a variety of objectives and motives. In some instances, institutions and individuals used adult education to further reformative and evolutionary change, and in other situations, they used education to maintain existing social, economic, and racial relationships.

References

Adams, E. C. *American Indian Education: Government Schools and Economic Progress.* New York: King's Crown Press, 1946.

Adams, F. *Unearthing Seeds of Fire: The Idea of Highlander.* Winston-Salem, N.C.: John F. Blair, 1975.

Adams, J. T. *Frontiers of American Culture: A Study of Adult Education in a Democracy.* New York: Charles Scribner's Sons, 1944.

Addams, J. *Twenty Years at Hull House.* New York: New American Library, 1961. (Originally published 1910.)

Adler, M. J. *Philosopher at Large: An Intellectual Autobiography.* New York: Macmillan, 1977.

Ahlstrom, S. E. *A Religious History of the American People.* New Haven, Conn.: Yale University Press, 1972.

Aiken, J. *Labor and Wages at Home and Abroad.* Lowell, Mass.: D. Bixby, 1849.

Akenson, J. E., and Neufeldt, H. G. "The Southern Literacy Campaign for Black Adults in the Early Twentieth Century." In H. G. Neufeldt and L. McGee (eds.), *Education of the African American Adult: An Historical Overview.* Westport, Conn.: Greenwood Press, 1990.

Albanese, A. G. *The Plantation School.* New York: Vantage Press, 1976.

Alcott, W. A. *Letters to a Sister; or, Women's Mission.* Buffalo, N.Y.: G. H. Derby, 1849.

Alexander, E. P. *Museums in Motion: An Introduction to the History and Function of Museums.* Nashville: American Association for State and Local History, 1979.

Alinsky, S. D. *Reveille for Radicals.* New York: Vintage Books, 1969.

Allen, J. S. *The Romance of Commerce and Capital: Capitalism, Modernism, and the Chicago-Aspen Crusade for Cultural Reform.* Chicago: University of Chicago Press, 1983.

Altenbaugh, R. J. *Education for Struggle: The American Labor Colleges of the 1920s and 1930s.* Philadelphia: Temple University Press, 1990.

Altenbaugh, R. J., and Paulston, R. G. "The Work People's College and the American Labor College Movement." In R. G. Paulston (ed.), *Other Dreams, Other Schools: Folk Colleges in Social and Ethnic Movements.* Pittsburgh: University Center for International Studies, University of Pittsburgh, 1980.

Anderson, J. D. *The Education of Blacks in the South, 1860–1935.* Chapel Hill: University of North Carolina Press, 1988.

Anderson, W. T. *The Upstart Spring: Esalen and the American Awakening.* Reading, Mass.: Addison-Wesley, 1983.

Apple, M. *Ideology and Curriculum.* New York: Routledge & Kegan Paul, 1979.

Aronowitz, S. "The New Labor Education: A Return to Ideology." In S. H. London, E. R. Tarr, and J. F. Wilson (eds.), *The Re-Education of the American Working Class.* Westport, Conn.: Greenwood Press, 1990.

Auwers, L. "Reading the Marks of the Past: Exploring Female Literacy in Colonial Windsor, Connecticut." *Historical Methods,* 1980, *13,* 204–214.

Back, K. W. *Beyond Words: The Story of Sensitivity Training and the Encounter Movement.* New York: Russell Sage Foundation, 1972.

Bailyn, B. *Education in the Forming of American Society.* Chapel Hill: University of North Carolina Press, 1960.

Bailyn, B. (ed.). *The Apologia of Robert Keayne: The Self-Portrait of a Puritan Merchant.* New York: HarperCollins, 1965.

Bailyn, B. *The Ideological Origins of the American Revolution.* Cambridge, Mass.: Harvard University Press, 1967.

Bailyn, B., and others. *The Great Republic: A History of the American People.* Boston: Little, Brown, 1977.

Bailyn, B. *The Peopling of British North America: An Introduction.* New York: Knopf, 1986.

Baker, R. *The First Woman Doctor.* New York: Julian Messner, 1952.

Ballard, A. B. *One More Day's Journey: The Making of Black Philadelphia.* Philadelphia: ISHI Publications, 1984.

Barlow, M. L. *History of Industrial Education in the United States.* Peoria, Ill.: Charles A. Bennett, 1967.

Barton, P. *Worklife Transitions: The Adult Learning Connection.* New York: McGraw-Hill, 1982.

Bates, R. S. *Scientific Societies in the United States.* (3rd ed.) Cambridge, Mass.: MIT Press, 1965.

Beals, R. A., and Brody, L. *The Literature of Adult Education.* New York: American Association for Adult Education, 1941.

Becker, C. L. "What Are Historical Facts?" In H. Meyerhoff (ed.), *The Philosophy of History in Our Time.* Garden City, N.Y.: Doubleday, 1959.

Beder, H. *Adult Literacy: Issues for Policy and Practice.* Malabar, Fla.: Krieger, 1991.

Beecher, C. *The Moral Instructor for Schools and Families.* Cincinnati: Truman and Knight, 1838.

Beecher, C. *The Evils Suffered by American Women and American Children: The Causes and the Remedy.* New York: HarperCollins, 1846.

Beecher, H. W. *Lectures to Young Men.* Boston: Jewett, 1846.

Bell, D. *The Coming of the Post-Industrial Society: A Venture in Social Forecasting.* New York: Basic Books, 1976.

Benne, K. D. "History of the T-Group in the Laboratory Setting." In L. P. Bradford, J. R. Gibb, and K. D. Benne (eds.), *T-Group Theory and Laboratory Method.* New York: Wiley, 1964.

Benne, K. D. "Conceptual and Moral Foundations of Laboratory Method." In K. D. Benne, L. P. Bradford, J. R. Gibb, and R. O.

Lippitt (eds.), *The Laboratory Method of Changing and Learning: Theory and Application*. Palo Alto, Calif.: Science and Behavior Books, 1975.

Bennett, C. A. *History of Manual and Industrial Education up to 1870*. Peoria, Ill.: Bennett, 1926.

Bennett, H. S. *English Books and Readers, 1558 to 1603*. Cambridge, England: Cambridge University Press, 1965.

Bentham, J. *An Introduction to the Principles of Morals and Legislation*. London: T. Payne, 1789.

Berkhofer, R. F., Jr. *The White Man's Indian: Images of the American Indian from Columbus to the Present*. New York: Knopf, 1978.

Berkhofer, R. F., Jr. "Cultural Pluralism Versus Ethnocentrism in the New Indian History." In C. Martin (ed.), *The American Indian and the Problem of History*. New York: Oxford University Press, 1987.

Berlin, I. *Slaves Without Masters: The Free Negro in the Antebellum South*. New York: Vintage Books, 1974.

Berrol, S. C. "From Compensatory Education to Adult Education: The New York City Evening Schools, 1825–1935." *Adult Education*, 1976, *26*(4), 208–225.

Berthoff, R. F. *British Immigrants in Industrial America, 1790–1950*. Cambridge, Mass.: Harvard University Press, 1953.

Berthoff, R. F. *An Unsettled People: Social Order and Disorder in American History*. New York: HarperCollins, 1971.

Bestor, A. E., Jr. *Backwoods Utopias: The Sectarian and Owenite Phases of Communitarian Socialism in America, 1663–1829*. Philadelphia: University of Pennsylvania Press, 1950.

Bittner, W. S. *The University Extension Movement*. U.S. Bureau of Education Bulletin no. 84. Washington, D.C.: U.S. Government Printing Office, 1920.

Black, N. *Social Feminism*. Ithaca, N.Y.: Cornell University Press, 1989.

Blair, K. J. *The Clubwoman as Feminist: True Womanhood Redefined, 1868–1914*. New York: Holmes & Meier, 1980.

Blakely, R. J. *To Serve the Public Interest: Educational Broadcasting in the United States*. Syracuse, N.Y.: Syracuse University Press, 1979.

Blewett, M. H. "The Sexual Division of Labor and the Artisan Tradition in Early Industrial Capitalism: The Case of New England Shoemaking, 1780–1860." In C. Groneman and M. B. Norton (eds.), *"To Toil the Lifelong Day": America's Women at Work, 1780–1980.* Ithaca, N.Y.: Cornell University Press, 1987.

Bloom, A. D. *The Closing of the American Mind: How Higher Education Has Failed Democracy and Impoverished the Souls of Today's Students.* New York: Simon & Schuster, 1987.

Bluemel, E. *Opportunity School and Emily Griffith, Its Founder.* Denver: Green Mountain Press, 1970.

Blum, J. M. *V Was for Victory: Politics and American Culture During World War II.* Orlando, Fla.: Harcourt Brace Jovanovich, 1976.

Bode, C. *The American Lyceum: Town Meeting of the Mind.* New York: Oxford University Press, 1956.

Bode, C. *The Anatomy of American Popular Culture, 1840–1861.* Berkeley and Los Angeles: University of California Press, 1960.

Bolt, C. *American Indian Policy and American Reform: Case Studies of the Campaign to Assimilate the American Indians.* London: Unwin Hyman, 1987.

Borden, P. *Civilian Indoctrination of the Military: World War I and Future Implications for the Military-Industrial Complex.* Westport, Conn.: Greenwood Press, 1989.

Bordin, R. *Woman and Temperance: The Quest for Power and Liberty, 1873–1900.* Philadelphia: Temple University Press, 1981.

Bowles, S., and Gintis, H. *Schooling in Capitalist America: Educational Reform and the Contradictions of Economic Life.* New York: Basic Books, 1976.

Bowman, R. A. "The National Committee for the Extension of Labor Education, 1942–1950: A Study of the Committee's Attempt to Establish a Labor Extension Service." Unpublished doctoral dissertation, Rutgers University, 1979.

Boyte, H. C. *CommonWealth: A Return of Citizen Politics.* New York: Free Press, 1989.

Bradford, L. P., Gibb, J. R., and Benne, K. D. "Two Educational Innovations." In L. P. Bradford, J. R. Gibb, and K. D. Benne (eds.), *T-Group Theory and Laboratory Method.* New York: Wiley, 1964.

Brewer, J. W. "Introduction." In R. W. Kelly, *Training Industrial Workers*. New York: Ronald Press, 1920.

Bridenbaugh, C. *Cities in Revolt: Urban Life in America, 1743–1776*. New York: Capricorn Books, 1964a. (Originally published 1955.)

Bridenbaugh, C. *Cities in the Wilderness: The First Century of Urban Life in America, 1625–1742*. New York: Capricorn Books, 1964b. (Originally published 1938.)

Bridenbaugh, C. *The Colonial Craftsman*. Chicago: University of Chicago Press, 1964c.

Bridenbaugh, C. *Vexed and Troubled Englishmen, 1590–1642*. New York: Oxford University Press, 1968.

Brint, S., and Karabel, J. *The Diverted Dream: Community Colleges and the Promise of Educational Opportunity in America, 1900–1985*. New York: Oxford University Press, 1989.

Brodsky, N. "The Armed Forces." In R. M. Smith, G. F. Aker, and J. R. Kidd (eds.), *Handbook of Adult Education*. New York: Macmillan, 1970.

Brown, A. W. *Always Young for Liberty: A Biography of William Ellery Channing*. Syracuse, N.Y.: Syracuse University Press, 1956.

Brown, R. D. *Modernization: The Transformation of American Life, 1600–1865*. New York: Hill and Wang, 1976.

Brown, R. D. *Knowledge Is Power: The Diffusion of Information in Early America, 1700–1865*. New York: Oxford University Press, 1989.

Brumbaugh, S. B. *Democratic Experience and Education in the National League of Women Voters*. New York: Teachers College Press, Columbia University, 1946.

Bryson, L. *Adult Education*. New York: American Book Company, 1936.

Buck, S. J. *The Granger Movement: A Study of Agricultural Organization and Its Political, Economic, and Social Manifestations, 1870–1880*. Cambridge, Mass.: Harvard University Press, 1913.

Bullock, H. A. *A History of Negro Education in the South from 1619 to the Present*. Cambridge, Mass.: Harvard University Press, 1967.

Bullock, P. *African American Periodical Press, 1838–1909.* Baton Rouge: Louisiana State University Press, 1981.

Burnaby, A. *Travels Through the Middle Settlements in North America in the Years 1759 and 1760, with Observations.* London: T. Payne, 1775.

Burstyn, J. N. "Catharine Beecher and the Education of American Women." *New England Quarterly,* 1974, *47,* 386–403.

Burstyn, J. N. *Past and Promise: Lives of New Jersey Women.* Metuchen, N.J.: Scarecrow Press, 1990.

Bushman, C. L. *A Good Poor Man's Wife: Being a Chronicle of Harriet Hanson Robinson and Her Family in Nineteenth Century New England.* Hanover, N.H.: University Press of New England, 1981.

Butchart, R. E. *Northern Schools, Southern Blacks, and Reconstruction: Freedmen's Education, 1862–1875.* Westport, Conn.: Greenwood Press, 1980.

Butterfield, L. H. (ed.). *Letters of Benjamin Rush.* 2 vols. Princeton, N.J.: Princeton University Press, 1951.

Calam, J. *Parsons and Pedagogues: The S.P.G. Adventure in American Education.* New York: Columbia University Press, 1971.

Calvert, M. A. *The Mechanical Engineer in America, 1830–1910: Professional Cultures in Conflict.* Baltimore: Johns Hopkins University Press, 1967.

Campbell, K. K. "Elizabeth Cady Stanton." In B. K. Duffy and H. R. Ryan (eds.), *American Orators Before 1900.* Westport, Conn.: Greenwood Press, 1987.

Caplan, R. M. "Continuing Educational and Professional Accountability." In C. M. McGuire and Associates, *Handbook of Health Professions Education.* San Francisco: Jossey-Bass, 1983.

Carlson, R. A. *The Quest for Conformity: Americanization Through Adult Education.* New York: Wiley, 1975.

Carnegie Commission on Educational Television. *Public Television: A Program for Action.* New York: Bantam Books, 1967.

Carnevale, A. P., Gainer, L. J., and Villet, J. *Training in America: The Organization and Strategic Role of Training.* San Francisco: Jossey-Bass, 1990.

Carr, D. "The Adult Learner in the Museum." In J. W. Solinger (ed.), *Museums and Universities: New Paths for Continuing Education.* New York: Macmillan, 1989.

Cervero, R. M. "Continuing Education for the Professions." In S. B. Merriam and P. M. Cunningham (eds.), *Handbook of Adult and Continuing Education.* San Francisco: Jossey-Bass, 1989.

Chafe, W. H. *The Unfinished Journey: America Since World War II.* (2nd ed.) New York: Oxford University Press, 1991.

Charner, I., and Rolzinski, C. A. (eds.). *Responding to the Education Needs of Today's Workplace.* New Directions for Continuing Education, no. 33. San Francisco: Jossey-Bass, 1987.

Charters, A. N. *Report on the 1969 Galaxy Conference of Adult Education Organizations.* Syracuse, N.Y.: Syracuse University Publications in Continuing Education, 1971.

Chen, C. "Citizens' Information Needs—A Regional Investigation." In R. D. Stueart (ed.), *Information Needs of the 80s.* Greenwich, Conn.: JAI Press, 1982.

Cheney, L. V. *Humanities in America: A Report to the President, the Congress, and the American People.* Washington, D.C.: National Endowment for the Humanities, 1988.

Choate, P. "Introduction." In L. J. Perelman, *The Learning Enterprise: Adult Learning, Human Capital, and Economic Development.* Washington, D.C.: Council of State Planning Agencies, 1984.

Clark, B. R. "Knowledge, Industry, and Adult Competence." In H. W. Burns (ed.), *Sociological Backgrounds of Adult Education.* Chicago: Center for the Study of Liberal Education of Adults, 1964.

Clark, H. F., "Foreword." In C. R. DeCarlo and O. W. Robinson, *Education in Business and Industry.* New York: Center for Applied Research in Education, 1966.

Clark, H. F., and Sloan, H. S. *Classrooms in the Factories.* Rutherford, N.J.: Institute of Research, Fairleigh Dickinson University, 1958.

Claxton, T. *Memoir of a Mechanic.* Boston: George W. Light, 1839.

Clopper, E. N. "The Ohio Mechanics' Institute: Its 125th Anniversary." *Bulletin of the Historical and Philosophical Society of Ohio,* July 1953, *11*(3), 178–191.

Cohen, A. M., and Brawer, F. B. *The American Community College.* (2nd ed.) San Francisco: Jossey-Bass, 1989.

Cohen, I. B. *Benjamin Franklin's Science.* Cambridge, Mass.: Harvard University Press, 1990.

Cohen, S. I. "History of Adult Jewish Religious Education in Four National Jewish Organizations." Unpublished doctoral dissertation, Yeshiva University, 1967.

Cohen, S. I. "Update on Adult Education in Jewish Synagogues: Adult Jewish Education, 1976." *Religious Education,* 1977, *72,* 143–155.

Cole, J. Y. "Storehouses and Workshops: American Libraries and the Uses of Knowledge." In A. Oleson and J. Voss (eds.), *The Organization of Knowledge in Modern America, 1860–1920.* Baltimore: Johns Hopkins University Press, 1979.

Colin, S.A.J., III. "Voice Beyond the Veil: Marcus Garvey, the Universal Negro Improvement Association, and the Education of African-American Adults." Unpublished doctoral dissertation, Department of Leadership and Educational Policy Studies, Northern Illinois University, 1988.

College Entrance Examination Board. *Future Directions for a Learning Society.* New York: College Entrance Examination Board, 1978.

Collins, Z. (ed.). *Museums, Adults, and the Humanities: A Guide to Educational Programming.* Washington, D.C.: American Association of Museums, 1981.

Commons, J. R., and others (eds.). *Documentary History of American Industrial Society.* 5 vols. Cleveland, Ohio: A. H. Clark, 1910–1911.

Conway, J. K. "Perspectives on the History of Women's Education in the United States." *History of Education Quarterly,* 1974, *14*(1), 1–12.

Cooper, A. M. *Employee Training.* New York: McGraw-Hill, 1942.

Cornell, F. "A History of the Rand School of Social Science—1906–1956." Unpublished doctoral dissertation, Teachers College, Columbia University, 1976.

Cotton, W. E. *On Behalf of Adult Education: A Historical Examination of the Supporting Literature.* Boston: Center for the Study of Liberal Education for Adults, 1968.

Counter, J. E. "The Montana Study: A Comparative Look at Seven Study Groups." In *Proceedings of the 30th Adult Education Research Conference*. Madison: University of Wisconsin, 1989.

Creighton, D. *Dominion of the North*. Toronto: Macmillan, 1944.

Cremin, L. A. *The Transformation of the School: Progressivism in American Education, 1876–1957*. New York: Vintage Books, 1965.

Cremin, L. A. *American Education: The Colonial Experience, 1607–1783*. New York: HarperCollins, 1970.

Culbert, D. "Why We Fight: Social Engineering for a Democratic Society at War." In K.R.M. Short (ed.), *Film and Radio Propaganda in World War II*. Knoxville: University of Tennessee Press, 1983.

Curoe, P.R.V. *Educational Attitudes and Policies of Organized Labor in the United States*. New York: Teachers College Press, Columbia University, 1926.

Curry, L. P. *The Free Black in Urban America 1800–1850: The Shadow of the Dream*. Chicago: University of Chicago Press, 1981.

Curti, M. *The Learned Blacksmith: The Letters and Journals of Elihu Burritt*. New York: Wilson-Ericson, 1937.

Curti, M. *The Social Ideas of American Educators*. Paterson, N.J.: Pageant Books, 1959.

Curti, M. *The Growth of American Thought*. (3rd ed.) New York: HarperCollins, 1964.

Curti, M., and Carstensen, V. *The University of Wisconsin: A History, 1848–1925*. Vol. 1: *The Wider Campus*. Madison: University of Wisconsin Press, 1949.

D'Souza, D. *Illiberal Education: The Politics of Race and Sex on Campus*. New York: Free Press, 1991.

Daniels, G. H. "The Process of Professionalization in American Science: The Emergent Period, 1820–1860." *Isis*, 1967, 57, 151–166.

Daniels, G. H. *Nineteenth-Century American Science: A Reappraisal*. Evanston, Ill.: Northwestern University Press, 1972.

Dann, M. (ed.). *The Black Press, 1827–1890: The Quest for National Identity*. New York: Putnam, 1971.

Davenport, S. "The Revisionist Perspective: A Critical Look at the History of Adult Education in the United States." In *Proceedings of the 23rd Annual Adult Education Research Conference.* Lincoln: University of Nebraska, 1982.

Davidson, T. *The Education of the Wage-Earners: A Contribution Toward the Solution of the Educational Problem of Democracy.* Boston: Ginn, 1904.

Davis, A. F. *Spearheads for Reform: The Social Settlements and the Progressive Movement, 1890-1914.* New York: Oxford University Press, 1967.

Davis, R. B. *Intellectual Life in the Colonial South, 1585-1763.* 3 vols. Knoxville: University of Tennessee Press, 1978.

Decker, L. E. *Foundations of Community Education.* Midland, Mich.: Pendell, 1972.

Degler, C. N. *At Odds: Women and the Family in America from the Revolution to the Present.* New York: Oxford University Press, 1980.

Degler, C. N. *Out of Our Past: The Forces That Shaped Modern America.* (3rd ed.) New York: HarperCollins, 1984.

DeLargy, P. F. "Public Schools and Community Education." In S. B. Merriam and P. M. Cunningham (eds.), *Handbook of Adult and Continuing Education.* San Francisco: Jossey-Bass, 1989.

Denker, J. *Unions and Universities: The Rise of the New Labor Leader.* Montclair, N.J.: Allanheld Osmun, 1981.

Dennis, W. D. "The Salem Charitable Mechanic Association." *Historical Collections of the Essex Institute,* 1906, *42*(1), 1-29.

Department of the Interior. *Public Libraries in the United States.* Washington, D.C.: U.S. Government Printing Office, 1876.

Diner, S. J. *A City and Its Universities: Public Policy in Chicago, 1892-1919.* Chapel Hill: University of North Carolina Press, 1980.

Ditzion, S. "Mechanics' and Mercantile Libraries." *Library Quarterly,* 1940, *10*(2), 198-200.

Dolan, J. P. *The American Catholic Experience: A History from Colonial Times to the Present.* Garden City, N.Y.: Doubleday, 1985.

Douglass, F. *Life and Times of Frederick Douglass.* New York: Collier Books, 1962.

Draves, B. *The Free University: A Model for Lifelong Learning.* Chicago: Association Press, 1980.

Drazek, S. J., and Associates. *Expanding Horizons . . . Continuing Education: The Golden Anniversary Publication of the National University Extension Association, 1915-1965.* Washington, D.C.: National University Extension Association, 1965.

Drucker, P. F. *The Age of Discontinuity: Guidelines to Our Changing Society.* New York: HarperCollins, 1978.

Dublin, T. "Women at Work: The Transformation of Work and Community in Lowell, Massachusetts, 1826-1860." Unpublished doctoral dissertation, Columbia University, 1975.

Dublin, T. "Women, Work, and Protest in the Early Lowell Mills: 'The Oppressing Hand of Avarice Would Enslave Us.'" In M. Cantor (ed.), *American Workingclass Culture: Explorations in American Labor and Social History.* Westport, Conn.: Greenwood Press, 1979.

DuMont, R. R. *Reform and Reaction: The Big City Public Library in American Life.* Westport, Conn.: Greenwood Press, 1977.

Dupree, A. H. "The National Pattern of American Learned Societies, 1769-1863." In A. Oleson and S. C. Brown (eds.), *The Pursuit of Knowledge in the Early American Republic: American Scientific and Learned Societies from Colonial Times to the Civil War.* Baltimore: Johns Hopkins University Press, 1976.

Dychtwald, K., and Flower, J. *Age Wave: The Challenges and Opportunities of an Aging America.* Los Angeles: Tarcher, 1989.

Dyer, J. P. *Ivory Towers in the Market Place: The Evening College in American Education.* New York: Bobbs-Merrill, 1956.

Edelson, P. "Codification and Exclusion: An Analysis of the Early Years of the National University Extension Association (NUEA), 1915-1923." Unpublished paper, State University of New York, Stony Brook, n.d.

Edgarton, S. C. "Female Culture." *Mother's Assistant,* 1843, *3,* 94-95.

Ehrenreich, B., and English, D. *For Her Own Good: 150 Years of the Experts' Advice to Women.* Garden City, N.Y.: Doubleday, 1978.

Elias, J. L. *The Foundations and Practice of Adult Religious Education.* Malabar, Fla.: Krieger, 1982.

Ellis, J. J. *After the Revolution: Profiles of Early American Culture.* New York: W.W.Norton, 1979.

Ely, M. L. *Adult Education in Action*. New York: American Association for Adult Education, 1936.

Emerson, G. B. "Mechanics' Institutions." *American Journal of Education*, 1827, *2*, 273-278.

Emerson, J. *Female Education*. Boston: Armstrong, Crocker and Brewer, 1822.

Eurich, N. P. *Corporate Classrooms: The Learning Business*. Princeton, N.J.: Carnegie Foundation for the Advancement of Teaching, 1985.

Eurich, N. P. *The Learning Industry: Education for Adult Workers*. Princeton, N.J.: Princeton University Press, 1990.

Evans, C. (ed.). *American Bibliography*. 14 vols. New York: P. Smith, 1941-1959.

Everett, E. *An Address Delivered as the Introduction to the Franklin Lectures in Boston, November 14, 1831*. Boston: Gray and Bowen, 1832.

Everett, E. *Importance of Practical Education and Useful Knowledge*. Boston: Marsh, Caper, Lyon and Webb, 1840.

Everett, S. *The Community School*. New York: D. Appleton-Century, 1938.

Farnham, C. "Sapphire? The Issue of Dominance in the Slave Family, 1830-1865." In C. Groneman and M. B. Norton (eds.), *"To Toil the Lifelong Day": America's Women at Work, 1780-1980*. Ithaca, N.Y.: Cornell University Press, 1987.

Faure, E. *Learning to Be: The World of Education Today and Tomorrow*. Paris: UNESCO, 1972.

Feinberg, W., and others. *Revisionists Respond to Ravitch*. Washington, D.C.: National Academy of Education, 1980.

Ferguson, E. S. *Early Engineering Reminiscences (1815-40) of George Escol Sellers*. Washington, D.C.: Smithsonian Institution, 1965.

Feuer, L. S. "The East Side Philosophers: William James and Thomas Davidson." *American Jewish History*, 1987, *81*, 287-310.

Fink, L. *Workingmen's Democracy: The Knights of Labor and American Politics*. Urbana: University of Illinois Press, 1983.

Fischer, D. H. *Albion's Seed: Four British Folkways in America*. New York: Oxford University Press, 1989.

Fisher, R. *Let the People Decide: Neighborhood Organizing in America.* Boston: Twayne, 1984.

Flanagan, H. *Arena: The Story of the Federal Theatre.* New York: Limelight Editions, 1985. (Originally published 1940.)

Flint, T. *Recollections of the Last Ten Years.* Reprinted and edited by C. Hartley Grattan, New York: Knopf, 1932. (Originally published 1826.)

Foner, P. S. *Organized Labor and the Black Worker, 1619–1973.* New York: Praeger, 1974.

Foner, P. S. *The Factory Girls.* Urbana: University of Illinois Press, 1977.

Foner, P. S. *Women and the American Labor Movement from World War I to the Present.* New York: Free Press, 1980.

Foster, G. E. *George Everett. Se-quo-yah, the American Cadmus and Modern Moses.* New York: AMS Press, 1979.

Frank, G. "The Parliament of the People." *The Century,* 1919, *98,* 401–416.

Franklin, B. *Reflections on Courtship and Marriage: In Two Letters to a Friend, Wherein a Practical Plan is Laid Down For Obtaining and Securing Conjugal Felicity.* Philadelphia: B. Franklin, 1746.

Franklin, J. H., and Moss, A. A., Jr. *From Slavery to Freedom: A History of Negro Americans.* (6th ed.) New York: Knopf, 1988.

Franklin, V. P. "In Pursuit of Freedom: The Educational Activities of Black Social Organizations in Philadelphia, 1900–1930." In V. P. Franklin and J. D. Anderson (eds.), *New Perspectives on Black Education History.* Boston: G. K. Hall, 1978.

Frederickson, M. "Citizens for Democracy: The Industrial Programs of the YWCA." In J. L. Kornbluh and M. Frederickson (eds.), *Sisterhood and Solidarity: Workers' Education for Women, 1914–1984.* Philadelphia: Temple University Press, 1984.

Freeman, E. J., and Brickner, D. G. "Labor Education: A Growth Sector in a Stagnant Industry." In S. H. London, E. R. Tarr, and J. F. Wilson (eds.), *The Re-Education of the American Working Class.* Westport, Conn.: Greenwood Press, 1990.

French, L. *Psychocultural Change and the American Indian: An Ethnocultural Analysis.* New York: Garland, 1987.

French, W. L. "The Emergence and Early History of Organization and Development with Reference to Influences upon and Interactions Among Some of the Key Actors." In D. D. Warrick (ed.), *Contemporary Organization Development: Current Thinking and Applications*. Glenview, Ill.: Scott, Foresman, 1985.

Frick, G. F. "The Royal Society in America." In A. Oleson and S. C. Brown (eds.), *The Pursuit of Knowledge in the Early American Republic: American Scientific and Learned Societies from Colonial Times to the Civil War*. Baltimore: Johns Hopkins University Press, 1976.

Fund for Adult Education. *A Ten Year Report of the Fund for Adult Education, 1951-1961*. White Plains, N.Y.: Fund for Adult Education, 1961.

Gainey, L. "Clandestine Learning Among Slaves: Evidence from the Federal Writers' Project." *Proceedings of the 27th Annual Adult Education Research Conference*. Syracuse, N.Y.: Syracuse University, 1986.

Galenson, D. W. *White Servitude in Colonial America*. New York: Cambridge University Press, 1981.

Garrison, D. *Apostles of Culture: The Public Librarian and American Society, 1876-1920*. New York: Free Press, 1979.

Gaustad, E. S. *A Religious History of America*. New York: Harper-Collins, 1990.

Genovese, E. D. *Roll, Jordan Roll: The World the Slaves Made*. New York: Pantheon Books, 1976.

Gibson, W. "Community Center Movement Late Nineteenth Century-1930s." In P. M. Melvin (ed.), *American Community Organizations: A Historical Dictionary*. Westport, Conn.: Greenwood Press, 1986.

Gill, T. "Scientific Libraries in the United States." In *Public Libraries in the United States*. Department of the Interior. Washington, D.C.: U.S. Government Printing Office, 1876.

Glasser, J. R. "Museum Studies in the United States: Toward Professionalism." In J. W. Solinger (ed.), *Museums and Universities: New Paths for Continuing Education*. New York: Macmillan, 1989.

Glen, J. M. *Highlander: No Ordinary School, 1932-1962*. Lexington: University Press of Kentucky, 1988.

Gluck, D. T. "The Independent Chautauquas Then and Now."

Henry Ford Museum and the Greenfield Village Herald, 1984, *13*(2), 42–51.

Glueck, E. T. *Community Use of Schools.* Baltimore: Williams & Wilkins, 1927.

Gould, S. J. *The Mismeasure of Man.* New York: W.W.Norton, 1981.

Gouldesborough, P. "An Attempted Scottish Voyage to New York in 1669." *Scottish Historical Review,* 1961, *40,* 56–62.

Grace, A. *Educational Lessons from Wartime Training: The General Report of the Commission on Implications of Armed Services Educational Programs.* Washington, D.C.: American Council on Education, 1948.

Graebner, W. *The Engineering of Consent: Democracy and Authority in Twentieth-Century America.* Madison: University of Wisconsin Press, 1987.

Grattan, C. H. *In Quest of Knowledge.* New York: Association Press, 1955.

Grattan, C. H. *American Ideas About Adult Education, 1710–1951.* New York: Teachers College Press, Columbia University, 1962.

Greeley, H. *Hints Toward Reforms.* New York: Fowlers and Wells, 1853.

Greeley, H. *An Address on Success in Business.* New York: S. S. Packard, 1867.

Greeley, H. *Recollections of a Busy Life.* New York: J. B. Ford, 1868.

Green, J. R. *Grass-Roots Socialism: Radical Movements in the Southwest, 1895–1943.* Baton Rouge: Louisiana State University Press, 1978.

Greene, T. A. *An Address Delivered Before the Members of the New Bedford Lyceum at Their First Meeting, December 18, 1828.* New Bedford, Mass.: The Lyceum, 1829.

Greenhalgh, P. *Ephemeral Vistas: The Expositions Universelles, Great Exhibitions and World Fairs, 1851–1939.* Manchester, England: Manchester University Press, 1988.

Greer, C. "Immigrants, Negroes, and the Public Schools." *Urban Review,* 1969, *3*(3), 9–12.

Griffin, C. S. "Religious Benevolence as Social Control, 1815–

1860." In D. B. Davis (ed.), *Ante-Bellum Reform*. New York: HarperCollins, 1967.

Grimke, S. *Letters on the Equality of the Sexes and the Condition of Women*. Boston: Isaas Knapp, 1838.

Gunderson, R. G. "Introduction : A Setting for Protest and Reform." In P. Boase (ed.), *The Rhetoric of Protest and Reform, 1878–1898*. Athens: Ohio University Press, 1980.

Gunther, C. F. "Museumgoers: Life-styles and Learning Characteristics." In J. W. Solinger (ed.), *Museums and Universities: New Paths for Continuing Education*. New York: Macmillan, 1989.

Gutman, H. G. *Work, Culture, and Society in Industrializing America*. New York: Knopf, 1976.

Gysel, L.J.C. "Whisper Out Loud! *Spirochete*, A Living Newspaper, 1937–1939, Produced by the Federal Theatre Project, An Instrument for Public Health Education in the War on Syphilis." Unpublished doctoral dissertation, Department of Adult and Continuing Education, Virginia Polytechnic Institute and State University, 1989.

Hall, D. D. "The Uses of Literacy in New England, 1600–1850." In W. L. Joyce and others (eds.), *Printing and Society in Early America*. Worcester, Mass.: American Antiquarian Society, 1983.

Hall, J. D. *Revolt Against Chivalry: Jessie Daniel Ames and the Women's Campaign Against Lynching*. New York: Columbia University Press, 1974.

Hamilton, E. "Post–World War II Manpower Training Programs." In H. G. Neufeldt and L. McGee (eds.), *Education of the African American Adult: An Historical Overview*. Westport, Conn.: Greenwood Press, 1990.

Handlin, O. *Liberty and Power, 1600–1760*. New York: Harper-Collins, 1986.

Hansome, M. "The Development of Workers' Education." In T. Brameld (ed.), *Workers' Education in the United States.* New York: HarperCollins, 1941.

Harris, N. "The Lamp of Learning: Popular Lights and Shadows." In A. Oleson and J. Voss (eds.), *The Organization of Knowledge in Modern America, 1860–1920*. Baltimore: Johns Hopkins University Press, 1979.

Harris, N. *Cultural Excursions: Marketing Appetites and Cultural*

Tastes in Modern America. Chicago: University of Chicago Press, 1990.

Harrison, J.F.C. *Robert Owen and the Owenites in Britain and America: The Quest for the New Moral World.* New York: Charles Scribner's Sons, 1969.

Hart, M. "Liberation Through Consciousness Raising." In J. Mezirow and Associates, *Fostering Critical Reflection in Adulthood: A Guide to Transformative and Emancipatory Learning.* San Francisco: Jossey-Bass, 1990.

Hartle, T. W., and Kutner, M. A. "Federal Policies: Programs, Legislation, and Prospects." In R. E. Peterson and Associates, *Lifelong Learning in America.* San Francisco: Jossey-Bass, 1979.

Haskell, T. L. *The Emergence of Professional Social Science: The American Social Science Association and the Nineteenth-Century Crisis of Authority.* Urbana: University of Illinois Press, 1977.

Hayes, C. B. *The American Lyceum: Its History and Contribution to Education.* Washington, D.C.: U.S. Government Printing Office, 1932.

Hefferman, J. M. *Educational and Career Services for Adults.* Lexington, Mass.: Lexington Books, 1981.

Heim, K. M. "Adult Services: An Enduring Focus." In K. M. Heim and D. P. Wallace (eds.), *Adult Services: An Enduring Focus for Public Libraries.* Chicago: American Library Association, 1990.

Heller, R. "Blue Collars and Blue Stockings: The Bryn Mawr Summer School for Women Workers." In J. L. Kornbluh and M. Frederickson (eds.), *Sisterhood and Solidarity: Workers' Education for Women, 1914–1984.* Philadelphia: Temple University Press, 1984.

Hendrickson, W. B. "Science and Culture in the American Middle West." *Isis,* 1973, *64,* 326–340.

Herberg, W. *Protestant-Catholic-Jew.* Garden City, N.Y.: Doubleday, 1960.

Higginbotham, E. B. *Righteous Discontent: The Women's Movement in the Black Baptist Church, 1880–1920.* Cambridge, Mass.: Harvard University Press, 1993.

Hindle, B. *The Pursuit of Science in Revolutionary America.* Chapel Hill: University of North Carolina Press, 1956.

Hindle, B. "The Underside of a Learned Society in New York, 1754–1854." In A. Oleson and S. C. Brown (eds.), *The Pursuit of Knowledge in the Early American Republic: American Scientific and Learned Societies from Colonial Times to the Civil War.* Baltimore: Johns Hopkins University Press, 1976.

Hirsch, E. D., Jr. *Cultural Literacy: What Every American Needs to Know.* Boston: Houghton Mifflin, 1987.

Hirsch, J. I. *The History of the National Training Laboratories: 1947–1986.* New York: Peter Lang, 1987.

Hirsch, S. E. *Roots of the American Working Class: The Industrialization of Crafts in Newark, 1800–1860.* Pittsburgh: University of Pennsylvania Press, 1978.

Hodgson, G. *America in Our Time.* New York: Vintage Books, 1978.

Holland, J. G. "The Popular Lecture." *Atlantic Monthly,* 1865, *15,* 362–371.

Holliday, C. *Women's Life in Colonial Days.* New York: Frederick Ungar, 1922.

Holmes, E. C. "Alain L. Locke and the Adult Education Movement." *Journal of Negro Education,* 1965, *34*(1), 5–10.

Hopkins, C. H. *History of the Y.M.C.A in North America.* New York: Association Press, 1951.

Horlick, A. S. "Phrenology and the Social Education of Young Men." *History of Education Quarterly,* 1971, *11*(1), 23–38.

Horton, A. I. *The Highlander Folk School: A History of Its Major Programs, 1932–1961.* Brooklyn, N.Y.: Carlson, 1989.

Houle, C. O. *Major Trends in Higher Adult Education.* Chicago: Center for the Study of Liberal Education for Adults, 1959.

Houle, C. O. *The External Degree.* San Francisco: Jossey-Bass, 1974.

Houle, C. O. *Continuing Learning in the Professions.* San Franciso: Jossey-Bass, 1980.

Houle, C. O. "Possible Futures." In M. R. Stern (ed.), *Power and Conflict in Continuing Professional Education.* Belmont, Calif.: Wadsworth, 1983.

Houle, C. O., Burr, E. W., Hamilton, T. W., and Yale, J. R. *The Armed Services and Adult Education.* Washington, D.C.: American Council on Education, 1947.

Howe, I. *World of Our Fathers: The Journey of the East European Jews to America and the Life They Found and Made.* Orlando, Fla.: Harcourt Brace Jovanovich, 1976.

Hugo, J. M. "Adult Education History and the Issue of Gender: Toward a Different History of Adult Education in America." *Adult Education Quarterly,* 1990, *41*(1), 1–16.

Hurd, D. H. *History of Essex County.* Philadelphia: J. W. Lewis, 1888.

Huse, E. F., and Cummings, T. G. *Organization Development and Change.* (3rd ed.) St. Paul, Minn.: West, 1985.

Ihle, E. L. "Education of the Free Blacks Before the Civil War." In H. G. Neufeldt and L. McGee (eds.), *Education of the African American Adult.* Westport, Conn.: Greenwood Press, 1990.

"Imperatives for Policy and Action in Lifelong Learning." Report of the 1976 Wingspread Conference on Lifelong Learning in the Public Interest. Washington, D.C.: Coalition of Adult Education Organizations, 1976.

Inkeles, A. H., and Smith, D. H. *Becoming Modern: Individual Change in Six Developing Countries.* Cambridge, Mass.: Harvard University Press, 1974.

Irving, W. *Wolfert's Roost and Other Papers.* (Rev. ed.). New York: Putnam, 1865.

Jackson, S. L. "Some Ancestors of the Extension Course." *The New England Quarterly,* 1941, *14*(3), 505–518.

Jacoby, R. M. "The Women's Trade Union League: Training School for Women Organizers, 1914–1926." In J. L. Kornbluh and M. Frederickson (eds.), *Sisterhood and Solidarity: Workers' Education for Women, 1914–1984.* Philadelphia: Temple University Press, 1984.

Jacoby, S. M. *Employing Bureaucracy: Managers, Unions, and the Transformation of Work in American Industry, 1900–1945.* New York: Columbia University Press, 1985.

Jarman, T. L. *Landmarks in the History of Education.* London: John Murray, 1970.

Jeffrey, J. R. "Women in the Southern Farmers' Alliance: A Reconsideration of the Role and Status of Women in the Late Nineteenth-Century South." In J. E. Friedman, W. G. Shade, and M. J. Capozzoli (eds.), *Our American Sisters: Women in Amer-*

ican Life and Thought. (4th ed.) Lexington, Mass.: D. C. Heath, 1987.

Jennings F. *The Invasion of America: Indians, Colonialism, and the Cant of Conquest.* New York: W.W.Norton, 1976.

Jensen, G., Liveright, A. A., and Hallenbeck, W. (eds.). *Adult Education: Outlines of an Emerging Field of University Study.* Washington, D.C.: Adult Education Association of the U.S.A., 1964.

Jernegan, M. W. *Laboring and Dependent Classes in Colonial America, 1607–1783.* New York: Frederick Ungar, 1931.

Johnson, F. E. "The Church an Educational Asset." In M. L. Ely (ed.), *Adult Education in Action.* New York: American Association for Adult Education, 1936.

Johnson, G. T., and Komer, O. "Education for Affirmative Action." In B. M. Wertheimer (ed.), *Labor Education for Women Workers.* Philadelphia: Temple University Press, 1981.

Jones, A. L. "Gaining Self-Consciousness While Losing the Movement: The American Association for Adult Education, 1926–1941." Unpublished doctoral dissertation, Department of Continuing, Adult, and Vocational Education, University of Wisconsin-Madison, 1991.

Jones, J. *Soldiers of Light and Love: Northern Teachers and Georgia Blacks, 1865–1873.* Chapel Hill: University of North Carolina Press, 1980.

Jordan, W. D. *White over Black: American Attitudes Toward the Negro, 1550–1812.* Chapel Hill: University of North Carolina Press, 1968.

Josephson, H. *The Golden Threads: New England's Mill Girls and Magnates.* New York: Russell and Russell, 1949.

Kahn, R. P. "Taking Our Maternal Bodies Back: *Our Bodies, Ourselves* and the Boston Women's Health Book Collective." In J. Antler and S. K. Biklen (eds.), *Changing Education: Women as Radicals and Conservators.* Albany: State University of New York Press, 1990.

Kaplan, A. C., and Veri, C. C. *The Continuing Education Unit.* DeKalb, Ill.: ERIC Clearinghouse in Career Education, 1974.

Karier, C. J., and others (eds.). *Roots of Crisis: American Education in the Twentieth Century.* Skokie, Ill.: Rand McNally, 1973.

Kathan, B. W. "Adult Learning in Church and Synagogue." *Religious Education*, 1977, *72*, 115–120.

Katz, M. B. *The Irony of Early School Reform: Educational Innovations in Mid-Nineteenth-Century Massachusetts*. Cambridge, Mass.: Harvard University Press, 1968.

Katz, M. B. *Class, Bureaucracy and the Schools*. New York: Praeger, 1975.

Keane, P. "Adult Education and the Cornish Miner." *British Journal of Educational Studies*, 1974, *22*(3), 261–291.

Keane, P. "Questions from the Past of Appropriate Methodology for Adult Learners." *Convergence*, 1984a, *28*(2), 52–63.

Keane, P. "Useful Knowledge and Morality." *Adult Education Quarterly*, 1984b, *35*(1), 26–50.

Keane, P. "Internationalism in Early Adult Education." *International Journal of Lifelong Education*, 1985a, *4*(3), 229–238.

Keane, P. "Financial Policy and the Mechanics' Institutes: Transatlantic Comparisons in Adult Education." *Studies in the Education of Adults*, 1985b, *17*(2), 156–167.

Keefer, L. E. *Scholars in Foxholes: The Story of the Army Specialized Training Program in World War II*. Jefferson, N.C.: McFarland, 1988.

Kelly, R. W. *Training Industrial Workers*. New York: Ronald Press, 1920.

Kelly, T. *A History of Adult Education in Great Britain*. Liverpool, England: Liverpool University Press, 1962.

Kendall, E. "Beyond Mother's Knee." *American Heritage*, 1973, *24*(4), 12–16, 73–78.

Kerber, L. K. "Science in the Early Republic: The Society for the Study of Natural Philosophy." *William and Mary Quarterly*, 1972, *29*, 264–265.

Kerber, L. K. *Women of the Republic: Intellect and Ideology in Revolutionary America*. Chapel Hill: University of North Carolina Press, 1980.

Kerber, L. K. "Why Should Girls Be Learn'd and Wise?" In J. M. Faragher and F. Howe (eds.), *Women and Higher Education in American History*. New York: W.W.Norton, 1988.

Kieffer, E. "Libraries in Lancaster." In *Papers, Lancaster County*

Historical Society. Lancaster, Pa.: Lancaster County Historical Society, 1944.

Kirby, D. "The Wage-Earning Woman and the State: The National Women's Trade Union League and Protective Labor Legislation." *Labor History*, 1987, *28*, 54-74.

Klingberg, F. J. *Anglican Humanitarianism in Colonial New York*. Philadelphia: Church Historical Society, 1940.

Knowles, M. S. *The Adult Education Movement in the United States*. Troy, Mo.: Holt, Rinehart & Winston, 1962.

Knowles, M. S. *A History of the Adult Education Movement in the United States*. (Rev. ed.). Huntington, N.Y.: Krieger, 1977.

Kobre, S. *The Development of the Colonial Newspaper*. Pittsburgh: Colonial Press, 1944.

Kohlstedt, S. G. "Savants and Professionals: The American Association for the Advancement of Science, 1848-1860." In A. Oleson and S. C. Brown (eds.), *The Pursuit of Knowledge in the Early American Republic: American Scientific and Learned Societies from Colonial Times to the Civil War*. Baltimore: Johns Hopkins University Press, 1976.

Korman, G. *Industrialization, Immigrants, and Americanizers: The View from Milwaukee, 1886-1921*. Madison: State Historical Society of Wisconsin, 1967.

Kornbluh, J. L. "The She-She Camps: An Experiment in Living and Learning, 1934-1937." In J. L. Kornbluh and M. Frederickson (eds.), *Sisterhood and Solidarity: Workers' Education for Women, 1914-1984*. Philadelphia: Temple University Press, 1984.

Kornbluh, J. L. *A New Deal for Workers' Education: The Workers' Service Program, 1933-1942*. Urbana: University of Illinois Press, 1987.

Kryder, L. G. "Humanizing the Industrial Workplace: The Role of the Early Personnel Manager, 1897-1929." *Henry Ford Museum & Greenfield Village Herald*, 1985, *14*(1), 14-19.

Kurland, N. D. *A National Strategy for Lifelong Learning*. Remarks prepared for the dialogue on Lifelong Learning, Institute for Educational Leadership, Postsecondary Education Convening Authority, George Washington University, Washington, D.C., 1976.

Lacy, D. "Liberty and Knowledge—Then and Now: 1776-1876-

1976." In H. Goldstein (ed.), *Milestones to the Present.* Syracuse, N.Y.: Gaylord Professional Publications, 1978.

Lagemann, E. C. "Introduction. Jane Addams: An Educational Biography." In E. C. Lagemann (ed.), *Jane Addams on Education.* New York: Teachers College Press, Columbia University, 1985.

Lagemann, E. C. "The Politics of Knowledge: The Carnegie Corporation and the Formulation of Public Policy." *History of Education Quarterly,* 1987, *27*(2), 205–220.

Lagemann, E. C. *The Politics of Knowledge: The Carnegie Corporation, Philanthropy, and Public Policy.* Middletown, Conn.: Wesleyan University Press, 1989.

Lamb, M. J. *The Career of a Beneficent Enterprise. Being a Historical Sketch of the General Society of Mechanics and Tradesmen of the City of New York.* New York: The General Society, 1889.

Larcom, L. *A New England Girlhood.* Boston: Houghton Mifflin, 1890.

Larson, M. S. *The Rise of Professionalism: A Sociological Analysis.* Berkeley: University of California Press, 1977.

Laurie, B. "Fire Companies and Gangs in Southwark: The 1840s." In A. F. Davis and M. H. Haller (eds.), *The Peoples of Philadelphia.* Philadelphia: Temple University Press, 1973.

Laurie, B. " 'Nothing on Compulsion': Life Styles of Philadelphia Artisans, 1820–1850." In M. Cantor (ed.), *American Workingclass Culture: Explorations in American Labor and Social History.* Westport, Conn.: Greenwood Press, 1979.

Laurie, B. *Artisans into Workers: Labor in Nineteenth-Century America.* New York: Hill and Wang, 1989.

Lazerson, M. *Origins of the Urban School: Public Education in Massachusetts, 1870–1915.* Cambridge, Mass.: Harvard University Press, 1971.

Lazerson, M., and Grubb, W. N. (eds.). *American Education and Vocationalism: A Documentary History, 1870–1970.* New York: Teachers College Press, Columbia University, 1974a.

Lazerson, M., and Grubb, W. N. "Introduction." In M. Lazerson and W. N. Grubb (eds.), *American Education and Vocationalism: A Documentary History, 1870–1970.* New York: Teachers College Press, Columbia University, 1974b.

Learned, W. S. *The American Public Library and the Diffusion of Knowledge.* Orlando, Fla.: Harcourt Brace Jovanovitch, 1924.

Leary, T. "Industrial Ecology and the Labor Process." In C. Stephenson and R. Asher (eds.), *Life and Labor: Dimensions of American Working Class History.* Albany: State University of New York Press, 1986.

Lee, R. E. *Continuing Education for Adults Through the American Public Library, 1833–1964.* Chicago: American Library Association, 1966.

Levin, D. *Cotton Mather: The Young Life of the Lord's Remembrancer, 1663–1703.* Cambridge, Mass.: Harvard University Press, 1978.

Levin, P. L. *Abigail Adams.* New York: St. Martin's Press, 1987.

Levine, H., and Hutton, C. M. "Financing Labor's Role in Education and Training." In H. Stack and C. M. Hutton (eds.), *Building New Alliances: Labor Unions and Higher Education.* New Directions for Experiential Learning, no. 10. San Francisco: Jossey-Bass, 1980.

Levine, L. W. *Black Culture and Black Consciousness: Afro-American Folk Thought from Slavery to Freedom.* New York: Oxford University Press, 1977.

Levine, S. "Labor's True Woman: Domesticity and Equal Rights in the Knights of Labor." *Journal of American History,* 1983, *70*(2), 323–339.

Levy, B. M. *Cotton Mather.* Boston: Twayne, 1979.

Lifelong Learning Project. *Lifelong Learning and Public Policy.* Washington, D.C.: U.S. Government Printing Office, 1978.

Lindeman, E. C. *Social Education: An Interpretation of the Principles and Methods Developed by the Inquiry During the Years 1923–1933.* New York: New Republic, 1933.

Liveright, A. A. *A Study of Adult Education in the United States.* Boston: Center for the Study of Liberal Education for Adults, 1968.

Locke, A. "Negro Needs as Adult Education Opportunities: Findings of the First Annual Conference on the Negro." In L. Harris (ed.), *The Philosophy of Alain Locke: Harlem Renaissance and Beyond.* Philadelphia: Temple University Press, 1989.

Lockridge, K. A. *Literacy in Colonial New England.* New York: W.W.Norton, 1974.

Lockwood, G. R. *The New Harmony Movement.* New York: Appleton, 1905.

Lockwood, M. "The Experimental Utopia in America," In F. E. Manuel (ed.), *Utopias and Utopian Thought.* Boston: Beacon Press, 1966.

Long, H. B. (ed.)."Adult Education in Colonial America." *Journal of Research and Development in Education,* 1975a, *8.*

Long, H. B. "Women's Education in Colonial America." *Adult Education,* 1975b, *25*(2), 90-106.

Long, H. B. *Continuing Education of Adults in Colonial America.* Syracuse, N.Y.: Syracuse University Press, 1976.

Long, H. B. "Educational Opportunities for Adults in London and Philadelphia in the Eighteenth Century." *Lifelong Learning,* 1984, *7*(7), 18-21, 27.

Lotchin, R. W. *San Francisco, 1846-1856: From Hamlet to City.* New York: Oxford University Press, 1974.

Lovejoy, E. P. *Women Doctors of America.* New York: Macmillan, 1957.

Luke, R. A. "Public School Adult Education." In M. S. Knowles (ed.), *Handbook of Adult Education.* Washington, D.C.: Adult Education Association of the U.S.A., 1960.

Luke, R. A. *The NEA and Adult Education: A Historical Review, 1921-1972.* Sarasota, Fla: R. A. Luke, 1992.

Lurie, R. L. *The Challenge of the Forum: The Story of Ford Hall and the Open Forum Movement, A Demonstration in Adult Education.* Boston: Badger, 1930.

Lusterman, S. *Education in Industry.* New York: The Conference Board, 1977.

Luther, S. *Address to the Working Men of New England.* Philadelphia: S. Luther, 1836.

Lutz, A. *Emma Willard: Daughter of Democracy.* Boston: Houghton Mifflin, 1964. (Originally published 1929.)

Lyell, C. *Travels in North America, 1841-42, with Geological Observations on the U.S., Canada, and Nova Scotia.* 2 vols. New York: Wiley, 1845.

Lynn, R. W., and Wright, E. *The Big Little School: Two Hundred*

Years of the Sunday School. (2nd ed.) Birmingham, Ala.: Religious Education Press and Nashville, Tenn.: Abingdon, 1980.

McBath, J. H. "The Platform and Public Thought." In P. H. Boase (ed.), *The Rhetoric of Protest and Reform, 1878-1898.* Athens: Ohio University Press, 1980.

McClymer, J. F. *War and Welfare: Social Engineering in America, 1890-1925.* Westport, Conn.: Greenwood Press, 1980.

McClymer, J. F. "The Americanization Movement and the Education of the Foreign-Born Adult, 1914-25." In B. J. Weiss (ed.), *American Education and the European Immigrant: 1840-1940.* Urbana: University of Illinois Press, 1982.

McCown, R. A. "The Development of the Tent Chautauqua." *Henry Ford Museum & Greenfield Village Herald,* 1984, *13*(2), 33-39.

McCurdy, F. "Women Speak Out in Protest." In P. Boase (ed.), *The Rhetoric of Protest and Reform, 1878-1898.* Athens: Ohio University Press, 1980.

McFeely, W. S. *Frederick Douglass.* New York: W.W.Norton, 1990.

Machlup, F. *The Production and Distribution of Knowledge in the United States.* Princeton, N.J.: Princeton University Press, 1962.

McHugh, C. "Midwestern Populist Leadership and Edward Bellamy: 'Looking Backward' into the Future." *American Studies,* 1978, *19*(2), 57-74.

Mackenzie, J. R. "Labor Education Growth and Development." In C. Klevins (ed.), *Materials and Methods in Continuing Education.* New York: Klevens, 1976.

McLaurin, M. A. *The Knights of Labor in the South.* Westport, Conn.: Greenwood Press, 1978.

Maclure, W. *Opinions on Various Subjects, Dedicated to the Industrious Producers.* 3 vols. New Harmony, Ind.: School Press, 1831-1838.

McWhiney, G. *Cracker Culture: Celtic Ways in the Old South.* Tuscaloosa: University of Alabama Press, 1988.

Maine Charitable Mechanic Association. *Constitution and History.* Portland: Bryant Press, 1965.

Maloy, W. L., Gager, W. A., Jr., and Sullivan, E. "Continuing Education Within the Department of Defense." In C. Klevins (ed.), *Materials & Methods in Continuing Education*. New York: Klevens, 1976.

Manuel, F. E. (ed.). *Utopias and Utopian Thought*. Boston: Houghton Mifflin, 1966.

Marable, M. "Alain Locke, W.E.B. DuBois, and the Crisis of Adult Education During the Great Depression." In R. J. Linneman (ed.), *Alain Locke: Reflections on a Modern Renaissance Man*. Baton Rouge: Louisiana State University, 1982.

Marquis, A. G. *Hopes and Ashes: The Birth of Modern Times, 1929-1939*. New York: Free Press, 1986.

Maskin, M. R. "Black Education and the New Deal: The Urban Experience." Unpublished doctoral dissertation, Department of History, New York University, 1973.

Mather, C. *Bonifacius: An Essay Upon the Good*. Cambridge, Mass.: Harvard University Press, 1966.

Mathews, D. G. *Religion in the Old South*. Chicago: University of Chicago Press, 1977.

Matthews, G. *"Just A Housewife": The Rise and Fall of Domesticity in America*. New York: Oxford University Press, 1987.

Matthews, J. D. "Arts and the People: The New Deal Quest for Cultural Democracy." *Journal of American History*, 1975, *62*, 316-339.

Mead, D. *Yankee Eloquence in the Middle West: The Ohio Lyceum, 1850-1870*. Westport, Conn.: Greenwood Press, 1951.

Meier, A. *Negro Thought in America, 1880-1915: Racial Ideologies in the Age of Booker T. Washington*. Ann Arbor: University of Michigan Press, 1966.

Meyerowitz, J. *No Sense of Place: The Impact of Electronic Media on Social Behavior*. New York: Oxford University Press, 1985.

Mickelson, P. "American Society and the Public Library in the Thought of Andrew Carnegie." *Journal of Library History*, 1975, *10*(2), 117-138.

Miller, E. R. "Adult Education in Religious Institutions." In M. Knowles (ed.), *Handbook of Adult Education in the United States*. Washington, D.C.: Adult Education Association of the U.S.A., 1960.

Miller, H. S. "Science and Private Agencies." In D. Van Tassel and

M. G. Hall (eds.), *Science and Society in the United States.* Homewood, Ill.: Dorsey, 1966.

Miller, P. *The Life of the Mind in America: From the Revolution to the Civil War.* New York: Harcourt Brace Jovanovich, 1965.

Mitchell, T. R. *Political Education in the Southern Farmers' Alliance: 1887-1900.* Madison: University of Wisconsin Press, 1987.

Moody, H. R. *The Abundance of Life: Human Development Policies for an Aging Society.* New York: Columbia University Press, 1988.

Moreland, W. D., and Goldenstein, E. H. *Pioneers in Adult Education.* Chicago: Nelson-Hall, 1985.

Morris, A. D. *The Origins of the Civil Rights Movement: Black Communities Organizing for Change.* New York: Free Press, 1984.

Morris, J.V.L. *Employee Training: A Study of Education and Training Departments in Various Corporations.* New York: McGraw-Hill, 1921.

Morris, R. B. *Government and Labor in Early America.* New York: Columbia University Press, 1946.

Morrison, T. *Chautauqua: A Center for Education, Religion, and the Arts in America.* Chicago: University of Chicago Press, 1974.

Moses, S. *The Learning Force: A More Comprehensive Framework for Educational Policy.* Syracuse, N.Y.: Syracuse University Publications in Continuing Education, 1971.

Moses, W. J. *The Golden Age of Black Nationalism, 1850-1925.* Hamden Court, Conn.: Archon Books, 1978.

Moss, J. W., and Lass, C. B. "A History of Farmers' Institutes." *Agricultural History,* 1988, *62*(2), 150-163.

Mott, F. L. *American Journalism: A History of Newspapers in the United States Through 260 Years: 1690 to 1950.* (Rev. ed.). New York: Macmillan, 1950.

Murray, C. *Losing Ground: American Social Policy, 1950-1980.* New York: Basic Books, 1984.

Nelms, W. E. "Cora Wilson Stewart and the Crusade Against Illiteracy in Kentucky, 1916-1920." *The Register of the Kentucky Historical Society,* 1984, *82*(2), 151-169.

Nelson, D. *Managers and Workers: Origins of the New Factory System in the United States, 1880-1920.* Madison: University of Wisconsin Press, 1975.

Neufeldt, H. G., and McGee, L. (eds.). *Education of the African American Adult*. Westport, Conn.: Greenwood Press, 1990.

Neumann, W. "Educational Responses to the Concern for Proficiency." In G. Grant and Associates, *On Competence: A Critical Analysis of Competence-Based Reforms in Higher Education*. San Francisco: Jossey-Bass, 1979.

Newsom, B. Y., and Silver, A. Z. (eds.). *The Art Museum as Educator*. Berkeley: University of California Press, 1978.

Noffsinger, J. S. *Correspondence Schools, Lyceums, Chautauquas*. New York: Macmillan, 1926.

Norton, M. B. *Liberty's Daughters: The Revolutionary Experience of American Women, 1750-1800*. Boston: Little, Brown, 1980.

Norton, M. B., and others. *A People and a Nation: A History of the United States*. Boston: Houghton Mifflin, 1982.

O'Gorman, A., and Coy, P. G. "Houses of Hospitality: A Pilgrimage into Nonviolence." In P. G. Coy (ed.), *A Revolution of the Heart: Essays on the Catholic Worker*. Philadelphia: Temple University Press, 1988.

Oleson, A., and Brown, S. C. (eds.). *The Pursuit of Knowledge in the Early American Republic*. Baltimore: Johns Hopkins University Press, 1976.

Oleson, A., and Voss, J. (eds.). *The Organization of Knowledge in Modern America, 1860-1920*. Baltimore: Johns Hopkins University Press, 1979.

Oliver, L. P. *The Art of Citizenship: Public Issues Forums*. Dayton, Ohio: Kettering Foundation, 1983.

Oliver, L. P. *Study Circles: Coming Together for Personal Growth and Social Change*. Washington, D.C./Cabin John, Md.: Seven Locks Press, 1987.

Oliver, R. T. *History of Public Speaking in America*. Needham Heights, Mass.: Allyn & Bacon, 1965.

Olmstead, F. L. *Journey in the Seaboard Slave States in the Years 1853-1854, With Remarks on Their Economy*. New York: Dix and Edwards, 1856.

Olson, J. S. "Booker T. Washington (1856-1915), Black Educator and Leader." In B. K. Duffy and H. Ryan (eds.), *American Orators Before 1900*. Westport, Conn.: Greenwood Press, 1987.

Olson, K. W. *The G.I. Bill, the Veterans, and the Colleges.* Lexington: University Press of Kentucky, 1974.

Ossoli, M. F. *Memoirs of Margaret Fuller Ossoli.* Boston: Phillips, Sampson, 1852.

Overstreet, H., and Overstreet, B. *Where Children Come First.* Chicago: National Congress of Parents and Teachers, 1949.

Owen, R. "Address Delivered by Robert Owen, April 27, 1825." *New Harmony Gazette,* Oct. 1, 1825, 1-2.

Owen, R. D. *Threading My Way: Twenty-seven Years of Autobiography.* New York: A. M. Kelley, 1967. (Originally published 1874.)

Park, R. E. *Race and Culture.* New York: Free Press, 1950.

Parry, J. H. *The Spanish Seaborne Empire.* New York: Knopf, 1966.

Payne, E. A. *Reform, Labor, and Feminism: Margaret Dreier Robins and the Women's Trade Union League.* Urbana: University of Illinois Press, 1988.

Peffer, N. *Educational Experiments in Industry.* New York: Macmillan, 1932.

Perkins, C. R. "City Council Members' Perceptions of Virginia Cooperative Extension Service." Unpublished doctoral dissertation, Department of Adult and Continuing Education, Virginia Polytechnic Institute and State University, 1978.

Perkins, L. M. "The Education of Black Women in the Nineteenth Century." In J. M. Faragher and F. Howe (eds.), *Women and Higher Education in American History.* New York: W.W.Norton, 1988.

Perrett, G. *Days of Sadness, Years of Triumph: The American People, 1939-1945.* Madison: University of Wisconsin Press, 1985.

Pessen, E. *Most Uncommon Jacksonians: The Radical Leaders of the Early Labor Movement.* New York: State University of New York Press, 1967.

Peterson, D. A. *Facilitating Education for Older Learners.* San Francisco: Jossey-Bass, 1983.

Peterson, D. A. "Toward a Definition of Educational Gerontology." In R. H. Sherron and D. B. Lumsden (eds.), *Introduction to Educational Gerontology.* (2nd ed.) Washington: Hemisphere, 1985.

Peterson, R. E., and Associates. *Lifelong Learning in America.* San Francisco: Jossey-Bass, 1979.

Polenberg, R. *War and Society: The United States, 1941–1945.* Philadelphia: Lippincott, 1972.

Porter, D. "The Organized Educational Activities of Negro Societies, 1828–1846." In A. Meier and E. Rudwick (eds.), *The Making of Black America: Essays in Negro Life and History.* Vol. 1: *The Origins of Black America.* New York: Atheneum, 1969.

Portman, D. N. *The Universities and the Public: A History of Higher Adult Education in the United States.* Chicago: Nelson-Hall, 1978.

Powell, J. W. *School for Americans: An Essay in Adult Education.* New York: American Association for Adult Education, 1942.

Prucha, F. P. *The Great Father: The United States and the American Indians.* Vol. 2. Lincoln: University of Nebraska Press, 1984.

Prucha, F. P. *The Great Father: The United States Government and the American Indians.* (Abridged ed.). Lincoln: University of Nebraska Press, 1986.

Quarles, B. *Frederick Douglass.* Washington, D.C.: Associated Publishers, 1948.

Quigley, B. A. "Shaping Literacy: An Historical Analysis of Literacy Education as Social Policy." In *Proceedings of the 32nd Adult Education Research Conference.* Norman: University of Oklahoma, 1991.

Quimby, I.M.G. "Apprenticeship in Colonial Philadelphia." Unpublished master's thesis, University of Delaware, 1963.

Quinn, D. B. (ed.). *The Roanoke Voyages, 1584–1590.* London: The Hakluyt Society, 1955.

Rachal, J. R. "Freedom's Crucible: William T. Richardson and the Schooling of Freedmen." *Adult Education Quarterly,* 1986, *37*(1), 14–22.

Rachal, J. R. "The American Library Adult Education Movement: The Diffusion of Knowledge and the Democratic Ideal, 1924–1933." In R. W. Rohfeld (ed.), *Breaking New Ground: The Development of Adult and Workers' Education in North America.* Proceedings of the Syracuse University–Kellogg Project's First Visiting Scholar Conference in the History of Adult Education,

March 1989. Syracuse, N.Y.: Syracuse University–Kellogg Project, 1990.

Raphael, M. L. *Profiles in American Judaism: The Reform, Conservative, Orthodox, and Reconstructionist Traditions in Historical Perspective.* New York: HarperCollins, 1984.

Rasmussen, W. *Taking the University to the People: Seventy-Five Years of Cooperative Extension.* Ames: Iowa State University Press, 1989.

Ravitch, D. *Revisionists Revised: A Critique of the Radical Attack on the Schools.* New York: Basic Books, 1978.

Ravitch, D. *The Troubled Crusade: American Education, 1945–1980.* New York: Basic Books, 1983.

Rayback, J. G. *A History of American Labor.* New York: Macmillan, 1959.

Reber, L. E. *University Extension in the United States.* U.S. Bureau of Education Bulletin no. 19. Washington, D.C.: U.S. Government Printing Office, 1914.

Reid, I. De A. *Adult Education Among Negroes.* Washington, D.C.: Associates in Negro Folk Education, 1936.

Reid, I. De A. "The Development of Adult Education for Negroes in the United States." *Journal of Negro Education,* 1945, *14*(3), 299–306.

Reilly, E. E. "The Wages of Piety: The Boston Book Trade of Jeremy Condy." In W. L. Joyce and others (eds.), *Printing and Society in Early America.* Worcester: American Antiquarian Society, 1983.

Reingold, N. "Definitions and Speculations: The Professionalization of Science in America in the Nineteenth Century." In A. Oleson and S. C. Brown (eds.), *The Pursuit of Knowledge in the Early American Republic: American Scientific and Learned Societies from Colonial Times to the Civil War.* Baltimore: Johns Hopkins University Press, 1976.

Rhees, W. J. *Manual of Public Libraries, Institutions, and Societies, in the United States and British Provinces of North America.* Philadelphia: Lippincott, 1859.

Richardson, P. L. "Lifelong Learning and Politics." *Convergence,* 1979, *12*(1-2), 95–103.

Rischin, M. *The Promised City: New York's Jews, 1870–1914*. Cambridge, Mass.: Harvard University Press, 1977.

Risley, R. F. "Adult Education in Business and Industry." In M. S. Knowles (ed.), *Handbook of Adult Education*. Washington, D.C.: Adult Education Association of the U.S.A., 1960.

Robbins, W. A. "The TVA as a Social and Educational Enterprise, 1933–1953." Unpublished doctoral dissertation, Teachers College, Columbia University, 1972.

Robinson, J. H. *The Humanizing of Knowledge*. New York: George H. Doran, 1924.

Rock, H. B. *Artisans of the New Republic: The Tradesmen of New York City in the Age of Jefferson*. New York: New York University Press, 1979.

Rockhill, K. "The Past as Prologue: Toward an Expanded View of Adult Education." *Adult Education*, 1976, *26*(4), 196–207.

Rogin, L., and Rachlin, M. *Labor Education in the United States*. Washington, D.C.: Labor Education Materials and Information Center, National Institute of Labor Education at the American University, 1968.

Rogow, F. *Gone to Another Meeting: The National Council of Jewish Women, 1893–1993*. Tuscaloosa: University of Alabama Press, 1993.

Rohfeld, R. W. "Preparing World War I Soldiers for Peacetime: The Army's University in France." *Adult Education Quarterly*, 1989, *39*(4), 187–198.

Rohfeld, R. W. (ed.). *Expanding Access to Knowledge: Continuing Higher Education, NUCEA, 1915–1990*. Washington, D.C.: National University Continuing Education Association, 1990.

Rorabaugh, W. J. *The Craft Apprentice: From Franklin to the Machine Age in America*. New York: Oxford University Press, 1986.

Rose, A. D. "Adults on Campus, the G.I. Bill and the Colleges." *Proceedings of the 30th Adult Education Research Conference*. Madison: University of Wisconsin, 1989a.

Rose, A. D. "Beyond Classroom Walls: The Carnegie Corporation and the Founding of the American Association for Adult Education." *Adult Education Quarterly*, 1989b, *39*(3), 140–151.

Rose, A. D. "Beyond Rhetoric: U.S. Literacy Campaigns in the

Twentieth Century." *Proceedings of the 31st Adult Education Research Conference*. Athens: University of Georgia, 1990.

Rose, S. N. "Collegiate-based Noncredit Courses." In B. L. Watkins and S. J. Wright (eds.), *The Foundations of American Distance Education: A Century of Collegiate Correspondence Study*. Dubuque, Iowa: Kendall/Hunt, 1991.

Rose, W. L. *Rehearsal for Reconstruction*. New York: Bobbs-Merrill, 1964.

Rosenberg, C. E. *No Other Gods: On Science and American Social Thought*. Baltimore: Johns Hopkins University Press, 1976.

Rosenberg, R. *Beyond Separate Spheres: Intellectual Roots of Modern Feminism*. New Haven, Conn.: Yale University Press, 1982.

Rosenwaike, I. *A Population History of New York*. Syracuse, N.Y.: Syracuse University Press, 1972.

Ross, E. D. *Democracy's College: The Land Grant Movement in the Formative Stage*. Ames: Iowa State College Press, 1942.

Ross, S. J. *Workers on the Edge: Work, Leisure, and Politics in Industrializing Cincinnati, 1788–1890*. New York: Columbia University Press, 1985.

Rossiter, M. W. "Benjamin Silliman and the Lowell Institute: The Popularization of Science in Nineteenth Century America." *The New England Quarterly*, 1971, *44*(4), 602–626.

Rossiter, M. W. "The Organization of Agricultural Improvement in the United States, 1785–1865." In A. Oleson and S. C. Brown (eds.), *The Pursuit of Knowledge in the Early American Republic: American Scientific and Learned Societies from Colonial Times to the Civil War*. Baltimore: Johns Hopkins University Press, 1976.

Rothman, S. M. *Women's Proper Place: A History of Changing Ideals and Practices*. New York: Basic Books, 1978.

Rowden, D. (ed.). *Handbook of Adult Education in the United States*. New York: American Association for Adult Education, 1934.

Rowden, D. (ed.). *Handbook of Adult Education in the United States*. New York: American Association for Adult Education, 1936.

Rowe, J. *Hard-Rock Men: Cornish Immigrants and the North*

American Mining Frontier. Liverpool, England: Liverpool University Press, 1974.

Rowse, A. L. *The Cousin Jacks: The Cornish in America.* New York: Charles Scribner's Sons, 1969.

Roydhouse, M. W. "Partners in Progress: The Affiliated Schools for Women Workers, 1928–1939." In J. L. Kornbluh and M. Frederickson (eds.), *Sisterhood and Solidarity: Workers' Education for Women.* Philadelphia: Temple University Press, 1984.

Rubin, J. S. *The Making of Middlebrow Culture.* Chapel Hill: University of North Carolina Press, 1992.

Rudolph, F. *Essays on Education in the Early Republic.* Cambridge, Mass.: Harvard University Press, 1965.

Rutkoff, P. M., and Scott, W. B. *New School: A History of the New School for Social Research.* New York: Free Press, 1986.

Salmond, J. A. *Civilian Conservation Corps, 1933–1942: A New Deal Case Study.* Durham, N.C.: Duke University Press, 1967.

Salt, H. P. *Life of Henry David Thoreau.* London: Walter Scott, 1896.

Schaefer, J. R. "Update on Adult Education in Churches and Synagogues: Roman Catholicism." *Religious Education,* 1977, *72,* 133–143.

Schiller, H. I. *Culture, Inc: The Corporate Takeover of Public Expression.* New York: Oxford University Press, 1989.

Schlesinger, A. M., Sr. "A Critical Period in American Religion, 1875–1900." In J. Mulder and J. F. Wilson (eds.), *Religion in American History: Interpretive Essays.* Englewood Cliffs, N.J.: Prentice-Hall, 1978.

Schlossman, S. L. "Before Home Start: Notes Toward the History of Parent Education in America, 1897–1929." *Harvard Educational Review,* 1976, *46*(3), 436–467.

Schlossman, S. L. "The Formative Era in American Parent Education: Overview and Interpretation." In R. Haskins and D. Adams (eds.), *Parent Education and Public Policy.* Norwood, N.J.: ABLEX, 1983.

Schweninger, L. "Prosperous Blacks in the South, 1790–1880." *American Historical Review,* 1990, *95*(1), 31–56.

Scott, A. F., and Scott, A. M. *One Half the People: The Fight for Woman Suffrage.* Philadelphia: Lippincott, 1975.

Scott, D. M. "The Popular Lecture and the Creation of a Public in Mid-Nineteenth Century America." *Journal of American History*, 1980, *66*, 791–809.

Scott, D. M. "Print and the Popular Lecture System, 1840–60." In W. L. Joyce and others (eds.), *Printing and Society in America*. Worcester, Mass.: American Antiquarian Society, 1983.

Scott, R. V. *The Reluctant Farmer: The Rise of Agricultural Extension to 1914*. Urbana: University of Illinois Press, 1970.

Scudder, T. *Concord: American Town*. Boston: Little, Brown, 1947.

Searcy, H. L. "Parochial Libraries in the American Colonies." Unpublished doctoral dissertation, University of Illinois, 1963.

Seller, M. S. "Success and Failure in Adult Education: The Immigrant Experience, 1914–1924." *Adult Education*, 1978, *28*(2), 83–99.

Seybolt, R. F. *Apprenticeship and Apprenticeship Education in Colonial New England and New York*. New York: Arno Press and the *New York Times*, 1969. (Originally published 1917.)

Seybolt, R. F. *The Evening School in Colonial America*. New York: Arno Press and the *New York Times*, 1971. (Originally published 1925.)

Sharp, D. S. "Yellowstone National Park and the Education of Adults." In *Proceedings of the 28th Adult Education Research Conference*. Laramie: University of Wyoming, 1987.

Sheehan, B. *Seeds of Extinction*. New York: W.W.Norton, 1974.

Sheldon, H. O. *The Lyceum System of Education*. Cincinnati: Ephraim Morgan, 1842.

Sidwell, R. T. "Writers, Thinkers and Fox Hunters: Educational Theory in the Almanacs of Eighteenth Century Colonial America." *History of Education Quarterly*, 1968, *8*(3), 275–288.

Sims, M. S. *The Natural History of a Social Institution—The Y.W.C.A.* New York: Women's Press, 1936.

Sinclair, B. *Philadelphia's Philosopher Mechanics: A History of the Franklin Institute, 1824–1865*. Baltimore: Johns Hopkins University Press, 1974.

Skidmore, T. *The Rights of Man to Property: Being a Proposition to Make It Equal Among the Adults of the Present Generation*. New York: T. Skidmore, 1829.

Smith, D. L. *The New Deal in the Urban South*. Baton Rouge: Louisiana State University Press, 1988.

Solinger, J. W. "Museums and Universities: Choices." In J. W. Solinger (ed.), *Museums and Universities: New Paths for Continuing Education*. New York: Macmillan, 1989.

Solomon, B. M. *In the Company of Educated Women: A History of Women and Higher Education in America*. New Haven, Conn.: Yale University Press, 1985.

Sparks, H. *Tradition, Transformation and Tomorrow: The Emerging Role of American Higher Education*. Occasional Paper 2. Washington, D.C.: National University Continuing Education Association, 1985.

Sperber, A. M. *Murrow: His Life and Times*. New York: Bantam Books, 1987.

Spicer, C. "Folk Education in the United States Today." *Option: Journal of the Folk Association of America*, 1991, *15*(2), 3–16.

Stack, H., and Hutton, C. M. (eds.). *Building New Alliances: Labor Unions and Higher Education*. New Directions for Experiential Learning, no. 10. San Francisco: Jossey-Bass, 1980.

Stavisky, L. P. "Negro Craftsmanship in Early America." *American Historical Review*, 1949, *54*, 315–316.

Stearns, B. M. "Early Factory Magazines in New England: The *Lowell Offering* and Its Contemporaries." *Journal of Economic and Business History*, 1930, *2*, 685–705.

Stearns, R. P. *Science in the British Colonies of North America*. Urbana: University of Illinois Press, 1970.

Steinmetz, C. S. "The History of Training." In R. L. Craig (ed.), *Training and Development Handbook*. New York: McGraw-Hill, 1976.

Stephens, M. D., and Roderick, G. W. *Post-School Education*. Dover, N.H.: Croom Helm, 1984.

Stephenson, C., and Asher, R. *Life and Labor: Dimensions of American Working Class History*. Albany: State University of New York Press, 1986.

Sternett, M. *Black Religion and American Evangelicalism: White Protestants, Plantation Missions, and the Flowering of Negro Christianity, 1787–1865*. Metuchen, N.J.: Scarecrow Press, 1975.

Stevens, E., Jr. "Social Centers, Politics, and Social Efficiency in the

Progressive Era." *History of Education Quarterly,* 1972, *12,* 16–33.

Stevens, E., Jr. "The Anatomy of Mass Literacy in Nineteenth Century United States." In R. A. Arnove and H. Graff (eds.), *National Literacy Campaigns: Historical and Comparative Perspectives.* New York: Plenum Press, 1987.

Stewart, D. W. "Interest Group Roles in the Development and Passage of the Mondale Lifelong Learning Legislation." *Adult Education,* 1978, *28*(4), 264–275.

Stiverson, C. Z., and Stiverson, G. A. "The Colonial Retail Book Trade: Availability and Affordability of Reading Material in Mid-Eighteenth-Century Virginia." In W. L. Joyce and others (eds.), *Printing and Society in Early America.* Worcester, Mass.: American Antiquarian Society, 1983.

Stokes, K. "Religious Institutions." In R. M. Smith, G. F. Aker, and J. R. Kidd (eds.), *Handbook of Adult Education.* New York: Macmillan, 1970.

Stokes, K. "Update on Adult Education in Churches and Synagogues: Protestantism." *Religious Education,* 1977, *72,* 121–132.

Storr, R. J. *Harper's University: The Beginnings.* Chicago: University of Chicago Press, 1966.

Strane, S. *Prudence Crandall and the Education of Black Women.* New York: W.W.Norton, 1990.

Struik, D. J. *Yankee Science in the Making.* (Rev. ed.). New York: Collier Books, 1968.

Stubblefield, H. W. "Continuing Education for Community Problem Solving: A Historical Perspective." In H. W. Stubblefield (ed.), *Continuing Education for Community Leadership.* New Directions for Continuing Education, no. 11. San Francisco: Jossey-Bass, 1981a.

Stubblefield, H. W. "The Idea of Lifelong Learning in the Chautauqua Movement." *Adult Education,* 1981b, *31,* 198–208.

Stubblefield, H. W. *Towards a History of Adult Education in America.* London: Croom Helm, 1988.

Stubblefield, H. W. "Is a Unified Field of Adult Education Possible? The Experience of the AEA, 1951–1960." Paper presented at the Visiting Scholar Conference in the History of Adult Education, Syracuse, N.Y., March 1990.

Stubblefield, H. W. "Learning from the Discipline of History." In
J. M. Peters and P. Jarvis (eds.), *Adult Education: Evolution and
Achievements in a Developing Field of Study*. San Francisco:
Jossey-Bass, 1991.

Stubblefield, H. W., and Keane, P. "The History of Adult and Continuing Education." In S. B. Merriam and P. M. Cunningham
(eds.), *Handbook of Adult and Continuing Education*. San Franciso: Jossey-Bass, 1989.

Stubblefield, H. W., and Rachal, J. R. "On the Origins of the Term
and Meanings of 'Adult Education' in the United States." *Adult
Education Quarterly*, 1992, *42*(2), 106–116.

Studebaker, J. W. *The American Way: Democracy at Work in the
Des Moines Forums*. New York: McGraw-Hill, 1935.

Susman, W. I. *Culture as History: The Transformation of American
Society in the Twentieth Century*. New York: Pantheon, 1984.

Sutton, F. X. "The Ford Foundation: The Early Years." *Daedalus*,
1987, *116*(1), 41–91.

Talbot, M., and Rosenberry, L.K.M. *The History of the American
Association of University Women, 1881–1931*. Boston: Houghton
Mifflin, 1931.

Taylor, E.G.R. *The Mathematical Practitioners of Tudor and
Stuart England*. Cambridge, England: Cambridge University
Press, 1954.

Taylor, R., Rockhill, K., and Fieldhouse, R. *University Adult Education in England and the U.S.A.* Dover, N.H.: Croom Helm,
1985.

Tebbel, J. *The Media in America*. New York: New American Library, 1974.

Tebbel, J. *A History of Book Publishing in the United States. The
Golden Age Between Two Wars, 1920–1940*. Vol. 3. New York:
R. R. Bowker, 1978.

Thistlethwaite, F. *The Anglo-American Connection in the Early
Nineteenth Century*. Pittsburgh: University of Pennsylvania
Press, 1967.

Ticknor, G. *Life, Letters, and Journals of George Ticknor*. Boston:
James R. Osgood, 1876.

Tjerandsen, C. *Education for Citizenship: A Foundation's Experience*. Santa Cruz, Calif.: Emil Schwarzhaupt Foundation, 1980.

Toffler, A. *Future Shock*. New York: Bantam Books, 1971.

Toll, W. "A Quiet Revolution: Jewish Women's Clubs and the Widening Female Sphere, 1870–1920." *American Jewish Archives*, 1989, *41*, 7–26.

Towner, L. W. "A Good Master Well Served: A Social History of Servitude in Massachusetts, 1620–1750." Unpublished doctoral dissertation, Northwestern University, 1955.

Towner, L. W. "The Indentures of Boston's Poor Apprentices: 1734–1805." *Publications*, Colonial Society of Massachusetts, 1966, *43*, 417–468.

Trachtenberg, A. *The Incorporation of America: Culture and Society in the Gilded Age*. New York: Hill and Wang, 1982.

Trachtenberg, A. "We Study the Word and Works of God: Chautauqua and the Sacralization of Culture in America." *Henry Ford Museum & Greenfield Village Herald*, 1984, *13*, 3–11.

Treffman, S. A. "Mechanics' Institutes in Nineteenth Century American Society." *Proceedings of the Twenty-second Adult Education Research Conference*. De Kalb, Ill.: Northern Illinois University, 1981, 224–229.

Tyack, D. B. "Ways of Seeing: An Essay on the History of Compulsory Schooling." *Harvard Educational Review*, 1976, *46*(3), 355–389.

Tyack, D., Lowe, R., and Hansot, E. *Public Schools in Hard Times*. Cambridge, Mass.: Harvard University Press, 1984.

Tyler, A. F. *Freedom's Ferment: Phases of American Social History from the Colonial Period to the Outbreak of the Civil War*. New York: HarperCollins, 1962. (Originally published 1944.)

Tyler, M. C. *A History of American Literature, 1607–1765*. 2 vols. Ithaca, N.Y.: Cornell University Press, 1949. (Originally published 1878.)

U.S. Department of Health, Education, and Welfare. "Perspectives of Adult Education in the United States and a Projection for the Future." Report for the Third International Conference on Adult Education sponsored by the United Nations Educational, Scientific and Cultural Organizations, Tokyo, Japan, July 25–Aug. 7, 1972. Washington, D.C.: U.S. Government Printing Office, 1972.

Ulrich, L. T. "Housewife and Gadder: Themes of Self-Sufficiency and Community in Eighteenth Century New England." In C.

Groneman and M. B. Norton (eds.), *"To Toil the Lifelong Day":*
America's Women at Work, 1780–1980. Ithaca, N.Y.: Cornell
University Press, 1987.

Urwick, L. F. *Management Education in American Business.* New
York: American Management Association, 1954.

Van Deusen, G. G. *Horace Greeley: Nineteenth-Century Crusader.*
Philadelphia: University of Pennsylvania Press, 1964.

Van Fleet, C. "Lifelong Learning Theory and the Provision of
Adult Services." In K. M. Heim and D. P. Wallace (eds.), *Adult*
Services: An Enduring Focus for Public Libraries. Chicago:
American Library Association, 1990.

Van Hise, C. "The University Extension Function in the Modern
University." *Proceedings of the First National University Exten-*
sion Conference, Madison, Wisc., Mar. 10–12, 1915.

Vaughn, S. L. *Holding Fast the Inner Lines: Democracy, National-*
ism, and the Committee on Public Information. Chapel Hill:
University of North Carolina Press, 1980.

Veeman, F. C., and Singer, H. "Armed Forces." In S. B. Merriam
and P. M. Cunningham (eds.), *Handbook of Adult and Contin-*
uing Education. San Francisco: Jossey-Bass, 1989.

Verner, C. "Introduction." In C. Verner (ed.), *Pole's History of*
Adult Schools (1816 ed.). Washington, D.C.: Adult Education
Association of the U.S.A., 1967.

Vincent, J. H. *The Chautauqua Movement.* Freeport, New York:
Books for Libraries Press, 1971. (Originally published 1886.)

Viola, H. J. *After Columbus: The Smithsonian Chronicle of the*
North American Indians. New York: Crown, 1990.

Walker, T. "Defense of Mechanical Philosophy." *North American*
Review, 1831, *33,* 123–125.

Walter, B. "The Cult of True Womanhood: 1820–1860." *American*
Quarterly, 1986, *18,* 151–174.

Walters, R. G. *American Reformers, 1815–1860.* New York: Hill and
Wang, 1978.

Wandersee, W. D. *On the Move: American Women in the 1970s.*
Boston: Twayne, 1988.

Ward, E. J. *The Social Center.* New York: Appleton, 1913.

Ware, S. *Holding Their Own: American Women in the 1930s.* Boston: Twayne, 1982.

Warner, P. D., and Christenson, J. *The Cooperative Extension Service: A National Assessment.* Boulder, Colo.: Westview Press, 1984.

Watkins, K. E. "Business and Industry." In S. B. Merriam and P. M. Cunningham (eds.), *Handbook of Adult and Continuing Education.* San Francisco: Jossey-Bass, 1989.

Webber, T. L. *Deep Like the Rivers: Education in the Slave Quarter Community, 1831–1865.* New York: W.W.Norton, 1978.

Webster, N. "An Essay on the Necessity, Advantages, and Practicality of Reforming the Mode of the Spelling and of Rendering the Orthography of Words Correspondent to Pronounciations." In *Dissertations on the English Language.* Boston: Isaiah Thomas, 1789.

Wecter, D. *The Saga of American Society: A Record of Social Aspiration, 1607–1937.* New York: Charles Scribner's Sons, 1937.

Welter, R. *The Mind of America, 1820–1860.* New York: Columbia University Press, 1975.

Wertheimer, B. M. (ed.). *Labor Education for Women Workers.* Philadelphia: Temple University Press, 1981.

Wesley, E. B. *NEA: The First Hundred Years.* New York: Harper-Collins, 1957.

Whipple, J. B. *A Critical Balance: History of CSLEA.* Boston: Center for the Study of Liberal Education for Adults, 1967.

Whiteaker, L. H. "Adult Education Within the Slave Community." In H. G. Neufeldt and L. McGee (eds.), *Education of the African American Adult.* Westport, Conn.: Greenwood Press, 1990.

Whitehill, W. M. "Early Learned Societies in Boston and Vicinity." In A. Oleson and S. C. Brown (eds.), *The Pursuit of Knowledge in the Early American Republic: American Scientific and Learned Societies from Colonial Times to the Civil War.* Baltimore: Johns Hopkins University Press, 1976.

Wilson, W. E. *The Angel and the Serpent: The Story of New Harmony.* Bloomington: Indiana University Press, 1964.

Windham, D. M., Kurland, N. D., and Levinsohn, F. (eds.). "Financing the Learning Society." *School Review,* 1978, *86*(3), 1978.

Winkler, A. M. *The Politics of Propaganda: The Office of War Information, 1942–1945.* New Haven, Conn.: Yale University Press, 1978.

Wong, S. S. "From Soul to Strawberries: The International Ladies' Garment Workers' Union and Workers' Education." In J. L. Kornbluh and M. Frederickson (eds.), *Sisterhood and Solidarity: Workers' Education for Women 1914-1984*. Philadelphia: Temple University Press, 1984.

Woods, T. A. *Knights of the Plow: Oliver H. Kelley and the Origins of the Grange in Republican Ideology*. Ames: Iowa State University, 1991.

Woytanowitz, G. M. *University Extension: The Early Years in the United States, 1885-1915*. Iowa City: National University Extension Association and the American College Testing Program, 1974.

Wroth, L. C. *The Colonial Printer*. (2nd ed.) Portland, Maine: Southworth-Anthoensen Press, 1938.

Wyllie, I. G. *The Self-Made Man in America: The Myth of Rags to Riches*. New York: Free Press, 1954.

Yankelovich, D. *Coming to Public Judgment: Making Democracy Work in a Complex World*. Syracuse, N.Y.: Syracuse University Press, 1991.

Young, M. "Pagans, Converts, and Backsliders, All: A Secular View of the Metaphysics of Indian-White Relations." In C. Martin (ed.), *The American Indian and the Problem of History*. New York: Oxford University Press, 1987.

Name Index

Subject Index

leges of, 224; Jewish, 178; and labor education, 269–270; and mechanics' institutes, 84; and reform, 160–161; and study circles, 281; women's, 162–164

Unitarians: and reform, 82, 88, 92; and self-culture, 60, 70–71; and utopian groups, 77; and women's education, 113

United Auto Workers, 269

United Christian Adult Movement, 226

United Council for Christian Democracy, 226

United Farm Workers Union, 276–277

United Kingdom: and apprenticeship, 35; and colonial learning, 19–20, 24, 27, 28, 29, 30, 31, 32, 310; and early adult education, 2, 12–14, 15; immigrants from, 102–103; libraries in, 143; and literacy, 63, 68, 71–72; lyceums in, 86–87, 89, 90; mechanics' institutes in, 81, 82; and Native American education, 44, 45; and reform, 58, 60, 74; and religious communities, 176; settlement houses in, 172; university extension in, 139; women's education in, 108, 116; women's groups in, 162; workers' education in, 161, 193, 222

United Neighborhood Houses (UNH), 186

U.S. Armed Forces Institute, 244, 246, 263

U.S. Bureau of the Census, 266

United States Catholic Conference, Division of Adult Education of, 289

U.S. Chamber of Commerce, Immigration Committee of, 183

U.S. Commissioner of Education, 100, 139, 232

U.S. Commissioner of Indian Affairs, 123, 237

U.S. Department of Agriculture (USDA), 146, 147, 157, 199

U.S. Department of Education, 240

U.S. Department of Health, Education and Welfare, 308; Administration on Aging in, 286

U.S. Department of Labor, 269, 270, 302; Labor Extension Service of, 300

U.S. Department of the Interior, 28, 66, 68, 123. *See also* Bureau of Education

U.S. Forest Service, 233

United States Naval Lyceum, 88

U.S. Office of Education, 233, 240, 302, 303–304; Emergency Education Program in, 231, 232, 236

U.S. Supreme Court, and abortion, 276

Unity Centers, 163–164

Unity Houses, 164

Universal African Legions, 216

Universal Lyceum, 89–90

Universal Negro Improvement Association (UNIA), 215–216

Universities: activities of, 198–201; collaboration by, 258; evening colleges of, 200–201; extension from, 138–141, 185, 198–200, 259–260; free, 259; and labor education, 268–269; in learning society, 256–259; outreach by, 257–258

University and College Labor Education Association, 268

University Labor Education Association, 268

UNO, 277

Urban order: adult education in, 171–188; in Americanism era, 180–187; community approach to, 173–174; and family expertise, 179–180; and immigrants, 171–180; and religion, 176–178; and settlement movement, 172–173; summary on, 187–188; and women's clubs, 174–175

Utopian groups, and literacy, 73–78